Key to the Northern Country

SUNY SERIES, AN AMERICAN REGION:
STUDIES IN THE HUDSON VALLEY

THOMAS S. WERMUTH, EDITOR

Key to the Northern Country

The Hudson River Valley in the American Revolution

Edited by
James M. Johnson,
Christopher Pryslopski,
and
Andrew Villani

excelsior editions
State University of New York Press
Albany, New York

On the cover: *Burgoyne's Surrender at Saratoga*, © 1911. Percy Moran.
Color photomechanical print. Library of Congress,
call number LOT 4412-FC [P&P]

Published by State University of New York Press, Albany

Printed in the United States of America

Excelsior Editions is an imprint of State University of New York Press

For information, contact State University of New York Press, Albany, NY
www.sunypress.edu

Production by Ryan Morris
Marketing by Fran Keneston

Library of Congress Cataloging-in-Publication Data

Key to the northern country : the Hudson River Valley in the American Revolution / edited by James M. Johnson, Christopher Pryslopski, and Andrew Villani.

p pages cm. — (SUNY series, an American region: studies in the Hudson Valley)

Includes bibliographical references and index.

ISBN 978-1-4384-4814-5 (pbk. : alk. paper) 1. New York (State)—History—Revolution, 1775–1783. 2. Hudson River Valley (N.Y. and N.J.)—History—18th century. I. Johnson, James M., 1947 June 28–, editor. II. Pryslopski, Christopher. III. Villani, Andrew, 1986–, editor. IV. Title: Hudson River Valley in the American Revolution.

E230.5.N4K49 2013
974.7'03—dc23
2012044466

10 9 8 7 6 5 4 3 2 1

To Dr. Frank T. Bumpus
Philanthropist, Aviator, Radiologist, and Supporter of
the Hudson River Valley Institute

Contents

PART II. SUFFRAGE AND SOCIETY

PART III. FORTRESSES, PRISONS, AND HUTS

PART IV. BATTLES AND WARFARE

Illustrations

Foreword

In 2009 the Hudson River Valley Institute at Marist College joined forces with SUNY Press to commemorate New York State's Quadricentennial, 1609–2009, with the book, *America's First River: The History and Culture of the Hudson River Valley*. The editorial staff selected for inclusion eighteen articles previously published in *The Hudson River Valley Review* and its predecessor the *Hudson Valley Regional Review* that showcased not only the Native American and Dutch experiences but the many dimensions of the Hudson River Valley itself.

This second volume in the SUNY Press series, *Key to the Northern Country: The Hudson River Valley in the American Revolution*, focuses on the War for Independence in the Hudson River Valley in honor of the 235th anniversary of America's second deadliest war, a war that brought the original thirteen colonies their independence and started the transformation of New York into the Empire State. Two hundred thirty-five years ago in 1777, the Northern Army defeated and captured a British army at Saratoga, in what would prove to be the turning point of the war when France recognized the United States of North America. The nexus of the conflict was New York's Hudson River Valley, the cockpit of the war for both sides. As you will read, this region saw major fighting, served as the granary of the colonies and formulated many of the key political ideas that would find their way into the Constitution and its Bill of Rights. New York and its Hudson River Valley were integral to the Revolutionary cause.

In this volume you will read why New York was so important. Articles will highlight the civil war that pitted Whigs against Loyalists, spawned new approaches to voting and taxation, and changed the role of women in society. You will explore key sites and battles such as Valcour Island, Fort Constitution, the Fleet Prison at Esopus, and Fort Montgomery. Finally, you will follow the lives of Americans who fought and died for their beliefs—for independence or for empire.

Join us as we once again explore the history of the Hudson River Valley.

Thomas S. Wermuth, Ph.D.
Director, Hudson River Valley Institute
Editor, SUNY Series: An American Region: Studies in the Hudson Valley

Preface

It is an honor to introduce this book, *Key to the Northern Country: The Hudson River Valley in the American Revolution*. We New Yorkers have always believed that the Hudson River Valley played the pivotal role in determining the outcome of the Revolutionary War and these twenty-one chapters support our case.

In 1996 Congress designated ten counties on the Hudson River as the Hudson River Valley National Heritage Area and one of our first, and likely most important accomplishments, was the establishment of a continuing partnership with Marist College. The Heritage Area has prospered through this partnership because of the extraordinary efforts of three Marist scholars: President Dennis Murray, Vice President and Dean Thom Wermuth, and Colonel (Ret.) Jim Johnson. These three dynamos, with the advice and assistance of Peter Bienstock, created the Hudson River Valley Institute at Marist College. Last year Dr. Frank T. Bumpus funded a chair at Marist in Hudson River Valley History. Colonel Johnson, the Military Historian of the Hudson River Valley and Executive Director of the Institute, is its distinguished first occupant.

I have read and enjoyed these twenty-one chapters about our wonderful and historic valley and trust that you will agree.

Barnabas McHenry, Esq.
Co-Chair, Hudson River Valley National Heritage Area
Vice Chair, Advisory Board, Hudson River Valley Institute

Acknowledgments

THE EDITORS would like to acknowledge the assistance of the following people, organizations, and groups. Dr. Thomas S. Wermuth, publisher of *The Hudson River Valley Review* and Director of the Hudson River Valley Institute, encouraged this project as the editor of SUNY Press's Hudson River series. Dr. Martin Shaffer, Dean of Liberal Arts, supported this project from its inception. Interns Gail Goldsmith, Marist '12, and Samantha McNerney, Marist '14, assisted with the scanning, organizing, and copy editing. Intern Christina Ritter, Marist '14, found and organized the original illustrations and did copy editing. Lois S. Johnson and interns Taylor Mullaney and Marygrace Navarra, Marist '14, joined the team as copy editors. Thanks to each of the authors for the research and scholarship that went into the original articles.

The editors would like to recognize the founders of *The Hudson River Valley Review* (then the *Hudson Valley Regional Review* published by the Bard Center), Richard Wiles and the late William Wilson.

Thanks also go to the Hudson River Valley National Heritage Area and Marist College for their continuing support of the Hudson River Valley Institute and *The Hudson River Valley Review.*

Introduction

JAMES M. JOHNSON

IF ANY BRITISH ARMY had chosen to play "The World Turned Upside Down" as it marched into captivity, it should have been Lieutenant General John Burgoyne's Convention Army. With its surrender to the American Northern Army commanded by Major General Horatio Gates on 17 October 1777, the diplomatic world did turn upside down. On 6 February 1778 Conrad Alexander Gerard, representing King Louis XVI of France, signed a Treaty of Amity and Commerce in Paris with the three American envoys, Benjamin Franklin, Silas Deane, and Arthur Lee. Not only did this document recognize the independence from Great Britain of the "United States of North America," it also pledged that the French would be America's principal ally should war develop between her and the British, "their common Enemy." General George Washington would call Fortress West Point on the Hudson River in New York "the key of America." From July 1776 until 25 November 1783, the Hudson River would be one of the most important strategic locations in the colonies. As the central seat of the war in the thirteen colonies, New York would be the center of political, social, and military activities throughout the war.

The North River Valley, as it was first known, was distinguished by its central role in the American Revolution, the region that George Washington referred to as the "Key to the Northern Country." The region was prized by the British for its strategic and tactical advantages, its central role in communication and trade, and its primary role as the major agricultural producer in North America. For the same reasons, the American revolutionaries mustered all of their resources to retain and control the region. From 1776–1780, the region was the central battleground of the Revolution, with major battles fought at White Plains, Saratoga, Fort Montgomery, and Stony Point. It also witnessed some of the most dramatic and memorable aspects of the war, including Benedict Arnold's failed conspiracy at West Point, the burning of the New York capital at Kingston, the chaining of the river, and the over 600-mile march of General George Washington and the Continental Army and Jean Baptiste Donatien de Vimeur, comte de Rochambeau and his French Expeditionary Corps—the *expédition particulière* to Yorktown, Virginia. All but three of the chapters in this volume have previously appeared in either the *Hudson Valley Regional Review* or *The Hudson River Valley Review*, published by the Hudson River Valley Institute. We have chosen 20 articles, from the more than 194 published in these two regional journals, which we believe illustrate the richly textured history of this supremely important place in the American Revolution. We hope that this anthology of representative pieces of writing about the Hudson River Valley will inspire you to enjoy many other issues of *The Hudson River Valley Review.*

OVERVIEW

"The American Revolution in the Hudson River Valley" by Dr. James M. Johnson and Dr. Thomas S. Wermuth provides an overview of the region's important role in the Revolutionary War and the reasons that it was one of the most embattled areas in North America. Ultimately, as "the nexus of the conflict," it was the region's strategic importance, rich bounty, proximity to New York City, and leading role in trade that led both Revolutionaries and Redcoats to prize the region.

POLITICS AND LOYALTIES

Kenneth Shefsiek's "A Suspected Loyalist in the Rural Hudson Valley" tells the story of New Paltz's Roeloff Josiah Eltinge, who was accused of being a Tory by his neighbors and the conspiracy commissioners. His primary crime seems to have been disinterest in the Revolutionary cause as revealed by his refusal to accept Continental currency. As Edward Countryman has pointed out, Eltinge was by no means unique among people in the region and elsewhere, who chose no side in the conflict and preferred to watch the growing struggle from the sidelines. The term "Tory" was usually understood by generations following the Revolution to mean someone who stayed loyal to the Crown—a "Loyalist." However, the term had much wider meaning during the war years and soon after. It connoted folks who were not "patriotic" enough or who simply seemed disinterested in the struggle. At times it referred to those who didn't seem to do their share to win the war, while other times it might be used to describe a local price-gouger. In the story of Roeloff Eltinge, we see the difficult world of the Revolutionary Hudson and how a citizen could be driven into the Loyalist camp by the harsh treatment of his neighbors.

In his article, "'Can you on such principles think of quitting a Country?' Family, Faith, Law, Property, and the Loyalists of the Hudson Valley during the American Revolution," Michael Diaz, a former intern at the Hudson River Valley Institute and the recipient of the Open Space Institute's first Barnabas McHenry Hudson River Valley Award, introduced the plight of key Loyalists (Tories) who sided with King George III against their neighbors, the Whigs, who were determined to separate themselves in a civil war from his control. Inspired by States Dyckman of Boscobel, Diaz looked at the most influential Loyalist families in the Hudson River Valley: the DeLanceys, the Philipses, the Van Cortlandts, the Coldens, the Van Schaacks, and the Robinsons. He concluded that rather than being "disaffected," the politics of the men in these families "were determined by strong social forces such as family ties, religious conviction, and a respect for civil obedience, law, and order."

Former West Point instructor Major Colin Williams in his article, "New York's Committees in the American Revolution," reveals the mysteries of the political system used by the Whigs during the *rage militaire* before the approval of the New York State Constitution in Kingston on 20 April 1777—the extra-legal committees of safety, "which ran the local governance in the colonies upstate counties." After gaining "legitimacy by giving as many residents as possible a role in fighting the rebellion," the committees "handled the challenges of local security, commodity distribution, military provisioning, and collecting the money needed to pay for the war." Ultimately, committees for detecting and defeating conspiracies "became the government's most powerful instrument in prosecuting New York's civil war."

Claire Brandt shows in "Robert H. Livingston, Jr.: The Reluctant Revolutionary" that Robert R. Livingston, Jr., "the Chancellor," might not deserve to be mentioned among the names of George Washington, Thomas Jefferson, George Clinton, and other prominent figures of the American Revolution. Nonetheless she gives him his due as she explores the numerous contributions that he made to the Whig cause in New York's Hudson River Valley.

He was the chancellor of New York, a nominal member of the committee that drafted the Declaration of Independence, the Secretary of Foreign Affairs, and the Minister to France as the United States negotiated the acquisition of the Louisiana Purchase. For a leader of the democratic Whig cause in America's first civil war, he proved to be a reluctant revolutionary who regarded the masses "as irresponsible, immoderate, and injudicious" and thus not to be trusted with political power. According to Brandt, Livingston hungered "for recognition, fame, and power" and in the end achieved only political ruination.

Lincoln Diamant, in his article about Skinners in the Neutral Ground of Westchester County, answers the question in his title—"Patriot 'Friends' or Loyalist Foes?"—as emphatically Loyalist foes. Diamant provides a penetrating analysis that rejects the legend started by James Fenimore Cooper that Cowboys were affiliated with the British and Skinners with the Patriots. The name Skinners in fact can be traced to Brigadier General Cortlandt Skinner, commander of a New Jersey Loyalist brigade. His article is a cautionary tale for all historians—find the bedrock evidence and avoid the quicksand of hearsay.

Dr. Thomas S. Wermuth in "The Central Hudson Valley and the American Revolution," originally published in *The Other New York*, focused his research on the central counties of the Hudson River Valley: Dutchess, Orange, and Ulster Counties. He found that "The Central Hudson Valley was one of the most contested battlegrounds in the War for American Independence." Except for the entrenched institution of African slavery, the turmoil of war caused economic and political change as "a far more democratic, egalitarian society" emerged. In the central Hudson new leaders rose from the middling classes and used their political power to confiscate and to redistribute Loyalists' lands. This "dramatic" development "opened opportunities for land ownership and free-hold status," which were truly revolutionary.

SUFFRAGE AND SOCIETY

Denis P. Brennan provides insights into the Revolutionary era newspaper business in New York and the other colonies in his article, "Open to All Parties: Alexander and James Robertson, Albany Printers, 1771–1777." Of particular interest, Alexander and James Robertson published Albany's first newspaper, *The Albany Gazette*, from 1771–1772. Although they initially appeared "to have been most interested in the newspaper as a tool of the enlightenment and not as a weapon of the political wars," the Albany Committee of Correspondence thought their later printing trade to be overly supportive of the Crown, causing James to flee Albany and Alexander and his apprentice to be imprisoned. Brennan concludes that they "deserve more than a footnote in Albany's history."

Jonathan Clark in "Taxation and Suffrage in Revolutionary New York" reexamines the relationship between taxation and the franchise in Revolutionary New York based on its Constitution adopted in the capital of Kingston on 20 April 1777. Investigating poll and tax lists in Dutchess County, Clark concluded that "the suffrage requirements may not have excluded as many men as currently accepted estimates would have it." He discovered that the Revolutionary founders may have "held somewhat more democratic leanings" as they allowed those who voted for assemblymen, unlike for governor or senator only, to have to "own a bit of land or pay taxes." They thus came close to universal manhood suffrage with the next best thing—taxpayer suffrage.

William P. McDermott examined voting patterns in Dutchess County in his article, "The Right to Choose: Suffrage During the Revolutionary Era in Charlotte Precinct." He sought to answer the question: "Was the Revolution and the events which followed, such as the Constitutional Convention held in Poughkeepsie in 1788, treated as a significant social movement by the average individual in the agricultural communities of Dutchess County?" Not so surprisingly, he revalidated the old axiom that all politics are local even among the Revolutionary English, Germans, and Dutch residents of the county. With votes on significant questions such as sending delegates to the Second Continental Congress, "a great majority of individuals in Dutchess County were opposed, neutral, or simply unwilling to commit themselves." In fact, 60% chose neutrality. Over the period that he studied, he found that, in Charlotte Precinct, the residents were "focused on local conditions, and interested in maintaining the status quo locally." Voting records led him to six other major conclusions about how those who cast ballots moved toward "more democratic representation in public office" and avoided class conflict as they aspired to social advancement themselves.

Dr. Thomas S. Wermuth's "The women! in this place have risen in a mob: Women Rioters and the American Revolution in the Hudson River Valley," tells the story of the popular disturbances and crowd actions that dominated Valley towns and villages in the years during the Revolution. While many crowd actions that occurred in the 1760s and 1770s were aimed at the Crown (Stamp Act Riots, Boston Massacre, etc.), it was far more common that eighteenth-century riots were aimed at local social and economic conditions. Boycotts of profiteering shopkeepers, "rough music" aimed at perceived social deviants, and riots against hoarding shopkeepers were not uncommon and in fact grew in number during the wars years. These riots, often related to economic woes and shortages of basic foodstuffs, were dominated by women who exerted their public voice around these issues. Although women did not fight on the battlefield, they were involved in important social and economic activities central to the Revolutionary process as "they threatened the ability of authorities to wage war."

Former Marist College graduate, professor, and Vice President for Academic Affairs, Dr. Edward J. Cashin used his article, "Three Officers and a Lady: The Hudson Highlands and Georgia During the Revolution," to tie together pieces of his own heritage as a Georgian educated in New York who returned to Dixie to teach at Augusta State University for thirty-eight years. The three officers were Major General Anthony Wayne, Major General Nathanael Greene, and Lieutenant Colonel "Light-Horse" Harry Lee. The lady was Greene's wife Catherine or Caty. While the inspiration for Cashin's talk, which became this article, was the 225th anniversary of the battle of Stony Point in the Hudson Highlands won by Wayne on 15–16 July 1779, Greene and Lee make their reputations in the southern theater of operations. While these four individuals made signal contributions to victory in the War for Independence, Cashin determined that their lasting legacy to the United States, as they all ended up in Georgia after the war, was to influence Georgians to join "in a stronger federal union" and to make New Yorkers more accepting of Georgia. Following in their footsteps, Dr. Cashin, who also lived in both states and died in Georgia, helped to bridge the Mason-Dixon Line with his own academic work.

FORTRESSES, PRISONS, AND HUTS

In "Lewis Graham's House in Pine Plains: A Revolutionary Log Building," Neil Larson offers a detailed examination of a house in Pine Plains, New York, originally constructed of pine logs during the American Revolution. The Graham-Brush Log House—now restored—survives as an example of eighteenth century domestic architecture—log construction—that Larson found to be "a near intuitive solution for a settler in a forest." Of interest to students of the War for Independence, the house appears "to be the only example of a log building built to military specifications during the Revolutionary War that retains sufficient architectural integrity to represent the character of the hundreds of log huts constructed by the Continental Army to house troops and refugees from Virginia to Maine temporarily, including the major encampments at New Windsor, Morristown and Valley Forge."

The fortress at West Point, called by General George Washington the "key of America," started inauspiciously as Constitution Fort on what is now Constitution Island across from the present-day United States Military Academy. In his article, "The Flawed Works of Fort Constitution," originally printed in *Engineer,* Colonel (Ret.) James M. Johnson found that the military engineer, Dutch-born Bernard Romans, produced flawed fortifications by improperly locating the works and by failing "to develop them effectively, expeditiously, and economically."

Hudson River Valley Institute Advisory Board member and genealogist Frank Doherty in his article, "The Revolutionary War Fleet Prison at Esopus," answered the call to research the prison ships on Rondout Creek. Using ships such as the *Camden* and the *Hudson* to incarcerate known or suspected Loyalists, the Committee for Detecting and Defeating Conspiracies and the Albany Committee of Correspondence "reduced the Loyalist threat" and freed up space in overcrowded jails in the surrounding counties. At least 176 prisoners spent some time confined aboard the ships. Doherty found that the Fleet Prison had "served its purpose, but for a relatively short period of time—just under six months." Aside for the uncomfortable confinement, he found that most Loyalists did not receive any harsher punishments.

BATTLES AND WARFARE

The Saratoga campaign of 1777 proved to be the turning point of the War for Independence and placed the Hudson River at the center of the naval action in 1776 and 1777. In November 1775, Congress passes a resolution authorizing the construction of a fleet of thirteen frigates to challenge the Royal Navy. New York would outfit and build the *Congress* and the *Montgomery*. As James M. Johnson argued in his article, "A Warm Reception in the Hudson Highlands," originally published in *Sea History*, these two ships, fighting and ultimately burning in the Hudson Highlands off Fort Montgomery, would contribute to Major General Horatio Gates's far-off victory at Saratoga.

R. Beth Klopott, in "Civil War in Schaghticoke: A Footnote to the Revolution in Upstate New York," ventures into the civil war between New York and New Hampshire within the larger civil war between Whigs and Loyalists over what would become the state of Vermont. She shows why "Schaghticoke residents split over support for Vermont or New York." While the Crown had sided with New York in the Order of Council in 1764, the area between the Hudson River and the border with New Hampshire, including Schaghticoke, saw raids by "Vermonters" confronted by New York militiamen until 1782. The issue was not fully resolved until Vermont became a state in 1790.

One of New York's greatest achievements during the 225th anniversary of the American Revolution was to reclaim Fort Montgomery near the Bear Mountain Bridge from the wilderness and to open it as Fort Montgomery State Historic Site. In "Interpreting the Battle for the Hudson River Valley: The Battle of Fort Montgomery," Gregory Smith and James M. Johnson describe the battle fought there and at its sister Fort Clinton on the south side of Popolopen Creek on 6 October 1777 and their "decisive role in the Saratoga campaign of 1777, 'the turning point of the American Revolution.'" Additionally, they explain the work of the Fort Montgomery Plan Team in clearing and interpreting the site's ruins so that visitors can learn about the forts, the battles fought there, and the sacrifices made by the men who defended their works.

Thomas C. O'Keefe in his article, "Revolutionary Road: Incident on Gallows Hill," focused on the former commander of the Hudson Highlands Department during the Saratoga Campaign of 1777, Major General Israel Putnam, to connect the Hudson River Valley to Redding, Connecticut. While General George Washington had assigned Putnam to command the Eastern Wing of the Continental Army in 1778, he clearly had lost confidence in his subordinate after he failed to prevent Lieutenant General Henry Clinton from running free up and down the Hudson. While the Court of Inquiry chaired by Major General Alexander McDougall had absolved Putnam of "any fault, misconduct, or negligence," Old Put was clearly under a cloud. During the harsh winter of 1778–1779, faced with a mutiny and threatened march on the Connecticut legislature in Hartford by troops from Brigadier Jedediah Huntington's brigade, Putnam chose to shoot a convicted spy, Edward Jones, and hang a deserter, John Smith, as, according to O'Keefe, "sacrificial lambs," to make an impression on the Connecticut troops. While he couched his conclusions as questions, O'Keefe clearly feels that General Putnam had "taken the hardest possible line," treating the two unfortunate prisoners as ring leaders of a mutiny, which they clearly were not. While a paralytic stroke in December 1779 would end Putnam's career, his legacy would be anchored on his earlier military service rather than the events at the Redding encampments.

Joseph Plumb Martin is perhaps the most famous enlisted soldier in the American Revolution because be published his experiences in the war. Another soldier, Moses Tuttle, from the Constitution State fought alongside Martin in the New York Campaign of 1776. In fact, William Sullivan in his article, "Soldier of '76: The Revolutionary Service of a Connecticut Private in the Campaign in New York," found that Connecticut provided over one-third of the men to defend New York against General William Howe's invading British army. Tuttle served in New York first as a militiaman and then as a levy in Captain Nathaniel Bunnel's 7th Company of the 5th Connecticut Battalion. He saw action at Kips Bay, Harlem Heights, and White Plains. Sullivan argues that Tuttle's "experience as a soldier during the campaign of 1776 demonstrates that while the performance of temporary troops proved dismal at times, their willingness to enter the field of battle against great odds and in spite of hunger, poverty, and disease helped sustain the Revolution through its early stages." He concluded that "the militia and levies had performed a valuable role in the New York campaign."

In his article, "Valcour Island: Setting the Conditions for Victory at Saratoga," Major Gregory M. Tomlin reassesses the 1776 Lake Champlain Campaign that led to the Battle of Valcour Island. A pyrrhic victory that ended with the loss of almost all of Brigadier General Benedict Arnold's fleet, the battle "delayed an earlier British attack in the fall of 1776, thereby providing the Americans with an additional year to prepare their defenses for the British northern invasion of New York." He concluded that "This unique naval battle fought on Lake Champlain . . . should be considered the opening phase of the Saratoga campaign, making it a relatively obscure engagement that deserves greater attention by students of the American struggle for independence." The Battle of Valcour Island thus "proved critical for setting the conditions for victory" in the turning point Saratoga Campaign the next fall, 1777. It also foretold the British military strategy in 1814 that would culminate in the American victory at Plattsburg.

1

The American Revolution in the Hudson Valley—An Overview

THOMAS S. WERMUTH AND JAMES M. JOHNSON

ALTHOUGH THE "shot heard 'round the world" that ignited the American Revolution occurred a few miles outside of Boston and the campaign that ended it took place in Virginia, the nexus of the conflict was New York's Hudson River Valley. Throughout the war, officers on both sides made it their top priority to gain control of the Hudson River—and to keep hold of it at any cost.

As a result, the Hudson Valley—the virtual center of the colonies—hosted many key figures, battles, and political events throughout the eight years of war, and its final drama was played out here with the British evacuation of New York City on November 25, 1783. In the years leading up to the Revolution, the Sons of Liberty, as active in New York as they were in Massachusetts, printed broadsides, encouraged boycotts, rallied, rioted, and dumped British tea into New York Harbor. Patriot housewives throughout the Valley threw their own "tea parties" at the expense of merchants and Loyalist neighbors. The region's social fabric was ripped apart, first by the struggle between the powerful coalitions of DeLanceys and Livingstons, and then by the clash between the Loyalists and Whigs (or Patriots).

The New York Provincial Congress established itself at the courthouse in White Plains in July 1776 and created the State of New York with its acceptance of the Declaration of Independence on July 9. New York adopted its constitution in Kingston on April 20, 1777, and on February 6, 1778, it ratified the Articles of Confederation, tying its fate to the rest of the United States of America.

PRELUDE TO WAR

On the eve of the American Revolution, the Hudson River Valley was among the most fertile and productive regions in North America. Its grain, flour, and dairy products were sent all over the world. The port towns of Albany, Poughkeepsie, and Kingston were thriving commercial entrepôts that served as regional hubs in the vibrant agricultural trade with New York City.

The Hudson Valley had been settled primarily by the Dutch in the mid-seventeenth century, and the English soon thereafter, with some French Huguenots and Germans following. Much of the Hudson's west bank was still ethnically and culturally Dutch, perhaps three generations removed from leaving Europe. Dutch customs prevailed, the Dutch Reformed Church dominated, and while the Second Continental Congress was approving the Declaration of Independence, Dutch was spoken more regularly in many Hudson Valley towns than English. Indeed, through 1774 the Ulster town of Kingston (a mere three years away from being the state capital) kept its official records in Dutch.

As late as 1763, residents of the Hudson Valley still felt strong bonds to the king of

England and his empire. A typical outpouring of this affection was the celebration in Kingston of George III's ascension to the throne in 1761. Hundreds of residents paraded through the streets and offered toasts and cannonades to "His most Royal and Sacred Majesty."[1] Similar celebrations were held throughout the region.

Nevertheless, relations between England and the colonies began to sour. Following the French and Indian War, the British government levied new taxes on the American colonies that were intended to defray its large war debt. The Stamp Act of 1765, which imposed a tax on a variety of goods and services, was viewed suspiciously by Valley inhabitants, as well as other colonists. In towns throughout the region, residents resisted the implementation of the act, and in Albany and New York City riots broke out in order to prevent the tax from going into effect.[2]

Calm returned to North America following the Stamp Act's repeal in 1766, and over the next several years there was a rapprochement of sorts between England and her colonies. Nevertheless, the quartering of British troops in Boston and New York inflamed tensions in both cities, leading to sporadic outbursts of violence. The Boston Massacre further ignited anti-British sentiment.

1763	Treaty of Paris concludes French and Indian War
1765	Stamp Act Riots in New York, Albany, and Boston
1766	Stamp Act Repealed
1770	Boston Massacre
1773	Boston Tea Party
1774	Coercive (or Intolerable) Acts Quebec Act
1775	Battle of Lexington (April); Battle of Bunker Hill (June)
1776	British Invasion of New York City
1777	Campaign for the Hudson River Valley
1778	Washington's Encampment at Pawling (Fredricksburg)
1779	Battle of Stony Point
1780	Fortress West Point threatened by General Benedict Arnold
1781	Battle of Yorktown
1782	Washington's army encamped at New Windsor
1783	Evacuation Day (November 25)

Fig. 1.1. Timeline, 1763–1783.

The primary debate in the 1770s continued to be over Britain's authority to tax the colonists. Britain asserted this right as essential to the process of governance. Although the colonial argument varied, in essence it recognized the empire's right to tax to regulate imperial relations, but not to raise revenue. Colonists generally agreed with Patrick Henry's famous declaration of "no taxation without representation." Such sentiment led to a variety of responses from British officials, one of the most interesting being the distinction between "actual" and "virtual" representation: The colonists were not physically represented in Parliament (and neither were many English subjects). However, the colonists *were* represented, so the argument ran, in the sense that Parliament represented the interests of all subjects of the realm.[3]

From 1770 through 1773, relations between the colonies and Britain were relatively stable, but events in late 1773 changed that. The newly enacted Tea Act, offering East Indian tea at reduced prices (and including a tax), inspired "tea parties" throughout the colonies, including the Hudson Valley. The most famous, of course, occurred in Boston, where members of the Sons of Liberty dressed as Mohawk Indians and dumped British tea overboard.[4]

The Coercive Acts of 1774, implemented to punish Boston following its Tea Party, ignited resistance throughout the colonies. New Yorkers had their own tea party on April 22, when "Mohawks" dumped tea from the ship *Hook* into New York harbor, forcing another ship, the *Nancy*, to return to England. In communities up and down the Hudson, committees of safety, observation, and inspection sprang into action to challenge recent British policies.[5]

Characteristic of this resistance was the Kingston Committee of Safety's anger over Parliament's attempt to establish "the Romish Religion in America," a feature of the Quebec Act of 1774. The Kingston committee was equally shocked by the "avowed design of the [British] ministry to raise a revenue in America." The New Windsor Committee of Observation articulated its fear of Parliament's desire to levy taxes "on us without our consent" and for asserting absolute legislative authority over the colonies. The committee resolved that such powers were "subversive of our natural and legal rights as British subjects, and that we would be deficient in point of duty to our King and the British Constitution were we to yield in tame submission to them."[6]

As war began in New England in 1775, the people of the Hudson Valley began to choose sides. Throughout the war, there were pockets of Loyalism in the region, but devotion to the Revolutionary cause remained strong. The Valley was able to muster several Continental and militia regiments.

THE CAMPAIGNS FOR THE HUDSON RIVER VALLEY

Control of the Hudson Valley was one of the primary strategic objectives of the British high command. The Valley's defense was equally important to General George Washington, whose army was to spend more than a third of the war in (or in close proximity to) the region. In 1776, Washington stated that "the importance of the river in the present contest and the necessity of defending it, are so well understood that it is unnecessary to enlarge upon them." Whereupon he proceeded to enlarge upon those reasons, citing its strategic significance for transportation and communication, as well as the importance of its agricultural production.[7]

That July, the largest armada the British Empire had ever sent abroad entered New York Harbor. Five hundred ships carrying more than 34,000 British Regulars, sailors, and German mercenaries under the joint command of the brothers Howe, Admiral Richard and General William, landed at the southern tip of Manhattan Island. Facing them across the East River, atop Brooklyn Heights, were some 20,000 Continentals and militia under Washington's command.[8]

In late August, Howe's army slipped around Washington and attacked from the rear. The Americans were driven across the river to Manhattan. In mid-September the two armies clashed again near Kip's Bay, sending Washington's army reeling northward up the island. In early October, the British again seized the advantage, striking Washington at Pell's Point; later that month, the two armies battled to a draw at White Plains. In just three months, the Continental Army had been pushed out of New York City and into the lower Hudson Valley.[9]

The British engaged in several small raids in the mid-Valley in 1776 and early 1777. Their subsequent campaign to control the region consisted of an elaborate three-pronged invasion. The main force, under General John Burgoyne, was to depart from Canada and push its way south through the Adirondacks to Albany, where it was to meet up with a combined British-Indian force pushing eastward along the Mohawk Valley. The third force was to be an expeditionary unit under the command of Sir Henry Clinton, who had been left in command of New York City when General Howe unexpectedly sailed south to Philadelphia in July 1777. Clinton's push up the Hudson aimed at either meeting with, or giving support to, Burgoyne's forces. Military scholars have often noted the lack of proper planning and coordination of this major invasion, whose failure led directly to the British defeat at Saratoga, "the turning point of the war."[10]

As Clinton's army made its way up the Hudson, about 700 soldiers from the 5th New York Regiment, Lamb's Artillery, and the Ulster and Orange county militia garrisoned Forts

Montgomery and Clinton. The state's new governor, Brigadier General George Clinton, commanded the posts. His brother, James, commanded the troops at Fort Clinton. On the morning of October 6, after a day of fierce fighting, British troops captured both forts and spent the next several days destroying them, along with an iron chain that had been stretched across the Hudson there. The main part of the American force was able to escape.[11]

Despite the British victory, Henry Clinton's troops suffered almost 200 casualties and were delayed by the action. They resumed their movement upriver and stopped at several points along the way, landing small units for limited forays against local militia units. British forces reached Kingston, the state capital, ten days later.

Advance British units approached Kingston before dawn on October 16. Many residents had already escaped in the days before the British arrival, and local militia were prepared to conduct a delaying action if large numbers of troops came ashore. Major General John Vaughan led a British raiding party of several hundred men that quickly drove local militia units west from the town in pre-dawn fighting. Determined to punish the region, British troops burned large portions of the town before departing later that afternoon. Henry Clinton's forces pushed another ten miles upriver over the next few days, dropping landing parties at various points (including the Livingston estate at Clermont, which, with the nearby Belvediere, was burned to the ground) before heading back to New York City. By this time, Burgoyne had surrendered and Clinton's northward movement had been made irrelevant.[12]

Although there was limited military action in the mid-Valley in 1778, the Hudson remained the primary target of both British and American strategists. In May 1779, Henry Clinton attempted a second invasion, seizing Stony Point. However, Washington kept his army between Clinton and the northern stretches of the Valley, and on July 15 he sent a force under General "Mad" Anthony Wayne to drive the British from Stony Point. The surprise nighttime attack was a huge success, and all British troops in the vicinity retreated downriver in the fall.[13]

It was the importance of maintaining control of the Hudson that had led Washington, in 1778, to order construction of fortress West Point—a complex of forts and redoubts that he dubbed "the key of America." A feature of the fortress was an iron chain, which was laid across the river to prevent any future British naval incursion upriver. In 1780, the British made one more attempt on the Hudson, when Henry Clinton opened secret negotiations with General Benedict Arnold, recently appointed commander of West Point, to gain control of the fort. Arnold's plans were discovered when Clinton's aide-de-camp, Major John André, was captured. He was hanged as a spy in Tappan; Arnold escaped to safety in New York City.[14]

In the last years of the war, the mid-Valley remained central to Washington's plans. After the British were defeated at Yorktown, they continued to occupy New York City for two more years, and their continued threat to the Valley kept Washington and his army stationed nearby. The Continental Army encamped in southern Ulster County, in and around the town of New Windsor, while Washington himself took up headquarters a few miles north, at Newburgh. In the summer of 1781, the French commander, the Comte de Rochambeau, marched his 5,000-man army from Rhode Island to Philipsburg, in Westchester, to join the Continental Army, first in the siege of New York and then in the pivotal Yorktown Campaign in Virginia.

WAR AND THE HOME FRONT

With the gradual collapse of New York's colonial government, the committees of safety, observation, and inspection emerged to fill the vacuum of power. In most towns, these developed alongside existing town boards and governments. In many communities, they maintained a strong presence by exerting their influence not only in the political sphere, but also in the economic arena. The committees regulated prices, controlled the importation and exportation of goods, and set maximum- and minimum-wage rates for local labor.

Often the powers invested in the committees were greater than those that town officials possessed. In 1776, the Provincial Congress gave the committees the authority to tax and appoint tax collectors and assessors. During the war, the committees gradually gained additional powers and became the de facto governing authority in many Valley towns. Besides control over local taxation and legislation, they also assumed judicial and police powers. The committees could use their authority over local militia units to enforce their rulings.[15]

Usually, the committees did not have to resort to displays of power; they were able to employ community pressures against those suspected of unpatriotic actions or of any activity seen as threatening. These punishments included public denunciations of those who were considered to be enemies of the cause, symbolic burnings of effigies, or boycotts of shopkeepers and tradesmen who seemed lukewarm to the Revolution. Committees instructed residents not to patronize businesses whose patriotism was suspect because "every shilling of property we put in their hands . . . enable them to purchase the chains to bind us in slavery."[16]

The issues upon which committees expended the most energy tended to be economic. Food shortages, inflated prices, currency of questionable value, rising taxes, and, on the Hudson's east bank, tenants demanding land redistribution all helped to shape some of the most revolutionary aspects of the Revolution. On the eve of the war, the local committees of observation supervised economic activities in their counties and towns. Initially, the role of the committees was to promote non-importation and the boycott of British goods. Once the war began and shortages and inflation became rampant, the local committees started to scrutinize and regulate the trade and economic activities of local shopkeepers to ensure that they engaged in business practices that promoted the war effort and supported a vibrant local economy.[17]

THE END OF THE WAR

Following the American victory at Stony Point, the British never directly threatened the Hudson Valley again. (The last engagement in the region occurred in the summer of 1779, when Chief Joseph Brant, leading a mixed band of Mohawks and Loyalists, conducted a raid on Minisink.) Following their dramatic victory at Yorktown, Washington and the Continental Army spent the last two years of the war encamped at New Windsor and Newburgh. On November 25, 1783, Governor George Clinton led the Americans into New York City after the British evacuation. And on December 4, the commander in chief bid a tearful farewell to his officers of the Continental Army at Fraunces Tavern in Manhattan. The war that started in Massachusetts and had centered in New York at last ended there.

This article originally appeared in *The Hudson River Valley Review*, Volume 20.1, summer, 2003.

NOTES

1. *New York Gazette*, February 1761.
2. Edward Countryman, *A People in Revolution: The American Revolution and Political Society in New York, 1760–1790* (Baltimore: Johns Hopkins University Press, 1981), 37–39; Joseph Tiedemann, *Reluctant Revolutionaries: New York City and the Road to Independence, 1763–1776* (Ithaca: Cornell University Press, 1997), 15–26.
3. Bernard Bailyn, *Ideological Origins of the American Revolution* (Cambridge: Harvard University Press, 1967), 166–71; Edmund S. Morgan, *The Birth of the Republic, 1763–89* (Chicago: University of Chicago Press, 1967), 23–24.

4. Alfred Young, *The Shoemaker and the Tea Party: Memory and the American Revolution* (Boston: Free Press, 1999), 99–107.
5. Countryman, 137–43.
6. "Resolves of the New Windsor Committee" in Peter Force, *American Archives* (Washington, D.C.: 1837–1853), 2:131–33.
7. Washington's comments are cited in Louis V. Mills, "Attack in the Highlands, the Battle of Fort Montgomery," *Hudson Valley Regional Review* (Sept. 2000), 39–40.
8. Barnet Schecter, *The Battle for New York: The City at the Heart of the American Revolution* (New York: Walker, 2002), 112–16.
9. William Polf, *Garrison Town: The British Occupation of New York City* (Albany: New York State Library, 1976), 5–7.
10. Mark Lender and James Kirby Martin, *A Respectable Army: The Military Origins of the Republic* (New York: Harlan Davidson Press, 1981), 83–87.
11. Robert Venables, *The American Revolution in the Hudson Valley* (Albany: New York State Library, 1975), 12–13.
12. Schecter, 286–99.
13. Venables, 18.
14. Willard Sterne Randall, *Benedict Arnold: Patriot and Traitor* (New York: Morrow, 1990), 526–37.
15. Countryman, 137–40.
16. "Minutes of Committee of Ulster, May 11, 1775" in Force, 2:833.
17. Thomas S. Wermuth, "The Central Hudson Valley and the American Revolution," in Joseph Tiedemann and Eugene Fingerhut, ed., *The Other New York: The Revolution Beyond New York City, 1763–1787* (SUNY Press, 2005), 137–38.

PART I

Politics and Loyalties

2

A Suspected Loyalist in the Rural Hudson Valley

The Revolutionary War Experience of Roeloff Josiah Eltinge

KENNETH SHEFSIEK

IN THE YEARS leading up to the War of Independence, battle lines were being drawn not only between the British government and its American colonies, but also among the colonial citizenry itself. For the radical revolutionaries who believed in the existence of a British governmental conspiracy to deprive the colonists of their liberty, as well as for those whose strong conservative stance enabled them to accept British authority in whatever form it was foisted upon them, matters of allegiance were fairly clear. But these two positions were the extremes, and the opinions of many resided in "the twilight zone between wholehearted support of the American cause and overt identification with the British."[1] Most of the populace, whether or not they eventually became Patriot or Tory, were thoroughly uncomfortable with the innovative methods Parliament had enacted to raise revenue directly from the colonies. As William Nelson states, in regard to taxation the Tories "were as indignant as other Americans as to what seemed an unjust and arbitrary exercise of British authority."[2] What separated the Revolutionaries from the Tories was not the belief that the British government was overstepping its bounds. Where they differed was in their opinion of the role of the British Crown and Parliament in relation to the elected governments of the colonies and the means open to them for resolving the controversy. There were, of course, Loyalists who actively fought on the side of the British. However, there were also many who considered themselves Loyalists because they felt negotiation and readjustment within the current imperial system was the proper approach to resolution. Then there were those who opposed the radical Revolutionaries because "they were alarmed at the prospect of strife between Britain and the colonies;" however, it took years for the "the issue of allegiance [to] crystallize."[3]

The issue of allegiance was particularly complicated in New York, where the heterogeneity of the population in terms of ethnicity, religion, and wealth resulted in a similar heterogeneity in political beliefs. Whereas the greater homogeneity of society and political belief in New England and Virginia resulted in a greater clarity of political divisions, the heterogeneity of New York resulted in a greater distribution throughout the possible range, from left to right.[4] Additionally, New York's extensive experience in dealing with political and social division resulted in a culture of negotiation and moderation.[5] The way of moderation was also followed in New York as a means of preventing a renewed outbreak of violence, like that experienced during the Stamp Act Riots of 1765.[6]

Once the war began, the situation became increasingly difficult for those who were unable to support the Patriot cause fully, and even for those "who have affected to observe . . . a dangerous and equivocal neutrality."[7] To a Revolutionary, there was no middle ground: moderates were considered potential Tories. It was these moderates who faced some of the greatest personal challenges of conscience during the war.

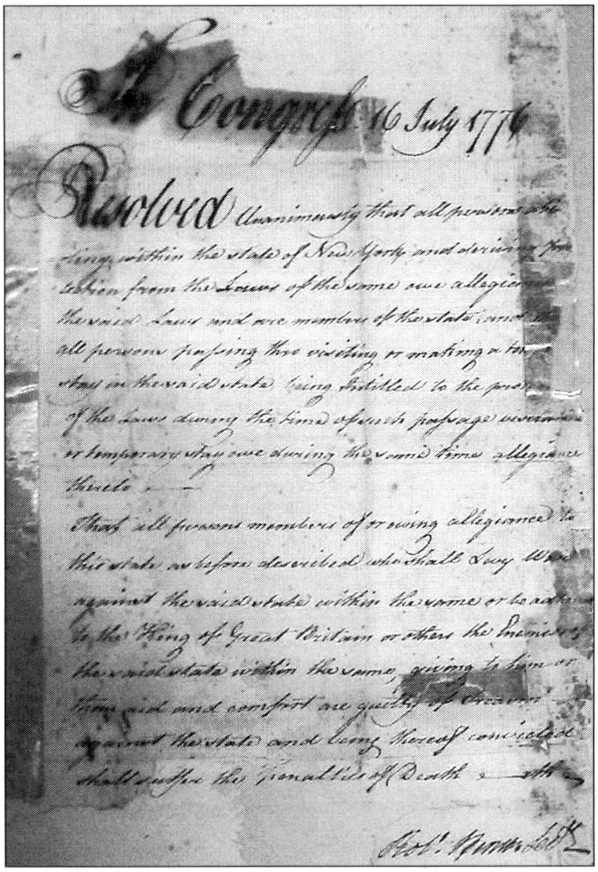

In Congress 16 July 1776

Resolved Unanimously that all persons abiding within the state of New York and deriving protection from the Laws of the same owe allegiance to the said Laws and are members of the state, and that all persons passing thro visiting or making a temporary stay in the said state being Intitled to the protection of the Laws during the time of such passage visitations or temporary stay owe during the same time allegiance thereto —

That all persons members of or owing allegiance to this state as before described who shall levy War against the said state within the same or be adhesions to the King of Great Britain or others the Enemies of the said state within the same, giving to him or them aid and comfort are guilty of Treason against the state and being thereof convicted shall suffer the penalties of Death

Robt. Benson Secy

Fig. 2.1. The Oath of Allegiance required of all New York citizens. Courtesy of NYS Office of Parks, Recreation and Historic Preservation, Senate House Historic Site.

IN CONGRESS 16 JULY 1776
Resolved Unanimously that all persons abiding within the state of New York and deriving protection from the laws of the same owe allegience (to) the said Laws and are members of the state, and that all persons passing thro visiting or making a temporary stay in the said state, being Intitled to the protection of the Laws during the time of such passage visitations or temporary stay owe during the same time allegience thereto— That all persons members of or owing allegience to this state as before described who shall levy War against the said state within the same or be adhesions to the King of Great Britain or others the Enemies of the said state within the same, giving to him or them aid and comfort are guilty of Treason against the state and being thereof convicted shall suffer the penalties of Death

Rob't Benson, Sec.

Fig. 2.2. Transcription of The Oath of Allegiance required of all New York citizens. Courtesy of NYS Office of Parks, Recreation and Historic Preservation, Senate House Historic Site.

Since the Revolutionaries, who held the reins of government and the law, would accept nothing less than full, unequivocal support, the moderates were forced to compromise their principles by choosing either the far left or the far right, or simply lying and stating that they supported the Patriots.[8] Those of questionable allegiance were particularly vulnerable in New York because the state was wedged between the British forces occupying New York City and the threat of invasion from the north. Both the British and the Americans believed that silent Tories would be encouraged to declare their true allegiance and threaten the state from within if the British forces were able to advance into the interior.

It was therefore incumbent upon the authorities in New York to find a method to deal with the Loyalist threat, whether real or phantom.[9] The government imprisoned suspected Tories, often in extremely substandard facilities and without due process of law. Particularly feared Tories were exiled, others were put to hard labor (although many authorities denounced such punishment). The property of some Loyalists was confiscated; Patriot vigilantes occasionally tarred and feathered their opponents. Alexander Flick contends that the treatment was "firm but comparatively moderate,"[10] and other historians also declare it "moderate and fair, all things taken into consideration."[11] Robert Calhoon is generally forgiving of the governmental organization charged with suppressing Loyalist activity; he notes that it was "more concerned with identifying persons of doubtful loyalty than with punishment or harassment." Tories, Calhoon adds, were given the opportunity either to take an oath of allegiance or "move to New York

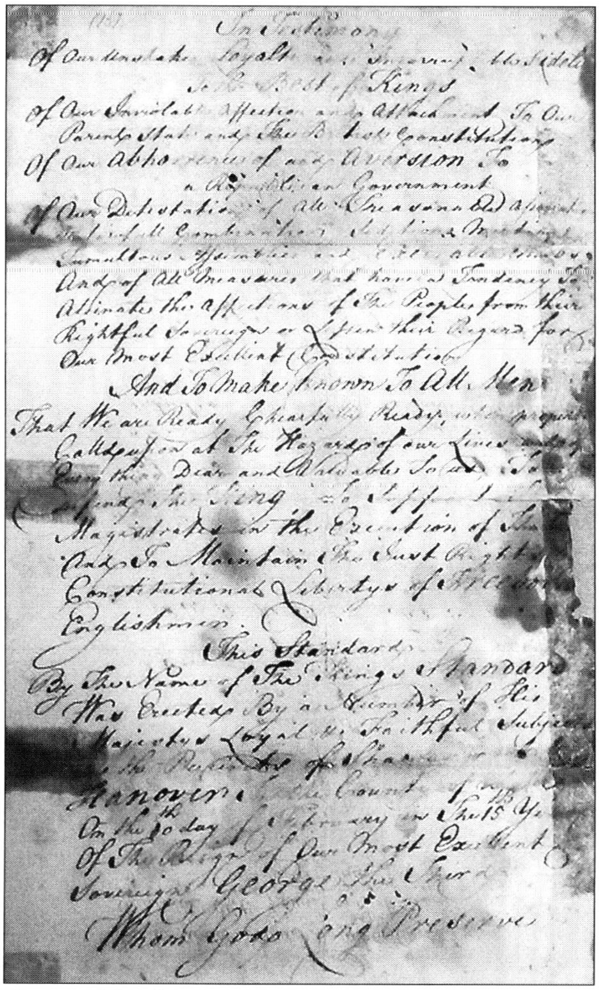

Fig. 2.3. The Oath of Allegiance to the King. Courtesy of NYS Office of Parks, Recreation and Historic Preservation, Senate House Historic Site.

In Testimony Of our Unshaken Loyalty and Incorruptible Fidelity To the Best of Kings Of our Inviolable Affection and Attachment To Our Parent State and The British Constitution Of our abhorrence of and Aversion To a Republican Government Of our Detestation of All Treasonable Associations Unlawfull Combinations Seditous Meetings Tumultuous Assemblies and Execrable Mobs And of All measures that have a Tendency To Alienate the Affections of The People from their Rightful Sovereign or Lessen their Regard for Our Most Excellent Constitution And To Make Known To All Men That We are Ready Chearfully Ready when properly Calld upon at The Hazard of our Lives and of Every thing Dear and Valualbe to us To Defend The King To Support The Magistrates in the Execution of The Laws And to Maintain The Just Rights of Constitutional Liberty of Freeborn Englishmen This Standard By The Name of The Kings Standard Was Erected By a Number of His Majestys Loyal & Faithful Subjects In the Precincts of Shawangunk & Hanover in the County of Ulster On the 10th day of February in the 15th Year Of The Reign Of Our Most Excellent Sovereign George the Third Whom God Long Preserve

Fig. 2.4. Transcription of the Oath of Allegiance to the King. Courtesy of NYS Office of Parks, Recreation and Historic Preservation, Senate House Historic Site.

City." (By "move," he means exile.)[12] Although exile is neither punishment nor harassment, it was rather harsh, especially when forced upon those who did not pose any real threat, even if they did have Tory leanings. Calhoon also states that in New England, county committees provided suspected Loyalists with the opportunity to end their "estrangement from the community through a recanting of any loyalistic statements," and thus "served to define the moral and inclusive character of a community in crisis."[13] The same was true in New York. Being given the chance to recant before a committee that had the power to punish hardly suggests the "inclusiveness" of a community in regard to political opinions. Philip Ranlet is not so forgiving, stating that the treatment of suspected Loyalists "was not kind."[14]

Many of the recent investigations into New York Toryism focus on sophisticated political ideology. The high-minded constitutional principles that were the basis for discussion and dispute were primarily the domain of the politicians and gentry. However, they were not the only Tories of the day: they were found in all ranks of society. It is more difficult to investigate the issue of allegiance for people of the middle and lower ranks of society because suspected Loyalists who were neither belligerent nor socially prominent were handled by local committees, and few of their records survive.[15] Jonathan Clark has attempted to define allegiance for residents of all walks of life in Poughkeepsie, but he categorizes so many as "occasional loyalist" or "occasional patriot" that it is apparent that the issue of allegiance is often unclear.[16] It is also difficult to investigate fully how such suspects were treated by the Revolutionary authorities. In the archives of the Huguenot Historical Society in New Paltz, a town of modest size during the eighteenth century, there survives a collection of documents relating to the wartime experience of one resident, Roeloff Josiah Eltinge (1737–1795), which substantially documents his treatment at the hands of the Revolutionaries. His story provides insight into both the mind of a man who was neither an avowed Patriot nor a staunch Loyalist and the methods and motives of Patriot authorities during the early years of the conflict.

Roeloff Josiah Eltinge was a third-generation resident of New Paltz, which had been founded by French Huguenot refugees in 1678 on a patent of nearly 40,000 acres. The first Eltinge who moved to New Paltz was Roeloff Josiah's grandfather, a man of Dutch descent also named Roeloff (1689–1746/7), who married Sara DuBois (1682–c.1746), the daughter of New Paltz Patentee Abraham DuBois (1657–1731). According to tradition, the first Roeloff's son, Josiah, began to operate a general store in New Paltz around 1740 and was considered the wealthiest man of the town.[17] Roeloff Josiah took over the business from his father and was involved in many entrepreneurial endeavors.[18] He was one of New Paltz's most prominent citizens, but his influence did not extend outside the town. Although it is difficult to say where Roeloff Josiah fit in the overall social structure of his time and region, New Paltz was a small, isolated, relatively unimportant town in the eighteenth century, thus his social position would have been restricted. His small house, with three above-ground rooms, still survives, and it attests to his modest social standing.

Fig. 2.5. The Roeloff Josiah Eltinge House in New Paltz. Photograph by Christopher Pryslopski.

Eltinge's Revolutionary War experience begins with his signing of the Articles of Association in May 1775. The articles had been prepared by the Committee of New York City on April 29, 1775, ten days after the battles at Lexington and Concord, and they had been transmitted to the counties of New York for signing in every town. The purpose of the association was to create a "firm union of its inhabitants in a vigorous prosecution of the measures necessary for safety (because) of the necessity of preventing the anarchy and confusion which attend a dissolution of the powers of government." It was a response both to Britain's taxation of the colonies and its subsequent aggression in Massachusetts. The association was an early statement of the independence movement, so many future Revolutionaries signed it. So, too, did many future Loyalists. This sometimes occurred because of pressure by the local committees and other townspeople, but moderates would have generally felt comfortable signing because it also stated that "we most ardently desire . . . a reconciliation between Great Britain and America on Constitutional Principles."

Whether or not Eltinge willingly signed the articles is unknown, but his signature ensured his continued safety for the following eighteen months. This was to change on October 26,

1776, when he was brought before the Ulster County Committee meeting at the home of his kinsman, Abraham DuBois.[19] This extra-legal governmental committee had been in existence since January 6, 1775, when five town committees had met in Hurley, near the county seat of Kingston. County, town, and district committees, some of which had been formed as early as 1774, were becoming increasingly central to the war effort and served to fill the function of regional and local government with the collapse of the colonial government. After the Declaration of Independence, they became the local governments in a free state until the new government was set up under the state constitution of 1777. Whether or not these committees were truly representative of the people is questionable. As Hugh Flick states, "In speaking for the people (in 1774–1775), active minorities were usurping the functions of local governments and, for the most part, without hindrance by the more passive conservative(s)."[20] And as Samuel Seabury noted at the time, "It is notorious that in some districts only three or four met and chose themselves to be a committee. . . ."[21] By the time Eltinge came before the Ulster committee in 1776, it probably was more representative of the public voice than in earlier years because sentiment against the British had been growing, especially since the struggles began in Massachusetts. Nevertheless, there was still a question in the eyes of many, particularly those with conservative tendencies, whether the committees had the right to assume governmental functions. Thus Eltinge might have approached his examination with severe misgivings.

The county committees were essentially the regional representatives of the New York Provincial Congress, and it was their responsibility to assist the Congress in its Revolutionary efforts. One of these activities was to confront the internal threat posed by those who were loyal to the British crown—the "disaffected." This became an increasing concern with the close proximity of British forces after the occupation of New York City in the fall of 1776, as well as the ongoing possibility of attack from the north. This effort to apprehend Tories had begun in May 1776, and it was stepped up with the creation of the Committee for Detecting and Defeating Conspiracies (to which the county committees were subordinate) on September 21, 1776. It was in its capacity as locator of Tories that Eltinge was brought before the Ulster County Committee.

Eltinge was forced to appear because he refused to take Continental currency in his store. According to his statement to the committee, he never entirely trusted the value of the currency, and although he initially received it, his trust in it subsequently eroded further. After the withdrawal of Continental forces from Long Island and a "general rumor amongst the people of [his] neighborhood that in a little time Congress money would be good for nothing as the King was likely to overcome," others came to his store to purchase goods with the currency, but he believed they did so simply because they also considered it would soon be worthless. Although he refused the currency, he told his customers that he would allow purchases on credit. According to the New York Provincial Congress, such actions were unacceptable according to their resolves passed on June 5, 1776, which indicated that those who prevented the circulation of paper money "were to be imprisoned, put under bond for good behavior, or removed from their localities on parole."[22] This local statement reflected the policy of the Continental Congress promulgated on January 11, 1776: those who did not accept currency should be treated as enemies. Although activities such as Eltinge's were nonbelligerent in nature, such an extreme position was taken because the acceptance of Continental money was absolutely necessary to fund the war effort, and the Revolutionaries feared that "Tories" such as Eltinge might influence others, directly and by example. The committee chose to take the most extreme action they could under the

Provincial Congress' resolves, and Eltinge was sentenced to the prison in Fishkill, Dutchess County.[23]

While Eltinge's refusal to take Continental currency was in itself unacceptable to the authorities, the fact that he was brought before the committee and soundly punished might also have been reflective of personal animosities in both New Paltz and nearby Kingston. Tradition has it that there was an ongoing feud between the Eltinges and another prominent local family, the Hasbroucks, whose progenitors—the brothers Jean and Abraham—had been founding members of New Paltz (along with Abraham DuBois). According to Ralph LeFevre, the disagreement between the families resulted from a dispute over a land grant received by Eltinge's uncle, Noah, which some landowners in New Paltz protested because they claimed that part of the land was contained in the New Paltz patent.[24] Jacob Hasbrouck, Jr. (grandson of Jean Hasbrouck), and Abraham Hasbrouck (grandson of patentee Abraham Hasbrouck) instigated proceedings over this dispute in 1748. Unfortunately for Eltinge, the woman from whom he first refused to take the Continental currency was Esther Hasbrouck Wirtz, the daughter of Jacob Jr. Both Jacob Jr. and Abraham were active Patriots. Jacob Jr. (of New Paltz) was a member of the Ulster County Committee and a major in the militia, while Abraham (of Kingston) was a colonel, and a rather petulant one at that.[25] Thus, Eltinge's run-in with the authorities might have had an extremely personal side to it, as small-town politics often do.

From that point until after the ratification of the peace treaty in 1784, Eltinge's freedom was circumscribed by the authorities. After a stay of more than a month at the jail in Fishkill, he was sent to New Hampshire for confinement.[26] He and others were exiled from New York, according to John Jay, a member of the Committee for Detecting and Defeating Conspiracies, because it was "indispensably necessary to remove a number of dangerous and disaffected persons, some of whom have been taken in arms against America, to one of the neighboring states."[27] The committee's prime concern was the men's proximity to the British stronghold of New York City. The Council of New Hampshire was willing to take them. Leaving Fishkill on December 4, 1776, Eltinge arrived in Atkinson, New Hampshire, on December 13. He was confined at the home of a Lieutenant Belknap for several days before being moved to the home of Lieutenant Colonel Joseph Welch until February 3, 1777, when he was placed in prison at Exeter.[28] Even though Eltinge and the other prisoners had been confined against their will, they remained responsible for their own "expenses and diet,"[29] a policy made necessary because of the limited financial resources of the provincial government.

While officials in New Hampshire were willing to take the prisoners, the New Hampshire Council had some misgivings about their guilt.

> Their clamours of being sent here without an examination at home and consciousness of their innocence which they assert, has had considerable influence among the people. . . . And as a great number of them make such protestations of their not being sensible of their having ever given occasion for any person to suppose them unfriendly to the American cause, we wish an impartial inquiry might be made into their characters . . .

wrote council President Meshach Weare.[30]

Eltinge remained in jail in Exeter until March 25, when he was released back to New York in response to a March 13, 1777, request by the Committee for Detecting and Defeating Conspiracies to return all prisoners except those who were "closely confined in Goal (sic),"[31] to administer an oath of allegiance. If the prisoners refused, they were to be forced to remove themselves behind enemy lines. Eltinge arrived in Poughkeepsie to see the commissioners on May 13, but there is no evidence that he was asked to take an oath at that point. Nevertheless, he was given an order on May 21 to report to the fleet prison in Kingston in six days. Opened on May 2, 1777, the prison originally consisted of two former privateer vessels anchored off Kingston, but as the need arose, other boats had been added. Initially intended to house prisoners whom the commissioners feared might lead rumored uprisings in Dutchess County, Westchester County, and Livingston Manor, the prison later swelled with detainees from Albany and Orange counties, as well as with those, like Eltinge, who had been recalled from New England. Eltinge remained on board until June 18, when he was paroled to the home in Hurley of Jacobus Hardenburgh, his brother-in-law, who had petitioned for his release. This was the first time in almost eight months that Eltinge was able to enjoy a modicum of freedom and be with family. It was to be short-lived.

In his diary, Eltinge does not record any dealings with the authorities for the subsequent four months, but on October 6, 1777, after being accused of breaking his parole, he was taken back to Kingston to appear before the Commission for Detecting and Defeating Conspiracies. He proved that he was innocent of the charge, and he was again paroled back to Hardenburgh's, although his parole was to last only a few more days. Forts Clinton and Montgomery, about forty miles south of Kingston, had been taken on October 6 by British forces under General Sir Henry Clinton; General John Burgoyne's forces were eighty miles north, at Saratoga. Meeting on October 8 in Kingston, the Council of Safety was not yet aware that Burgoyne's forces had been defeated on October 7, and in its eyes, the northern and southern armies were too close for comfort. Fearing that inactive Loyalists would be emboldened to act if British forces pushed into the region, the council felt it was necessary to remove all prisoners in and around Kingston to Hartford, Connecticut. Within hours, the militia was at the home of Jacobus Hardenburgh, where it again took Eltinge into custody. It also detained Eltinge's luncheon companion, Cadwallader Colden Jr., who was on parole to the Van Deusen House in Hurley. From that moment on, the wartime fates of these two men would be bound together.[32]

Colden was the son of Cadwallader Colden Sr. (1688–1776), of Coldengham, near Newburgh. The elder Colden had been a member of the Governor's Council from 1721 through 1776 and lieutenant governor from 1761 until his death. During several periods—most importantly throughout the Stamp Act crisis of 1765–1766—he filled the position of acting governor. He was the owner of a great deal of land, although not to the extent of families such as the DeLanceys or Livingstons. He was a thorough supporter of royal authority and prerogative, and as a high-ranking royal official he made considerable use of the power of his office in furthering the interests of both himself and his family. The Colden name was synonymous with the colonial royal government, and the family was soon to be considered the enemy of the Revolution, which they were.

David Colden, Cadwallader Jr.'s younger brother, was a resident of Long Island who "actively supported royal government, and as a leader of the Loyalists who outnumbered whigs in Flushing, [he] prevented the creation of local protest committees in 1775 and '76."[33] Also, as the leader of 1,293 freeholders and inhabitants of Queens County who had "steadfastly maintained their royal principles,"[34] he petitioned the governor for the reinstitution of royal government when the British took New York City. After the war, David Colden was denied admission to the State of New York (as an active Loyalist, he had been forced to flee when the British evacuated New York City), and his property was confiscated after his death in 1784.

The Loyalist activities of Cadwallader Colden Jr. were not as forward as those of his brother, possibly because the smaller number of Tories in Ulster County made it extremely difficult and dangerous to be so blatant. Nonetheless, his sympathies were identical. On April 14, 1775, he, Walter DuBois, and Peter DuBois[35] published a protest in response to the election of delegates from Ulster County to the Provincial Congress. They stated that the election was bogus because it had been executed by a group that in no way represented the eligible voters, and that the only legal governmental body was the Assembly. (Both were common Loyalist complaints.) They also declared that they would remain loyal "to our Parent State and British Constitution."[36] Although Colden signed the Articles of Association in April because of pressure from the local committee, he continued to espouse his Loyalist rhetoric. He was arrested by the committee in June 1776 so they could disarm him. (Because he was considered an active Loyalist, he was assumed to have a large cache of guns at his home. Only a broken gun and his son-in-law's fowling piece were found.) On July 4, he was asked to sign an oath stating that he would abide by the Association. He refused to sign when a codicil was added stating that, if necessary, he would bear arms against the British army. As a result, he was sentenced to jail as a Loyalist. On August 22, 1776, his case was given to the state Committee for Detecting and Defeating Conspiracies. His troubles with the authorities would last throughout the war, as would Roeloff Eltinge's. Although Colden consistently claimed that he would obey the rules of the state and remain neutral throughout the struggle, he later stated that he could never swear an oath to the state in God's name, since his oath to the king was completely binding and could not be superseded. During the Revolutionary War, however, neutrals in New York were believed to be "cowardly tor(ies)"[37] and could not be countenanced. While Eltinge's condemnation as a Loyalist was not based on any overt support of the power of the king and Parliament, keeping company with an avowed Loyalist—especially one from such a hated family—was extremely compromising.

After the militia burst in on the luncheon at the Hardenburghs, it took Colden and Eltinge to Kingston along with other parolees it picked up along the way. Meeting in the Ulster County Courthouse in Kingston, the Committee for Detecting and Defeating Conspiracies issued a list of those who were to be sent out of state; for some unrecorded reason, Colden and Eltinge were left off. They were ordered by the "officer of the guard to come out of the ranks and (were) left on the street."[38] Not knowing what to do, both returned to Hurley, obeying their parole.[39]

Eltinge was taken by guard back to Kingston on October 12 and confined to "close goal by the Council of Safety till further orders."[40] He remained there for only a short time, as he and the other prisoners were removed on October 16, and "As soon as we got out of town it was in flames."[41] The British forces under Major General John Vaughan arrived in Kingston on October 15, having been sent by Sir Henry Clinton in the Highlands to meet up with Burgoyne at Saratoga. Burgoyne had already asked for surrender terms on the 13th, but Clinton had been unaware of this when he dispatched Vaughan. On the 16th, the residents of Kingston had fled, and Vaughan's forces burned the town nearly to the ground.

Colden was still under parole in nearby Hurley at the time of the burning, and he was subsequently sent to appear before the State Council of Safety meeting in Marbletown. He stated before the council a few days later that he was bound by oath to the king, but would remain neutral and subject to the laws of the state. The council responded that he must remain a prisoner if he was a subject of the king, and it paroled him to the Hardenburghs'. Eltinge had been held as a "close prisoner" at the house of Johannes Tack, in Marbletown, since the burning of Kingston.[42] On November 5, an order was issued by the Council of Safety that both men were to be sent away to a remote district of Dutchess County called the Nine Partners. There were so few Tories in that region, it was felt, that the two would have little opportunity to influence others.

Although they petitioned the council for a reprieve or postponement, Colden and Eltinge did not receive a response and arrived in Nine Partners, near the Connecticut border, on December 9. On January 27, 1778, they went to Poughkeepsie to confront the state legislature. Since their arrival in Nine Partners, Colden had been campaigning to be allowed to return home. He had approached the council, spoken with and written letters to Governor George Clinton (his former lawyer), and contacted many others, including his "old friend Coll [Levi] Pawling," an important Patriot. His entreaties were apparently of no avail.[43] With the reorganization of the state government under the new constitution of 1777, there was a question of jurisdiction regarding the cases of the men. Colden attempted to use the influence that he thought he possessed with Clinton and others to have the state legislature decide their case, but that body decided that their fates should be under the purview of the reorganized Commission for Detecting and Defeating Conspiracies, which had not yet met. Colden and Eltinge contacted the two available members of the old committee, who agreed to allow them a two-week parole to their own homes until the new commission met. Eltinge left for New Paltz on January 30.

During the period of Eltinge's incarceration, which had begun back in October when he was initially to be sent to Connecticut, it is obvious that various governing bodies were unsure about how to deal with him, as well as with Colden. While the two did not pose any direct threat to the war effort, their being designated Loyalists required that their influence on others be contained. Furthermore, the jurisdiction that was to deal with their situation—whether local, county, or state—was unclear, and there was no defined protocol to be followed on any level. Thus the two were in a state of legal limbo that would last a few months longer.

As directed, Eltinge returned to Poughkeepsie on February 13, but he was not accompanied by Colden, who had received a one-month extension because he anticipated he would not be able to cross the ice-bound Hudson. This was probably a ploy to remain home longer, as Eltinge had been able to make the crossing. Eltinge was also given an additional month at home, quite possibly because the commission considered the two cases to be a single issue. Colden arrived in Poughkeepsie on March 15, Eltinge on the 18th. According to Eltinge, he was "detained"[44] until March 23, but Eugene Fingerhut states that "For four days Colden parked himself outside the Assembly door, awaiting his fate,"[45] so the status of their level of freedom is unclear. Colden was told that he could return home until further orders, while Eltinge "was . . . permitted to remain at my place of abode . . . till I could be exchanged for some well-affected citizen or prisoner with the enemy."[46] While Colden's status was still uncertain, Eltinge's situation was apparently coming to a head.

On June 30, the legislature passed "An Act More Effectively to Prevent the Mischieffs ariseing from the Influence and Example of Persons of Equivocal and Suspected Character in this State." No longer would the state accept neutral persons in its midst; with British forces so close, it felt the risk was too great. While people like Eltinge and Colden never aided British forces or bore arms against the Revolutionaries, the state thought it would be better to be rid of them. However, they were given one last chance to regain their freedom and stay: Loyalists were given a final opportunity to take an oath of allegiance to the laws of New York. If they refused, they would be banished. This oath would also require the person to declare that the state had a right to be free and independent. Colden was the first person to be dealt with under the new law, and on July 4 he declined to take the oath. Although he could abide by the state laws, his oath to the king could not be superseded. On July 6, Eltinge also refused to take it.

Following Eltinge's refusal, he was paroled back to New Paltz, but on July 26 he received a notice from the Commission for Detecting and Defeating Conspiracies. "Pursuant to the act of the Legislature," he was to appear at Fishkill on August 3 "in order to effect his removal within the Enemy's lines, that he be permitted to take with him his family (males capable of bearing arms excepted) one week's provisions and as much of his effects as together with his family and provisions as would be transported in two wagons."[47] Colden also was to appear on August 3 for the same purpose. Eltinge met up with him at Coldengham, and when they arrived in Fishkill they remained there for two days because no one knew how their transport would be effected. It was decided that they would travel to New York City on a sloop that had been obtained by another banished Loyalist, William Smith Jr., under the guard of Colonel Aaron Burr.[48] Even though Eltinge had been permitted to take his family, they remained in New Paltz, and he arrived in New York City on August 11. On September 8, 1778, he indicated that he "took (his) boarding at Anthony van Noorstrandt in Wolves Hollow on Long Island in Queens County," where it appears from his diary that he primarily remained throughout the war, although he made trips into the city every few months.

Also living in New York was Eltinge's younger brother Solomon (1742–1809). He, too, had been in trouble with the authorities. On November 8, 1776, he had been sent by the conspiracy commissioner to Exeter, New Hampshire, for being "notoriously disaffected to the American cause, which [he has] evinced by refusing to receive in payment the Continental currency, and endeavouring to depreciate the same"—the same charge originally levied against his brother.[49] Solomon followed Roeloff in his refusal to take the oath of allegiance on August 1, 1778, and he, too, was banished. Records indicate that the brothers were in close contact during their exile.[50]

Although some account information concerning Roeloff Eltinge's financial situation during his exile survives, no descriptive information about his day-to-day life exists. His financial situation must have been precarious, since it would have been impossible for him to perform his livelihood as a merchant. To earn money, it appears that he turned to crafts such as "patching shoes" and "making a slay." Additionally, from January 1780 through March 1783 he left a considerable amount of "stoves," pails, piggins, "koolers," sugar boxes and "canteens" to be sold at various locations. This provided him with a steady, albeit small, income.[51] Food, other essential goods, and housing were difficult to come by because of a significant surge in Loyalist refugees and the large garrison of British troops. Making matters worse, inflation rates were dramatic. However, Eltinge appears to have survived reasonably well. The last entry in his wartime diary and account book indicates that in 1784 (presumably at the conclusion of his exile) he had amassed £26.2.8.

Provisional articles of peace between Britain and the United States were signed at Paris on November 30, 1782, thus beginning the process for Loyalists either to emigrate or reconcile with and remain in the new nation. Article five provided for "the restitution of . . . the estates, rights, and properties of persons resident in districts in the possession of his Majesty's arms and who have not borne arms against the said United States," but this provision was only to be "earnestly recommended . . . to the legislatures of the respective states." The provisional articles were included in the final treaty, which was signed by representatives of both countries in Paris on September 3, 1783. Because the agreement concerning the appropriate treatment of Loyalists was not binding on any state, Roeloff Eltinge's position in relation to New York remained unaltered at the conclusion of the war. In other words, he remained banished. Thus, when the British army began the process of evacuating New York City in the spring of 1783, it was necessary for him to leave the state. A letter from Eltinge to his son (probably his eldest, Ezekiel) dated September 29, 1783, indicates that he and Solomon had moved to Achquechkononck, New Jersey (now Passaic). In this letter, he informed his son that "if any of my friends want to see me [they] may come here, because I see no probability as yet to come to see them with Safety."[52] He and Solomon were still there on January 11, 1784, as indicated in a letter Roeloff wrote to his wife. He stated that "I [will] not be able to come home as soon as I had expected on account of the definitive triety [sic] not being published . . . and not knowing yet . . . whether [the state government] will or can do anything for us."[53]

The peace treaty was ratified by Congress on January 14, 1784, but New York refused to consider its recommendations regarding the treatment of Loyalists. On February 12, 1784, Roeloff and Solomon Eltinge petitioned the state legislature to be "released from the disagreeable situation to which they have been so long exposed and humbly pray the Honorable Legislature to make such order in their behalf as may remove the effect of the law under which they suffer and enable your Petitioners to return with safety to their families."[54] Several other banished Loyalists, including Cadwallader Colden Jr., also submitted petitions. The Assembly voted to reject them all, and the Senate voted to postpone consideration. According to Alexander Flick, "In early 1784 the wartime policy of the state legislature was still clear and certain." It had no intention of revoking the banishment of Loyalists.[55]

On May 12, however, Roeloff and Solomon Eltinge and 25 others (including Cadwallader Colden Jr.) were permitted to return to their homes. This permission was passed in conjunction with an anti-Loyalist act that upheld the banishment of those who actively took part in the war on the side of the British. Only 36 Loyalists had their banishments revoked in 1784. It was not until 1792 that all of those who had been exiled were allowed to return.

The exact date of Roeloff Eltinge's return to New Paltz is unknown, but it is likely that he returned forthwith. Few records survive that indicate the process of his reintegration into society. Because he never took an active part on the side of the British, his property was never confiscated, nor did he face persecution extreme enough for him to emigrate from his native land. According to Alexander Flick,

> Those whose worst crime was open loyalty, who had been arrested, imprisoned, exiled, or paroled, but never charged with treason, were found in every community, and, although subjected to more or less abuse, were for the most part allowed to remain after the war was over, and to keep their property. While never fully forgiven, in time they came to be looked upon as true Americans, and were given full political rights.[56]

Roeloff Eltinge's experience in New Paltz supports Flick's assertion. Within a few years he was respected enough to serve in several elected government positions, first as overseer of the poor in 1790 and then "as one of the New Paltz Twelve Men for the share of Louis DuBois from 1791 until his death in 1795."[57] He also returned to his mercantile activities in partnership with his son Ezekiel.

It is clear that the Revolutionary authorities believed that Eltinge was a Tory, but were they accurate in their perception? His refusal to take the oath of allegiance clearly indicates that he did not embrace the Patriot cause, but in and of itself that might not indicate that he harbored pro-British sentiments. Before the issue of Eltinge's allegiance is considered in depth, his involvement in an earlier dispute concerning the relation between the colonies and Europe must be considered.

Eltinge was a lifelong member of the Dutch Reformed Church, having joined the Kingston congregation in 1762, at the age of 25. In 1737, the same year as Eltinge's birth, a controversy began to develop in the Dutch Reformed congregations in the colonies. The governing organization of the church, which was responsible for doctrine, ordination, dispute resolution, and all general ecclesiastical business, was the Classis of Amsterdam. Because of its distance from the colonies, a movement began in the 1730s to establish an organization in America to conduct church business, but this organization—the Coetus—would remain subordinate to the

Classis. When the Coetus was formed in 1737, several congregations refused to send representatives because they believed that some congregations had obfuscated their true intention of ultimate independence from the Netherlands. Indeed, in 1754 the Coetus expressed its belief that it should serve as an independent, American Classis. The result was a schism in the colonial churches, with those that desired maintaining ties with Amsterdam forming a separate, smaller body of congregations called the Conferentie, meaning "conference." The schism was not mended until 1772, when the Articles of Union (which resulted in virtual independence of Dutch Reformed congregations in America) was signed by the American congregations with the approval of the Classis.

The New Paltz congregation sided with the Coetus, but there were residents who wished to remain subordinate to the Classis, and this resulted in the formation of a new, Conferentie congregation on August 29, 1766. Ten of the original 15 members of this new church had never been official members of the New Paltz church, but rather were congregants in the Dutch church in Kingston. (However, it appears likely that these Kingston members attended services in New Paltz on a regular basis.) The other five were members of the New Paltz congregation, although four of them had previously been members in Kingston. Although there was a great deal of strife in the Kingston congregation, it officially remained in the Conferentie party. Interestingly enough, one of the protagonists in the dispute within the Kingston congregation was Colonel Abraham Hasbrouck (of the reputed Eltinge-Hasbrouck feud), who was attempting to force the church in the direction of the Coetus. This would have placed the Eltinges in opposition to the Hasbroucks once again.[58] The founding members from the Kingston church had been granted a dismissal by the Kingston consistory in order to form the new church, as "they [were] living too far away from the church of Kingston to dutifully and statedly attend divine worship there . . . in the pure doctrine of the truth, and to lead them to the communion of a Reformed (and to the Reverend Classis of Amsterdam subordinated) congregation."[59]

A leading member of the new congregation was Roeloff Josiah Eltinge's father, Josiah Eltinge, who provided a large portion of the funds for construction of a house of worship. Roeloff Josiah (who was a member of the Kingston congregation) and his three brothers joined the church the year after its creation. Roeloff Eltinge was active in his new congregation, serving as both elder and deacon at various times. The last elections for elder and deacon of the second church in New Paltz for which evidence survives is dated December 16, 1776, four years after the Articles of Union had been signed, but the churches did not unite until May 25, 1783.[60]

The fundamental question in this dispute was whether or not the colonial church should remain subordinate and dependent on the mother country or should it, as a result of growth and maturation and the need to manage its own affairs, become independent. That these issues were being faced in the Dutch church at the same time that the political independence movement was gaining momentum was not coincidental. American society in many ways was considering its position in relation to Europe, with many in America leaning toward separation. That Roeloff Josiah Eltinge sided with the Conferentie party suggests a conservative mindset; when faced with the issue of political independence, the implication is that he would have possessed more of a Loyalist mentality.

While it is true that members of the Conferentie faction were cultural conservatives, those who were opposed to the Coetus party were not necessarily political conservatives as well. The controversy concerning religious independence did develop at the same time as the political independence movement, and both movements were guided by similar principles regarding American and European relationships. But it also occurred at a time when Dutch culture and language was being diminished by the dominating English influence, and those who expressed a desire to remain subordinate to Amsterdam might have been led by an equal desire to retain their cultural identity. Additionally, there were many in the Coetus who tended toward evangelical style of worship, thus encouraging those "uncomfortable with the vagaries of revivalism" to join the Conferentie opposition.[61] Thus, all members of the Dutch conservative faction, including Eltinge, were not necessarily anti-Revolutionaries by definition since they were also being influenced by other cultural and spiritual concerns.

What, then, is the evidence that sheds light on Eltinge's allegiance? His involvement in the conservative faction of the Dutch church suggests that even before the American political independence movement began he was a proponent of continued cultural connections with Europe. However, the incident that marked him as a Loyalist in the eyes of the Patriots—and by the definition of the Continental Congress—was his refusal to take Continental currency. At his trial, he never stated any support for the British government other than indicating that he did not feel that the Patriots would prevail. His decision not to take the currency was based on economic pragmatism and his belief that he was being taken advantage of. If he was truly a Loyalist, at that point it is likely that he would have made statements to that effect; both his involvement in the less-powerful Conferentie faction and his future refusal to take the oath suggest that he was a man of principle who was willing to declare publicly his ideology, whether it was popular or not. It must also be remembered that in the fall of 1776, even though independence had been declared, Loyalist and Patriot ideologies had not yet polarized the people into two camps. It is likely that, given his conservative mindset, Eltinge leaned toward the Loyalist side without fully committing to it—at least in 1776.

When he refused to take the oath in 1778, however, the situation had changed. By that time, a person had to be either a Loyalist or a Patriot because it had become a matter of one party against another, rather than an issue of a somewhat fluid ideology. Refusing to take the oath in itself was not a clear statement of pro-British sympathies; it could also have been an anti-Revolutionary declaration. During the previous two years, Eltinge had been shuttled around from place to place, confined in prisons, and in general treated poorly by authorities whose right to punish was questionable, particularly in the early years before the state had been officially formed. If we keep in mind that he did not declare pro-British opinions (if he in fact possessed them) when he would likely have done so, it is quite possible that his treatment at the hands of the Patriots hardened his heart against them and made it too galling for him to take the oath. Thus, it is likely that he was a conservative forced into the Loyalist camp by the harsh treatment to which he was subjected for a perceived offense that was simply a matter of financial self-preservation.

The other piece of evidence that might suggest a Loyalist stance was Eltinge's relationship with Cadwallader Colden Jr. Although the two were at least acquainted with each other before the war, their close interaction did not begin until both had difficulties with the Patriot committees. While it appears that the committees treated the two almost as a unit, suggesting that they believed the men shared a common ideology, there is no evidence to suggest that Eltinge held the same staunch Loyalist outlook that Colden did. Their relationship, then, was substantially a matter of circumstance. Finally, Eltinge's lack of involvement in the Patriot movement might have been a response to the active part played by such influential Ulster County leaders as Major Jacob Hasbrouck Jr. and Colonel Abraham Hasbrouck. If indeed there was a feud between the two families, it is possible that Eltinge was loath to support the Patriots in Ulster County due to personal conflicts.

Eltinge's political ideology will, unfortunately, never be known. During the Revolution itself, it is quite likely that his position was equally unclear in the eyes of his community, and his treatment was a direct result of this ambiguousness. To the authorities, his actions would have marked him as a suspicious person, but because he did not pose any clear threat, they were at a loss to determine an appropriate method of containing him. Had he taken up arms against the Patriots, or otherwise blatantly assisted the British, the appropriate punishment would have been clear. But Eltinge's suspiciousness placed him in limbo, and his resulting treatment might have influenced his inability to sign an oath that would have resolved his predicament and allowed him to return home.

It is also clear that Eltinge's ambiguousness was considered a substantial threat; otherwise, he would not have been removed from the area whenever the possibility of British invasion increased. This highlights a different dimension of the activities of committees in relation to the Loyalists from that suggested by Jonathan Clark, who states that their primary goal was "to enforce a patriotic consensus" within the community by requiring that suspicious individuals "choose between acting like Patriots and silent acquiescence."[62] Unfortunately, pretending to be a Revolutionary and/or keeping one's mouth shut would not have been sufficient to satisfy the Patriots. Even if oaths were taken by those whose actions suggested a Loyalist mentality, "Many participants remarked upon the difficulty of knowing who had sworn the oath with conviction, and who was simply being pragmatic in order to save his property or his skin."[63] Because those of ambiguous allegiance—many of whom did take an oath of allegiance—were still feared as potentially active Tories, the committees were additionally required to deal with the silent threat that they posed.

It is difficult to compare Eltinge's experience with that of others whose political allegiance was unclear, as there is little modern research on the subject other than that which concerns key figures, or the experience of Tories in general. But certainly Eltinge would not have been alone. In Poughkeepsie, Clark contends that 130 out of the 239 residents whose allegiance can be sufficiently determined were not fully supportive of the Patriot cause, although the level of their support (or lack thereof) varied.[64] He also states that "Perhaps the most unjustly treated victims of patriotic justice were men who belonged . . . in one of the 'occasional' categories."[65] This is likely because they were seen as unknown quantities and therefore unpredictable. As to the experience of Loyalists, or suspected Loyalists, after the war, Alexander Flick contends that nonbelligerents were generally accepted back into their communities, although not always fully forgiven.[66] Clark's investigation suggests a similar postwar treatment in Poughkeepsie, possibly because "Ties to family, to farms, and to the community . . . proved to a surprising extent stronger than political causes," although they were excluded from political affairs.[67] Eltinge was apparently successfully reintegrated, possibly more so than many in similar circumstances in Poughkeepsie, but this might have been because the affairs of New Paltz were heavily influenced by the original founding families through the organization known as "The Twelve Men," and Eltinge was the dominant member of the line of patentee Abraham DuBois. As long as his family accepted him, he would retain a position in the community.

Even though Eltinge's experience was far from unique, his story is rare for its completeness given his social standing. It demonstrates the sticky issue of allegiance, both in its time and in retrospect, as well as the motivations of a suspicious community in an anxious time. While those in the higher ranks of society were involved in an ideological struggle to understand how, and if, the colonies should remain attached to Great Britain, there were many in the middle ranks whose allegiance—although not always without philosophical foundations—was also determined by small-town politics, familial animosities, suspicion, and pride.

This article originally appeared in *The Hudson River Valley Review*, Volume 20.1, summer, 2003.

NOTES

1. Robert M. Calhoon, *The Loyalists in Revolutionary America, 1760–1781* (New York: Harcourt Brace Jovanovich, 1973), 300.
2. William H. Nelson, *The American Tory* (Oxford: Oxford University Press, 1961), 5.
3. Calhoon, xii.
4. Nelson, 41.
5. Nelson, 43–45; Philip Ranlet, *The New York Loyalists* (Knoxville: University of Tennessee Press, 1986), 10–25.
6. Ranlet, 26–51.
7. Robert Benson, "To Aaron Burr," 2 Aug. 1778, Matthew L. Davis, ed. *Memoirs of Aaron Burr* (New York: Da Capo, 1971), 131.
8. Michael Kammen, "The American Revolution as a *Crise de Conscience:* The Case of New York," in Richard M. Jellison, ed., *Society, Freedom, and Conscience: The Coming of the Revolution in Virginia, Massachusetts, and New York* (New York: Norton, 1976), 125–89.
9. Both British and American authorities of the period felt that New York was rife with Loyalist sympathizers. Most modern historics follow the lead of Alexander Flick who contended that half of all New Yorkers were against the Patriot cause [*Loyalism in New York During the American Revolution* (1901; New York: Arno Press, 1969), 180–82]. Most historians who followed Flick accepted his analysis until Ranlet questioned this accepted view in his 1986 reevaluation of the issue [*The New York Loyalists*]. He suggests that "New York was probably similar to the other Revolutionary states in its degree of loyalism" (186–87). The issue of Tory strength in New York is sticky at best and irresolvable at worst, since it would have been almost impossible to determine allegiance of many at the time, let alone hundreds of years hence.
10. Alexander Flick, *Loyalism in New York During the American Revolution,* 71.
11. University of the State of New York, Division of Archives and History, *The American Revolution in New York: its Political, Social and Economic Significance* (Albany: The University of the State of New York, 1926), 225.
12. Calhoon, 410.
13. Calhoon, 304–05.
14. Ranlet, 162.
15. The only extensive group of documents related to a local committee are those of the Albany Committee.
16. Jonathan Clark, "The Problem of Allegiance in Revolutionary Poughkeepsie," in David D. Hall, John M. Murrin, and Thad W. Tate, eds., *Saints & Revolutionaries: Essays on Early American History* (New York: Norton, 1984), 285–317.
17. Ralph LeFevre, *History of New Paltz and its Old Families* (Albany: Fort Orange Press, 1903), 487.
18. The archives of the Huguenot Historical Society and Senate House (Kingston, New York) contain a great deal of information about Roeloff Josiah Eltinge's financial activities, but these have yet to be fully studied.
19. Roeloff Eltinge's paternal grandmother was Sara DuBois, daughter of Abraham DuBois (1657–1731), one of the holders of the patent of New Paltz. Also, his mother was Magdalena DuBois, his father's first cousin. As there were several men with the name of Abraham DuBois alive in 1776, the familial relationship between Eltinge and this Abraham DuBois is unclear.

20. Hugh Flick, "The Rise of the Revolutionary Committee System," in *History of the State of New York"* (New York: Columbia University Press, 1933) III, 232.
21. Quoted in H. Flick, 230. However, Seabury's analysis cannot be entirely trusted because his staunch Loyalism might have clouded his perceptions. Additionally, in his desire to discredit the Revolutionaries, he might have overstated his case.
22. A. Flick, 67.
23. According to his parole of June 17, 1777, he had been "confined since last Fall." Additionally, his diary attests to his leaving Fishkill on December 3, 1776. *Roeloff and Ezekiel Eltinge Family Papers,* Huguenot Historical Society, New Paltz, N.Y.
24. LeFevre, 485. While this supposed feud is a matter of folklore, it is said in New Paltz today that animosity extended well into the twentieth century.
25. Abraham Hasbrouck resigned his position as commander of the Ulster Fourth Regiment because he had been passed over for generalship in favor of George Clinton. The return of his commission was described as "childish" by the provincial government [quoted in Marius Schoonmaker, *The History of Kingston, New York* (New York: Burr Printing House, 1888), 175].
26. Prisoners were also sent to Connecticut, Massachusetts, and Pennsylvania.
27. New York State, Commission for Detecting and Defeating Conspiracies, 1777–1778. *Minutes of the Committee and of the first Commission for Detecting and Defeating Conspiracies in the State of New York,* Minutes of Committee, October 13, 1776, The New-York Historical Society, *Collections* (New York, 1918), 414.
28. Lt. Col. Welch was an officer of New Hampshire who had been assigned to New York by Washington and was made responsible for removing the prisoners to New Hampshire. It is not clear from the Minutes exactly to whom Welch had been assigned, but he had a great deal of interaction with the Committee of Conspiracies in 1776–1777.
29. Receipt of February 15, 1777, from Roeloff Eltinge to Joseph Stacy of the Exeter Gaol. *Eltinge Papers.*
30. Meshach Weare, President of the Council of New Hampshire, "To William Duer, Chairman of the Committee for Conspiracies," December 27, 1776, *Minutes of the Committee. . . . Defeating Conspiracies,* 417–18.
31. Commissioners for Conspiracies, "To the Honourable Committee of Safety of New Hampshire." March 13, 1777, *Minutes of the Committeee . . . Defeating Conspiracies,* 433–35.
32. Eugene Fingerhut suggests in *Survivor: Cadwallader Colden II in Revolutionary America* (Washington, University Press of America, 1983), 27, that the two might have become acquainted while involved in court cases in Kingston in the previous years, when Colden served as a judge. Their first recorded meeting of a personal nature occurred on June 18, 1777, when Eltinge was paroled and left several items, including eating and cooking utensils, in the care of Colden, who remained incarcerated on the prison ships. *Eltinge Papers.*
33. Fingerhut, 40.
34. Quoted in A. Flick, 97.
35. Peter DuBois was Roeloff Josiah Eltinge's third cousin. Walter DuBois is not identified in the published DuBois family genealogy.
36. Cited in Fingerhut, 44.
37. Fingerhut, 92.
38. *Eltinge Papers.*
39. It is not clear if Eltinge returned to Van Deusen's house in Hurley with Colden or if he returned to Hardenburgh's, also in Hurley. His diary simply states "went to Hurley again."
40. *Eltinge Papers.*
41. *Eltinge Papers.*
42. *Eltinge Papers.*
43. Quoted in Fingerhut, 88.
44. *Eltinge Papers.*

45. Fingerhut, 92.
46. *Eltinge Papers.*
47. In his diary, he recorded that he was to report on July 30. *Eltinge Papers.*
48. William Smith Jr. (1728–1793) was a prominent lawyer and historian who had been appointed to his father's seat in the Governor's Council in 1767 and subsequently served as Chief Justice of the Province of New York (appointed in 1780 by the royal governor during the British occupation of New York). He left for Canada after the British evacuation of New York City and was appointed Chief Justice of Quebec in 1786. While Smith was also banished from the State of New York for refusing to take the oath of allegiance, and while he was adamantly against independence, he was also staunchly opposed to Parliamentary taxation and was for the "cause of truth and liberty," as he stated in the first issue of his 1752 weekly, *The Independent Reflector* [as quoted in William Sabine, introduction, *Historical Memoirs of William Smith from 12 July 1776 to 25 July 1778* (Hollis, N.Y.: Colburn & Tegg, 1958), 2–3]. He was a close colleague of many other patriot radicals, including John Morin Scott, the Livingstons (to whom his wife belonged), and Alexander McDougall.
49. *Minutes of the Committee . . . .Defeating Conspiracies*, 11.
50. Eltinge's diary indicates that he loaned Solomon six half guineas in April 1781, and two letters written from New Jersey in September 1783 and January 1784 state that they were together there pending the decision regarding their being allowed to return to New York. Roeloff had additional contact with his family during his exile; his wife, Maria, visited him in the company of Mrs. Colden, who was given permission to visit her husband in April 1781 for a total of 11 days. Eltinge's eldest son, Ezekiel, who was eighteen years of age, began the journey with his mother but was sent home when the American General William Heath detained their sloop at West Point. Additionally, when the general found "a quantity of provisions . . . over and above what appeared necessary to support the families on their way to the enemy," he seized the goods and put them in the public stores [New York State. *Public Papers of George Clinton* (New York and Albany: State of New York, 1899–1914) VI, 756].
51. A piggin, or pipkin, is a small wooden vessel with a handle. A "stove" probably refers to a foot-stove or footwarmer. A "kooler" might refer to a wooden vessel for cooling wine, and a canteen is a type of wooden keg. While Eltinge's account book does not definitively state that he made these objects himself, it is quite likely that he did; if he was serving as a middleman, he would probably have dealt in a greater variety of objects.
52. *Eltinge Papers.*
53. *Eltinge Papers.*
54. *Eltinge Papers.*
55. Fingerhut, 125.
56. A. Flick, 165.
57. Eric Roth, "Finding Aid, Elting Family Papers," Huguenot Historical Society Archives. The Twelve Men was a quasi-governmental organization in New Paltz that was charged with the administration of the land patent received in 1678 by the twelve founders of the town. Organized in 1728, the Twelve Men were primarily involved in dividing land in the early years, but by the 1790s they were generally only responsible for resolving disputes concerning land titles. They were elected by the freeholders of the town, with each man serving as the representative of the share of one of the original twelve patentees. Only a person descending from an original patentee could represent the share of his ancestor, in this case, Louis DuBois, Roeloff Eltinge's great-great-grandfather.
58. Abraham Hasbrouck, a supporter of the

Coetus, forced the domine (the minister) of the Kingston church to take an oath of allegiance to the king, which he felt would nullify any connection between the American churches and the Classis since the oathtaker would be forced to declare "that no foreign prince, person, prelate, State or potentate had, or ought to have, any jurisdiction, power, superiority, dominion or authority ecclesiastical or spiritual within this realm" (quoted in Schoonmaker, 216). It was later determined that Abraham Hasbrouck had no right to administer an oath.

59. D. Veersteeg, *Records of the Reformed Dutch Church of New Paltz, N.Y.* (New York: Knickerbocker Press, 1896), 9. If they felt that they were too far from Kingston to worship, that would have been the case even prior to the internal disputes, thus suggesting that they had been previously attending the New Paltz church without becoming official members.

60. The last two elections are recorded on a single sheet of paper, rather than in a book or other such longer document, suggesting haphazard record keeping. It is possible there were additional elections for which no records survive.

61. Randall Balmer, *A Perfect Babel of Confusion: Dutch Religion and English Culture in the Middle Colonies* (New York: Oxford University Press, 1989), 147.

62. Clark, 306.

63. Kammen, *Crise,* 156.

64. Clark, 296. Clark created four categories of allegiance: Patriot, Loyalist, Occasional Patriot, and Occasional Loyalist. He states that "While another investigator might, in a very few instances, decide to assign to an individual an allegiance slightly different from the one I assigned, the general conclusions regarding allegiance would, I am confident, still stand" (310). Clark probably would have categorized Eltinge as a Loyalist, considering that he refused an oath. But as we have seen, Eltinge's allegiance is questionable. Using Clark's categories, I would define him as an "Occasional Loyalist."

65. Clark, 306.

66. A. Flick, 165.

67. Clark, 309.

3

"Can you on such principles think of quitting a Country?"

Family, Faith, Law, Property, and the Loyalists of the Hudson Valley during the American Revolution

MICHAEL DIAZ

MUCH HAS BEEN SAID of the importance of New York's Hudson Valley during the war of the American Revolution. As both a natural invasion corridor and the nexus of the Continental Army's primary supply routes, the American and British commands spent much of the war vying for control of the region. However, these campaigns were waged primarily by people from outside the colony, be they garrisoning New England Rebels or invading British troops. To native New Yorkers, the battle for control of the Hudson Valley merely accented a far more local and personal struggle. As the Revolution swept through the colonies, longstanding political divisions in New York merged into the greater conflict between rebellion and loyalty to the crown. The result was the creation of a relatively large, diverse, and powerful Loyalist population within the colony. The American Revolution for many residents of the Hudson Valley was thus first and foremost a civil war.

The enormity and bitterness of the ensuing struggles inevitably leads one to ask "Why?" What motivated so many of the region's residents to choose a distant government over their friends and neighbors? An examination of the Loyalists' own words yields an answer. The loyal population of the Hudson Valley was not simply "deluded" or "disaffected," as they are often described in period accounts; rather, their politics were often determined by strong social forces such as family ties, religious conviction, and a respect for civil obedience, law, and order. Woven through all of these forces was often an interest in the defense or pursuit of profit and property. These forces guided the behavior of the Hudson Valley's Loyalists, and also greatly informed their treatment by their more numerous, and ultimately victorious, Rebel neighbors.

The term "Loyalist" describes an American who broke with the sentiments of his or her countrymen and believed that submitting to British rule was the best way to ensure peace and prosperity for the Thirteen Colonies. It is worth noting that many of these reviled "Tories" had taken part in the anti-tax protests of the 1760s and early 1770s, as there were few Americans who supported Parliament's efforts to raise revenue-generating taxes on the Colonies. However, as the anti-tax movement grew more radical, people began questioning not just whether or not Parliament had the right to tax Americans, but whether Britain should rule America in the first place.[1] For the Loyalists, such talk pushed matters too far, and they began to view themselves as politically separate from those advocating outright rebellion. Almost immediately, they were viewed with suspicion and loathing by self styled "Patriots" calling for Revolution.

Years before the Declaration of Independence proclaimed a final break with Britain, the more rebellious Americans began taking steps to ferret out those who did not show appropriate umbrage at Parliament or, even worse, voiced support of the British government. The

Fig. 3.1. States Dyckman. Courtesy of Boscobel House and Gardens, Garrison, NY & DS Blaney.

most widespread and (to the Loyalists) threatening of these measures was the Continental Association. Drafted by the First Continental Congress in 1774, the Association was a formal protest of Britain's policies in America, and announced a universal boycott on British goods. In a draft of the Association adopted in the Orange County town of New Windsor, which paraphrases the original version approved by the Congress, the Parliament is accused of conceiving "a plan adopted and invariably pursued for a number of years past, by the *British* Parliament, for enslaving us, by levying taxes on us without our consent, and declaring they [the Parliament] are fully vested with power to make laws obligatory on us, in all cases whatsoever."[2] The Congress also asked that committees to oversee the adoption of the Association be formed "in every county, city, and town" in New York.[3] In addition to drafting their own versions of the Association, these committees were to take note of those who refused to sign the Association, and jail them if they stood to be dangerous or disruptive to the protest movement.[4] These non-signers were the first to be legally identified, and thus persecuted, as Loyalists. As protest gave way to open rebellion, independence, and revolution, an increasing number of Americans felt that their disgruntled countrymen were pushing the matter too far. Their number eventually included as much as twenty to thirty percent of the Valley's population,[5] and fractured the region so deeply that it took decades for the political and emotional scars to fade.

Of these forces that guided the Loyalists, the most powerful and prevalent were family ties. In his *History of Westchester County*, historian J. Thomas Scharf notes the importance of family to New York politics in this way: "In no other American colony did their exist such great kinship . . . no one can write the history of New York under the English without first making himself, or herself, the master, or the mistress, of at least the leading facts of this kinship of the different governing families of New York."[6] As such, it is not surprising that the most significant Loyalists and Rebels in the Hudson River Valley belonged to well-established clans that had a tradition of being politically opposed to each other. Outside of these large clans, families were often divided in their loyalties. How these families' political positions informed their actions is a large part of the Loyalists' story.

The largest and most influential of the region's families were the DeLanceys, the Livingstons, the Philipses, and the Van Cortlandts. The latter three had been granted extensive land holdings in the Hudson Valley by the crown, and as such enjoyed tremendous wealth and political influence.[7] The DeLanceys were minor French Huguenot nobility that married into the Van Cortlandts and enjoyed a meteoric rise to prominence in the colony.[8] While all held property in New York City, the DeLanceys and Philipses owned much of present-day Westchester, Putnam, and Dutchess Counties, whereas the Livingstons held much of modern Columbia County.[9] Of these great clans, the DeLanceys were the most successful in gaining government and religious office, holding both civil service positions (including the Lieutenant-Governorship of James DeLancey II from 1753–1755, and again from 1757–1760[10]) and serving as wardens and vestrymen in Westchester's Anglican churches.[11] The Philipses filled much the same role for their holdings in upper Westchester and lower Dutchess (now Putnam). The Livingstons, by contrast, were largely Presbyterian and headed a political party in opposition to the DeLanceys.[12]

When the Revolution began, there was little doubt as to which side the DeLanceys would support. Fortunately for them, much of the family lived in New York City, where a strong British presence and the authority vested in their civil positions kept them safe. However, there were family members scattered throughout the colony, and these had to be more careful in their politics. When asked of the various committees' harassment of suspected Loyalists, Stephen DeLancey of Westchester answered that his family "regard not anything the Committee does with them, so long as they have their liberty," and thus was left largely unmolested prior to the signing of the Declaration of Independence.[13] James DeLancey, also of Westchester, was more vocal in his loyalty to the king, and as such faced attacks on his home.[14]

When the British occupied New York City in the summer of 1776, the DeLancey family was well-poised to take up leadership positions among the Loyalist refugees streaming into the city. Oliver DeLancey, one of the clan patriarchs who had served with distinction during the French and Indian Wars, was made a brigadier general by General William Howe.[15] In doing so, he became one of the only Americans to reach flag rank in the British Army during the Revolution. General DeLancey was authorized to form a brigade of Loyalist troops, and quickly raised some 1,500 men.[16] This unit served with distinction throughout the war, with the 1st Battalion distinguishing itself at the defense of Savannah in 1779.[17] General DeLancey also was able to assist his nephew, James, in raising his own unit, officially called the Westchester Chasseurs, but better known by their nickname "DeLancey's Cowboys."[18] This band of cavalry raiders helped turn Westchester County into a dangerous no man's land between British-held New York City and the Rebel-held Hudson Highlands.[19] The peculiar nickname was earned by their habit of stealing the cattle of any suspected Rebel sympathizers they could find in Westchester.[20] At its peak, the unit mustered 500 men, all raised from Westchester and Dutchess counties.[21] James DeLancey had no military experience prior to raising the Chasseurs, and thus relied on his family connections to secure this vital commission.

Other family members also benefited from Oliver DeLancey's influence. His eldest son, Stephen, served as a lieutenant colonel in the 1st Battalion of DeLancey's Brigade.[22] Oliver's second son, Oliver Jr., had already been a lieutenant in the prestigious 17th Light Dragoons when the war began, but was transferred to a series of positions on the British command staff. After the death of Major John André, Oliver Jr. became adjutant general to the British Army in North America, and as such head of espionage operations in the Hudson Valley.[23] Again, if not for the influence of his relations, it is extremely doubtful that an American who began the war as a junior officer would have achieved such a position on the British command staff.

Despite the power and influence the DeLanceys enjoyed, their family was not without political division. The Westchester branch, cousins to General DeLancey's branch of the family, was split over whether or not to support the king. The family's eldest son, Stephen, served as the recorder of Albany before the war, and was arrested with other Loyalists (among them States Dyckman) in Albany in 1775.[24] The family's eldest daughter, Alice, married Ralph Izard, one of South Carolina's representatives to the Continental Congress. While this is not in and of itself a direct statement of her political leanings, the fact that she never joined her family in New York City or British forces in South

Carolina can be taken as such. There is no such ambiguity, however, in the politics of the family's seventh son, James DeLancey, of the aforementioned Chasseurs, or of family's youngest, Oliver. At the start of the war, Oliver was an officer in the British navy. However, after American blood was shed in Massachusetts in 1775, he resigned his commission, refusing to fight his fellow Americans.[25] Thus, even the most powerful and influential of the Hudson River Valley's Loyalist families faced the same internal strife and discord that sundered many of the region's families.

The DeLanceys were not the only high-profile Hudson River Valley family to face hardship and division during the Revolution. On June 24, 1776, Cadwallader Colden Jr., the son of New York's lieutenant governor, was arrested at his house in Orange County by committeemen from Newburgh and New Windsor. The militia was dispatched to Colden's house when it was decided that he was under "suspicion of being an enemy to the liberties of *America*."[26] This suspicion was borne of two factors: his highly-recognizable family name, which already brought him under intense scrutiny, and his refusal to accept Continental currency in the payment of a debt owed to him by John Hill of New Windsor.[27] Hill, who described himself as "a friend to my country," wrote to the Provincial Congress, the colony's revolutionary government, to inform them of Colden's refusal of American money in February of 1776.[28]

Escorted under guard before the joint Newburgh-New Windsor Committee, Colden was outraged to find he had been arrested on "nothing but a grand suspicion of my being inimical to the *American* cause."[29] In his defense, Colden pointed out that the Newburgh-New Windsor Committee had no right to bring charges against him, as he lived under the jurisdiction of the committee of the town of Hanover. However, the Newburgh-New Windsor group felt that the committeemen of Hanover were "too remiss in their duty, and under some undue influence."[30] In an attempt to receive some manner of fair trial, Colden appealed for a public hearing before the Committee of Ulster County. In the resultant proceedings, Colden admitted that he was opposed to independence (he had previously opposed the election of officials to the Provincial Congress and "had made no secret of my principles and opinions on these matters"[31]) but agreed to sign the Association and maintain his public silence on political dealings. Unconvinced, the committee also demanded that he swear to take up arms to oppose any British invasion of the region. This Colden refused to do; as such, he was condemned as a Loyalist and remained in custody.[32]

While men like Colden were made targets due to their names, others loudly proclaimed their loyalty and thus received similar treatment. For example, Peter Corne of Westchester County is described by several sources as "an obstinate Tory."[33] A retired merchant and privateer, Corne ran a farm and mill near Peekskill when the Revolutionary crisis began.[34] As was common for those who had fought for king and country in previous wars (the aforementioned privateering took place during the War of Austrian Succession, 1743–1748), Corne made his loyalty to the British government clear from an early stage.[35] He was signatory of an early Loyalist protest published in the Westchester County town of Rye in April 1775.[36] As the Rebels sought to weed out Loyalists in the summer of 1776, he was named on a list of suspected persons published by the Provincial Congress.[37] As a result, he was issued a summons to appear before either the Provincial Congress or a local committee on July 5.[38] The arrival of the British invasion force in the area may have proved enough of a distraction for Corne to ignore the summons. Sources reveal that he did spend part of the war in England.[39] However, he did so only after attempting to remain on his Westchester property.

In both cases, Corne and Colden turned to their families in an attempt to retain their property. After Colden was arrested, his son, Cadwallader Colden III, moved into the family mansion in Ulster (now Orange) County. From there, he was able to both maintain the Coldens' extensive land holdings and lobby for his father's release. Despite sharing his father's name, Cadwallader III was considered a "decent young man" by the Rebel authorities.[40] Though no direct statements of his politics survive, both this appraisal by the Ulster County Committee and his marriage to Elizabeth Fell, a daughter of a prominent Rebel family, speak of his acceptance among the Whigs.[41] Following a petition written by him in the summer of 1776, the Ulster County Committee released the elder Colden from jail. However, suspicion of his loyalties continued to dog Cadwallader II throughout the war, and he was jailed once more in November 1776, and again in March 1777, a stay that may have extended into 1780.[42] Cadwallader III spent these years securing his father's property and doing his utmost to obtain his release. Through these efforts, the Colden family's holdings in Ulster County remained in the family's hands, unlike so many other Loyalists' farms. Remarkably, Cadwallader II was allowed to return to the farm unmolested after the war. He died there in February 1797.[43]

Likewise, Peter Corne turned to Rebel family members to defend his property. After initial Rebel scrutiny, he signed his farm over to his son-in-law, Dennis Kennedy. Kennedy was, at least on the surface, more attached to the Rebels' cause, holding a commission in the local militia.[44] However, either because of Corne's clear displays of loyalism or of the favorable placement of his farm,[45] the property eventually was seized.[46] Peter Corne was banished from the colony, and Dennis Kennedy fled to Canada following accusations of being "strongly connected with the enemy."[47] In this instance, the Cornes/Kennedys had neither the political connections nor the Rebel "credentials" to escape scrutiny, and they suffered for it.

While Loyalists with the most prominent family names were the first to be targeted by Rebel committees, those belonging to fringes or branches of some of the bigger Loyalist families were approached in a somewhat more circumspect manner. The Rebel committeemen often hoped to lure those with power and influence to their cause, as the Revolution was always in need of money and capable leadership. An example of the gentler hand the committees showed the seemingly neutral can be seen in case of another of the Hudson River Valley's prominent Loyalists, Beverly Robinson. The interactions between Robinson and the revolutionary committees again bring out the importance of family to the thinking of many Loyalists.

Beverly Robinson was born in Virginia in 1732. He enlisted in the king's service to fight in the War of Austrian Succession. In this capacity, he came to New York near the war's end in 1748, and became associated with the Philipse and DeLancey families. He married Susannah Philipse in July 1748 and entered into the merchant trade. His marriage brought him a 60,000-acre plot of land on the eastern side of the Hudson Valley, encompassing much of what are now the towns of Garrison, Philipstown, Kent, and Patterson.[48] In the early 1760s (possibly 1763), Robinson retired to his estate, assuming direct control of the property. It included extensive forests, comprising as much as half of the property, and 146 tenants.[49] Many of these tenants were Presbyterians, but there was a notable Anglican minority, to which Robinson himself belonged.[50]

In the Highlands, Robinson rose to local prominence, holding office as the supervisor of Dutchess County's Southern Precinct from 1763 to 1765, and of the Philipse Precinct from 1772 to 1774, and Judge of the Inferior Court during 1775.[51] He also was an important force in the region socially, donating land and funds for the construction of St. Philip's Chapel in Garrison to serve the Anglicans among his tenants.[52] As a public servant of the British crown, he attempted to discharge his duties faithfully, including traveling to Poughkeepsie to aid Sheriff Philip Livingston in tearing down a liberty pole.[53] However, there were those who hoped that he would take the side of the Rebels as the political crisis worsened. He was offered a colonelcy in command of the Dutchess County Militia in September 1775 but chose to decline the commission.[54] Since Robinson later raised and commanded a Loyalist regiment, one can assume that his objection was not based on distaste for military service. Rather, the decision appears to have been a political one. Even in 1775, the militias of the Hudson River Valley were firmly in control of the Rebels,[55] and to accept a command in them would have made a clear political statement in opposition to the royal government. This was one of the few clear political gestures he gave prior to 1777.

However committed to the British rule as he may have been, Robinson was not as "obstinate" as others during the early days of the crisis. The historical record reveals little of his activities prior to 1776, while many more vociferous Loyalists came under persecution. As late as October 1775, well after blood had been shed on both sides at Lexington and Concord and Bunker Hill, he did not object to the Rebel authorities building fortifications on his property.[56] By being so agreeable, it appears that Robinson was able to avoid any major scrutiny until 1777. At that point, with the British preparing to invade the Hudson River Valley from their newly taken base in New York City, the Provincial Congress began forming committees specifically to ferret out Loyalists, eventually brought together as the Committee to Detect and Defeat Conspiracies. When the Congress relocated to Fishkill after the fall of New York City in 1776, they felt they had to be sure where Robinson's loyalties lay. As such, they issued a summons for him on February 20, 1777.[57]

In his appearance before the Committee to Detect and Defeat Conspiracies, both Beverly Robinson and John Jay, the committee's chair, made frequent mention of the importance of family. Early in the questioning, Robinson's politics were probed through the behavior of his son, Beverly Jr., who had fled to New York City to join the British.[58] Robinson points out that his son's treatment at the hands of the local committees, which was apparently rough,[59] drove him into the British camp, "as it is natural when a man is hurt to kick."[60] As such, he showed no approbation at the young man's actions. Seeing that separating the elder Robinson's politics from his son's was not working, Chairman Jay tried a different tack. He stated directly that America had "passed the Rubicon and it is now necessary every man Take his part, Cast off all allegiance to the King of Great Britain and take an oath of Allegiance [an updated version of the aforementioned Continental Association] to the States of America or Go over to the Enemy for we have declared ourselves Independent."[61] Robinson replies that he is hesitant to take such a drastic step, and explains his reasoning for wishing to stay out of the conflict:

> Sir, I cannot take the Oath but should be exceeding Glad to Stay in the Country, to Inable me to Stay in the Country, and Expecting that there would be a great Deal of Trouble about the forts [Montgomery and Clinton] in the Spring have already Sent Some of my Goods farther back in the Country to Patersons [now the Town of Patterson] and I should be extremely unhappy to go over to the enemy, for I have no way to maintain my family there, but I have here. If I go to the enemy, can I carry with me any of my effects? It is very uncertain who will Rule yet, for the matter is not Determined.[62]

Once again, note how central family is to Robinson's thinking. His reply to a direct statement about American independence and adherence to the crown makes no mention of higher legal concepts or ideology. Rather, Robinson is chiefly concerned with ensuring the peace and comfort of his family. Despite his offer to move away from the strategically important riverfront where he lived, Robinson was never sufficiently assured of his family's security if he did not take the oath. As such, he chose to cast his lot with the British.

Shortly after this hearing, Robinson fled to New York City, leaving his wife and remaining children at their estate.[63] From there he sent a letter to John Jay, informing him of his decision. While that letter does not survive, Jay's response does. Interestingly, Jay writes not to Beverly, but to his wife, Susannah.[64] In this letter, he appeals to her sense of family, invoking some very strong imagery of the suffering her children might endure if her husband did not reverse his decision and join the rebellion:

> When your Friends reflect, that not only Mr. Robinson's Estate, but the reputation and Influence he has just acquired; would become the Inheritance of children who promise to do honor to their parents; they can entertain few Ideas more painful, than those which Arise from the Danger of your family's being deprived of Expectations so well founded & so valuable; and of a Lady's being subjected to all the anguish and misfortune & . . . Mr. Robinson has put his own, and the happiness of his family at hazard, and for what? For the sake of a fanciful regard to an Ideal Obligation to a prince, who on his part disdains to be fettered by any obligation, a prince who with his Parliament, arrogating the attributes of Omnipotence, claims a right to bind you and your children in all cases whatsoever . . .
>
> Can you on such principles think of quitting a people who respect you, a Habitation and a Country which afford you every Convenience? Remember that should you carry your numerous Family to New York, Famine may meet you and incessant anxiety banish your peace . . . Picture to your imagination a city besieged, yourself and your children mixt with contending armies—Should it be evacuated, where and with whom and in what manner are you next to fly—can you think of living under the restless wings of an army—Should heaven determine that America should be free, in what country are you prepared to spend the remainder of your days and provide for your children. These things it is true may not happen, but don't forget that they may—admit they should not—suppose heaven unjust—Britain Victorious, and the Americans bound in all cases whatsoever, will you ever Madam be able to reconcile yourself to the mortifying Reflection of being the Mother of Slaves . . .
>
> For the sake of everything dear to you Madam be persuaded to prevail on Mr. Robinson to return, and advise him to take an open, decisive part with his Country . . . Be pleased to assure him that I shall always think myself happy in being useful to him in every occasion consistent with the Duties I owe to that important cause to which after the most mature consideration, I have cheerfully devoted myself, Family, and Fortune.[65]

Clearly, Jay's intent was to use familial obligations to overcome the Robinsons' political convictions. Unfortunately for all parties involved, this method failed, and Beverly Robinson went on to become an extremely useful asset to the British. Twice his actions put the Rebel cause in great danger: once by helping plan and lead the British attacks on Forts Clinton and Montgomery in 1777,[66] and again by acting as the main contact between Benedict Arnold and John André during the former's defection to the British in 1780.[67]

By the end of 1777, much of the Hudson Valley's Loyalist population had joined the Robinsons in their exile in British-held New York City. After the expulsion of the Rebel army, the area effectively became British territory once again (though one under military control). As could be expected, there were many families who had members on either side of this new border. Interestingly, these families continued the pattern of helping each other, even when communication could be difficult or dangerous.

The Dyckmans of the lower Hudson Valley offer an interesting take on such a relationship for two reasons. First, it was unusual to have two brothers, Samson and States, well-placed on either side of the political divide. The elder brother, Samson, was a wealthy and influential Rebel in southern Dutchess County. He was recommended to General Washington as a person who was "well affected" to the American cause in 1780, when Washington was in the area investigating the Benedict Arnold affair.[68] He frequently acted as a messenger for local Committees of Safety,[69] and seemed to enjoy the trust of the influential body.[70]

States Dyckman chose a different path during the American Revolution. On June 4, 1776, he was arrested with a group of other Loyalists in Albany.[71] Mostly civil servants and officials,[72] these men had gathered in force to celebrate the king's birthday at the King's Arms Tavern.[73] Such a numerous gathering of Loyalists was a tempting target for Albany's Committee of Safety. A Rebel mob descended on the gathering, arresting all involved.[74] Dyckman, a minor catch compared to the mayor of Albany and other high-ranking officials present, was released shortly afterward on the condition that he stay in the city and promise not to carry arms for the British.[75] The latter was an easy promise to keep, as Dyckman never showed any inclination for military service. His confinement in Albany, however, was at some point broken, as he fled to New York City in January 1777.[76] There he was one of the few Americans to find gainful employment in the British army, working as an accountant for the corrupt Quartermaster Department. In this capacity, Dyckman was tasked with hiding the full extent of the department's corruption.[77]

At the direction of department officials, Dyckman and the other accountants were to maintain a "clean" set of books, which masked the fact that the quartermasters were lining their own pockets with the crown's funds. The sensitive nature of this work necessitated that the accountants were well-compensated for their discretion. On paper, Dyckman was paid two shillings sixpence a day (at a time when the common British soldier made only eight pence a day), but off-the-books supplements hugely increased his earnings.[78] In this capacity, he certainly made substantially more than his brother.[79] Such was States' newfound prosperity that his sister, Catalina, was sent to live with him, though she herself seemed to have more rebellious leanings.[80] States' duties with the Quartermaster Department necessitated that he travel to London in 1779 and 1781,[81] but even this did not deter him from aiding his family. He made sure that, should anything befall him on his travels across the Atlantic, his Rebel family would have a handsome share of his British profits.[82] In a seemingly unparalleled move, States actually met Samson in Westchester's neutral ground, no man's land between the two armies, in 1780, hand-delivering a £100 loan.[83] States contributed so much to his family that he had to request a raise from one of his employers, Quartermaster General William Erskine. In a letter written in May 1788 (five years after the war's end), he asked Erskine to consider that "I have reduced [my earnings] considerably by assisting a Mother and Brother who suffered as much [by] the American War as I benefited."[84] It should be noted that Dyckman was far from completely "reduced" by his charity, as he still managed to find money to buy several hundred pounds' worth of English fineries to wear or resell in America every time he crossed the Atlantic.[85] Still, this is an unusual and informative statement, as there were few Loyalists who would have gone so far to help those who had rebelled against the crown and even fewer who had "benefited" enough to offer help.

The date on Dyckman's letter shows that States' actions during the war continued to affect the Dyckman family for years afterwards. States was in London when the Revolutionary

Fig. 3.2. Front Façade of Boscobel Mansion. Courtesy of Boscobel House and Gardens, Garrison, NY & DS Blaney.

War ended in 1783 and remained there until 1788.[86] However, even before the war's end, he turned his eyes towards resettling in America. In 1782, States wrote to Samson and asked that he purchase a small farm for States' retirement.[87] By the end of 1783, Samson was "well pleased" by the property he had secured for his brother.[88] Britain's defeat, and America's subsequent independence, slowed States' return by years. Also slowing his return was the increased scrutiny the Quartermaster Department was subject to, as the angry British public was eager to use the corrupt and costly department as a scapegoat for Britain's defeat.[89] States and the other accountants were called to defend the quartermasters from a Parliamentary Commission appointed to investigate their business dealings. In this capacity, the exiled Loyalist was instrumental in ensuring that his employers avoided disgrace and as such secured from them a substantial annuity.[90]

Dyckman's success in obtaining his annuity highlights another reason some Americans chose to side with the British government: profit. The British army was a vital organ of one of the wealthiest empires on the planet; the Continental Army barely subsisted on whatever scraps the perennially bankrupt Congress could send its way. Obviously, working for the crown appeared to offer Americans opportunities for economic and social advancement that seemed flatly impossible under the ill-funded Rebels. While the vast majority of Loyalists had their hopes of riches dashed at the end of the war, States Dyckman provides one of the only examples of an American who made a fortune working for the British who was then able to enjoy that bounty in the colony of his birth. Dyckman's pension funded not only his eventual return to America in 1788, but also bankrolled the construction of a lavish mansion, named Boscobel,[91] where he hoped to live out his last days. Built on a small plot of land at Montrose Point on the Hudson, the house was finely built and elaborately furnished with luxuries Dyckman shipped back from London.[92] While he kept largely to himself for the last few years of his life at Boscobel, States Dyckman was able to enjoy the comfort and luxury his loyalty to Britain had bought him.

Knowing that their wayward relation was now the wealthiest man in the family, States Dyckman's Rebel family members took an active role in his eventual return to the newly United States. In addition to procuring States the aforementioned farm in Westchester, his family kept him informed of the political climate of the Hudson River Valley, and how likely he was to face persecution if he returned. Interestingly, one of the most helpful of States' relations in this regard was his new brother-in-law, Daniel Hale. The husband of States' younger sister, Catalina, Hale had sided with the Rebels and supposedly been an officer in the Continental Army during the war.[93] In a letter written to States on January 17, 1784—less than two months after the last British troops left New York City—the Rebel Hale describes himself as the Loyalist States' "Friend and Brother."[94] In another letter, written several months later, he informs States of a recent election for the state Legislature in which "men of prudence and moderation" were elected that would surely overturn the "unconstitutional or unjust" anti-Loyalist laws passed by revolutionary "firebrands."[95] Hale gave States his assurances that the exiled Loyalist soon could safely return to America.[96] Later still, he informed States that "it would give me real pleasure to see you at home in my little family."[97] It is surprising to hear such language directed at a Loyalist from one who had taken up arms against the king. Hale's enthusiasm for his brother-in-law's return makes more sense when one remembers that Hale hoped to rely upon Dyckman to finance several business ventures.[98] Dyckman apparently was forthcoming as ever with lending money, and as such helped the ex-Rebel start a new business in Albany.[99] Tempered by economic interest, family once again superseded political differences.

States Dyckman's habit of spending his annuity on family members was not limited to Hale or the years after the war. In fact, Dyckman spent lavishly on his family both before and after his return to the United States in 1788. Such was his generosity that Dyckman had to request an increase in pay from his clients to adjust for the amount of money he was giving to his family while he was still in London. Back in America, he noted that "On my return to this country, I found numerous sets of relations all ruined and beggared by the war. It was natural for me to assist them, but probably imprudent to the extent that I did."[100] Following the Revolution, the success of the Dyckman family, which had sided so prominently with the Rebels during the war, was funded in large part by British money. Political disagreements could not break family ties, and money helped a "black sheep" like States return to the fold.

The intermixing of money, family, and politics also can be seen in the story of Samuel and Judith Verplanck. Wealthy landlords of a nearly 40,000-acre tract around Fishkill Landing[101] and owners of a fine mansion on Wall Street in New York City, the Verplancks had much to lose by picking the wrong side in the Revolution. However, with the British holding New York City and the American Rebels the Hudson Valley, the Verplancks were trapped in a position that forced them to support one side or the other, giving the offended side an excuse to seize the "traitors'" property. However, the Verplancks found a way to keep possession of both properties while maintaining their social prominence: separation. In early 1776, Samuel Verplanck moved to the family's Fishkill holdings, splitting his time between his own home,

Mount Gulian, and his recently deceased brother's. While in the valley, Samuel took several measures to ingratiate himself with the Rebels' military and social hierarchy, including becoming a member of the local Committee of Safety and allowing Baron Friedrich von Steuben, inspector general of the Continental Army, to use Mount Gulian as his headquarters. Judith, on the other hand, stayed with the couple's children at their Wall Street house and became one of occupied New York's most famous hostesses. General Howe, British commander in chief during the first phase of the war, was a frequent guest at Mrs. Verplanck's balls. Despite the fact that Judith Verplanck had entertained much of the British high command, the family was allowed to retain all of their property during and after the war due to Samuel's political connections, making the Verplancks one of the very few moderate or Loyalist families to make it through the Revolution unscathed.[102]

While family played a huge and important role in the lives of many Loyalists, it was not the only societal institution to factor into the Loyalist community. Religion, namely in the form of the Anglican faith, informed the politics of many of the Hudson River Valley's Loyalists. Likewise, the Anglican Church itself was a center for loyal protest and support for the crown. However, while the majority of the church hierarchy remained strongly loyal, many Anglicans sided with the Revolution. Internally divided and viewed with suspicion by their neighbors, most of the region's Anglican churches closed their doors during the Revolutionary crisis.[103]

It was only natural for the Anglican Church to be a rallying point for support of the British government. George III's many titles included his positions as Defender of the Faith and head of the Church of England. As such, loyalty and submission to the king was more than a matter of civic responsibility; it was an act of faith.[104] In addition to this, the Anglican community in New York was led by those with strong civil and economic ties to Great Britain, men who were ill-disposed toward thoughts of rebellion and separation. The political party that powerful Anglicans like the DeLanceys, Philipses, and others led in the Provincial Assembly, which opposed the rebellion up until the assembly's dissolution in 1776, was frequently called "the Episcopalian Party."[105] The Anglican Church, then, was a center for loyal thought and conduct, as well as a forum for voices within the Loyalist community.

Anglicans were particularly powerful in Westchester, which had more Anglicans per capita than the rest of the colony.[106] Correspondingly, it was one of the more loyal areas of the Hudson Valley, and its inhabitants noisily protested the Revolution from its earliest days. In 1775, Anglicans in Rye gathered at a church to sign a protest against Rebel activities in nearby White Plains.[107] One Anglican minister, Epenetus Townsend of Salem, testified that he used his pulpit for "reading Homilies against the Rebellion, and . . . to give my Parishioners and others a Just Idea of the Sacred Obligation laid upon us by Christianity to be good and peaceable Subjects . . ."[108] Perhaps more so than anywhere else in the colony, the Anglican Church in Westchester was the focal point of the county's Loyalist movement.

Beverly Robinson was also a loyal Anglican and acted to spread the faith into the Hudson Highlands. The area in general, and Robinson's patent in particular, did not have a numerous Anglican population.[109] To give himself and his few Anglican tenants a place to worship, Robinson sponsored the construction of St. Philip's, a small chapel in the Highlands that was affiliated with St. Peter's Church in Westchester.[110] The church minutes of St. Philip's from the period survive and illustrate just how divided the Anglican Church could be.

With such fundamental ties to the King of England and the clear loyalty of the chapel's first warden, Beverly Robinson, it is surprising that the vestry and, in all probability, the membership of St. Philip's was so deeply divided by the war. The chapel's second Warden, Charles Moore, elected in 1772, was a Loyalist. While he never took up arms for the king like his predecessor, he was obnoxious enough to his Rebel neighbors that he had to relocate to North Carolina after the war.[111] The other four wardens of the Revolutionary generation, all elected well after the war when the chapel reopened, were Rebels, some prominently so. Two of them, William Denning and Pierre Van Cortlandt, served in the Provincial Congress. (The latter was named lieutenant governor after the war.)[112] A third, Jeremiah Drake, served in the Rebel militia.[113]

The vestry was likewise divided. Of these, eight were Loyalists and six were Rebels.[114] Two of the vestry's Loyalist members served in the military.[115] Fredrick Philips, one of the more militant vestrymen, joined the King's American Dragoons. He was elected to the vestry in 1812, well after Revolutionary passions had cooled.[116] Francis Pemart initially served in the Rebel army but defected to the British for unknown reasons. He served as a spy and boat pilot until the war's end. Convicted *in absentia* of treason, Pemart had his property confiscated. After the war he relocated to Canada.[117] Two other vestrymen, Henry Purdy and Peter Corne (the grandfather of States Dyckman's wife), also had their properties confiscated.[118] The remaining two suspected Loyalist vestrymen, Pierre Van Cortlandt (a different person from the lieutenant governor) and Silvanus Haight, show little cause or consequence of being branded Loyalists, besides being noted as such in the church records. Neither had their property confiscated nor appears to have been forced into exile after the war.[119] It is possible, then, that these men were moderates who had been falsely accused of being Tories, or at the very least were not sufficiently attached to the royal cause to sever their ties with the land of their birth after the Rebels' victory. This general passivity on the part of St. Philip's loyal members demonstrates a sharp contrast to the Rebel vestrymen, several of which served in the local militia and the Continental Army.[120]

While the case of St. Philip's shows that the members of the Anglican Church were somewhat divided, there was no such dissension in the ranks of the Anglican ministry. Almost to a man, Anglican ministers in the Hudson River Valley consistently preached a message of loyalty until their parishes were closed. Of the 250 Anglican ministers in America prior to the war, ninety percent remained loyal to the crown.[121] In the Hudson River Valley, the Anglican ministry was particularly supportive of the loyal cause. Anglican ministers in the Highlands Patent, Fishkill, Poughkeepsie, and Westchester closed their churches and left the area after their congregations either turned against them or faced persecution by their non-Anglican neighbors.[122] Two ministers from Dutchess County, John Doty of Robinson's Highland Patent and John Beardsley of Poughkeepsie, joined the Loyalist military as chaplains of the King's Royal Regiment and the Loyal American Regiment, respectively.[123] All of these men felt that the oaths that consecrated them as ministers bound them to the king, even in the face of enormous popular pressure.

The region's most outspoken Anglican minister made his voice heard not only from the pulpit but also in print. Rev. Samuel Seabury, from Westchester, was one of the few Loyalists who put pen to paper to answer the flood of Rebel propaganda.[124] Taking the pen name A. W. Farmer [A Westchester Farmer] in 1774, he laid out a series of logical arguments against the rising tide of resistance and separation from the British government. One of these, 1774's *The Congress Canvassed*, was a scathing attack on the extra-legal Congress, the concept of boycotting British goods, and of the hypocrisies of the Rebel leadership. Seabury phrases his argument as a common farmer might and thus sheds light on the doubts and concerns that many average New Yorkers felt during this period.[125]

Seabury appeals to the good nature, humanity, and reason of New Yorkers in his writings. When arguing against the boycott proposed by the Continental Association of 1774, he asked his neighbors to consider the human cost of their actions:

> The manufacturers of Great-Britain, the inhabitants of Ireland, and of the West-Indies, have done us no injury. They have been no ways instrumental in bringing our distresses upon us. Shall we then revenge ourselves upon them? Shall we endeavour to starve them into a compliance with our humours? Shall we, without any provocation, tempt or force them into riots and insurrections, which must be attended with the ruin of many—probably with the death of some of them? Shall we attempt to unsettle the whole British Government—to throw all into confusion, because our self-will is not complied with? . . . Good God! Can we look forward to the ruin, destruction, and desolation of the whole British Empire, without one relenting thought? Can we contemplate it with pleasure; and promote it with all our might and vigour, and at the same time call ourselves his Majesty's most dutiful and loyal subjects [as the Continental Association did]?[126]

Seabury also reminds New Yorkers that Britons do not respond well to threats, and that damaging their economy will only further anger the British government. He also states the common wisdom about America's military prospects, should the conflict between colony and parent come to blows. The British army could with "[a] single campaign . . . ruin us effectually," while the mighty Royal Navy could easily "embarrass our trade in the Mediterranean with Spain, Holland &c."—nations with which the nascent independence movement hoped to trade.[127] Further defiance of Parliamentary authority thus risked not only the financial well-being of Hudson Valley farmers, but quite possibly their lives as well.

The pamphlet goes on to list reasons to distrust the powers behind the Association. Many of the Congressmen were merchants who stood to make huge profits as scarcity drove up the price of goods during the boycott. Moreover, how could a people trust an extra-legal body that was doing its best to stifle dissent and close the courts of law? Such actions stood to leave all New Yorkers at the mercy of radicals and "Rascal[s] from New England,"[128] who had long laid claim to New York lands, though they had "no more right to it than the Pope of Rome."[129] With no legal recourse, even Americans who supported the Congress could find themselves victimized and taken advantage of.

However logical Seabury's complaints were, his comments were not well-received by the Rebel majority of New Yorkers. His writings, and ultimately his person, were attacked by Rebel committees. Revolutionary committees in Westchester, Orange, and Ulster Counties acted to confiscate and burn the reverend's writings. At a Committee meeting in Wallkill, Ulster County, the pamphlet was read aloud, found to be "replete with falsehoods, artfully calculated to impose upon the illiterate and unthinking, to frustrate the Resolves of the Congress, and to destroy the union so necessary for the preservation of our constitutional liberty." The committee then resolved, "[t]hat the said Pamphlet, in abhorrence and detestation of such infamous publications, be now burnt, and that the authors, publishers, and circulators of such performances be henceforth deemed enemies to their country." The pamphlet was then tossed into the fire.[130]

Reverend Seabury himself fared little better. On November 22, 1775, he was seized by a party of armed men at a house in Westchester where he taught a grammar school. They eventually met up with another party of militia, the whole commanded by Isaac Spears, a hotheaded leader of the Sons of Liberty from New York City. These militia men escorted Seabury to New Haven, some seventy miles from his home, and out of "Loyalist" New York.[131] There he stood trial for being "against the liberties of America."[132] Despite his protest to the contrary, he was found guilty and was held in Connecticut for seven weeks.[133] Seabury went on to become the chaplain for the King's American Regiment. After the War, he became the first American named a bishop of the Episcopal Church.

Finally, a sense of civic duty and a respect for law and order motivated many to turn against the Rebel committees, which often seemed to skirt the edge of anarchy and lawlessness. Most notable among these were the Hudson Valley's numerous civil servants and lawyers. In a very immediate and practical way, these men relied upon the crown for their livelihoods and their social position. For them, supporting the British government was more than a philosophical argument: it was the only way to secure their future in what they hoped would be a British America. A high percentage of civil servants were active Loyalists during the Revolution and took leadership roles both during and after the war. Likewise, many lawyers, who had spent years of their lives (and no small amount of money) learning their trade, felt that English law was the best and fairest on the planet, and that the loosely organized Rebel mobs trying to separate America from Britain could not possibly protect a man's rights and property as well as the British legal system.

Civil servants were one of the most unanimously loyal segments of the population. As such, they were held under careful scrutiny by their more numerous Rebel neighbors. This lesson was learned all too well by the small but influential body of Loyalists arrested at a tavern in Albany with States Dyckman on the night of June 4, 1775. Among these was Royal Mayor Abraham Cuyler, Albany County Clerk Stephen DeLancey, and county Postmaster John Moiner.[134] One of the many toasts raised that night was for "damnation to the enemies of the King," whose birthday the men were celebrating. Even this relatively mild gesture drew an immediate and harsh response from the city's enraged populace. A mob quickly descended on the pub. The partygoers were arrested and promptly brought before Albany's Committee of Safety.[135] At the subsequent trials, the Albany Committee provided a lengthy list of charges against Cuyler and DeLancey, the night's two biggest arrests. The two were ultimately banished to Hartford, Connecticut.[136] The order of banishment, sent to Hartford's Committee of Safety, included quotes made by the men, as well as a careful accounting of their social activities. For example, Abraham Cuyler was charged with "openly and avowedly countenancing of, and associating with, such persons as were suspected of being unfriendly to the *American* cause, without having regard to the rank or character of such persons, and frequently speaking in the most violent terms against the cause of *America.*" His apparent treason was based mainly upon his statements that "he was a friend to the Constitution of *Great Britain*, and good order and Government; and that *England* never meant to distress *America*, and that we brought the war upon ourselves; and that the *Americans* were acting in open rebellion; and that many of the Congress had sinister views, and meant only to make their fortunes . . ." Even speaking against the Congress was now a crime for someone in his position, a frightful prospect for those dedicated to enforcing British law in the colonies. Stephen DeLancey was similarly charged with making "free and indecent speeches against the Congress, our Army, and America." The charges against him also included meeting "more frequently than previously" with Sir William Johnson, an influential Loyalist of the Mohawk Valley.[137] The fact that civil servants like Cuyler and DeLancey were so carefully monitored showed they were regarded as particularly dangerous by the Rebel authorities.

Both men were eventually released into British-held New York City. While Stephen DeLancey apparently did his best to stay out of any future trouble, retiring either to London or New York City,[138] Abraham Cuyler, took the opposite tack and tried to raise a regiment, the Loyal Refugee Volunteers, to fight for the king.[139] This unit, which never recruited its full complement of men,[140] guarded British supply bases in New York and New Jersey, thus freeing British regulars to fight elsewhere.[141] Cuyler is only one of many civil servants who remained in British service and attempted to restore British rule to the Hudson River Valley.

One of the Hudson River Valley's foremost legal minds also felt that British rule was the best course for the Thirteen Colonies. Peter Van Schaack of Kinderhook, a King's College (later Columbia University) schoolmate of John Jay, was one of the many Americans who protested Parliament's actions but found the movement toward independence a step too far. Early on, he supported protesting Parliamentary taxation and sat on several committees in Kinderhook and New York City.[142] However, as the crisis between Britain and American worsened, Van Schaack became increasingly worried about the violent and lawless turn the Revolution was taking. In 1775, militia men from Claverack, New York, and Western Massachusetts raided Kinderhook, where they "disarmed, dragooned, and generally ill-treated" anyone suspected of being a Loyalist, including moderates like Van Schaack.[143] Such behavior played on Van Schaack's fears of anarchy and rule by the mob. As such, he eventually fled to England.

While he had been driven to England by necessity and conviction, Van Schaack still considered himself first and foremost an American. He returned to the United States after the war, and written records exist of both the scrutiny he faced upon his return and his own personal thoughts on life in a newly independent nation. When asked to explain his actions during the war, he responded that, "I repent not what I have done . . . my Heart condemns me not for any Part of my political Conduct."[144] However, he later added, "My attachment to her [Great Britain] (great indeed as it was) was founded in the relation she stood in to America, and the happiness I conceived America derived from it."[145]

Van Schaack also voices a rather surprising opinion of the new United States in a letter to his friend States Dyckman. Writing in 1785, shortly after his return to America, Van Schaack describes the country, and its situation:

> I really see no change in the country—or if there is any, it is no more than there is in the same man in a change of clothes—the stuff is the same and the cut is the same, nor is there less embroidery, I assure. Society has indeed lost many valuable members, but let us consider this subject upon a large scale and free from prejudice, and how many will there be found who are ornaments to the community and have become so by means of this very Revolution, without which they would perhaps have languished into obscurity? Believe me there is no dearth of merit here. I have now had time to look about me and though the idea of England excites many a tender thought and recalls many a found remembrance, yet nothing but dire necessity could persuade me to quit my native country again. I have been treated with great attention by all descriptions and I may say without vanity by all ranks of people here. My time has been spent in one continuous Round of Social Easures, my Friends are numerous, my circumstances better than I expected, and to crown all, my Children!—blessed be God for this the greatest of all his mercies—are good, amiable, and promising.[146]

Van Schaack's glowing account of the post-war United States speaks for many Loyalists who still wished to call America home. As this article has argued, a great number of Loyalists were concerned not with subjugation to the king but to practical and moral concerns about their families, their faith, and their protection under law. Once these vital rights were secured in the United States, many of these Loyalists sought nothing more than to be left in peace. Men like Peter Van Schaack, States Dyckman, and Peter Corne gladly returned to America after the violence ended. Others, like the Colden family, fought to ensure that they never had to endure the pain of exile. Unfortunately, there were those, like the Robinsons and the DeLanceys, who sided too strongly with Britain and thus were lost to the United States forever. While these men chose different paths in their attempts to remain loyal to the British government, they were moved and motivated by the same factors. Family, faith, and law shaped their worlds, and the Loyalists supported a government they felt best served these interests. The actions taken by the Loyalists made up the heart of the civil war in the Hudson River Valley. As such, they were a vital chapter in the greater story of the American Revolution.

This article originally appeared in *The Hudson River Valley Review*, Volume 28.1, autumn, 2011.

NOTES

1. Edward Countryman, *The American Revolution* (New York: Hill and Wang 1985), 35–42.
2. *American Archives* Series 4, Volume 2, 0131, "Meeting of Freeholders and other Inhabitants of New-Windsor, in Ulster County, New-York Declare their attachment to the King, to whom they would be deficient in duty if they submit to the power assumed by the Parliament. Approve and will abide by the Association of the Continental Congress. Condemn sundry Publications by James Rivington, a Ministerial hiring, and an enemy to his Country." http://www.lib.uchicago.edu/efts/AmArch; Countryman, 100.
3. Countryman, 100; Philip Ranlet, *The New York Loyalists* (Lanham, Maryland: University of America Press 2002) 40.
4. Ranlet, 41.
5. There is significant debate over the how loyal New York remained during the American Revolution. Alexander Flick, one of the first historians to examine the question, boldly states that half of all New Yorkers were loyal. While this is still a commonly cited figure, later historians, such as Bernard Mason and Philip Ranlet, have more conclusively shown the number to be substantially lower. The figure cited above is the most commonly accepted by current researchers.
6. J. Thomas Schaarf, *History of Westchester County vol I.* (Philadelphia: L. E. Preston and Co. 1886/reprint Camden, ME: Picton Press 1992) 130.
7. Scharf, 26.
8. Scharf, 864.
9. Sung Bok Kim, *Landlord and Tenant in Colonial New York: Manorial Society 1664–1775* (Chapel Hill: University of North Carolina Press 1978), 39; Scharf, 26, 91.
10. Scharf, 864.
11. Scharf, 91, 130, 169, 864–69.
12. Alexander Flick, *Loyalism in New York During the American Revolution* (New York: AMS Press 1901), 18–20.
13. Scharf, 352.
14. George DeLancey Hanger, "The Life of Loyalist Colonel James DeLancey," *Nova Scotia Historical Review* #3:2(1983), 40.
15. Scharf, 868.
16. Ranlet, 100.
17. Robert S. Allen, "The Loyalist Provincial Corps," printed in Robert S. Allen, ed., *The Loyal Americans* (Canada: National Museum of Man/National Museums of Canada 1984), 42.
18. Allen, 42; Scharf, 868.
19. Ranlet, 135.
20. Ranlet, 135; it should be noted that many of the outlaws and bandits wreaking havoc in Westchester during the war would claim to belong to DeLancey's Cowboys when robbing Rebels, despite the fact that they had no real connection to the unit.
21. Ranlet, 135.
22. Lorenzo Sabine, *The American Loyalists* (Boston: Little and Brown 1847), 255.

23. Scharf, 869.
24. Albany Committee of Correspondence: Tory Friends and Associates, "Minutes of the Albany Committee of Correspondence 1775–1778, Proceedings June 6th 1776," Institutional Records, Boscobel Restoration Inc., Garrison, NY.
25. Scharf, 868.
26. *American Archives* Series 4, Volume 6, Page 1111, "June 27, Letter from Colonel Clinton to General Washington, requesting his instructions about the arrest of some suspected persons." http://colet.uchicago.edu/cgi-bin/amarch/getdoc.pl?/projects/artflb/databases/efts/AmArch/IMAGE/.17561.
27. *American Archives* Series 4, Volume 4, Page 1532 "Letter from John Hill to New-York Congress, complaining of Cadwallader Colden, son of the Lieutenant Governour." http://colet.uchicago.edu/cgi-bin/amarch/getdoc.pl?/projects/artflb/databases/efts/AmArch/IMAGE/.12294.
28. Ibid.
29. *American Archives* Series 4, Volume 6, Page 1112, "Letter from Cadwallader Colden, Jr., to the Committee for Ulster County, New-York, complaining of the treatment he had received from the Committee of Newburgh and New-Windsor, and asking for an immediate hearing before the County Committee." http://colet.uchicago.edu/cgi-bin/amarch/getdsoc.pl?/projects/artflb/databases/efts/AmArch/IMAGE/.17562.
30. *American Archives* Series 4, Volume 6, 1112
31. Ibid.
32. Edwin R. Purple, *Genealogical Notes of the Colden Family in America* (New York: Privately Printed 1873); Ranlet, 145.
33. Edmund Clowes Chorely, *History of St. Philip's Church in the Highlands* (New York: Edwin S. Gorham 1912), 168; Thomas Flexner, *States Dykman: American Loyalist* (New York: Fordham University Press, 1992), 132.
34. Chorely, 394.
35. Flexner, 130.
36. *American Archives* Series 4, Volume 2, 0321, "Protest of the Inhabitants and Freeholders of Westchester County, New-York, against the Proceedings of the Meeting held at the White Plains, on the 11th instant, for the appointment of Deputies to the Provincial Congress, Subscribers to the Protest from Westchester County." http://colet.uchicago.edu/cgi-bin/amarch/getdoc.pl?/projects/artflb/databases/efts/AmArch/IMAGE/.2321.
37. *American Archives* Series 4, Volume 6, 1152, "Committee met in the Assembly Chamber, Philip Livingston chosen President, List of suspected persons." http://colet.uchicago.edu/cgi-bin/amarch/getdoc.pl?/projects/artflb/databases/efts/AmArch/IMAGE/.17668.
38. *American Archives* Series 4, Volume 6, 1179, "Summons issued to Charles Nicoll Donald MeClean, Peter Graham, Richard Morris, Solomon Fowler, and William Smith, as persons of equivocal character, Summons issued against Theophylact Bache, Charles Arden, John Moore, Sen., Benjamin Williams, Nathaniel Underhill, James Horton, Jun., William Sutton, Peter Corne, Peter Huggeford, William Barker, Joshua Purdy, and Absalom Gidney, persons inimical to the cause and rights of America." http://colet.uchicago.edu/cgi-bin/amarch/getdoc.pl?/projects/artflb/databases/efts/AmArch/IMAGE/.17716.
39. Flexner, 130.
40. Purple, 19.
41. Ibid.
42. Purple, 17–18.
43. Purple, 18; "Elizabeth Fell Colden," *Eighteenth Century Personnel Files*, New Windsor Cantonment State Historic Site, Vails Gate, NY.
44. Flexner, 132.
45. The Rebels were able to make significant confiscations in Westchester County, as the DeLancey and Philipse clans remained loyal to the Crown. Having a suspected Loyalist island in a newly Rebel sea would do little to serve the local committees in charge of

the confiscation. Thus they may have been unusually committed to seizing the Corne property.

46. Flexner, 132.
47. "Stephen Ward to Governor George Clinton," Dyckman Ancestors, Descendants, Relatives Re: Dennis Kennedy, Institutional Records, Boscobel Restoration Inc.; Flexner 130, 132; Barbara Glassman, *The Dyckman Family in America*. Institutional Archives, Boscobel Restoration Inc., Garrison, NY, 18.
48. Chorely, 120.
49. Chorely, 182–84.
50. Chorely, 118–22; Ranlet, 130.
51. Chorely, 118–22, 126.
52. Chorely, 118–22.
53. Chorely, 126.
54. Chorely, 120–26.
55. This is evidenced most clearly by the fact that none of the region's militias did anything to impede Rebel activity during this period or aid the British when they landed in 1775.
56. *American Archives* Series 4, Volume 3, 1274, "Letter from Beverly Robinson, dated Highlands, October 2. The point of land on which the Fort is erecting belongs to Mrs. Ogilvie, and not to him, were it his, the publick should be welcome to it." http://colet.uchicago.edu/cgi-bin/amarch/getdoc.pl?/projects/artflb/databases/efts/AmArch/IMAGE/.8155.
57. Chorely, 130.
58. Catherine S. Crary, *The Price of Loyalty* (New York: McGraw-Hill 1973), 148.
59. A Mr. Robinson had been arrested in Ulster County in the fall of 1776 for trying to organize a band of Loyalists to march down to New York City and enlist in the King's service. It is unclear if this figure is Beverly Robinson Jr., or even if he is of the same Robinson family. Ms. Crary believes this Robinson to be Beverly Jr.; however, one wonders why the committee makes no specific mention of the man's arrest and capture. For more on this arrest, and a fascinating look at the works of Jay's Committee to Detect and Defeat conspiracies, see the account of Enoch Crosby in John C. Dann, ed., *The Revolution Remembered: Eyewitness Accounts of the War for Independence* (Chicago: The University of Chicago Press 1980). Crosby's account begins on page 340, and the part of it specifically concerning the Robinson affair begins on page 343.
60. Crary, 148.
61. Ibid.
62. Crary, 149.
63. Chorely, 130.
64. Most likely, this was simply because Susannah still lived in Rebel-held territory. One could hardly expect a postman from a Rebel committee to simply walk into New York City.
65. Chorely, 130–33.
66. For a more complete examination of Robinson's role in the campaign's planning and his brave personal leadership at the Battle of Fort Montgomery, see Dave Richard Palmer, *The River and the Rock: The History of Fortress West Point* (New York; Hippocrone Books 1991), 101–16.
67. Robinson's role in the André-Arnold affair is often passed over. Arnold was staying in the Robinson house, across the Hudson from West Point, at the time, and Robinson hid letters from André in his own letters to Arnold inquiring after the state of his property. For more, see Richard J. Koke, *Accomplice in Treason: Joshua Hett Smith and the Arnold Conspiracy* (New York: New York Historical Society 1973).
68. States Morris Dyckman Papers, B1. MD1780.11 Boscobel Restoration Inc., Garrison, NY.
69. *American Archives* Series 4, Volume 4, Page 1025, "Congress having refused to make the Loan requested by this Colony an emission of Paper Money to be prepared immediately. Committee directed to despatch three Vessels for Ammunition and

Medicines. Artillery Company ordered to be raised for the defence of the Colony." http://colet.uchicago.edu/cgi-bin/amarch/getdoc.pl?/projects/artflb/databases/efts/AmArch/IMAGE/.11523; "Samson Dyckman," Institutional Archives, Boscobel Restoration Inc., Garrison, NY.

70. One of the first messages that Samson delivered was a Summons to Oliver DeLancey and his wife calling them before the Committee to Detect and Defeat Conspiracies; "Samson Dyckman," Institutional Records, Boscobel Restoration Inc., Garrison, NY.
71. The aforementioned Stephen DeLancey was arrested at the same time; Albany Committee of Correspondence: Tory Friends and Associates, "Minutes of the Albany Committee of Correspondence 1775–1778, Proceedings June 6th 1776" Institutional Records, Boscobel Restoration Inc., Garrison, NY.
72. It is unclear exactly what Dyckman was doing with this group. There is no conclusive evidence to States' occupation during this time, or why a man whose family lived in lower Westchester was in Albany. However, States' later employment as an accountant for the British Quartermaster Department may give a hint to his occupation during this time.
73. Albany Committee of Correspondence: Tory Friends and Associates, "Minutes of the Albany Committee of Correspondence 1775–1778, Proceedings June 6th 1776" Institutional Records, Boscobel Restoration Inc., Garrison, NY; Ranlet, 110.
74. Flexner, 19; Ranlet, 110.
75. Albany Committee of Correspondence: Tory Friends and Associates, "Minutes of the Albany Committee of Correspondence 1775–1778, Proceedings June 18th, 1776" Institutional Records, Boscobel Restoration Inc., Garrison, NY.
76. Calendar of Historical Manuscripts relating to the War of the Revolution in the office of the Secretary of State, Albany, NY, Vol. 1 (Albany, 1868), 674.
77. Specifically, the Quartermaster Department would secretly buy wagon companies, then contract with themselves to carry supplies. The number of wagons contracted for bore only a passing resemblance to the number of wagons that were actually sent out, allowing the quartermasters to pocket the rest of the money. Thomas Flexner describes the scam, and the ensuing scandals, much more completely in chapters 3–7 of his *States Dyckman: American Loyalist.*
78. Flexner, 50, 63.
79. Flexner, 30.
80. As indicated by the fact that she left New York City shortly after States moved to London, and later married a Rebel officer. Flexner, 40, 87; Dyckman Papers, B1.MD.1780.7.
81. Both times, to defend his employers from governmental inquires into the conduct of the quartermasters.
82. Flexner, 64.
83. Flexner, 71.
84. "States Dyckman to William Erskine," *Erskine, Bruen, Quartermaster Accounts & Misc. Correspondence*, Institutional Files, Boscobel Restoration Inc., Garrison, NY.
85. Flexner, 72, 80, 103–04.
86. Flexner, 84, 108.
87. Flexner, 82.
88. States Morris Dyckman Papers, B2.1783.43, Boscobel Restoration Inc., Garrison, NY.
89. Flexner, 58–61.
90. Flexner, 102–03.
91. After the Boscobel Oak, a large tree in which the future Charles II hid himself from the armies of Oliver Cromwell during the English Revolution.
92. Flexner, 208.
93. Hale claimed, and was referred to as such by one of States' Loyalist friends, the rank of major in the Continental Army. However, his name does not appear on any lists of New York regular army officers. It is possible that Hale served only in the militia, or

in a regiment from another colony, Flexner, 118.

94. Daniel Hale to States Morris Dyckman, Jan. 17, 1784. States Morris Dyckman Papers, B3.JA1784.8. Boscobel Restoration Inc., Garrison, NY.
95. Daniel Hale to States Morris Dyckman, May 5, 1784. States Morris Dyckman Papers, B3.JA.1784.18. Boscobel Restoration Inc., Garrison, NY.
96. Hale to Dyckman, May 5, 1784. B3.JA. 1784.18.
97. Daniel Hale to States Morris Dyckman, July 3, 1786. States Morris Dyckman Papers, B3.1786.29. Boscobel Restoration Inc., Garrison, NY.
98. Hale to Dyckman, Jan. 17, 1784 B3.JA1784.8; Flexner, 89–91.
99. Flexner, 89–90.
100. Flexner, 116–17.
101. Modern-day Beacon, New York.
102. Visit to Mount Gulian Historic Site, Beacon, NY, 6/29/11; Robert W. July, *The Essential New Yorker: Gulian Crommelin Verplanck* (Durham: Duke University Press 1951), 4–6.
103. Chorely, 210.
104. Flick, 1.
105. Flick, 18.
106. Ranlet, 131–32.
107. *American Archives* Series 4, Volume 2, Page 0321, "Protest of the Inhabitants and Freeholders of Westchester County, New-York, against the Proceedings of the Meeting held at the White Plains, on the 11th instant, for the appointment of Deputies to the Provincial Congress, Subscribers to the Protest from Westchester County." http://colet.uchicago.edu/cgi-bin/amarch/getdoc.pl?/projects/artflb/databases/efts/AmArch/IMAGE/.2321.
108. Ranlet, 132.
109. Chorely, 36.
110. Chorely, 115.
111. Chorely, 155.
112. Chorely, 156, 158.
113. Chorely, 156.
114. Chorely, 140–73.
115. Chorely, 167, 173.
116. Chorely, 173.
117. Chorely, 167.
118. Chorely, 166. I would be remiss in not pointing out that, as most of these vestrymen were tenants, not landowners, they may not have had property to seize. However, the fact that only two men were singled out and subsequently disappeared from the church records points towards this being a special case.
119. Chorely, 161–73.
120. Chorely, 163.
121. Crary, 89.
122. Chorely, 39, 80–81, 86.
123. Chorely, 81; Frank Hasbrouck, ed., *The History of Dutchess County* (Poughkeepsie, NY: S.A. Matthieu, 1909), 211.
124. Ranlet, 43.
125. Otto Hufeland, *Westchester County During the American Revolution* (Privately Printed, 1926), Chapter 2.
126. Samuel Seabury, "The Congress Canvassed" http://anglicanhistory.org/usa/seabury/farmer/01.html.
127. Seabury, "The Congress Canvassed."
128. Philip Ranlet speaks extensively of the longstanding feuds between New Yorkers and New Englanders. See his already much-cited *The New York Loyalists* for more.
129. Seabury, "The Congress Canvassed."
130. *American Archives* Series 4, Volume 1, 1201, "Meeting of Freeholders in the Precinct of Wallkill, Ulster County, New-York. Approve of the Association of the General Congress.- 'Free Thoughts on the Resolves of the Congress,' burnt." http://www.lib.uchicago.edu/efts/AmArch.
131. Crary, 100–01.
132. Crary, 102.
133. Janice Potter, *The Liberty We Seek: Loyalist Ideology in Colonial New York and Massachusetts* (Cambridge: Harvard University Press 1983) 30.
134. Stefan Bielinski, "The Beginning of the

End" http://www.nysm.nysed.gov/albany/or/or-be.html; Flexner, 19; Ranlet, 110.

135. Albany Committee of Correspondence: Tory Friends and Associates, "Minutes of the Albany Committee of Correspondence 1775–1778, Proceedings June 6th 1776" Institutional Records, Boscobel Restoration Inc.
136. *American Archives* Series 4, Volume 6, Page 1072, "List of charges against the person sent this city to Hartford, in Connecticut." http://www.lib.uchicago.edu/efts/AmArch.
137. *American Archives*, "List of charges against the person sent this city to Hartford, in Connecticut."
138. Catherine Williams to States Morris Dyckman, 1781. States Morris Dyckman Papers, B1.1781.28.
139. "Loyal Refugee Volunteers Recruiting Notice." http://www.royalprovincial.com/military/rhist/lrv/lrvrecruit.htm.
140. Cuyler to Ward, January 9, 1780. http://www.royalprovincial.com/military/rhist/lrv/lrvlet1.htm.
141. "Attack on Refugee Post," http://www.royalprovincial.com/history/battles/lrvrep1.shtml.
142. Ranlet, 36, 112.
143. Ranlet, 112–13.
144. Mary Beth Norton, *The British Americans: The Loyalist Exiles in England 1774–1789* (Boston: Little, Brown and Company 1972), 128.
145. Ibid.
146. Peter Van Schaack to States Morris Dyckman, States Morris Dyckman Papers, B3.1785.34.

4

New York's Committees in the American Revolution

COLIN WILLIAMS

ON 21 MARCH 1775, "Friends to Liberty" outside of Poughkeepsie, New York, wanting to protest Britain's invasive colonial policies, raised a flag with THE CONGRESS AND LIBERTY on one face and THE KING on the other. By proclaiming the not-yet-convened Second Continental Congress instead of Parliament, these Hudson River Valley agitators were not just exercising their rights as British citizens: they were declaring their allegiance to local government instead of transoceanic rule. When Royal officials learned about the display, they decried it as "a public nuisance" and instructed the Dutchess County sheriff to cut it down.[1] Although the flag was removed peacefully, tensions between the colonists and British troops remained high. Less than a month after the incident, Massachusetts minutemen clashed with British regulars at Lexington and Concord. As resistance across the continent escalated into armed conflict, political legitimacy in New York came to be determined, in part, on how communities fought the war.

Since English warships took the Dutch trading post of New Amsterdam in 1664, threats both outside and inside the colony had challenged the legitimacy of New York's established government. The province's external hazards emerged from England's struggles with other European monarchies. In 1673, the Netherlands recaptured its old settlement on Manhattan Island, only to be forced to return it a year later when the Treaty of Westminster ended the Third Anglo-Dutch War. In a more persistent struggle, France fought a series of wars against England from 1688 until 1783 in, among other places, New York.[2]

Like its external threats, the first serious internal challenge to New York's legitimacy originated from European politics. When news of England's Glorious Revolution crossed the Atlantic in 1689, Lieutenant Governor Francis Nicholson fled the colony, allowing Jacob Leisler, a local merchant, militia captain, and Calvinist minister, to assume control of the province. For over a year, Leisler attempted to solve New York's myriad problems by taking bold action. Most significantly, he called for the continent's first intercolonial conference to discuss defense against common threats and opposed the Dominion of New England, a corporate polity designed to tighten the Crown's control over its colonies. Proclaiming to govern the colony in the name of William of Orange, the Dutch stadtholder who had invaded England, he refused to surrender the city fort to Major Richard Ingoldsby, an English officer who had arrived in advance of Henry Sloughter, the new provincial governor. When Sloughter, bearing credentials signed by King William, disembarked several days later, Leisler submitted to his authority. The new governor, viewing the militia captain's lack of immediate deference as an assault on his authority, repaid the ambitious merchant by executing him for treason.[3]

With the threat from Leisler suppressed, Sloughter and subsequent Royal governors, when not directing military action against the

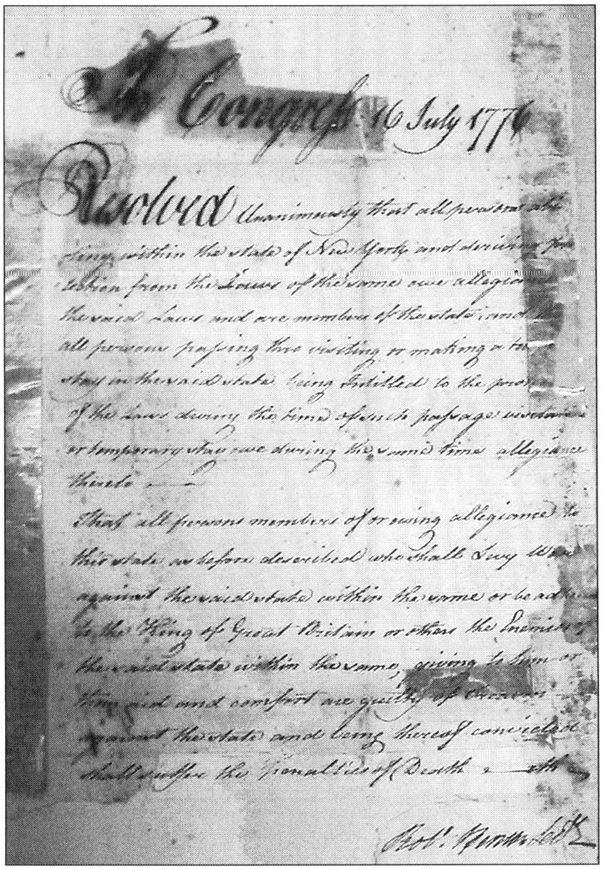

In Congress 16 July 1776

Resolved Unanimously that all persons abiding within the state of New York and deriving protection from the laws of the same owe allegiance to the said laws and are members of the state; and all persons passing thro visiting or making a temporary stay in the said state being entitled to the protection of the laws during the time of such passage visitation or temporary stay owe during the same time allegiance thereto —

That all persons members of or owing allegiance to this state as before described who shall levy war against the said state within the same or be adherent to the King of Great Britain or others the enemies of the said state within the same, giving to him or them aid and comfort are guilty of treason against the state and being thereof convicted shall suffer the penalties of Death —

Robt. Benson Secy

Fig. 4.1. The Oath of Allegiance required of all New York citizens. Courtesy of NYS Office of Parks, Recreation and Historic Preservation, Senate House Historic Site.

French, concentrated on solidifying their control over the province and securing personal wealth. In order to achieve these aims, they granted large expanses of land to English noblemen in exchange for yearly quitrents. Hoping that new property holders would recruit numerous immigrants to work their land, governors also looked to enlarge the colony's population, increase tax revenue, and bolster their influence with London. With Leisler's Rebellion demonstrating their need for power and control, governors granted manors as a way of beholding the powerful to them. By the beginning of the eighteenth century, manors dominated New York's agricultural system, dividing society into those who owned land and those who worked it.[4]

The geography of upstate New York supported the creation of manors and neo-manorial social practices.[5] The Hudson River enabled grain to be transported profitably to New York City from as far north as Albany, but only if milled and shipped in mass quantities. Milling, transportation, and selling grain were the responsibilities of the manor lord. For the privilege of working a farm on their lord's land, tenants paid a yearly rent and rendered respect to their social superiors. This homage was based on more than just economic position. In order to gain direct control of the area north of New York City, they invested upstate gentry with the authority to exercise courts leet and baron—jurisdictional and civil law—over their tenants. Although landlords and tenants usually interacted peacefully, contracts governing their relationships often indebted farmers for as long as ninety-nine years, creating obligations that were passed from generation to generation.[6]

Tensions inherent in the manorial system devolved into land riots during the 1750s and 1760s that, in addition to challenging the established social order, pitted New York's possession of the east bank of the Hudson River against Massachusetts' jurisdictional claim to the land. On certain manors, confrontations between landlords and tenants became violent and deadly. Incursions by armed bands from both sides of the ill-defined border between New York and Massachusetts likewise resulted in the deaths of tenants and squatters. When, in 1766, a large mob led by disenchanted farmer William Prendergast began to evict tenants loyal to their manor lord, Governor Henry Moore deployed the 28th Regiment to Dutchess County and detachments from the 46th, 19th, and 26th Regiments to Albany County.[7]

Why did Moore use British regulars to staunch the unrest? Riots and uprisings were commonplace in mid-eighteenth-century Britain, often the only method in which the disenfranchised could voice their disgruntlement.[8] Although jurisdictional problems between landlords and tenants were persistent and violent, the two groups targeted each other, not the provincial government.[9] What Moore probably realized, however, was that class-based agrarian unrest threatened the province's order and stability. New York's social structure was hierarchically based. Rank was paramount among a people that had no police to enforce the will of the governor (disseminated via sheriffs) or the rights of property owners. Correspondingly, its jurisdictional issue with Massachusetts also had a hierarchical component to it. Both colonies were corporate bodies in competition with each other over economic power at home and influence with the home office. More importantly, Moore believed that he was protecting the province's hierarchical social organization. At bottom, Moore used troops to keep the peace because, according to his understanding, anarchy and its economic and political consequences could result if he did not.[10]

At the same time that upstate New York was erupting in violence, Parliament enacted the 1764 Sugar and 1765 Stamp Acts. The Sugar Act mandated that the royal navy and admiralty courts enforce a three-pence-per-gallon tax on molasses, a levy that merchants in New York City believed would ruin them. The Stamp Act affected even more people. According to the broad-ranging regulation, colonists would have to pay a surcharge on everything from commercial and legal documents to cards and dice.[11]

In New York, resistance to the Stamp Act gave rise to new political actors who radicalized the lawyer-based Livingston faction and enervated support for the merchant-based DeLancey clan.[12] Agitators such as Isaac Sears, John Lamb, Alexander McDougall, and the Sons of Liberty allied with the Livingstons to form committees of observation and inspection that enforced the colony's adherence to the non-importation movement, a continent-wide protest against duties on imported items of everyday use.[13] After Parliament repealed most of these levies in 1770, committees focused on tea, the one commodity still taxed. On 22 April 1774, despite attempts by conservative colonists to prevent an incident, unknown radicals associated with the committee of observation dumped tea from the British merchant vessel *Nancy* when it hove to the waters off Sandy Hook.[14]

During the Stamp Act crisis, a series of extralegal political bodies directed committees of observation and inspection, spoke for the resistance movement, corresponded with similar organizations in other provinces, and chose members to attend an intercolonial congress. In April 1775, after the Battles of Lexington and Concord, the city's Committee of Sixty allied with Rebels in eastern Massachusetts and invited representatives from New York's other jurisdictions to join it in representing the province.[15] Later that year, when Governor William Tryon left his factious colony to govern from a ship in New York Harbor, the committee proclaimed that, since the king's representative had vacated New York without disbanding or proroguing the (by now defunct) provincial assembly, it was justified in exercising the authority that the colonial legislature had once held.[16]

New Yorkers' long history of questioning the legitimacy of established authority suggests that the rebellion was merely a point along a continuum of political unrest. This assumption is both true and misleading: resistance to authority did not abate with the codification of legal authority in 1777; instead, it became institutionalized in political expression. The pressures that war brought to upstate New York during these two years created a caldron in which local leaders of middling backgrounds faced dramatic events and responded to them in ways that relied as much on expediency as on precedent. Between April 1775 and April 1777, with the success of the rebellion in doubt, reactions instead of policies characterized how upstate New York's committees addressed the unpredictability of war.

Scholars have not neglected the contentious nature of New York politics during the late colonial period. Since Carl Becker famously divided the rebellion into domestic and imperial conflicts, historians have studied how the committee system arose and what it meant to the nascent republic.[17] Using the existence of these powerful boards as empirical evidence, they have investigated subjects as disparate as social change resulting from military conflict and General George Washington's partisan war.[18] Yet, except for Hugh M. Flick's 1933 *The Rise of the Revolutionary Committee System* and Bernard Mason's *The Road to Independence*, no historical work has addressed how committees exercised power or controlled the populace. Even Flick's and Mason's monographs, although valuable, have a serious shortcoming: they rely on provincial (rather than county or local) records, a decision that led them to overly simplistic theses.[19]

Most works on local governance during the rebellion underestimate the pressures that war placed on leaders. During its first two years of conflict, the colony experienced British penetration from three directions. The most permanent incursion followed the Battles of Long Island and New York in the summer of 1776 and lasted until British forces evacuated Manhattan Island on 25 November 1783. The proximity of Westchester County to these troops, commanded until May 1778 by Major General William Howe, as well as to the province's Loyalist coastal areas, would torment its residents throughout the war. In a second operation, Lt. Col. Barry St. Leger moved eastward along the Mohawk Valley in the summer of 1777 with a force of Tories and Indians, devastating many Tryon County residents in the costly Battle of Oriskany. At the same time, Charlotte County, Albany County's recently-established northern neighbor, experienced invasion when Major General John Burgoyne led an army south from Montreal headed for the City of Albany and union with St. Leger and Clinton moving up from New York City. Thus by 1777, counties in the Hudson Valley constituted a no man's land between British encroachments and Rebel strongholds. It was at these places of friction where the conflict's military and political outcomes were determined.

As the most populous urban area in upstate New York and the seat of the most populous upstate county, Albany was *primus inter pares* among the colony's northern political jurisdictions. Over 100 miles up the Hudson River from Manhattan, the city was uniquely situated. Close to British Canada and closer still to the powerful Iroquois Confederacy, Albany and its environs would be the central theater for the northern Continental Army throughout much of the war.[20] Shortly before conflict began in 1775, two new jurisdictions had been formed from territory previously in Albany County. Governor Tryon, the eponymous founder of Tryon County, established the new county out of Albany's western lands in 1772. At the same time, he partitioned off the county's Lake Champlain region and named it for Britain's Queen Charlotte.[21] Ulster, Orange, Dutchess, and Westchester counties, on the other hand, could all trace their histories back to the late seventeenth century.[22]

This chapter examines the committee system that ran local governance in the colony's upstate counties and attempts to explain how they achieved, solidified, and used legitimacy to wage war against the British. It begins with the outbreak of war on 19 April 1775 and concludes with the enactment of the state constitution on 20 April 1777.[23] Its first section, "Committee Formation: Initial Attempts at Establishing Legitimacy," describes how these legislative bodies organized themselves, established loose hierarchical relationships with the provincial council, and defined their purpose and scope. This section also traces the proactive measures such as Association-signing and election-holding that they took to justify their existence. The second section, "Wartime Governance: Securing Legitimacy by Addressing Domestic Issues," explains how the winter of 1775 to 1776 challenged committees. Surviving the difficulties inherent in a wartime economy strengthened their claims of authority. In the second year of the war, proactive attempts to forge legitimacy combined with aggressive reactions to local problems to enable committees to deal with upstate New York's large disaffected population. Always a goal of committee governance, eliminating the Tory problem became feasible only after the boards had won a degree of legitimacy. By the end of the conflict's second year, the authority of the committee system had been accepted by politically-active upstate New Yorkers. The legacy of committee governance would affect how this segment of the population would react to the 1777 state constitution, the rise of a popular governor from its own ranks, and the structuring of politics in postwar society.

COMMITTEE FORMATION: INITIAL ATTEMPTS AT ESTABLISHING LEGITIMACY

After Lexington and Concord, Rebels in New York's northern counties found themselves in a precarious position. Alexander White, Tryon County's law enforcement officer, vigorously supported King George III and Governor William Tryon's supremacy over the colony. An opponent of the non-importation movement, the sheriff had affixed his name to a 16 March 1775 declaration censuring the "violent and designing men" in Boston who "had committed an outrageous and unjustifiable act on the private property of the [East] *India* Company" a year and a half earlier.[24] Published in the *New-York Gazetteer* by James Rivington, a newspaper editor suspected of having Tory sympathies, the proclamation became public shortly before violence erupted in eastern Massachusetts. White, whose political sentiments were now widely known, "repeatedly insulted" residents who supported rebellion.[25] Unsure of their legitimacy in an area dominated by ardent Tories such as Sir John Johnson and his clan, members of the nascent Tryon County Committee refrained from acting against White.[26] In addition to wanting to avoid a confrontation, they had another reason for reticence: Guy Johnson, Sir John Johnson's brother-in-law and Britain's superintendent for Indian affairs, held good relationships with the Iroquois tribes surrounding the county's western communities. According to him, challenging the Johnsons subjected residents to Indian attacks, a potential tragedy that would result not only in death and destruction but also the loss of residents' tentative support for the committee.[27]

Committee members need not have worried. On 20 July 1775, a month after White had arrested John Fonda for assaulting a constable, 100 vigilantes broke into the county jail (located on the Johnsons' property) and freed the prisoner. The mob then searched for the sheriff but, fearing an attack by Johnson retainers, disbanded before locating him. Recognizing that he was a marked man, White fled to Johnson Hall, a fortified Tory stronghold in Johnstown, Tryon County.[28]

After consulting with the Albany Committee and Major General Philip Schuyler, commander of Continental forces in the Northern Department, the Tryon Committee decided to arrest the wayward sheriff.[29] Hoping that the display of Rebel fervor on the twentieth had attenuated Johnson's allegiance to the Crown, the committee sent messengers to Johnson Hall demanding White's surrender. Rebuffed by Sir John Johnson, the envoys returned to the board, which then considered organizing an assault on the house.[30] Rejecting the idea due to lack of firepower, it instead apprised Schuyler that armed Tories had massed at Johnson Hall. At Crown Point and busy directing an invasion of Canada, the general could not afford to send Continentals to Tryon County.[31]

Deciding that he could no longer live in the county, White attempted to escape to Canada. Apprehended on 13 August 1775 by William Gilliland, a rebellion-friendly manor lord in Charlotte County, the captured sheriff challenged the committee in several ways. First—and most basic—the board had to decide where to hold the prisoner. It could not lodge him in the county jail. Second, the legitimacy of the arrest was questionable. Not only was the committee's authority assumed, but White, who had broken no law, was still the only individual legally responsible for enforcing order in the county. Although the sheriff's apprehenders had found letters from Sir John Johnson on his person, no mittimus existed authorizing them to imprison him.[32] Moreover, Gilliland held no jurisdiction over Tryon County residents and could not legally execute a warrant even if he possessed one. The committee resolved the first problem by asking its Albany counterpart for assistance. The Albany Committee agreed to help, dispatching a detail to escort the sheriff back to its own jail.[33] Tryon's board never addressed the second problem, trusting that Albany's more Whig-friendly population would be less disturbed over White's questionable imprisonment.

Schuyler shared the committees' concern for the lack of due process in White's arrest. Writing a letter to the Albany board, he informed them that he "would not wish to give the least shadow of appearance to any that are unfriendly to the Cause of America to alledge that we forceably set aside the Laws which can never be the intention of true friends."[34] The general requested that the committee keep the sheriff "closely confined" and suggested that it ask the Provincial Council for a retroactive writ justifying the arrest. The committee dashed off a missive the same day, recommending that the province take responsibility for the prisoner.[35]

Over the next few weeks, the Albany Committee took steps to legalize White's arrest. On 1 September 1775, it decided to remind the county jailer that he was not to release the prisoner before his proper disposition had been determined.[36] After learning that the Provincial Council would accept White after he had paid a proper bail, the committee wrote its Tryon counterpart, suggesting that it replace the sheriff "in the usual manner by way of Petition to the Governor"—a disingenuous course of action that, because it claimed the executive power previously exercised by the Royal governor, redounded the responsibility for filling the office back upon the board.[37] Tryon County followed its neighbor's advice, deposing White from office, electing a new sheriff, and justifying its actions in a long letter to the Provincial Council.[38] On 20 September, the Albany Committee resolved to furnish its prisoner "with Copies of every thing in the Possession of this Board with which he is charged," a decision that allowed it to claim that it had followed due process in handling the former sheriff's case.[39]

At the bottom of the problem of what to do with White were the committees' perceived need for legality and their desire to win the approbation of their residents. Committeemen acted only in the wake of popular sentiment, as when the uprising of 20 July sanctioned their decision to accost the sheriff. Ironically, the vigilantes' release of Fonda made White's arrest impossible: by fleeing to Johnson Hall, the sheriff ensured that the Tryon Committee could not apprehend him forcibly. It is also possible that the board had held off demanding that Sir John Johnson surrender his fellow Tory until they knew it would be impossible to assault the stronghold. Once the futility of taking action was apparent, it could increase the rhetoric against Tories and solidify its leadership of the county's Rebel-minded residents without risking the loss of life or image. When Gilliland captured White escaping to Canada, the committee had both opportunity and cause to incarcerate the sheriff; however, it worried if it had the legal justification to do so. Procedural and jurisdictional questions mattered to the committeemen who, especially at this point of the conflict, worried about the legality of their governance.

Concern over how the public interpreted its actions impelled the Albany Committee to free White from imprisonment. When the sheriff's wife pleaded for her husband's release in October 1775, she reminded the board of what had precipitated her husband's apprehension: his lawful arrest of one county resident for physically assaulting another.[40] Implicit in Elizabeth White's entreaty was not only the legitimacy of her husband's actions but the illegality of his imprisonment. Less than a month later, committeemen interviewed the former sheriff and treated him with respect. The board voted his parole after he assured it "that he will bare no part against America in its present struggle for Liberty."[41]

The gentlemen's agreement between the Albany Committee and White did not last throughout the war. Imprisoning the Tory twice more over the next few years, the board forced him to submit a 500-pound bond for good behavior on 19 December 1776, when the Rebel military campaign was at its nadir, and move to Kingston on 27 August 1777, when British forces threatened Tryon and Albany counties from several directions.[42] Eventually, White managed to escape to Canada, a relocation that received no protest from upstate New York's Rebel leadership.[43]

The manner in which Tryon and Albany counties handled White and the threat that he posed typified how local committees grew in influence and importance. Residents in upstate New York first organized committees during the Stamp Act crisis to oppose—but not replace—Royal authority. These inchoate assemblies became crucial to the success of the non-importation movement, facilitating collective action, developing a cadre of leadership, and publicizing the atrocities of British troops.[44] In addition to helping a neighboring colony, these initial efforts at organization enabled Rebels to form local governance before Tory-minded opponents had the chance to do so. After Lexington and Concord, the goals of these boards became more political. With military conflict a reality, blocking voices of moderation and loyalty became the *sine qua non* of committee existence.[45]

The two battles initiated a *rage militaire* that spread across the colonies and increased the committees' legitimacy and confidence.[46] "A Tryon-County Freeholder," the author of a handbill posted in May 1775, asked his countrymen to "sleep no longer in a State of Supineness and Inattention . . . Behold Rapine and Murder, Blood and Slaughter, have already entered into the Bowels of a neighboring Province . . . Necessity urges us to Battle, we cannot escape it."[47] Yet this enthusiasm expressed itself mostly at the county level. When the Albany Committee received a request to provision colonists who were voluntarily guarding Fort Ticonderoga in sparsely-populated Charlotte County, it decided instead to concentrate on the situation within its borders.[48] *Rage militaire*'s unifying effect in Tryon County was local in nature. After four attempts, geographically-disbursed Rebel leaders in Tryon County assembled in one place for the first time in Canajoharie on 24 May.[49] A Provincial Council, centered in New York City and growing out of that municipality's Committee of Sixty, began corresponding with local leaders during this period of heightened concern, asking, in a circular dated 29 May, for all counties, districts, and precincts to establish committees "in order to carry into execution the resolutions of the Continental and this Provincial Congress."[50]

Tryon County Rebels were in no position to carry out the Provincial Council's resolution. Because the Johnsons had begun mobilizing residents before an anti-British faction could assemble, efforts to organize resistance were immediately challenged. After Guy Johnson fortified his home in Johnstown, he had his armed servants intercept travelers along the nearby King's Road. Not having the force to handle this threat militarily, the committee chose a diplomatic approach, sending the Indian commissioner a letter asking why he was harassing the people of the county.[51] After receiving an evasive response in which Johnson claimed only honest intentions, the committee decided not to engage him in a debate and dropped the issue.[52]

The Provincial Council helped local communities in the Hudson River Valley by standardizing a method for determining the political sentiment of every adult male in their communities. Well-thought-out, the plan involved local committees presenting each denizen with a petition onto which he could sign his commitment to the rebellion. If an individual would not pledge his fidelity to republican government, his name would go on a list of disaffected residents. Known as Association-signing, this procedure took a great deal of time, causing many local boards to miss the deadline of 15 July set by the Provincial Council.[53] Henry Van Schaack of Kinderhook (Albany County), for instance, had to request an extension of the deadline because of difficulties in getting people to sign.[54] Other districts in the county had little trouble in obtaining names of signers (and non-signers). Lists from Coxsackie, Schaghticoke, Little Hoosick, Claverack, Kinderhook, and the Township of Schenectady arrived in Albany on 29 June, two weeks before the Provincial Council wanted them.[55]

The Tryon Committee, like other county-level organizations, tried to have people sign "voluntarily" instead of "by Motives of Force or Fear."[56] More often than not, however, committeemen had to take measures—such as restricting commercial interactions with recalcitrant citizens—in order to obtain signatures.[57] Because applying pressure to individual residents took time, the Albany Committee downplayed the subversive nature of the Association. In a response to Cambridge and Quasakoke residents who had inquired if signing meant repudiating "the Execution of Law and Administration of Justice in his Majesty's Name," for example, it replied on 29 June that "the course of Justice ought . . . [to] continue in the usual Course and in the King's Name.[58]

Attempting to put every man on one of their lists, district committeemen not only helped the council proportion resources but also, by applying face-to-face pressure to neighbors, drew support from many who otherwise would not have opposed British rule. Once a resident whether persuaded, pressured, or deceived—had signed the Association, evidence existed that professed his allegiance to the rebellion. Since signatories had no control over this potentially incriminating document, self-interest induced them to support the fight against Great Britain.[59]

Although Association-signing helped legitimize the rebellion, propagating lists did not necessarily legitimize committees. Instead, committeemen rested their authority on a more republican mechanism for securing legitimacy: elections. All boards feared the "oligarch" label and looked to increase, or at least maintain, the size of their organizations. In September 1775, after some members of the Saratoga Committee had left to serve in military units, the Albany Committee permitted the town to elect five more persons.[60] The next year, Albany expanded the number of representatives sitting on its Cambridge and Livingston Manor boards by six and five seats, respectively.[61] On 12 August, the Tryon Committee decided to increase the membership of its Palatine Committee by two members, most likely to replace men currently sitting in its own body.[62]

Frequent elections helped validate claims of disinterested service. An opinion piece published in the 20 June edition of *The New-York Journal* expressed the common sentiment that, "If elections are free and regular, it will be impossible to shake a popular government."[63] Albany, like most counties in upstate New York, held an election every six months, asking people to re-legitimize its authority (and the authority of its district committees and Provincial Council representatives) in November 1775, March 1776, and November 1776.[64]

Committees used printed broadsides to announce an election's time and place, as well as the names of gentlemen eligible for office, while sheriffs and constables—putatively disinterested because they did not normally stand for election—tallied votes. Despite attempts to make elections as open and conspicuous as possible, committees still experienced criticism, as when a disagreement over when to cast votes caused the "Contraverted Election in Kinderhook District [Albany County]." In a sign that the people in the district cared as much about electoral legitimacy as their committeemen did, 270 out of the 278 men who did vote signed a petition requesting that the county accept the elected slate, a recommendation that the committee readily followed.[65] Ulster

County residents shared their northern neighbor's sensitivity to election legitimacy. A letter of 2 December 1777 written to the Provincial Council by Daniel Graham, the Ulster County committee chairman, related that it was "very disagreeable for many of the present members to serve in committees when at the same time the people tell them they have no right to act in that station on the footing they now stand."[66] The people in Graham's county, having heard about the new state constitution, no longer felt that the war empowered the committee to tell them what to do. Without being led to do so, the people of Ulster had included themselves in the democratic process of establishing legitimate government.

Understanding the importance of inclusion, upstate New York's committees tried to gain legitimacy by giving as many residents as possible a role in fighting the rebellion. For example, in November 1776, the Albany Committee placed a number of the county's citizens under its control by creating fire master posts for the town of Albany. Appointing six middling individuals (none of whose names had an "Esq" behind it or a "Mr." in front of it) to these important positions widened the committee's ambit.[67] The Schenectady Committee also used local governance to expand its control over people. Holding an election on 1 April 1777, it vested twenty townsmen—two assessors, one collector, four overseers of highways, two fire masters, four constables, two "fense vewers," two poor masters, one town clerk, and two pound masters—with interest in the outcome of the contest.[68] On 6 November 1777, the Albany Committee appointed two chimney viewers for each ward of the city, established the frequency of their inspections, and authorized them to fine residents twelve shilling for each deficient fireplace.[69] Later in the year, it assumed purview over the city's Fire Engine Company.[70]

Civic assignments bound only a few townsmen to the rebellion, however. The Albany Committee's establishment of a "Strong Watch well Armed and under proper Discipline," on the other hand, involved many more upstate New Yorkers in a "we-are-all-in-this-together" mindset.[71] Regimented by this vaguely defined duty in late May 1775, it appointed John Ostrander as "Town Serjeant" in charge of managing the rotation and armament of the nightly officer of the watch.[72] Codifying watch participation on 12 June, the committee mandated periodic service, declaring "That if any Person willfully neglect or refuse to Watch agreeable to the Resolves . . . he shall be deemed an Enemy to his Country, Peace and good order unworthy the Protection of this Committee, and that his Name be held up to the public in Hand Bills to be dispersed through the different Parts of this City and County."[73] By issuing this statement, the committee was deciding who should serve, what they should protect, how they should be armed, and the responsibilities of the officer of the watch and town sergeant.[74]

Although the Albany Committee had instituted a night watch just weeks after Lexington and Concord, Schenectady's committee did not follow suit until enjoined to do so in early April 1777.[75] Following standard procedure, it included all men over sixteen years of age on this duty and set clear standards for the conduct of the watch, including the frequency of inspection rounds and the oath sworn before assuming duty. Instigated for practical reasons, the duty also must have increased the cohesiveness of the rebellion. Although the committee authorized the watch to levy fines on fellow townsmen for unruly or dangerous behavior, no record of this happening ever appeared in the county's minutes.[76]

By the end of 1775, committees across upstate New York had corralled enough legitimacy to quiet their opponents in all places except Tory safe havens like Queens County.[77] When Loyalists attempted to win the Albany people's hearts and minds by distributing printed flyers proclaiming loyalty to the Crown and Lord Howe's regiments, residents did not react.[78] After the marginalization of the Johnson party in Tryon County, opposition could only manifest itself in destructive ways. For Loyalist-minded residents in upstate New York, this meant joining units attached to British regulars.

As town, district, and county committees used local issues to establish themselves in their communities, the Provincial Council used the necessity of collective action to establish its tentative superiority over the counties.[79] On 9 August 1775, it disseminated standards for militia establishment and command—a necessity clearly illustrated by events in eastern Massachusetts—and recommended a committee organizational structure for counties yet to form boards. These instructions arrived in Albany on 15 August and directed committees to oversee each militia company's election of ensigns, lieutenants, and commander. The same missive authorized counties to select field officers and form companies into regiments.[80] Several weeks later, the council authorized counties to tax citizens.[81] Collecting money was not a groundbreaking precedent; nevertheless, doing so at the behest of the council signified the degree to which the province was moving away from Royal control.[82]

The Provincial Council's relationship with its county committees entailed more than passing down authorizations to collect weapons, form militias, and tax citizens. Although ostensibly hierarchical, relationships among committee levels varied in complexity and degree of dependency. After the council had established itself at Kingston in the spring of 1777, the Ulster Committee adopted a noticeably subordinate role. Permitting the council to direct the town's night watch and use its manpower to guard provincial prisoners, the committee relinquished control over its own county's citizens.[83] During this stage of the conflict, when the nearness of British troops caused increasing unrest, the council deployed the militia of one county to a neighboring county in order to quell Tory activity.[84] In one inter-county police action, the council moved two Ulster regiments to Dutchess County's Rhinebeck precinct to suppress a Tory uprising. Six days later, it directed the regimental colonels via commissioners to subdue Paulding's Precinct before heading home.[85] In September 1775, the council had to resolve a jurisdictional dispute between its committee for detecting conspiracies and Ulster's committee over the guilt of one Abraham Brinckerhoff. Embarrassed by this quarrel, the council sided with its commissioners, probably because they had advocated treating the suspected Tory more leniently.[86]

By the end of 1775, after each county had established a viable committee, the Provincial Council began to address specific issues instead of issuing generalized directives.[87] On 12 December, it authorized county committees to come to each other's aid without first requesting provincial-level permission to do so. In the same session, it allowed the Dutchess Committee to arrest and detain residents who refused to cooperate with investigations.[88] Although it did not normally intercede in intra-county issues, in October 1775, the council resolved a dispute in Orange County by directing the New Windsor board to reimburse Newburgh's committee for the latter's help in apprehending Stephen Wiggins and David Purdy, two confessed Tories.[89]

The working relationship that emerged between local committees and the Provincial Council grew as each defined its purpose, established its scope, and standardized its procedures. After Lexington and Concord, committees of correspondence renamed themselves committees of safety and assumed governmental as well as political roles.[90] Although elected leaders organized the fight against British incursions and Tory insurrections, electors did not know to what degree their ballot was empowering the gentlemen they chose to represent them. Because they acted in an ever-changing political landscape, without a written constitution to guide them, representatives did not know themselves. Ad hoc wartime decisions (made because somebody needed to decide something—and quickly) characterized committees' exercise of power.[91]

Originally, committees existed for two reasons: to gather intelligence on the movement of British troops and armed Tories, and (when possible) police their jurisdiction for Tory activity.[92] Sometimes, the Provincial Council received word of potential unrest before local committees did, as when, on 25 October 1775, several members reported "a conspiracy of a great number of people from Haverstraw [Orange County] to [go to] Hackensack [NJ], to join the King's troops." The council immediately notified the town, requesting that it inquire about the threat with "as little violence as the nature of it will permit."[93]

As the war progressed, New York's committees grew to exercise extensive legislative and judicial powers.[94] Even before Lexington and Concord, the Albany Committee had argued that it needed "full Power to transact all such matters" that it "shall conceive may tend to promote the Weal of the American Cause."[95] A couple of months later, Tryon committeemen voted regulations defining their jurisdiction and responsibilities.[96] Because Tryon County began the war with a large number of Tory-minded residents, citizens sometimes ignored writs demanding that they appear before the committee.[97] In such divided localities, committees needed to confront the British with tools more effective than legislative statutes and judicial decisions. In order to compel people to comply with their edicts, committees needed to command the militia—the one institution capable of controlling recalcitrants. Committees established their authority over militias by organization—forming units, offering commissions to officers, and paying soldiers a per diem for time served.[98]

Sometimes boards frustrated Continental Army leaders, such as when the Albany Committee halted four companies of New York's Second Continental Regiment from moving north from Fort George to Fort Ticonderoga.[99] Although the commanders—John Visscher, Joel Pratt, Hezekiah Baldwin, and George White—understood that they were officers in the Continental Line, they were all from Albany County and had recruited their soldiers from there. Upon receiving word from the committee, they dutifully turned their units around and retraced their route of march back to Fort George. Distressed by the committee's jurisdictional myopia, the commander of Fort Ticonderoga sent a letter to Albany complaining that the "departure [of the line] leaves us in a very defenceless situation."[100] At other times, civilian control of the militia had a more salubrious effect, such as when the Provincial Council, concerned that soldiers were abusing civilians and turning sentiment against the Rebel cause, restrained enlisted soldiers from appropriating goods or articles from residents. Attempting either to sway or comfort the populace, the council published this decision in the 22 April 1776 edition of *The New-York Gazette; and Weekly Mercury*.[101]

When Continental commanders stationed units in the Hudson River Valley, local committees were responsible for feeding the visiting soldiers — a duty that increased the scope of their power. Setting this precedent early in the war, John Hancock, president of the Continental Congress, wrote a letter to the Albany Committee dated 1 June 1775, directing that upstate New York provision Connecticut troops stationed at Fort Ticonderoga.[102] Logistical concerns were the reason why the intercolonial body had appointed Schuyler, a merchant and native of Albany, as commander of the Continental Army's Northern Department. Throughout his time in command, Schuyler involved himself in committee business, exerting influence, requesting support, and passing along information.[103]

Schuyler was one of the few individuals outside of the committees to be privy to their deliberations.[104] Members from each board met, discussed, and voted regulations in sessions that were closed to the public. To ensure privacy and enable the free expression of ideas, they all swore oaths of secrecy to God (and each other).[105] These oaths were taken seriously. In Albany County, when a contrite Peter W. Yates confessed that he had announced Schuyler's arrival to a friend outside the committee, fellow board members expelled him from the organization.[106] Even though committees elected chairs to their meetings and appointed individuals to correspond with each other, decisions were arrived at equitably, with all the members present voting on every issue.[107] When James Gordon informed Albany's committee that the people of Balls Town had chosen him to handle all of their correspondence, Albany replied that it would recognize only egalitarian committees, not individuals.[108]

One of the reasons why committeemen kept their meetings secret had to do with the sensitive nature of some of the information they handled. The Tryon Committee, in addition to mobilizing and supplying militia units, also deployed scouts to gather intelligence on Indians and the Johnson clan.[109] On 6 November, it expanded this reconnaissance by adding a two- to three-man "Spyguard" to announce the enemy's approach in time for Whig residents to mobilize.[110]

In addition to obtaining intelligence on known and potential enemies, committees appropriated private arms for the common defense. Taking the lead in carrying out this policy, the Albany Committee appointed a subcommittee of three men to take a census of all arms, ammunition, and other accouterment owned by county residents. By 25 May, it had learned the whereabouts of approximately 400 firearms and had started to redistribute weapons owned by Rebels who were exempt from militia service.[111] At the same time, the Provincial Council decided to equip volunteers for New York's Continental regiments with weapons appropriated from those who refused to sign the Association.[112]

Security concerns forced Hudson River Valley committees to use travel passes to control movement across county lines. The Albany Committee first implemented this procedure on 17 July 1776 by charging a four-man commission with inquiring into the reasons why every visitor was in the city.[113] Soon, however, requesting and receiving travel passes became routine and the procedure no longer effectively checked the transmission of information and counterfeit money by Tories. Fearing not just the printing of false currency but also the forging of passes themselves, the Provincial Council resolved on 7 November 1776 to crack down on these "great abuses" by standardizing the forms and procedures county committeemen used to permit residents to travel.[114] Unlike the rest of upstate New York, Tryon County never issued *pro forma* passes. When James Cameron wanted to travel outside of the county in November 1775, for example, he had first to appear before the committee and defend his Association with Guy Johnson.[115]

Rage militaire allowed precincts and counties to establish committees and begin organizing a defense against British forces. Taking advantage of this short-lived enthusiasm, committees conducted Association-signing campaigns to increase the number of residents who had a stake in the rebellion's success. At the same time, they validated their mandate by subjecting themselves to scrutiny from above (the Provincial Council) and below (elections), and made decisions only when the needs of war required them to do so. During the first winter of the conflict, food shortages and economic distress tested the committees' newly forged strength. Not only did New York's committee government need to combat the British and gain prepotency over the Tories, it needed to appease distraught supporters so they would not return to a state of disaffection.

WARTIME GOVERNANCE: SECURING LEGITIMACY BY ADDRESSING DOMESTIC ISSUES

By the summer of 1776, a shortage of tea began to unsettle upstate New Yorkers. Understanding its importance in people's daily lives and the difficulty of importing quality Bohea tea leaves from China, the Albany Committee appointed a commission "to discover and bring to an [end to the] Indiscriminate Sale of Tea in this City and County."[116] Within a week and a half, this subcommittee had begun seizing incoming shipments in order to distribute leaves among county residents equally.[117] The New Windsor Committee (Orange County) took similar action when it found out that a Mrs. Jonathan Lawrence had sold tea for profit and, along with her husband, was manipulating its supply. The Provincial Council, after receiving an inquiry on how to handle the situation, advocated acting "spiritedly against all such as shall be convicted of that offence [pricing tea in excess of regulation]."[118]

As summer turned to fall, the Provincial Council took a more stringent stance, directing county committees to expropriate all quantities of Bohea tea in excess of twenty-five pounds (from both merchants and households) and to appoint a respected citizen to sell allotments of no more than twelve pounds per household at the regulated price of six shillings per pound.[119] Unfortunately for the committees, this measure did not satiate the thirst of upstate New Yorkers. When word spread that the Provincial Council was storing tea in Kingston (Ulster County), mobs descended on the town, broke down doors to public buildings, and forcibly entered private residences until they had found the precious commodity. As reported by Johannis Sleght, the Kingston Committee chairman, rioters had taken "that detestable article called tea" and "divided or distributed [it] in such manner as they think fit."[120]

Domestic crises such as tea shortages became intertwined with efforts to rid the colonies of British forces within six months from the outbreak of hostilities. Residents suffering from the inconveniences of war looked to committees for solutions partly because they represented the war effort and partly because, by the end of 1775, they were the only decision-making bodies extant in the region. How these extralegal organizations addressed and handled the challenges of local security, commodity distribution, military provisioning, and collecting the money needed to pay for the war would determine if the tentative legitimacy won at the beginning of the conflict would last.

Paying for the war was perhaps the most challenging duty undertaken by the committee system, requiring tough decisions on priorities and reviving persistent fears of losing legitimacy. Assembling for their first sessions, committeemen had to decide how to reimburse themselves. In a move that increased the number of citizens who could serve in the Provincial Council, Tryon's committee voted to pay each member it sent to New York City a *per diem*. To fund this cost, the committee established "the first raising [of] Taxes for our county's Expences," although it did not elaborate on how they planned to collect revenue.[121] The Albany Committee, without any specie or hard currency in the summer of 1775, began to purchase items "on the credit of this colony."[122] On 12 July 1775, it sent Jeremiah Van Rensselaer to Lake George, Ticonderoga, and Crown Point "with the sum of £332 — out of the Paper Emission of this Committee" to compensate county militia for their services.[123] These promissory notes delayed the need to reimburse soldiers immediately and helped give everyone receiving "payments" a stake in the rebellion's success.

Residents who violated price controls attenuated the Albany Committee's ability to manipulate the county's commerce for war purposes. To prevent merchants from selling goods for more than set prices, the board posted handbills on 8 March 1776 listing congressionally dictated rates.[124] A month later, it published its own prices, a move that not only reflected "the Rise of West India produce and Bohea Tea" but also established a degree of autonomy from higher echelons of colonial governance.[125] In addition, the committee determined the price of meat in the county, regulating costs per quantity as well as mandating that butchers slaughter all the animals in their shops.[126]

Complaints of price gouging dominated much of the Albany Committee's meeting time during the stressful summer of 1776.[127] Despite declaring that manipulators John Boyd Sr. and Absalom Woodworth Jr. "ought to be considered as [enemies] . . . to the American Cause," recommending "that all Persons break off all commercial intercourse" with them, and resolving that John Roff "be immediately apprehended and confined in Tory Goal till farther ordered by this Board" for illegally raising the price on Bohea tea, it could only regulate foodstuff distribution, not increase supply.[128]

In addition to creating food shortages, the war forced New York's upstate committees to handle one of the most perilous exertions of power: collecting taxes. Simple revenue-raising ploys like the Albany Committee's decision to fine members for non-attendance did not provide much income.[129] Hoping to have other locations help pay its costs, the committee learned on 10 August 1776 that it could charge to Congress no more than 175,000 dollars. Less than committee members had hoped for, this figure provoked a debate over whether or not to lay a tax to fund the balance of the county's expenses.[130] Perhaps due to concerns over its legitimacy, they decided not to burden residents.[131]

Committees could most readily buttress local currencies by extorting money from Tories and the disaffected. Adopting this method, the Albany Committee attempted to bolster the tender used in the county by resolving "That every person [who] . . . shall sell anything for a less Sum in Gold or Silver Money that in Continental or other Paper Money now passing Currently in this county shall be considered as a Depreciator of the Paper Currency and treated accordingly."[132] In March 1777, the Provincial Council enacted fifteen resolves that used the indebtedness of New Yorkers to bind their interests to the rebellion's success. In the third resolve, the council declared that all debts owed to Britain's colonial government were payable to a newly appointed treasurer. The fifth article absolved New Yorkers from paying debts to creditors who could not be reached (such as Tories who had fled). Instead, the province would collect those private debts. Citizens who could not immediately "reimburse" the council, according to the eighth resolve, would pay when they could—at one-half percent interest on the principal. The thirteenth resolve increased the difficulty for individuals to collect money owed them by the Colony. The Provincial Council published this legislative legerdemain in a broadside printed by Samuel Loudon of Fishkill on 1 May 1777.[133]

Tea shortages—especially of the Bohea variety—excited people living in upstate New York because the drink bespoke a minimum level of comfort, civility, and gastronomic pleasure. Salt, however, figured decisively in revolutionary New Yorkers' diet, being essential in making food edible and preparing meats for winter. Rochester (Ulster County) fell precariously short of this commodity during the hard winter of 1776. In November of that year, Jacob Hornbeck, the Rochester Committee chairman, wrote the Provincial Council beseeching any amount of salt it could spare for his community. In the request, Hornbeck reminded council members that "the season of the year is now for killing their [Rochester residents'] winter provision and pork for next summer." The council received his plea at the same time it recorded a note from Orange County reminding it that the survival of a great number of poor people from the lower west side of the Hudson River depended on receiving food from the colony during the winter.[134] The elimination of New York City as a market and a port made many upstate residents dependent on committees for sustenance and, *ipso facto*, political leadership.

Counties began to experience a shortage of salt as early as the summer of 1776, when decreasing supply tempted some merchants in Albany County to raise prices above the congressionally mandated rate.[135] Responding to economic pressures, the committee adjusted the cost, lowered the maximum quantity one buyer could purchase, and appropriated a large quantity from Joshua Watson, a resident who had hoarded salt at his residence. The committee then appointed Anthony A. Bratt to parcel out the salt, allowing him a cut of the proceeds but not reimbursing Watson.[136] The committee pursued a similar course of action when, on 15 November 1777, members learned that Teunis Swart, a disaffected resident, had purchased fifty-seven quarts of salt in Schoharie. Immediately authorizing the town to seize it, the committee then distributed the salt "among the well-affected agreeable to the Resolutions of the Convention."[137]

Whether effective or not, committees' strident attempts to resolve shortages of critical commodities such as salt and tea reflected an exercise of power that many found acceptable. Committee representatives energized themselves over these problems not just because they wanted to curry favor with the electorate but because they viewed supporting people as their *raison d'etre*. The survival of the populace was more dependent on the leadership of local committeemen than it was on the actions of delegates to the Continental Congress or decisions made by officers in the Continental Army. Whether duty or altruism motivated board members, the fact that they lived through the same conditions as those they represented made them empathetic toward their communities. As the war continued, the number of impoverished dependents increased in every community, widening the committees' scope of power once again. Authorizing counties to appoint commissioners of the poor, the Provincial Council allowed local leaders to draft up to 500 pounds of state currency to alleviate the sufferings of the destitute.[138] Later, it agreed to provide for families of those slain and imprisoned at the Battle of Fort Montgomery.[139] Because many hardscrabble citizens in the Hudson River Valley had spent time in debtors' prison at least once in their lives, committees did not vigorously prosecute indebtedness during the conflict. Instead, when the fight against Tories heated up, committees released prisoners charged with insolvency to make room for the disaffected.[140]

Just as salt was critical to the survival of upstate New York's communities, gunpowder was indispensable to the forces that committees formed to protect their localities. On 27 May 1775, the Albany Committee replied to a letter from Governor Jonathan Trumbull of Connecticut, apologizing to him for not being able to send any gunpowder. According to the authors of the missive, all but a small reserve had already been sold to residents of Massachusetts and his own colony.[141] When 1,247 pounds of powder was "brought in" on 14 June of the following year, it decided to parcel out quantities to each of the county's communities.[142] Despite the importance of gunpowder to the county's defense and the Rebel cause at large, the Albany Committee always gave quantities to visiting Indians in an attempt to buy their friendship. Leaders in the county did not unanimously agree upon this policy and, in June 1775, the committee had to investigate whether Rebels from outside the organization had attempted to stop a transaction.[143] Even though most tribes of the Iroquois Confederacy never seriously considered aligning with the Rebels, the Albany Committee was still giving them gunpowder as late as January 1777.[144] The supply was so critical that when Albany served as a depot for the Northern Army's movement into Canada, the transportation of 1,400 pounds of gunpowder up the Hudson and its storage in Albany were kept secret from those outside the committee.[145]

Attempting to remedy the gunpowder shortage, the Provincial Council tried to persuade mill owners to produce it locally. In one of its largest printing projects, it hired Samuel Loundon in January 1776 to engross copies of "Essays Upon the Making of Salt-Petre and Gun-Powder." Although most of the articles in this compendium required burying toxic offal and then waiting years for the nitrate content to build, Henry Wisner's testimonial claimed that he had created two tons of excellent-grade saltpeter in just a couple of months.[146] Although probably more braggadocio than fact (high-quality gunpowder was very difficult to make), Wisner's account prompted others to mimic his "success." Even with a proper site, such as at the

Livingstons' mill in Claremont, an inadequate supply of the necessary components (saltpeter in this case) prevented large-scale production.[147]

Still, projects to build powder mills along the Hudson River received the Provincial Council's repeated attention. After requesting that counties identify ideal construction locations, it received a petition on 18 April 1776 from John Carpenter and Henry Wisner to construct a mill in Cornwall. Three months later, after moving the site to a different location along the Wallkill River, the Orange Committee reported that the mill had produced 200 pounds of good powder in one day of operation. On 11 September 1776, the county bragged that that it had milled 1,459 pounds of good powder in seven consecutive days.[148] At the same time that Wisner was exercising his entrepreneurial spirit, Matthew Adgate, the Kingston Committee chairman, sent the council a proposal to "erect works to manufacture sulpher." The council approved the petition on 16 September and, without even acquainting itself with the plan's details, allocated 100 dollars for the project.

The committee system's promotion and support of entrepreneurial efforts indicate how desperate it was to supply its soldiers with what they needed to combat the British. When these ad hoc governments did have quantities of powder on hand, militia units guarded them closely. On 31 July 1776, the Provincial Council detached Captain Melancton Smith and seven of his men from the Dutchess County militia to guard a powder mill and magazine in Orange County.[149]

Since committees met in secret, they needed ways to disseminate regulations on issues such as salt rationing and gunpowder storage to the communities they represented. The quickest way to inform the public was to have printers publish handbills or broadsides for posting in pubic gathering places, a procedure frequently used by New York City's non-Association committees before the war.[150] When armed rebellion forced Governor Tryon out of the colony, for instance, the Provincial Council issued a broadside stating that since he had not prorogued or dissolved the assembly before "quitting" the province, it had a legal right to assume its governing responsibilities.[151] Even before this declaration of empowerment, the council employed a broadside to announce that it was assuming control over extant militia units and asking "every County, City, manor, Town, Precinct, and District, within this colony" to form militias if they had not done so already.[152]

The council also used newspapers to publicize standards for dealing with disaffection. On 4 September 1775, it released minutes from its 28 August meeting to the *New-York Gazette; and Weekly Mercury* to inform the colony that residents who abetted British forces "shall be punished at the Discretion of the Committee before whom he or they shall be found guilty . . . not [to] exceed three Months Imprisonment." Those arrested for a second offense of aiding the enemy "shall be banished from this colony for the term of seven Years." Speaking ill of any level of committee government would receive the same punishment as taking up arms against the united colonies: an indefinite jail sentence.[153] The Provincial Council also felt it necessary to broadcast its travel restrictions in a Samuel Loudon broadside.[154]

The Provincial Council was not the only committee to advance its interests through the medium of print. When the Hanover Committee won Sheriff Thomas Colden's support for the rebellion, the Ulster Committee published his confession for acting "in such a manner as to draw the resentment of all those that have appeared friends to the true interest of the United Colonies."[155] Although less than a full-throated support of independence, Colden's volte-face showed the people of New York that a relative of former lieutenant governor Cadwallader Colden had acceded to the legitimacy of committee rule.

A broadside could announce a policy but could not enforce people's compliance with it. Similarly, although taxes and price controls could unite residents, they could also turn sentiment against committee rule. Despite efforts to suppress opposition at all levels of colonial governance, some New Yorkers remained disaffected or outright Tories. To frustrate its enemies' schemes, the colony's committee system needed to go beyond the exercise of legitimate power: it needed to use that power to enforce its rule over the region.

DEALING WITH THE DISAFFECTED: EMPLOYING POWER TO SOLIDIFY LEGITIMACY

Counterfeiting schemes posed one of the most difficult Tory subterfuges for committee governments to unearth, even though revolutionary delegates universally despised their pernicious effect on the war effort. Replying to a letter from Saratoga asking "How is the Person to be dealt with, that counterfeits or forges the Albany committee Currency, or the Continental Currency, or the Boston Notes [?]" the Albany Committee answered that a "Magistrate" needed to determine the accused's guilt or innocence and then, if the former, send him to the "gaol."[156] Although clear and reasonable, this procedure was not easily followed: counterfeiters evaded Rebels by running printing presses in Tory-controlled New York City and then smuggling the faux bills up the Hudson River.[157]

Despite challenges, committees sometimes foiled counterfeiting plots. On 19 April 1776, Colonel Gilbert Drake notified the Provincial Council that counterfeited Continental currency was circulating in Westchester County, although he could not implicate anyone in its production.[158] Several weeks later, the council learned from Charles Friend of Westbury (Queens County) that several men were secretly printing Continental currency in Cold Springs, on Long Island. Sending Captain Wool and a guard to uncover the scheme, it then proceeded to spend two days hearing testimonies from the four men caught red-handed.[159] Reviewing the evidence a couple of weeks later, a newly elected committee decided by a nineteen to ten vote to charge a fifth man, Philip Youngs, even though a search of his house had found no evidence that he supported his relative, Issac.[160] Although the board quelled this plot, James Rivington, the Loyalist printer who likely instigated and oversaw the operation, remained under British protection in New York City.[161] Counterfeiting plots continued, whether independent or under Rivington's aegis.[162]

Although committees responded quickly when Tories challenged their authority, rarely would board members personally accost or apprehend a Tory. Instead, they relied on sheriffs, militia, or rangers, a special police force in the employ of the Rebel government, to keep order, control the supply of food, ferret out Tories, pressure the disaffected, and guard critical sites. As the fight against counterfeiters illustrated, only force or the threat of force could make some Loyalists submit.

Committees used different forms of law enforcement, depending on what they needed to accomplish. For civil issues not directly related to the war, they often employed sheriffs and constables who, because they had once been functionaries of the imperial government, did not need to legitimate their authority. Sheriffs and constables acted as they had previously, except they now took orders from a different hierarchy. The need to maintain continuity with the past was why Tryon's committee spent so much time worrying about Sheriff Alexander White and Dutchess County concentrated on pressuring Sheriff Thomas Colden. For larger threats, committees mobilized militias for set periods of time. Eventually, they formed rangers—quickly mustered, select militia units capable of handling a variety of tasks. These three branches of police power—sheriffs, militia, and rangers—gave committees the tools with which to pressure the disaffected, combat armed Tories, and resist incursions by the British.

Although the offices of sheriff and constable were legacies of the imperial system, residents in upstate New York were familiar with them; correspondingly, county committees kept men in the positions, expecting them to execute writs, mittimuses, and warrants: duties that required little independent decision making. Except in special circumstances, as when John Frey replaced White in Tryon County, these law enforcers did not stand for election.[163] Instead, they provided continuity in communities, usually also managing polling sites on election day.[164]

When a county committee needed the sheriff of another county to arrest one of its citizens, it maintained jurisdictional integrity by routing communication through the Provincial Council. For example, the Newburgh Committee (Orange County) sent a request to the council asking it to direct the Ulster Committee to have Egbert Dumon, Ulster's sheriff, arrest Elnathan Foster, "a person notoriously disaffected to the liberties of America."[165]

When apprehending Tories required more force than a sheriff could provide, committeemen relied on militias to make arrests. Most of the time, these units followed committee instructions since the boards paid—and had formed—them. In May 1775, however, two non-board members in Albany County formed their own companies. As the committee began to centralize all civil and military power over the next couple of months, it tried to persuade the two individuals to subordinate their units to committee oversight. The commander of the Association Company of the City of Albany agreed, marching his unit to Ticonderoga when asked to do so by the county board.[166] Also recognizing the committee's legitimacy, Benjamin Hicks, the commander of the second formation, consented to disband his company on the condition that, if ever mobilized by the board, "he would rely upon the Credit of the colony for his Pay."[167] Fortunately for the Albany Committee, officers and soldiers from both of these units accepted committee legitimacy. Once clearly in charge of the county's rebellion-minded population, the committee required prospective militia commanders, such as Elisha Benedict of Balls Town, to obtain its approval before they organized companies.[168]

In Tryon County, where Tory and rebellion-minded residents lived side by side, militia formation was more decentralized. The county committee immediately set about finding arms and ammunition so it could organize its residents into military units.[169] Soon, communities were petitioning the board for permission to form their own units.[170] Despite the willingness of some to align their fortunes with the rebellion, others proved intractable. Declaring that it would hear any dispute that a militia commander did not think himself authorized to handle, the Tryon Committee established itself as the final judicial authority over those it had enlisted. In units, order depended on the ability of militia commanders to apply pressure on malcontents in their formations. Captain Jacob Seeber learned that he held the responsibility for instilling this discipline when he took Charles Gordon and Lawrence Zimmermann, two of his citizen-soldiers, before the committee after they had refused to drill. To Seeber's embarrassment, the committee sided with the soldiers. The commander never brought another problem to the board's attention.[171]

Since Commander in Chief Washington rarely detached Continental soldiers to protect individual communities from British activity, counties needed to marshal as much of their population for defense as they possibly could.[172] Save for residents in a few clearly defined professions, committees assumed control over all men of military age. Provincial-level exemptions existed only for judges and sheriffs, although it did allow those chosen to serve to hire a substitute and pay the council a monthly fine.[173] Local exemptions covered only those considered too valuable to fight.[174] The Albany Committee, for example, decided "that Thomas Holliday who is employed in making Coals for the use of the Blacksmiths who are employed in making spades &c for the use of the Continental Army remain at home."[175]

Even with mandatory service and popularly elected officers, disputes arose over which commander residents were supposed to serve. John Salsbury, an Albany County militia captain, created several jurisdictional issues for his committee to settle. First, on 2 February 1776, he and another company commander argued over who was authorized to recruit one Ephraim Kidder Jr.[176] Two weeks later, Claverack's board complained that Salsbury was enlisting recruits from within its district, an act that prompted the Albany Committee to request that he appear before it and explain his actions.[177] In investigating the captain's character, it learned that when Peter Wiesman had asked the county sheriff to force Nicholas Grott to pay a debt owed to him, Salsbury and friends had physically prevented the law officer from discharging his duty. Taking matters into his own hands, Wiesman then seized a mare and colt from his debtor to hold as collateral. Salsbury responded by forcibly returning the animals to Grott, saying that "People there [in Spenser Town and Noble Town] would not be sued for they must go to war."[178] In a similar complaint, Christiaen Smith related an incident where he had tried to execute a warrant on one Jacob Lottewall who proceeded to escape into the captain's protection. Salsbury then threatened to tar and feather Smith if he ever accosted Lottewall again.[179] Coenraedt Peterson reported a similar story to the board. According to Peterson, Salsbury had refused to accept that he already belonged to a militia company. When he shared news of this encounter with Louranc[e] Hogeboom, Salsbury called Peterson a liar, "tied him with a Rope, and Carried him about a Mile" before releasing and forcing Peterson to confess that he, not Salsbury, was telling untruths.[180] When the committee heard Salsbury testify on his recruiting methods, it learned that the captain's commission to raise a minute company conflicted geographically with regular militia enlistment. Instructing Salsbury to stop recruiting soldiers, it then wrote the Provincial Council, requesting permission to disband its minute companies.[181]

Neither the Albany Committee nor the Provincial Council recorded a resolution to this matter, but Salsbury was mentioned in the Albany Committee minutes a few months later, having returned to his strong-armed recruiting tactics. According to Colonel Stephen Hogeboom and a Major Ford, "Mr. Salsbury of Kings District was extremely busy in recruiting from that and some adjoining Districts a Company of Minute Men, and thereby kept the Militia Officers in those Districts in Continual Confusion."[182] During the war, Salsbury activated his company "to attend the Kinderhook Election," for "apprehending disaffected Persons," for "apprehending certain dangerous Persons," and for unknown service, but never for engaging the enemy in combat.[183]

After the distressing experience of handling Salsbury's imbroglios, the Albany Committee formed ranger companies, which were easier to control because they were activated to perform specific tasks.[184] For example, when the committee felt that a military supply depot needed protecting, it formed two ranger companies on 9 August 1776 "to Guard the Stores of this City."[185] The next month, it sent Captain Baldwin's rangers to Coxsackie to apprehend persons "turbulent and Dangerous to Safety" who were terrorizing "the good People of that District."[186] As the war progressed, these companies effectively became the committee's private armed police force, used most often to hunt down elusive Tories.

Albany County employed rangers prudently but frequently. When the county committee learned that Gerrit Seeger, Staats Bratt, and Gerrit Slingerlandt might have Loyalist sympathies, it detailed a ranger unit to bring the three gentlemen before it. After questioning, all three men "Voluntarily Swore allegiance to the free and Independent States of America" and were released.[187] On 5 February 1777, the committee resolved to send ranger companies to guard Fort Ticonderoga. Whether they did not see the necessity of guarding a distant fort in another county, worried that a long posting would cause them to miss the spring harvest, were concerned about an Indian or British attack on their homes, or feared performing a duty so dangerous, twenty-four soldiers in Captain Alexander Baldwin's company refused to go. Perhaps a little fearful of such a large number of irate fellow Rebels, the board compromised and deployed fewer men, kept them within the county, and rotated their service.[188]

Dealing with upset Rebels caused less of a problem for the committees than the Tory question did. One of the biggest questions committees faced between April 1775 and April 1777 was what to do with those who did not support the rebellion. Sometimes a resident clearly proclaimed his disaffection by his actions or speech. More often, disaffection expressed itself in half-heartedly signing the Association or attempting to avoid the oath all together.

Throughout the war, the Albany Committee vigorously attempted to unearth disloyal behavior. On 4 September 1775, it received a letter from Daniel B. Bratt of the Hoosick Committee recounting his efforts to verify the Monro family's suspected Toryism. Bratt and others approached John and Daniel Monro's residence, entered their house, searched trunks of paperwork for a rumored royal commission, asked the Monros some questions, and then left. According to Bratt, "During the whole [of the] Transactions, Mr. Monro's behavior was very manly, & we cannot think he is in the least Guilty & have entirely discharge him on that Account."[189]

Investigations that ascertained no evidence of sympathy toward Tories, like the search on the Monro house, did not solve the problem of what to do with the disaffected. Even though the Albany Committee decided to jail Peter Everat for refusing to sign the Association, the county had too many disaffected residents for it to establish a precedent from Everat's sentencing.[190] On 2 May 1777, the committee, in a frustrated burst of anti-Tory fervor, ordered subordinate boards to inquire about residents currently out of their districts, reaffirmed the Manor of Rensselaerwyck's authority to use militias to arrest and suppress suspected Tories, and targeted named antagonists (such as Jacob Van Aernam) and distinct populations (such as "disaffected Persons [who] skulk in and about Hellebergh").[191] A couple of days later, it clarified its position on the disaffection by resolving to disarm "Persons within this county Inimical to the Liberties of America, or who have not associated and refuse to associate." Acting on this legislation, the committee directed the Cambridge District to disarm Peter Miller after he had taken an oath "to join the Kings Troops when called upon by any of his Officers, and to kill his best Friends if they were in opposition to him."[192]

The Provincial Council played an inconsistent role in directing the fight against Tories, sometimes advocating action and sometimes recommending restraint. When the Westchester Committee wrote the colonial body to ask what it should do with two equivocating Loyalists who had tried to instigate a peaceful, weaponless protest against its rule, the council never officially replied.[193] A year later, with British troops occupying New York City, disaffection grew in Dutchess and Westchester counties. As in northern and western New York, Rebels had organized citizens into militias, actions that imperiled the committees' safety when those formations began to agitate against committee rule. Hearing that the militia in Dutchess County's Rhinebeck Precinct not only refused orders to defend the Highlands but also "most contumaciously prevent[ed] those who were well affected, from obeying the said resolutions," the Provincial Council responded with force. Apologizing to the county committee for infringing on its jurisdiction, it sent two regiments of Ulster militia into Dutchess County, along with an advisory board of seven commissioners, any four of whom could direct the outside force first to fire on any resistance and then "to take such ways and means, as they [the commissioners], in their discretion, shall think proper to discover, arrest and secure the principals in the said riot and disaffection." Residents who were not killed or arrested would be forced to declare their loyalty to the rebellion. In order to prevent conflicts-of-interest, the council sent units from northern Ulster County precincts and gave the commissioners the power to fine malingerers. To fund the operation, the council voted the militia a payment of 300 pounds.[194]

As committee rule became more stable and legitimate, but before constitutionally elected bodies began representing the people, incidents of disaffection received increasingly harsh legal action. For example, on 12 May 1777 William Young, chairman of the Hanover Precinct Committee (Ulster County), reported Hugh Doughardy's arrest for speaking out against committee government.[195] Also, in Albany County, the committee began disarming all "who have been with the Enemy, and not taken the Oath of Allegiance to this state, or other ways evinced their Sincerity to the Cause of America" on 1 April 1778.[196]

When Royal forces were close by, as they permanently were in Westchester County, disruptions of the civilian population rarely abated. Washington's decision to store supplies for the Continental Army in the county made the land all the more volatile. When the commander in chief sent Major General Charles Lee to New York to call up local militias and prepare to defend the city, the new arrival worked with the Provincial Council to assemble 1,850 bushels of peas, 1200 barrels of "good salted pork," and other foodstuffs in the county.[197] In the winter of 1776, after Washington had lost New York City, the Westchester Committee wrote the Provincial Council relating three ways that the nearness of the British plagued the county. First, a Tory raiding party (approximately 700 men) led by Robert Rogers of French and Indian War fame destroyed farm produce, took livestock, and injured people. Second, the Continental Army had appropriated all of the militia commanders' troops in its defense of New York City, and third, Continentals would not defend residents from Tory incursions.[198] After the British had settled in New York City, Westchester County turned into a true no-man's land.[199] Early in May 1777, the Provincial Council sent three-man commissions into the county, authorizing them to issue writs and judge defendants.[200] Without the ability to assure the protection of residents, however, these commissions did little to help the Rebels' cause.[201]

From the summer of 1776, when British ships began arriving in New York Harbor, to the spring of 1777, when Major General John Burgoyne started advancing south from Montreal, the Orange and Dutchess committees were constantly suppressing Loyalist unrest in their counties. In June 1776, the Provincial Council received word that the majority of Captain Avery Blauvelt's Haverstraw precinct militia (Orange County) had "refused to suffer drafts to be made from said company for reinforcing the army at New-York." Fearing pre-battle disaffection and disloyalty, the council, meeting in an unusual Sunday afternoon session, instructed Colonel A.H. Hay to arrest "seven of the most refractory men of said company" and officially authorized Continental commanders to impress New York militia whenever they deemed it necessary "for the defense of this Colony."[202] Due to concerns raised in Newburgh about farmers planning to sell wheat to the British army, the Provincial Council, in a clever move, sent assistant commissioner Henry Scherck to purchase the "wheat and flour in any public or private store" in the county.[203] By purchasing excess foodstuffs, the council had provided an assured and immediate market for disaffected farmers and, by paying them in Continental currency, had wedded their financial interests to the rebellion's success. At the same time, Loyalists in Dutchess County, learning of Burgoyne's southward-advancing army, began to show their true colors. To combat these "conspirators," landowner Robert R. Livingston and others wrote the Provincial Council to suggest that both militia officers and General Thomas Gage hold courts-martial to identify, disarm, and displace the local enemy.[204]

British army movements during the summer of 1777 imperiled Albany County residents to a greater degree than it endangered its neighbors in Orange and Dutchess counties. In Albany, the committee lowered the standard for disloyalty as the county prepared to receive two of Britain's three-pronged New York advances. According to Committee resolution of 16 July 1777, "every Person in this County who has not publickly exerted himself in aiding the defense of this much injured Country, and purchasing any more Provisions than he or they were formerly used to do for their Families, shall [be] . . . sent to the Fleet Prison, and all such provision so found as aforesaid be seized & appropriated to public use."[205] On 7 August 1777, one day after the Battle of Oriskany, the committee ordered a portion of its militia to the eastern part of the Manor of Rensselear to "apprehend and destroy all such Persons who shall be found in Arms against the State."[206]

Public opinion provided the only check on the committee's ability to arrest disaffected persons during the first two years of the war. Most imprisoned Loyalists had found their way into jail either by denouncing revolutionary government or proclaiming the king. Committees arrested other Loyalists for passing messages for the British or, more detrimental, for counterfeiting state or Continental currencies. A few prisoners, however, earned their sentences by attempting to foment rebellion against committee government. When the Tryon Committee learned that Abram C. Cuyler, Albany's Loyalist-leaning mayor, had escaped north out of the city—possibly carrying military stores, arms, and ammunition—it began to mount offensive military action in order to hunt him down.[207] The Tryon Committee jailed prisoners at the incarcerated individual's expense.[208] Tryon County had reason to treat the disaffected harshly: of New York's upstate counties, its residents suffered the most during the war, with neighbor fighting neighbor and British-instigated Indian raids depopulating the county. As many as two-thirds of the county's residents died in the Battle of Oriskany, the destruction of German Flats, and the Cherry Valley Massacre.[209]

In the property-conscious enlightened thinking of the day, seizing Tory land reflected an expansive exercise of power. As in other measures, the Albany Committee took the lead. In a 27 November 1776 letter to the Provincial Council on frauds committed by flour manufactures, it requested guidance on how to handle wives who prevented Rebels from seizing their Loyalist husbands' property.[210] Not able to wait for an answer, it decided the next day to have representatives from each of its districts inventory all abandoned Loyalist property and "secure the same till the farther order and directions therein from the Convention of this State shall be known."[211] Perhaps because it was operating without a constitution, the Provincial Council favored inventorying property as opposed to outright seizures and redistributions, as evidenced by correspondence that instructed the Kingston Committee to "make an inventory of all personal property in the town . . . belonging to any person or persons gone over to the enemy" but not to dispose or dispense any of it until told to do so by the Providence.[212]

The Provincial Council did not officially permit the confiscation of vacated Tory property until 6 March 1777, and the State Assembly did not sanction the seizure of occupied Tory property until 22 October 1779.[213] Arrogating privately owned property was so antithetical to the spirit of the rebellion, however, that counties did not immediately act on these authorizations. The Albany Committee, for example, did not affirm its right to seize vacated Tory property until 15 May 1777, after a constitution existed to legalize the action. Even then, debate ensued over whose property was to be taken and what was to be done with it.[214]

Because committeemen understood that winning disaffected support solidified their rule, they tried to exercise power in ways that would win the politically lethargic to the rebellion. On

10 May 1777, the newly elected State Assembly issued an ordinance pardoning any Tory who renounced his prior ways and pledged allegiance to New York's new government.[215] In at least one instance, the Albany Committee commuted a prisoner's sentence after he decided to enlist in the Continental Army.[216]

Although several areas of provincial life reflected the progression of committee power over the two years covered in this survey, its development is most visible in how communities handled the disaffected. Starting with Association-signing efforts, committees worked hard to discern who was and who was not friendly to the rebellion. As boards grew in confidence and power, they began to restrict peoples' travel, a control that, when enforced, significantly reduced the ability of Tories to organize. Social pressure, in the guise of neighborly visits to disaffected houses or inquisitions before the local committee, won over the politically apathetic who sought the easiest response to the question of whether or not to support the fight against the British. Because militia and night-watch duty banded residents together, one risked alienating the rest of his community if he decided to oppose the rebellion. As some communities and counties became more inclusive, non-Association signers found themselves facing greater ostracization. Although Toryism became a jailable offense, more often than not, the application of social and economic pressures reduced the need for incarceration. With the war limiting farming, hurting commerce, and creating shortages of salt, tea, and meat, the committees' control over distribution gave them power with which to pressure the disaffected. Filling quotas for Continental enlistments and the need to tax residents further empowered New York's committee system.

THE 1777 CONSTITUTION: CODIFYING LEGITIMACY

On 20 April 1777, the Provincial Council enacted a constitution establishing New York as a political entity separate from the British crown. Drafted mostly by John Jay, James Duane, and other conservative lawyers from New York City, the document created a powerful executive who served three-year terms and exercised significant influence over the state's politics, laws, and militia.[217] Although it included an assembly, the constitution did not institutionalize county or local committees. Furthermore, in a spirit contrary to the democratic principles that many Rebels were fighting for, it restricted franchise only to those residents who rented or possessed land.[218]

After two years of fighting a war against authoritarian rule, why did New York's committees agree to such a conservative government? The foremost reason is that the Provincial Council left them out of the ratifying process. Determining that it was in its purview both to compose and enact a constitution, the council presented the document to committees as a fait accompli. Committeemen accepted the new plan of government partly because they had no viable alternative and partly because they had always conceived their service as based on the necessity of war and, therefore, temporary. Whereas committees had not been a permanent governmental structure in colonial times, the Provincial Council was, in effect, the colonial assembly with changed membership. In addition, upstate boards readily identified New York as their dominant political identity.[219] With the 1777 campaigning season already begun, committeemen had more pressing issues on which to focus. By summer, when the state held its first gubernatorial election, British forces occupied New York's northern, western, and southern regions. Geographically restricted, the election was decided by only 4,000 residents.

The election did not have the result that many in the Provincial Council had predicted it would. Instead of Schuyler, George Clinton, an Ulster County native of middling antecedents who had achieved success as a militia and Continental general, won the majority of votes.

Presented with a conservative government, Hudson River Valley voters reacted by choosing a representative of their own social class to head it.[220]

Clinton's rise from local to state importance occurred *pari passu* with the increasing effectiveness of local boards and the men who served on them. Establishing itself in 1775 when *rage militaire* pervaded the colony, the committee system claimed broad authorizations because, if it had not, the rebellion would have failed. Sensitive to public opinion, local boards acted tentatively where the legitimacy of their governance was challenged—such as in Tryon County—and took proactive measures where it had less competition. Spurred by the Provincial Council, they pursued an Association-signing campaign to determine who supported the fight against Britain and who did not. When the first winter of the war created hardships for upstate communities, they were the only governmental body that could address issues of food supply and military provisioning. Efforts to remedy these problems, if not actually solving them, secured their position in society. Even the food shortage-induced riots in front of meeting sites and raids on warehouses legitimated committee governance: protestors only agitate against organizations they think can better their lives. By the end of the war's first year, a combination of proactive and reactive measures had solidified committees' rule of their communities. With their legitimacy less in doubt, these ad hoc organizations could now exercise their new-found power in purging the colony of its Tories.

Committees conducted their campaign against Loyalists by employing sheriffs, mili tia, and rangers in accordance with the situation, capabilities of each force, and jurisdictions involved. Sheriffs quelled riots and public disturbances while rangers guarded sensitive sites and rousted counterfeiters from safe havens. In the neutral ground of Westchester and Orange counties, militias from neighboring counties deracinated and suppressed Tories. When the military situation reached its nadir in the summer of 1777, these local forces helped to oppose General John Burgoyne's movement along Lake Champlain; to keep General William Howe tied to his lines of communication and supply in New York City; and, in the Oriskany campaign, to stop the eastward march of Lieutenant Colonel Barry St. Leger's armed Tories and Indians through Tryon County.

At this propitious time, the Provincial Council foisted statehood on New York, a move that, whether it was intended to or not, intensified the fight against Tories. Facing threats from all directions, the Assembly relied on the legitimacy forged by two years of local assertiveness to revive committees for detecting and defeating conspiracies. Consisting of fewer representatives than its predecessors, these commissions—organized at both the state and county levels—became the government's most powerful instrument in prosecuting New York's civil war. Once Tories began to depart the state en mass, the Whig government used its constitution-imbued legality to pass a series of laws—the Confiscation Act of 1779, Citation Act of 1782, and Trespass Act of 1783—that robbed Tories of their citizenship and redistributed their lands among those with strong Rebel credentials.[221] Many former tenants received legal title to their farms after their landlords fled to Canada, a development that historians such as Edward Countryman view as significant.[222]

Social change resulting from the diminution of the manor system was not the only legacy of upstate New York's committee system, however. Large landholders continued to dominate life in the Hudson River Valley and, although an increase in the number of freeholders resulted in a larger electorate, restrictions in the 1777 constitution prevented this change from being sizable.[223] More important to the future of the state, committees had bequeathed a spirit of political freedom to the Hudson River Valley. Unlike Jacob Leisler in 1689, upstate New Yorkers would favor the reality, as well as the appearance, of republicanism.

This article originally appeared in *The Hudson River Valley Review*, Volume 28.1, autumn, 2011.

NOTES

1. "Extract of a Letter from Canada, Dated Montreal 24th March, 1775," *The New-York Gazette; and Weekly Mercury*, America's Historical Newspapers, American Antiquarian Society (10 April 1777).
2. The town of Schenectady was attacked in both King William's War (1689–1697) and King George's War (1740–1748). Fighting also occurred on New York's northern border during Queen Anne's War (1702–1713) and around Lake George during the French and Indian War (1754–1763).
3. Parliament later exculpated Leisler. David William Voorhees believes that the minister was motivated by religion. According to him, New York's Voetian Calvinists, led by Leisler, were incapable of secularizing their response to the Glorious Revolution. Once in a position of power, these Reformed Congregationalists initiated a crusade against non-believers, upsetting the crown's wishes for peace and moderation in the province. See David William Voorhees, "'In Behalf of the true Protestant religion': the Glorious Revolution in New York," Ph.D. diss., New York University, 1988. Jerome R. Reich, on the other hand, views Jacob Leisler's actions as more ethnically than religiously motivated. He credits the rebellion with initiating party politics in New York City. Jerome R. Reich, *Leisler's Rebellion: A Study of Democracy in New York, 1664–1720* (Chicago: The University of Chicago Press, 1953).
4. In neighboring New England provinces, individual farmers owned most of the arable land. The best work on the growth of social and economic systems in colonial New York is Michael Kammen, *Colonial New York: A History* (New York: Charles Scribner's Sons, 1975). Kammen posits that economic stagnation kept wealth away from New York during its formative years, giving the colony a secular and authoritarian culture. The arrival of a lawyer and newspaper class altered social dynamics in New York City but not in the upstate region, creating differences between the two localities.
5. I use "upstate" to refer to Tryon, Albany, Orange, Ulster, Dutchess, and Westchester counties. Although the term does not appear in committee journals, it is less cumbrous than listing counties. I use "Hudson Valley" to refer to Orange, Ulster, Dutchess, and Westchester counties.
6. I have relied on Sung Bok Kim's *Landlord and Tenant in Colonial New York: Manorial Society, 1664–1775* (Chapel Hill: The University of North Carolina Press, 1978) for my understanding of New York's manor system.
7. Patricia U. Bonomi offers a detailed account of New York's agrarian riots in "New York's Land System: Problems and Opportunities," her sixth chapter in *A Factious People: Politics and Society in Colonial New York* (New York: Columbia University Press, 1971). In addition to Bonomi, three other authors have written authoritative works on the Hudson Valley uprisings: Kim's *Landlord and Tenant in Colonial New York*; Irving Mark's *Agrarian Conflicts in Colonial New York, 1711–1775* (New York: Columbia University Press, 1940); and Thomas J. Humphrey's *Land and Liberty: Hudson Valley Riots in the Age of Revolution* (DeKalb: Northern Illinois University Press, 2004). Mark's study of personal correspondence and newspaper articles leads him to blame the unrest on manor lords' attempts to establish absolute power and control over their tenants. Kim views the riots through political and economic lenses, blaming the violence on conflicts with Massachusetts residents. Humphrey interprets the same evidence as Kim does but posits that land

riots were too complex to be attributed just to a border dispute between two colonies. According to him, prospective tenants did not care which colony granted them a title, as long as they could demonstrate proof of ownership.

8. Pauline Maier, *From Resistance to Revolution: Colonial Radicals and the Development of American Opposition to Britain, 1765–1776*, Norton Paperback edition (New York: W. W. Norton & Company, 1991), 5. According to Maier, "in certain circumstances, it was understood, the people would rise up almost as a natural force, much as night follows day, and this phenomenon often contributed to the public welfare," ibid., 3. Pauline Maier sees a natural progression from disillusionment over the British representative system to the formation of an American one, as symbolized by the "institutionalizing" of extralegal institutions such as New York's wartime committees. I believe that the existence of armed conflict after April 1775 accelerated this process, making for a less-than-perfect lineage between protest movements in Britain and unrest in America.
9. Before deploying British troops, Moore had ordered Albany Sheriff Harmanus Schuyler to recruit 105 men and suppress an uprising on the Van Rensselaer manor. Schuyler and his posse engaged sixty rioters in an inconclusive firefight that left four dead and many wounded. Bonomi, 222–23.
10. In colonial America, upsetting the social order was seen as a violation of a jurisdiction's law and order. According to Gordon S. Wood, "county courts were the places where the local communities reaffirmed their hierarchical relationships and reconciled their various obligations," *The Radicalism of the American Revolution*, (New York: Vintage Books, a division of Random House, Inc., 1991), 72. The existence of courts leet and baron made class imbalance in upstate New York greater than in other colonies. Although the gentry served as judges in other colonies (like in New York, often without any formal law training), they did not necessarily own the property worked by the defendant.
11. "The New-York Pocket Almanack For the Year 1766," Early American Imprints, Series I, Evans Digital Library, 1775. See also Edmund S. and Helen M. Morgan, *The Stamp Act Crisis: Prologue to Revolution*, 2d ed. (New York: Collier Books, 1962), especially chapters three and five.
12. Carl Lotus Becker, *The History of Political Parties in the Province of New York*, (Madison: The University of Wisconsin Press, 1960; reprint, No. 286 of the Bulletin of the University of Wisconsin History Series, Vol. 2, No. 1, 1909), 49–51. According to Roger James Champagne, local victories mattered more to the Livingstons and DeLanceys than resisting the British. See Roger James Champagne, "The Sons of Liberty and the Aristocracy in New York Politics, 1765–1790," Ph.D. diss., University of Wisconsin, 1961.
13. See Becker, chapter three.
14. Bernard Mason, *The Road to Independence: The Revolutionary Movement in New York, 1773–1777* (Lexington: University of Kentucky Press, 1967), 19.
15. *The Road to Independence*, 44.
16. Daniel L. Hulsebosch, *Constituting Empire: New York and the Transformation of Constitutionalism in the Atlantic World, 1664–1830*, Studies in Legal History (Chapel Hill: The University of North Carolina Press, 2005), 182.
17. According to Becker, colonists in New York took up arms in order to answer "the question of home rule" as well as to determine "who should rule at home," Becker, 22. For a comprehensive—if dated—bibliographic essay on revolutionary New York scholarship, see Bernard Mason, "The Heritage of Carl Becker: The Historiography of the Revolution in New York," *New-York*

Historical Society Quarterly Vol. 53, No. 2 (1969): 127–47.

18. See Edward Countryman, *A People in Revolution: The American Revolution and Political Society in New York, 1760–1790* (New York: W. W. Norton & Company, 1981) and Mark V. Kwasny, *Washington's Partisan War, 1775–1783* (Kent, Ohio: The Kent State University Press, 1966).
19. See Hugh M. Flick, *The Rise of the Revolutionary Committee System, History of the State of New York* (New York: New York State Historical Association, 1933) and Mason, *The Road to Independence.* Several local histories have addressed the committee system as a secondary thesis, including Michelle P. Figliomeni, *The Flickering Flame: Treachery and Loyalty in the mid-Hudson During the American Revolution* (Washingtonville, New York: Spear Printing, 1976) and chapters five through eight of *The Other New York: The American Revolution Beyond New York City, 1763–1787*, ed. Joseph S. Tiedemann and Eugene R. Fingerhut, SUNY series, *An American Region: Studies in the Hudson Valley,* ed. Thomas S. Wermuth (Albany: State University of New York Press, 2005). Jacob Judd wrote chapter five "Westchester County." Thomas S. Wermuth wrote chapter six "The Central Hudson Valley: Dutchess, Orange, and Ulster Counties." Stefan Bielinski wrote chapter seven "Albany County." Robert W. Venables wrote chapter eight "Tryon County."
20. Demographically, Albany County held more people than any other upstate New York polity, with almost 43,000 non-Indian residents by the beginning of the conflict. Bielinski, in Tiedemann and Fingerhut, 155.
21. I do not consider sparsely-populated Charlotte County or the New Hampshire Grants in this study.
22. According to Daniel L. Hulsebosch, governors created counties in New York to act as "ballast" against proprietary rule. Hulsebosch, 50.
23. The Provincial Council voted the constitution into effect on 20 April 1777. James Sullivan, ed., *Minutes of the Albany Committee of Correspondence, 1775–1778, Volume I*, The University of the State of New York (Albany: J.B. Lyon Company, General Printers, 1923), 898 (20 April 1777). Appointments and elections occurred over the next two months. Walter Stahr, *John Jay: Founding Father* (New York: Hambledon and London, 2005), 80. The new government was supposed to convene on 1 August but George Clinton, the newly-elected governor, prorogued the assembly until later that month. Kwasny, 154.
24. "Declaration of the Grand-Jury and Magistrates, Etc. at the Court of Quarter-Sessions, at Johnstown, Tryon County, New-York March 16, 1775," in Peter Force, ed., *American Archives*, 4th Ser., II, 151. All citations from this collection were obtained by using Northern Illinois University's on-line database at http://dig.lib.niu.edu/amarch/; *Rivington's New-York Gazetteer*, America's Historical Newspapers (American Antiquarian Society), 6 April 1775.
25. "Schenectady (New-York) Committee to General Schuyler," ibid., 4th Ser., II, 1730 (14 September 1775). I use "rebellion" instead of "revolution" because colonists who were opposed to British rule wanted London to withdraw its soldiers from the continent. They did not necessarily want a radical change in the colonial government.
26. Committees titled themselves "Committees of Safety," "Councils," "Congresses," and "Commissions." Oftentimes the same assembly would go by several names, depending on the quorum it voted in effect. In this paper, I use "committee" or "board" for all town, district, and county organizations and "Provincial Council" for the colonial organization. I reserve the term "congress" for the intercolonial Continental Congress.

27. "Letter from Colonel Guy Johnson to New-York Congress: opened and read by the Albany Committee, and a copy sent to General Schuyler," 8 July 1775, Force, 4th Series, II, 1669.
28. James F. Morrison, *A History of Fulton County in the Revolution*, Bicentennial Project of the County of Fulton (Gloversville, New York: Fulton County Bicentennial History Committee, 1977), 1.
29. Journals, Volume I, 166–67 (22 July 1775). Tryon committeemen often consulted their brethren in Albany during the war's early months, perhaps because the county had been part of Albany before 1772.
30. Morrison, 1.
31. "Extract of a Letter dated Crown Point, August 14, 1775," Force, 4th Series, III, 135.
32. "Letter from Sir John Johnson to Alexander White," ibid., 4th Series, II, 1726 (25 July 1775); "Letter from Sir John Johnson to Alexander White, Sheriff of Tryon County," ibid., 4th Series, III, 223 (unknown date).
33. Ibid.; Albany, Volume I, 196–97 (15 August 1775), 199 (16 August 1775).
34. Ibid., 204 (20 August 1775); "Letter from the Albany Committee to the New-York Congress," Force, 4th Series, III, 223 (21 August 1775).
35. Ibid.
36. Albany, Volume I, 220 (1 September 1775).
37. Proper bail: Ibid., 229 (5 September 1775); petition: Ibid., 242 (13 September 1775).
38. John Frey, a committee member from Palatine (Tryon County) and one of the two men who approached Johnson Hall to demand that Sir John Johnson surrender White, won election as sheriff. "Tryon County Committee to New-York Congress," Force, 4th Series, III, 660 (7 September 1775).
39. Albany, Volume I, 247 (20 September 1775).
40. Ibid., 273 (19 October 1775); "Petition of Elizabeth White," Force, 4th Series, III, 923 (3 October 1775).
41. Albany, Volume I, 292 (11 November 1775).
42. Ibid., 643 (19 December 1776); 836 (27 August 1777).
43. Morrison, 1.
44. Counties also formed committees to stay informed on events occurring in other colonies. In its second meeting, the Albany Committee altruistically resolved to collect donations to support the "Poor at Boston." Albany, Volume I, 9 (21 March 1775).
45. Alexander Clarence Flick, *Loyalism in New York During the American Revolution*, Studies in History, Economics and Public Law, ed., the Faculty of Political Science of Columbia University, Volume XIV, No. 13 (London: P.S. King & Son, 1901), 102.
46. *Rage Militaire* was first applied to the American Revolution by Charles Royster in *A Revolutionary People at War: The Continental Army and American Character, 1775–1793*, Institute of Early American History and Culture, Williamsburg, Virginia (Chapel Hill: The University of North Carolina Press, 1979).
47. A Tryon-County Freeholder, "To the Freeholders and Inhabitants of the County of Tryon," Early American Imprints, Series I, Evan's Digital Library (20 May 1775).
48. Albany, Volume I, 31 (11 May 1775).
49. Larry R. Gerlach, ed., *The American Revolution: New York as a Case Study*, The American History Research Series (Belmont, California: Wadsworth Publishing Company, Inc., 1972), 12.
50. *Journals*, Volume I, 18 (29 May 1775).
51. Tyron, 18–23 (2 June 1775).
52. The committee's decision to ignore Johnson's response shows his dominance on the New York frontier, ibid., 81–82 (26 October 1775), 83–84 (27 October 1775).
53. *Journals*, Volume I, 18 (29 May 1775). The Provincial Council's decision to request lists of non-signers as well as signers eliminated ambiguity: every resident contacted had to declare for either the Rebels or the Tories.
54. Albany, Volume I, 85–86 (11 June 1775).
55. Ibid., 113–14 (29 June 1775).

56. Samuel Ludlow Frey, ed., *The Minute Book of the Committee of Safety of Tryon County, the Old New York Frontier, Now Printed Verbatim for the First Time, With an Introduction by J. Howard Hanson* (New York: Dodd, Mead, and Company, 1905), 31 (14 June 1775).
57. According to the minutes of the Canajoharie District (Tryon Country) for 29 May 1775, "Resolved unanimously by this Committee, that [affected citizens should not] . . . from this Day have any Dealings or other Connections in the Way of trade with any person or persons whatsoever, who have not signed the Association entered into by this District," ibid., 16 (29 May 1775).
58. Ibid., 115 (29 June 1775).
59. According to Charles Royster, " . . . the main purpose of an oath was to compromise people in the eyes of the British and deter them from fighting for the British. A man who swore loyalty to Congress and his state would be a documented rebel if he fell into British hands," Royster, 105.
60. Ibid., 230 (5 September 1775), 231 (7 September 1775).
61. Ibid., 413 (22 May 1776), 418 (28 May 1776).
62. Tyron, 47 (12 August 1775).
63. Spartanus, "The Interest of America," *The New-York Journal; or, The General Advertiser*, America's Historical Newspapers (American Antiquarian Society), 20 June 1775.
64. Albany, Volume I, 281 (30 October 1775), 446 (30 March 1776), 601–02 (8 November, 1776). Representatives were often reelected, with the same individual and family names appearing in each session.
65. Ibid., 304 (5 January 1776).
66. *Journals of the Provincial Congress, Provincial Convention, Committee of Safety and Council of Safety of the State of New-York, 1775–1776–1777, Vol. I* (Albany: Thurlow Weed, Printer to the State, 1842), 1,096 (10 December 1777).
67. Albany, Volume I, 617 (25 November 1776).
68. Alexander C. Flick, ed., *Minutes of the Albany Committee of Correspondence, 1775–1778, Volume II and Minutes of the Schenectady Committee, 1775–1779*, The University of the State of New York (Albany: J.B. Lyon Company, General Printers, 1925), 1085–86 (28 March 1777).
69. Albany, Volume I, 861–62 (6 November 1777).
70. Ibid., 883 (11 December 1777).
71. Ibid., 24 (3 May 1775).
72. County minutes do not stipulate if the rest of the watch rotated with the officer or if some other method existed for sharing the duty, ibid., 56 (30 May 1775).
73. Ibid., 75 (12 June 1775).
74. Ibid., 241 (13 September 1775). The town sergeant's duties grew over time. On 22 April 1777, the committee instructed Jacob Kidney, the serving town sergeant, to order butcher Anthony Vain "to desist from killing any Cattle &c in his present Slaughter House and that he also remove filth with the greatest dispatch." Whether the committee decided upon this measure for health reasons, because of a malodorous smell, or to punish Vain, is not clear. Still, the restriction reflected the board's strength after two years in existence. Ibid., 729 (22 April, 1777).
75. The Albany Committee had instigated a night watch early in the conflict more out of fear that "Negroes" would act wildly at the thought of war than to defend against the British Army or armed Tories, ibid., 24 (3 May 1775).
76. Albany, Volume II, 1089–91 (13 and 19 April 1777).
77. According to Charles Royster, *rage militaire* gave committee governments "instant legitimacy," Royster, 43. The *Constitutional Gazette* published an article against revolutionary committees on 6 December 1775, stating that "there is not a more cruel tyranny, than that which is exercised under the shadow of laws, and with the colour of justice, when the unfortunate sufferers, are drowned, as it were on the very plank, then had taken to save themselves." Few writings

express the disaffected opinion better than this. "To the Inhabitants of Queen's County," *The Constitutional Gazette*, America's Historical Newspapers (American Antiquarian Society), 6 December 1775.

78. The committee questioned the city's printers but failed to find out who published the tracts. Albany, Volume I, 672. Most likely, Tories printed the handbills in New York City and smuggled them up the Hudson River.
79. I use "superiority" as opposed to "authority" because the first term suggests a natural geographic hierarchy while the second implies a degree of subordination that was not always present.
80. *Journals*, Volume I, 104 (9 August 1775); Albany, Volume I, 193–94 (15 August 1775).
81. Approving resolutions proposed by its Ways and Means subcommittee, the Provincial Council mandated "that the county committees be considered as supervisors" and that "they, with the assessors, under oath, and collectors, do proceed to assess, raise and collect their respective quotas," *Journals*, Volume I, 134 (2 September 1775).
82. Dutchess County had a long history of taxing its citizens, for example. See Ellen A. Sellingsloh, "A More Equal Proportion: Public Finance and the Social Order in Rumbout Precinct and the Town of Fishkill, N.Y., 1737–1800," Ph. D. diss., State University of New York at Albany, 1984.
83. *Journals of the Provincial Congress, Provincial Convention, Committee of Safety and Council of Safety of the State of New-York, 1775–1776–1777, Vol. II* (Albany: Thurlow Weed, Printer to the State, 1842), 424 (25 April 1777).
84. Loyalism, 62.
85. The Paulding's Precinct Committee likely welcomed the presence of Ulster troops since, only three days earlier, Committee Chairman Nathan Pearce had requested a ten-man guard from outside the county to protect meetings. *Journals*, Volume I, 766 (9 January 1777).
86. Ibid., 839. Several months into the war, events and personal experience made county committeemen less sensitive to legitimacy issues than the council and conspiracy commission, which could afford to be more dispassionate.
87. The tone of the Provincial Council also began to sound less authoritarian. Although the reason for this change is not clear, it may have been a result of new leadership or more upstate representation.
88. Ibid., 214, 215 (12 December 1775).
89. The Newburgh Committee most likely appealed directly to the Provincial Council because it thought that the Orange Committee was either feckless or not Whig enough. *Journals*, Volume II, 97 (27 October 1775); "Newburgh (New-York) Committee to the Provincial Congress," Force, 4th Series, III, 1206 (27 October 1775). Although the minutes do not explicitly state why Wiggins and Purdy were arrested, it might have been because both had twice refused to sign the Association. "Signers in Newburg, Orange County," Force, 4th Series, III, 595 (14 July 1775).
90. In Albany County, for example, Abraham Yates, Jr., chairman of the county committee, declared on 29 April 1775 that "it [is] absolutely necessary that there should be a meeting of the Committee of this County" and that, until it sat, "a Committee of Safety, Protection & correspondence should be appointed" from the existing body, Albany, Volume I, 14–15 (29 April 1775).
91. I am indebted to Professor Harold E. Selesky for this analysis.
92. *Journals*, Volume I, 131–32 (1 September 1775).
93. Ibid., 185 (25 October 1775). Although the conspiracy included a plan to "take up the Committees and Congres men, and deliver them [to British officers]," no challenge to the committee system arose at this time, Force, 4th Series, III, 1305 (25 October 1775).

94. In *The People's Welfare*, William J. Novak argues that, despite their label, state (police) powers were exercised mostly at the local level. Although he focuses his research on post-conflict America, Novak reads his observations back to cover the fight against the British, *The People's Welfare: Law & Regulation in Nineteenth-Century America*, Studies in Legal History (Chapel Hill: The University of North Carolina Press, 1996), 3–13. For the most part, New York's upstate communities support this extrapolation: although boards lacked the permanence or legal standing to merit the term "police powers," they did relay on regulatory measures to prosecute the war. In this essay, I use "police powers" to refer to the enforcement of regulations, not the committee decisions which authorized them.
95. Albany, Volume I, 18 (1 May 1775).
96. Tryon, 51–52 (26 August 1775).
97. Roger Baxtor, Thomas Baxtor, Charels Gordon, and Christian House never appeared for questioning., ibid., 63–66.
98. A complete record of militia payments was included in Volume 40 of *Manuscripts of the Colony and State of New York in the Revolutionary War, 1775–1800.* Along with the other fifty-one volumes in the series; however, Volume 40 burned in the Capitol fire of 1911. Note by James Sullivan, Albany, Volume I, 965.
99. Ibid., 88 (12 June 1775).
100. Benedict Arnold to the Albany Committee, received on 12 June 1775. Ibid., 88.
101. A soldier or non-commissioned officer had to have written permission from his commanding officer to take civilian property. The *Gazette* was published in New York City; editions would not have made their way up the Hudson for some time after publication. *New-York Gazette; and Weekly Mercury*, America's Historical Newspapers (American Antiquarian Society) 22 April 1776.
102. Albany I, 77 (1 June 1775).
103. Ibid., 127 (6 July 1775).
104. When in the province, Washington and Major General Charles Lee were also kept well-informed. Of course, the Provincial Council was in constant communication with the Continental Congress.
105. The members of the Tryon Committee, in particular, thrice swore oaths of secrecy in the first year of the war. Tryon, 40 (13 July 1775), 49 (August 1775), 72, 75 (13 September 1775). With enemies closer than in other counties, the Tryon Committee probably feared that security leaks would incite Tories and the disaffected to retaliate.
106. Albany, Volume I, 159 (17 July 1775). Yates, from a prominent Albany family, regained his political standing after the war, serving in the state assembly and Continental Congress. At least three other members from the Yates clan were in politics after the war: one as mayor of Albany, one as governor of New York, and one as a delegate to the constitutional convention.
107. Journal minutes rarely included "yea" and "nay" counts.
108. Ibid., 68 (7 June 1775).
109. On 13 July 1775, the assembled representatives voted to have all routes leading into the county watched by residents loyal to the committee, Tryon, 41 (13 July 1775).
110. Ibid., 92 (6 November 1775).
111. The subcommittee—Henry Wendell, Col. Goose Van Schaick, and Jeremiah Van Rensselaer—reported that a fourth of all arms needed major repair and instructed owners to take each weapon to a gunsmith. The gentlemen judged the remaining weapons to be in poor shape but salvable with a bit of at-home maintenance, Albany, Volume I, 32 (18 May 1775), 33 (25 May 1775).
112. The Provincial Council mandated that "the person or persons, who shall have the charge of the carrying this resolution into execution in each county" furnish

the owners with a written receipt for the appropriation. The council directed that Captain Dutcher's militia accomplish this task in the Tory stronghold of Westchester County. *Journals*, Volume I, 149, 150 (16 September 1775).

113. The commission consisted of Jeremiah Van Rensselaer, Gerit Langingh Jr., Jacob Roseboom Jr., and Rutger Bleecker. Albany, Volume I, 493 (17 July 1776). It is not clear why the Albany Committee—which had fewer threats to its existence than other Hudson Valley committees—waited until the fifteenth month of the war to gather this information. Perhaps the influx of new faces due to dislocations from other communities influenced the decision.
114. *Journals*, Volume I, 706 (7 November 1776). Although the council offered no evidence of illegal inter-county travel, the date of the resolution—7 November 1776—suggests that it was a consequence of Britain's occupation of New York City.
115. Tryon, 101 (24 November 1775).
116. Ibid., 521 (10 August 1776).
117. Ibid., 527 (21 August 1776).
118. It is not clear if communication between the district and the council skipped the Ulster Committee or not, *Journals*, Volume I, 494–95 (14 June 1776).
119. The authorized merchant would receive 3d. per pound for his responsibilities; the original owner would receive no compensation, ibid., 682 (17 October 1776).
120. *Journals*, Volume II, 229–30 (18 November 1776); *Journals*, Volume I, 714 (23 November 1776). According to Barbara Clark Smith, upstate new Yorkers rioted on ten occasions between the start of the war and the end of 1777, Barbara Clark Smith, "Food Rioters and the American Revolution," *The William and Mary Quarterly* 3rd Ser., Vol. 51, No. 1 (January 1994): 35–36.
121. Tryon, 80 (26 October 1775). More-established communities in upstate New York, such as Dutchess County's Rombout Precinct, had taxed residents before the war. See Sellingsloh.
122. Albany, Volume I, 51 (28 May 1775); "on the public Credit of this Colony" ibid., 61 (2 June 1775).
123. Ibid., 142 (12 July 1775).
124. It is not clear what was put on the handbills but reason suggests that it was aimed at the purchaser, either a list of prices or a *caveat emptor* warning, ibid., 353 (8 March 1776).
125. The county-published handbills listed prices for West India rum, Jamaica spirits, molasses, New York rum, coffee, loaf sugar, chocolate, sugar (1st quality), good coarse salt, pepper, and Bohea tea, ibid., 385 (20 April 1776).
126. Ibid., 496 (18 July 1776).
127. Ibid., 351 (6 March 1776), 387 (24 April 1776), 400 (8 May 1776), 483 (10 July 1776), 493 (17 July 1776).
128. Ibid., 400 (8 May 1776), 483 (10 July 1776).
129. Ibid., 18 (1 May 1775). Fining for non-attendance also helped maintain quorums.
130. The Continental Congress, with no income source of its own, either had to authorize expenditures against its credit or use foreign loans to back that credit, ibid., 185 (10 August 1776).
131. This observation is based on negative evidence.
132. Ibid., 661 (21 January 1777).
133. "In Committee of Safety for the State of New York," Fishkill, New York: Printed by Samuel Loudon, Early American Imprints, Series I, Evans Digital Library, 1 March 1777. The eighth resolve did not state when the one-half percent interest would compound.
134. *Journals*, Volume II, 316 (November 1776).
135. In my research, I did not come across the source of upstate residents' salt, other than indications that it was an imported commodity.
136. Albany, Volume I, 512 (3 August 1776).

Joshua Watson could have been a Tory or a profiteer.

137. Ibid., 868 (15 November 1777).

138. *Journals*, Volume I, 916 (8 May 1777). Most of upstate New York had long been supporting the poor. Referring to Dutchess County's Rumbout Precinct, Ellen A. Sellingsloh writes, "While growing pressure to provide a sufficient amount to support the poor reached a high point during the Revolution, it is important to note that there was a long time of increasing need for poor relief revenues," Sellingsloh, 48.

139. Ibid., 1096 (10 December 1777).

140. In one example, the Provincial Council ordered the sheriff of Orange County to release Andrew Bostwick after he spent eighteen months in jail, despite the fact that he could not repay his debtors, ibid., Volume I, 688 (23 October 1776).

141. The authors were Peter W. Yates, Peter Van Ness, Jeremiah Van Rensselaer, and Leonard Gansevoort. Albany, Volume I, 50 (27 May 1775), 58 (1 June 1775).

142. It is unclear from the journal entry where the powder came from. East Camp received 10 pounds, the Manor of Livingston 50, Claverack 50, Kinderhook 20, Kings District 32, East Manor of Rensselaerwyck 50, Hoosick 30, Cambridge 50, Schaghticoke 20, Balls Town 60, Half Moon 50, Schenectady 250, West Manor of Rensselaerwyck 100, Schohary 250, Coxsackie 50, Groat Imbocht 15, the three wards of the City of Albany 60 (total), Saratoga 100, ibid., 451 (14 June 1776).

143. The investigation revealed that Indians could not have received any gunpowder because there was none in the county stores to give them. According to those investigated, "We wish them [the Indians] well and would gladly supply them with Powder if we had any to spare," ibid., 58–59 (1 June 1775).

144. Ibid., 656 (9 January 1777). The journal entry does not specify which tribe received the powder.

145. Ibid., 267–68 (9 October 1775).

146. "Essays Upon the Making of Salt-Petre and Gun-Powder," compiled by Thomas Tredwell, printed by Samuel Loudon in New York, Early American Imprints, Series I; Evans Digital Library (17 January 1776).

147. Letter to the Provincial Council from John R. Livingston. *Journals*, Volume I, 287 (27 January 1776).

148. *Journals*, Volume II, 167 (18 April 1776), 302 (16 July 1776), 322 (11 September 1776).

149. *Journals*, Volume I, 551 (31 July 1776). Melancton Smith became one of New York's leading anti-Federalists after the war. See Staughton Lynd, *Anti-Federalism in Dutchess County, New York: A Study of Democracy and Class Conflict in the Revolutionary Era* (Chicago: Loyola University Press, 1962).

150. Whig newsprint—whether in article or broadside form—may have accomplished more than just disseminate communications, analyze the war effort, and define Continental events. By unifying opinion, it may have helped upstate New Yorkers form an identity separate from Britain, easing the psychological burden of separation. See Benedict Anderson, *Imagined Communities: Reflections on the Origin and Spread of Nationalism*, revised edition (New York: Verso, 1991), especially page 35.

151. A Free Citizen, "Petition to the Honourable the Committee of Safety for the Colony of New York," New York: printed by John Holt, Early American Imprints, Series I, Evans Digital Library, 1775.

152. William Walton, "Resolves from the Committee Chamber," Early American Imprints, Volume I, Evans Digital Library, 22 August 1775.

153. Robert Benson, "A True Copy from the Minutes," *New-York Gazette; and the Weekly Mercury*, America's Historical Newspapers,

4 September 1775. The council had the resolution reprinted in *The New-York Journal* on 14 September 1775, America's Historical Newspapers, American Antiquarian Society.

154. Robert Benson, "Extract from the Minutes," Fishkill, Dutchess County: printed by Samuel London, Early American Imprints, Volume I, Evans Digital Library, 7 November 1776.
155. *The New-York Gazette*, America's Historical Newspapers, 11 December 1775.
156. Albany, Volume I, 291 (11 November 1775).
157. For a detailed exposition of counterfeiting schemes, see Kenneth, Scott, *Counterfeiting in Colonial New York*, New York: The American Numismatic Society, 1953.
158. *Journals*, Volume I, 414 (19 April 1776).
159. Ibid., 413–17 (14–15 May 1776). The four men were Israel Youngs, Issac Youngs, Issac Ketcham, and Henry Dawkins (names appear as spelled in the council minutes).
160. Ibid., 471 (3 June 1776).
161. Although Rivington printed tracts for the British in New York City, I have come across no definitive proof that he was involved in counterfeiting plots.
162. Efforts to capture falsifiers continued as well. For example, a Captain Slawsen led troops into Thomas Heden's house to seize illegal currency in early April 1777. From *Calendar of Historical Manuscripts relating to the War . . . Secretary of State*, Albany, N.Y., II, page 91, Scott, 157 (5 April 1777).
163. John Frey received 89 out of 134 votes cast. Tryon, 55–59 (26 August 1777), 67 (7 September 1775); committee member from the Palatine District: "List of the Committees for the several Districts in Tryon County, New-York," Force, 4th Series, II, 878 (2 June 1775); delivered the demand: Fulton, 1.
164. *Journals*, Volume I, 917 (8 May 1777).
165. *Journals*, Volume II, 444 (29 May 1777).
166. Albany, Volume I, 41 (26 May 1775).
167. Ibid., 61 (2 June 1775).
168. Ibid., 56 (30 May 1775).
169. Tryon, 35 (3 July 1775).
170. Tryon County's Conajoharie District recorded that it needed to review its newly enlisted citizen-soldiers on 15 June 1775 to ensure the formation was "agreeable to the Regulations of our Provincial Congress," ibid., 29 (15 June 1775).
171. Ibid., 72 (26 October 1775).
172. Flick, *Loyalism*, 70.
173. John M'Kesson, "By Order of the Council," Kingston, New York, printed by John Holt, Early American Imprints, Series I, Evans Digital Library (31 July 1777).
174. For a detailed investigation of service exemptions, see Arthur J. Alexander, "Exemption From Militia Service in New York State During the Revolutionary War," *New York History*, New York State Historical Association Volume 27, No. 2 (April 1946): 204–12. In *Washington's Partisan War*, Kwasny argues that "better" laws would have fielded New York more soldiers, Kwasny, 168. I believe that *different* laws might have increased the number of men serving in the militia but that such a policy would come at an unacceptable cost to communities and their committees. Kwasny's failure to research local sources biases his interpretation, Kwasny, 168,193.
175. Albany, Volume I, 586 (24 October 1776).
176. Ibid., 325 (2 February 1776).
177. Ibid., 339 (18 February 1776).
178. Ibid., 344 (1 March 1776).
179. Ibid.
180. Ibid., 345 (1 March 1776).
181. Ibid., 485–86 (12 July 1776).
182. Ibid., 549 (11 September 1775).
183. Salsbury's company received a total of £25–12–3 for these four mobilizations, ibid., 487 (12 July 1776), 774 (31 May 1777), 794 (14 June 1777), 883 (11[12] December 1777).
184. Few secondary works analyze rangers in upstate New York. My understanding of

how provinces used these forces comes from James M. Johnson's *Militiamen, Rangers, and Redcoats: The Military in Georgia, 1754–1776* (Macon, Georgia: Mercer University Press, 1992).

185. Ibid., 519 (9 August 1776).
186. Ibid., 551–225 (14 September 1776).
187. Since the committee's proceeding made no mention of a connection between the two apprehended Bratts and John A. Bratt, a ranger commander, any familial relationship must not have been too direct, ibid., 599 (6 November 1776).
188. Ibid., 677, 681–82 (11 February 1777).
189. Bratt dated his letter 29 August 1775, Albany, Volume I, 227–28 (4 September 1775).
190. Ibid., 435 (6 June 1776). The Albany Committee did not imprison every resident that refused to sign the Association. Most non-signers probably would have temporized when questioned about their motives. When Everat did not, the committee had little choice but to make an example out of him.
191. Ibid., 741 (2 May 1777).
192. John Younglove informed the committee of Miller's oath to the king. The board did not consider any other evidence before taking action, ibid., 403, 413 (10 May 1777).
193. *Journals*, Volume II, 95 (22 November 1775). The White Plains Committee (Westchester County) charged Jeremiah Travis and Jeremiah Travis, Jr. with "warning a number of people to appear at *Peekskill*, and with appearing and embodying in arms to oppose the Congress and Committee." "Letter from the Committee of White-Plains," Force, 4th Series, III, 1763 (22 November 1775). Both father and son ended up spending time in the Westchester County Jail. "Letter from the Committee for Westchester County," Force, 5th Series, I, 1145 (24 August 1776).
194. *Journals*, Volume I, 757–58 (30 December 1776).
195. *Journals*, Volume II, 447 (12 May 1777).
196. Albany, Volume I, 956 (1 April 1778).
197. Letter of the Provincial Council replying to Major General Lee, *Journals*, Volume I, 336 (4 March 1776), ibid., 350 (12 March 1776).
198. *Journals*, Volume II, 259 (23 December 1776).
199. Michelle P. Figliomeni covers this civil, internecine fighting in *The Flickering Flame: Treachery and Loyalty in the mid-Hudson during the American Revolution* (Washingtonville, New York: Spear Printing, 1976).
200. Flick, *Loyalism,* 125.
201. Thomas Smith, a former member of the County of New York's Committee who had moved to Haverstraw after the British had occupied his home, wrote to Brigadier General George Clinton on 27 April 1777, reporting that "The people from Tappen and Clarks Town have applied to General M'Dougal for Troops to protect them from the Enimy in the English nighbourhood and Hackensack, but have received for answer that he could give them no assistance; this I fear will Induce many of them to make the best Terms they can to protect their Persons and Property," Tomas Smith to George Clinton, *Public Papers of George Clinton, First Governor of New York, 1777–1795—1801—1804*, Volume I, with an introduction by Hugh Hastings, state historian (Albany: State of New York, 1899).
202. *Journals*, Volume I, 512 (30 June 1776).
203. *Journals*, Volume II, 409.
204. *Journals*, Volume I, 918–20, (Spring, 1777). Livingston was probably acting in his own interest as much as out of loyalty to the rebellion.
205. Albany, Volume I, 812 (16 July 1777).
206. Ibid., 822 (7 August 1777).
207. Tryon, 35–36 (3 July 1775).
208. Ibid., 75 (13 September 1775).
209. J. Howard Hanson in the introduction to ibid., xviii.

210. Albany, Volume I, 626 (27 November 1776).
211. Ibid., 627–28 (28 November 1776).
212. *Journals*, Volume I, 821 (1 March 1777).
213. Harry B. Yoshpe, The *Disposition of Loyalist Estates in the Southern District of the State of New York* (New York: AMS Press, Inc., 1967), 113.
214. Committee minutes did not clarify to whom Loyalist property would go, Albany, Volume I, 755 (15 May 1777). In her 1984 dissertation, Ellen A. Sellingsloh argues that the rebellion necessitated an expansion of tax revenue and, therefore, a widening of taxable properties, Sellingsloh, 95.
215. *Journals*, Volume II, 446–47, 449 (10 May 1777).
216. Albany, Volume I, 954 (30 March 1778).
217. Forrest McDonald remarks that, in general, America's first state constitutions reflected a fear of centralized executive power. New York was an exception, with a governor who was not elected annually and who—through an awkward formation called the Council of Revision—possessed limited veto powers, *Novus Ordo Seclorum: The Intellectual Origins of the Constitution* (Lawrence: University Press of Kansas, 1985), 85–86. The authoritarianism of New York's first state constitution has traditionally been imputed to John Jay, one of America's most conservative founding fathers. According to Walter Stahr, however, most of the thirteen other Provincial Council delegates who helped author the document shared Jay's understanding of the type of government that the new state needed, Stahr, 74, 76.
218. According to Chilton Williamson, the authors of the constitution thought that, "without residence and property tests, Tories, Hessians, and other undesirables would have made more difficult the election of safe and sound Whigs," *American Suffrage from Property to Democracy, 1760–1860* (Princeton: Princeton University Press, 1960), 198.
219. Residents considered themselves to be citizens of New York, not of their county (or, after 1776, country). See James H. Kettner, *The Development of American Citizenship, 1608–1870*, The Omohundro Institute of Early American History and Culture (Chapel Hill: The University of North Carolina Press, 1978), especially chapter five, "Naturalization and the Colonies." Daniel L. Hulsebosch sees a provincial identity emerging in New York during the middle of the eighteenth century due to a local constitution, or a "shared political vocabulary and grammar," Hulsebosch, 75.
220. Stahr, 81.
221. Hulsebosch, 192; McDonald, 155.
222. Countryman, 288. Countryman sees the rise of a new political and social class as being the most radical change that the war brought to New York, ibid., 289–92.
223. Williamson, 197.

5

Robert R. Livingston, Jr.

The Reluctant Revolutionary

CLARE BRANDT

Robert R. Livingston, Jr. was a member of an extraordinary generation of American statesmen, a generation which included, among others, Thomas Jefferson, John Adams, James Madison, George Washington, and John Jay. It is to their breadth of mind, erudition, foresightedness, dedication, and courage that the success of the American Revolution may be largely ascribed.

Most of these political and military midwives, who supervised the delivery of our infant nation during a long and hazardous labor, were very young at the onset. Thomas Jefferson turned thirty-three the year he wrote the Declaration of Independence; that same year, 1776, Madison turned twenty-five, John Jay thirty-one, and Robert R. Livingston, Jr., of New York, thirty.

The name of Robert R. Livingston, Jr. does not, of course, usually appear with these others on the standard list of America's founding fathers. Anywhere outside the Hudson Valley, the inclusion of his name is generally greeted with "Robert who?" But here today, *in* the Hudson Valley, and in the process of examining the Livingston family's role in American history, we may choose to ask a different question about Robert: Why did this man, so eminently qualified, so strategically positioned, and so highly motivated, *fail* to gain a place in his country's pantheon of revolutionary demigods?

Chancellor Livingston was unquestionably a man of accomplishment, and the present inquiry is intended neither to deny nor to diminish those accomplishments. In fact, our investigation may result in a better appreciation of his real achievements—a clearer vision of what the Chancellor *was* by delineating what he was *not*.

Unfortunately, these are very muddy waters—due, in part, to a bad habit we all have of answering the question "Robert who?" by citing, first and foremost, Robert's membership on the committee that drafted the Declaration of Independence. We do that, of course, because the committee is instantly recognizable; it is an efficient way to put Robert on the historical map. The trouble is that we are also, at least by implication, claiming a distinction for Robert that does not belong to him. We all know that Robert neither wrote nor edited a word of the document. Most modern historians have concluded that he was appointed to the committee simply in order to get the name of a prominent New Yorker publicly attached to the Declaration, thereby forcing the faction-torn New York Provincial Assembly into a firm commitment to independence. Robert was a pawn in a political maneuver, and he served on the committee not because of his eloquence and erudition (which he had in good measure), but because he was a delegate from a colony that could not make up its mind. Yet his membership on that committee has come to be his principal claim to fame. He is best known, even in his own family, for something he did not really do.

This is both ironic and emblematic. It is ironic because in the process of magnifying Robert's national historical significance, we often

Fig. 5.1. *Robert R. Livingston*, oil on canvas portrait, 1795 c. Attributed to Gilbert Stuart, CL.1974.56. Courtesy of Clermont State Historic Site, New York State Office of Parks, Recreation and Historic Preservation.

minimize his real accomplishments—or at least put them badly out of focus. It is emblematic because this tendency to overinflate Robert—to try to turn him into something he wasn't—is a tendency to which he himself consistently yielded.

Robert R. Livingston, Jr. was unlucky enough to be born into what the old Chinese curse calls "interesting times." He graduated from King's College in June of 1765, only a few weeks after the promulgation of the Stamp Act, and his commencement oration was aptly entitled "On Liberty." But what he and most of the rest of his family, including his father, Judge Robert R. Livingston, Sr., meant by liberty in 1765 was not independence for the American colonies but rather a return to the *status quo ante*, before traditional colonial rights had been usurped by the terms of the Stamp, Currency, and Sugar Acts. These conservative Whigs stood firm against independence at this stage not just because of its short-term dangers, but, much more important, because they firmly believed it was contrary to the best long-term interests of the thirteen colonies. Instead, they sought—and fought for, in a whole series of extra-legal congresses and committees during the decade leading up to the war—the restoration of their traditional rights as British citizens.

As late as May 1775, a month *after* colonial lives had been lost at Lexington and Concord, Judge Robert R. Livingston wrote to his son at the Second Continental Congress in Philadelphia, "Every good man wishes that America might *remain* free [emphasis added]: in this I join heartily; at the same time I do not desire, she should be wholly independent of the mother country. How to reconcile their jarring principles, I profess I am altogether at a loss."[1] For the judge, as for many patriotic colonials, the notion of an independent America was never the greater good, only the lesser evil. They were extremely reluctant revolutionaries.

What disquieted them as much as the act of insurrection itself was the stated political goal of the American revolt: the establishment of a democratic republic. Democracy was not a congenial concept to Judge Robert R. Livingston, Sr. or to his son. They did not share the faith of Thomas Jefferson in the virtue and educability of the people. Quite the contrary, they regarded the masses as irresponsible, immoderate, and injudicious—an attitude which they and other members of their family came by quite naturally, after three generations of exercising political power in the Province of New York and social and economic power in the manorial world of the Hudson Valley.

New York had been founded in the mid-seventeenth century as a commercial colony. From the outset, its goals and values were commercial and its politics, quite unabashedly, were the politics of self-interest. During the Leisler interlude of the 1680s and '90s, New York's political picture was further disfigured by the stain of social snobbery. By 1765, when the first pre-revolutionary crisis hit the colony, New

York was politically divided into two passionately opposed parties: the so-called "merchant faction," led by the powerful DeLancey family of New York City, and the party of the upriver landed aristocracy, dominated by the Livingstons. These parties disagreed not so much on policy, or even goals, as they did on pedigree. The DeLanceys were descended from a supporter of New York's onetime self-appointed Lieutenant Governor, Jacob Leisler, a man whom Robert Livingston, the first manor proprietor, had called "ye vulgar sort."[2] Because the parties' differences were social and personal rather than ideological, members of both were perfectly capable of shifting ground when the occasion demanded. (As Philip Livingston, the second manor proprietor, put it, "We Change Sides as Serves our Interest best.")[3] In addition, the parties themselves veered from one end of the ideological spectrum to the other in the interest of expedience—a phenomenon amply demonstrated by the following capsule summary of the political events of the late 1760s.

In 1765, concurrent with the Stamp Act riots in New York City, there occurred a tenant uprising in the Hudson Valley which directly threatened both the life and property of Robert Livingston, the third manor proprietor. The proprietor's Clermont cousin, Judge Robert R. Livingston, was appalled not only by the effrontery of the insurgents but also by the fact that, after the uprising was quelled by British troops and its leader, William Prendergast, convicted and sentenced to death, he was granted a full pardon by His Majesty George III, King of England. This, coming so soon after the contretemps with His Majesty over the Stamp Act, was naturally received by the Livingstons and their fellow landed conservatives as a humiliating royal slap in the face. Their sovereign, whom they had always regarded as their natural ally against the forces of domestic radicalism, had finally, publicly, slammed the door in their faces. When they turned to look for new allies among their own countrymen, they discovered an unpleasant truth. While they had been preoccupied with the tenant uprising and with the Stamp Act congresses, their committees and their moderate addresses to the king, the political opposition had been busy in the streets. The DeLancey party, recognizing the potential of the newly aroused populace of New York, had successfully wooed the radical leadership and manipulated its followers in order to control votes. It was all quite cynical: the DeLanceys were no more dedicated to the radical cause than were the Livingstons (even less, as it turned out). But they did recognize an electoral bonanza when they saw one, and they mined it with ruthless ingenuity.

In a series of stunning electoral victories between 1767 and 1770, the DeLancey party assumed political control of the Province of New York and in the process confirmed all the conservatives' fears about the baseness of popular politics. In pursuit of votes, they employed all the time-honored political techniques: oversimplification of issues, concoction of scapegoats, and inflammatory catchwords, not to mention intimidation, bribery, and titillation. Exploiting their party's merchant origins and urban orientation, they depicted the Livingstons as aloof highbrows and would-be intellectuals lolling on their vast country acres. In one election, they attacked the entire legal profession, largely because of the prominence and popularity of Judge Livingston and his cousin William. In another they exploited the issue of religion, depicting all Anglicans as snobs and royalists, in contrast to the Presbyterians as men of the people. They even tried to defame a Livingston political ally, John Morin Scott, as a homosexual; one of their political broadsides read: "[He] dances with, and *kisses (filthy beast!)* those of his own sex."[4]

The Livingstons and their allies naturally fought back, indulging in a little mud-slinging of their own. But they didn't have their hearts in it; and by the end of the campaign of 1770, the DeLanceys and their allies were firmly established as the political darlings of the crowd and undisputed masters of the Provincial Assembly.

It was from this unassailable position that they were able to unseat from the assembly both the popular Judge Livingston and his powerful cousin Philip, leaving the family unrepresented in the assembly for the first time since Livingston Manor had been given its seat, fifty-four years before. The judge, deprived of his voice and vote at a time when his country's fate was hanging in the balance, suffered what he called "melancholy and dejection"; and he concluded sorrowfully, "This country appears to have seen its best days."[5]

Within a few years, however, the situation had reversed itself, in a preposterous sequence that went roughly as follows. After the death of Governor Sir Henry Moore in 1769, the new acting governor, Cadwallader Colden, in an attempt to ape his sovereign, withdrew gubernatorial support from the upriver landlords—the Livingston party—and in the process perforce allied himself with the opposition. This meant that the DeLanceys, in order to capitalize on his support, had to endorse his measures in the assembly, even unpopular legislation such as a £2,000 appropriation bill for the provisioning of British troops in New York City. The Livingstons naturally exploited these issues to wean the populace away from the DeLancey party but then, in order to solidify their gains with the voters, found themselves toeing the popular line on almost every issue.

This is, of course, an oversimplified description of a very complex shift. Suffice it to say that after the political seesaw tilted once again, the Livingston and DeLancey parties found themselves at the opposite ends of the political spectrum from where they had started, with the Livingstons, perhaps to their own surprise as much as anyone else's, holding down the left. If this seems unlikely, just remember that this was New York, where politics was practiced with mirrors, and logic, loyalty, and principle stood regularly on end in obeisance to power.

It was in this political tradition that Robert R. Livingston, Jr. was raised, so perhaps it is understandable that he should instinctively distrust the people as a political force. He shared the desire of his colleague, Thomas Jefferson, for the people, but good government by the people was, to him, a self-contradiction. He was not alone in this; many of his contemporaries—including some of our more eminent founding fathers—distrusted the people. What set Robert apart—and what finally prevented him from achieving preeminence in the political democracy his colleagues created—was that he lacked not only the head for democracy but also the stomach. His disdain for the people was both intellectual and visceral. He harbored a deeply felt, personal aversion to the people—an aversion that was a strong element of Livingston family tradition, bred into the family's collective subconscious as part of the manorial experience.

The Hudson Valley society into which Robert was born had almost as much in common with European Fifteenth century medieval society as it did with the Eighteenth century European Enlightenment. His perception of the character of the people was inevitably colored by his family's traditional perception of the tenants of Livingston Manor—a perception which had gotten off to a bad start, three generations before the Chancellor was born, when the relationship between his great-grandfather, the manor's founder, and a group of Palatine refugees ran on the rocks of greed, wishful thinking, and ineptitude. Their story has been told elsewhere in all its heartrending detail, and I will not repeat it here. By the end of it, the first proprietor of the manor had reached the conclusion that his Palatine tenants were, to a man and woman, nothing more than shiftless parasites, out to bleed the Livingston family and its resources to death. He called them (among other things) "worse than northern savages"[6]—which, in the context of the bloody French and Indian Wars, was probably the worst thing he could think to say about them.

This profound suspicion of the tenantry, laced with fervent contempt, was inevitably passed along to the next generation of Livingstons, and the next, until in the family vocabulary tenant came to mean parasite, and the people became synonymous with scoundrels. An examination of Livingston descriptive language over several generations leaves little doubt of the validity of this conclusion. One good example is the second manor proprietor's injunction to his son: "Our people are hoggish and brutish[;] they must be humbld."[7] And in the next generation, Walter Livingston simply categorized the tenantry as "Pests of Society."[8]

Naturally, the feeling was mutual. One of the third manor proprietor's tenants, escaping capture by his lordship's constables during a tenant uprising, yelled over his shoulder as he ran into the woods, "Robert Livingston: Kiss his ass!"[9]

In this context, Robert R. Livingston, Jr.'s assessment a few years later seems quite moderate. In 1779 he wrote, "From habit & passion I love and pity my fellow creatures would to God I could esteem them."[10]

The Chancellor's misgivings about his fellow men were not alleviated by the demeanor of the Livingston tenantry during the Revolutionary War. In 1775, when the Articles of Association were circulated, Robert informed his friend, John Jay, that "many of our Tenants here refused to sign . . . and [have] resolved to stand by the King . . . [But] since troops have been raised changed their battery."[11] Later in the war, bands of Tory tenants roamed the valley; and Robert's mother, Margaret Beekman Livingston, reported, "Some say their number is 4000 . . . They have taken a Congress Member . . . and carried him off to no one knows where, they have three boxes of gun powder that has been sent to them by some as bad as themselves."[12]

That letter was written on July 6, 1776, two days after the final draft of the Declaration of Independence had been sent to the printer in Philadelphia. Robert R. Livingston, Jr. was already on his way back to New York to steer ratification of the declaration through the faction-torn Provincial Assembly. The assembly managed without him, however. Acting expeditiously for perhaps the first and only time, it approved the declaration after one morning of debate; and Robert, arriving days later, was permitted to contribute nothing, not even his vote. Having thus forfeited this mark of distinction in the history books of his home state, he proceeded to lose his rightful place on his country's most exclusive roll of honor. Becoming engrossed in urgent business at home, he was unable to return to Philadelphia in time to sign the declaration, a ceremony which took place (popular legend notwithstanding) on August 2. His cousin Philip was there to give the Livingston seal of approval, and he is known in the family to this day as "Philip the signer." Robert's posterity, on the other hand, has had to be content with the inadvertent, but devastatingly accurate, designation on a plaque in the town of Rhinebeck, where he is memorialized as

ROBERT R. LIVINGSTON
DRAFTEE OF THE
DECLARATION OF INDEPENDENCE

Despite his increasing concern, even abhorrence, at the democratic complexion of his newly independent country, Robert R. Livingston, Jr. served both the nation and his state with great steadfastness and personal courage throughout the war. During late 1776 and early 1777 he labored unceasingly, at considerable personal risk, to secure the defenses of New York State, particularly of the Hudson Valley, the military key to the war. (He was rewarded by having his magnificent new Hudson River mansion burned to the ground in October 1777, during the British army's only successful foray into the valley.) Concurrently, he served on the committee to draft New York State's first constitution. A predictably conservative document—penned largely by John Jay, with Robert's assistance—it was accepted by the constitutional convention at Poughkeepsie only after considerable amendation from the floor, engineered by a large group of delegates from the new political class: mechanics, small farmers, and country lawyers. Observing the process, Robert complained to his friend Edward Rutledge:

> In this state we are to form a government under which we are to spend the remainder of our lives, without that influence that is derived from respect to old families wealth age &c.—we are to contend with the envy of some, the love of power in others who would debase the government as the only means of exalting themselves and above all with that mixture of jealousy and cunning into which Genius long occupied in trifles generally degenerates when unimproved by education and unrefined by honor . . . I am sick of politics and power, I long for more refined pleasures, conversation and friendship. I am weary of crowds and pine for solitude nor would in my present humor give one scene of Shakespeare for one thousand . . . Lockes, Sidneys and Adams to boot. If without injuring my country I could once return to my own farm and fireside, I aver, I would not change any situation to be Great Mogul or President of the Congress.[13]

Unfortunately for Robert's peace of mind, the latter was not true. He hungered for recognition, fame, and power; so despite his revulsion, he stayed on.

To Robert's horror, the winner of the New York gubernatorial election a few months later, over the patrician Philip Schuyler, was George Clinton, a country lawyer and the son of a farmer. Meanwhile, the tenants of the Hudson Valley had staged an uprising in support of the British army which, although easily quashed, nonetheless confirmed the Livingstons' perception of their tenants as ungrateful, unreliable, and short-sighted. Robert's mother may have summed up the family attitude best when, in a New Year's greeting to her son, she prayed for "Peace and Independence and deliverance from the persecutions of the Lower Class."[14]

Robert R. Livingston, Jr. became his country's first Secretary for Foreign Affairs in 1781; but within a year of taking office he had reached the conclusion that the position was not commensurate with his political abilities and social standing, so he resigned. The implications of this action, as well as the motives behind it, did not escape his political colleagues—men such as George Washington, John Adams, and Thomas Jefferson, who would become the first three presidents of the United States of America. Robert's now firmly established reputation for pride, disdain, and ambivalence probably cost him the high positions in their administrations which he felt he deserved. Robert was not only unprepared to share power with the hoi polloi, he was even more squeamish about submitting himself to their political judgment as a candidate for public office. Yet at the same time, he hungered for eminence at the national level. Torn between ambition and repugnance, poor Robert never satisfactorily sorted out his muddled set of goals, motives, and loyalties. It was perhaps nature's little joke to have given him one blue eye and one brown.

Robert's inevitable frustration at not receiving the recognition he thought he deserved soon began to express itself in behavior that was petty, foolish, transparent, and utterly self-defeating. For example, shortly after administering the oath of office to George Washington at the first presidential inauguration in April 1789, Robert conceived a burning notion that a major post in Washington's first cabinet was his due. During the early weeks of the new administration, he and his sister, Janet Montgomery, waged a strenuous behind-the-scenes campaign to secure one of the coveted places. But although President Washington solicited Robert's advice on a variety of matters, the expected offer of a cabinet post did not ensue. Finally, Robert swallowed his pride and applied to Washington directly, letting it be known that he preferred one of two offices: Secretary of the Treasury or Chief Justice of the Supreme Court. The president's reply to his letter was swift, tactful, and devastating:

> When I accepted of the important trust committed to my charge by my Country, I

gave up every idea of personal gratification that I did not think was compatible with the public good. . . . However strong my personal attachment might be to anyone—however desirous I might be of giving a proof of my friendship—and whatever might be his expectations, grounded upon the amity, which had subsisted between us, I was fully determined to keep myself free from every engagement that could embarrass me in discharging this part of my administration."[15]

The depths of Robert's disappointment and humiliation are easily measured. Within a year he had launched a vicious public attack on the man who had received the job of Chief Justice, his one-time bosom friend, John Jay, and he had taken himself and the entire Clermont branch of the Livingston family out of the Federalist Party and into an alliance with its political foes. This put him in the ridiculous position a few years later of supporting George Clinton for governor of New York, not because of any personal enthusiasm for the farmer's son but because his opponent, the Federalist candidate, was John Jay. A sixteen-page diatribe entitled, "John Jay Exposed for What He Is," appeared over Robert's name. The Clinton victory (a highly questionable one, after the votes from two large Federalist districts were invalidated on a technicality) must have been a bittersweet triumph for Chancellor Robert R. Livingston.

During the next decade, as Jay went from triumph to triumph at the national level, Robert continued to serve as chancellor of New York State. He refused President Washington's invitation to become minister to France in 1794; and five years later, when he was nominated to run for governor of New York against Jay, he waged only the most perfunctory of campaigns and lost by the largest majority in the state's history.

Throughout this period, he professed to find entirely satisfactory the life of an enlightened eighteenth-century gentleman. In 1793 he began construction of a new and elegant mansion at Clermont. He read the classics. He studied mechanics, particularly steam propulsion, and formed a partnership with his brother-in-law to build a prototype steam vessel in the North Bay near Tivoli. He studied botany and conducted experiments in agriculture, horticulture, and animal husbandry. He wrote public papers and corresponded extensively with other members of an elite transatlantic fraternity of like-minded intellectuals, including Arthur Young and William Strickland. His literary output during this period is remarkable for both its volume and variety, as demonstrated by the following representative titles: "Reflections on Peace, War and Trade"; "Thoughts on Lime and Gypsum"; "Reflections on the Site of the National Capital"; "Complaint on the Postal Service"; "The Use of Ashes and Pyrite as Manure"; "Reflections on Monarchy" (written in 1793 in response to the guillotining of Louis XVI); "Notes on Alkal"; "Thoughts on Coinage and the Establishment of a Mint"; "Oration on the Fine Arts"; a plan regarding "the discovery of the Interior parts of this Continent & establishing the Indian trade in that Quarter"; "Notes on Winds"; and many, many others. His name was known and esteemed in the fraternity of learned men as well as in judicial and legal circles, where his performance on the bench drew continued regard.

It was not enough, of course—not for a spirit in which inner contentment was so dependent on outward acclaim. Living the private life that he professed to find ideal, Robert burned when others' public lives outshone it.

In 1801, Robert accepted President Thomas Jefferson's appointment as minister to France. His primary diplomatic objective—negotiating United States purchase of West Florida and the Port of New Orleans—quickly bogged down in French bureaucratic red tape and the whims of First Consul Napoleon Bonaparte (whom Janet Montgomery dubbed "the Wary Corsican.")[16] None of this was Robert's fault. Nevertheless, in 1803, President Jefferson dispatched James Monroe to Paris as a special envoy to get the negotiations back on track. Within forty-eight hours of Monroe's arrival in the capital, Napoleon summoned the two American diplomats to his presence and stunned them with an offer to sell not only New Orleans but the whole of the Louisiana Territory, a tract of some 825,000 square miles, whose acquisition would double the size of the United States. Livingston and Monroe, with no instructions from home, took a deep breath and accepted, and the formal agreement was drafted and signed within a fortnight.

It was a diplomatic *coup* of major dimensions—a political jewel to fit nicely into Robert Livingston's well-earned crown—except that his cursed, battered pride rose up and knocked it away. After all his months of patient toil behind the scenes, Robert obviously felt upstaged by Monroe's dramatic entrance just before the denouement and so he altered the dates in his official record book to indicate that Napoleon had offered to sell Louisiana three days earlier than he actually did, the morning *before* Monroe's arrival in Paris. To drive the point home, Robert leaked a "secret" memorandum to the same effect to the New York press.

The State Department in Washington issued a vigorous denial and then made public Robert's own official correspondence, which revealed the true timetable in his own handwriting. Public outrage was intense and long-lived. Robert's bungled lie cost him the credit he rightly deserved for negotiating the Louisiana Purchase, and it gave the *coup de grace* to his political reputation. It also cost him the position that he had ardently desired for years, the governorship of the State of New York. A few weeks before the scandal broke, his party, virtually assured of victory in the approaching election, had promised the nomination to Robert. Now the offer was withdrawn for good, and a few months later Robert learned that the post had gone to a man of distinctly inferior intellect and attainments, his own brother-in-law, Morgan Lewis.

When Robert returned to Clermont in the summer of 1805, it was easy for him to become embroiled in domestic details: his handsome house had to be enlarged to accommodate the new furniture and fittings he had purchased in France; he spent hours supervising the care of the merino sheep he had imported from the famous flock at Rambouillet; and he worked enthusiastically with Robert Fulton on the final stages of their steamboat, which made its triumphant maiden voyage in 1807, the year of Robert's sixtieth birthday. Two years later he published the charming "Essay on Sheep." He suffered a series of strokes in late 1812 and died at Clermont in February of 1813.

Back in 1768, when Robert was twenty-two years old, his father had written a letter to his mother as follows: "My son Robert must not live in the country, he has talents, if he will use them, to make a figure at the head of his profession, a farm would ruin him."[17]

In a way the farm did ruin him, although perhaps in ways that even his wise father had not imagined. It ruined him, in the first place, by elevating his expectations. Robert always assumed that, as a Livingston of Clermont, he would automatically achieve primacy in every undertaking. At the same time, "the farm"—Clermont—effectively saw to it that these dazzling prospects could never be fulfilled by instilling in him a manorial attitude that was utterly out of place in the new republican America.

"The farm" also provided him with a refuge from disappointment. Clermont's attraction for Robert went far beyond its pastoral serenity and much deeper than the satisfaction he received from its socially redeeming intellectual activities—husbandry, botany, mechanics, etc. At Clermont he was utterly secure: his status there was guaranteed by his name. On "the farm," the lower orders kept their places, and nobody dared to visit on him the humiliations he experienced in the outside world. Because of "the farm," Robert expected perhaps more than was his due, but he ended by settling for less. The son of the manor was also its victim.

This article originally appeared in the *Hudson Valley Regional Review*, Volume 4.1, March, 1987.

NOTES

1. Robert R. Livingston to Robert R. Livingston, Jr., May 5, 1775. Livingston-Bancroft Transcriptions, Broadside Collection, Astor, Lenox and Tilden Foundations, The New York Public Library.
2. Letter from Robert Livingston, November 27, 1690. Livingston-Redmond Papers, F.D.R. Library, Hyde Park, New York.
3. Philip Livingston to Jacob Wendell, October 17, 1737. Livingston Papers, Museum of the City of New York.
4. Broadside Collection, New York Public Library.
5. Judge Robert R. Livingston to Robert R. Livingston, Jr., September 18, 1767, Livingston-Bancroft, op. cit.
6. Robert Livingston to Alida Livingston, May 31, 1713. Lieurance Translation, Livingston-Redmond, op. cit.
7. Philip Livingston to Robert Livingston, Jr., June 1, 1745, Livingston-Redmond, op. cit.
8. Walter Livingston to Robert Livingston, December 29, 1766, Livingston-Redmond, op. cit.
9. E.B. O'Callaghan, *The Documentary History of the State of New-York* (Albany, N.Y.: Weed, Parson & Co., 1849–1851, 4 vols.), Vol. III , p. 753.
10. Robert R. Livingston, Jr. to John Jay, February 2, 1779. Robert R. Livingston Papers, New-York Historical Society.
11. Robert R. Livingston, Jr. to John Jay, quoted in Staughton Lynd, "The Tenant Rising at Livingston Manor, May 1777," *The New-York Historical Society Quarterly*, Vol. XLVIII, No.2, April 964, p. 167.
12. Margaret Beekman Livingston to Robert R. Livingston, Jr., July 6, 1776. Livingston Family Papers, Broadside Collection, New York Public Library.
13. Robert R. Livingston, Jr. to Edward Rutledge, October 10, 1776. Bancroft, op. cit.
14. Margaret Beekman Livingston to Robert R. Livingston, Jr., December 30, 1779. Robert R. Livingston Papers, op. cit.
15. George Washington to Robert R. Livingston, Jr., May 31, 1789. Robert R. Livingston Papers, op. cit.
16. Janet Montgomery to General Horatio Gates, December 4, 1803. Emmet Collection, New York Public Library.
17. Robert R. Livingston to Margaret Beekman Livingston, January 11, 1768, quoted in E.B. Livingston, "The Livingstons of Livingston Manor" supplement, handwritten manuscript, Clermont State Historic Site.

6

Skinners

Patriot "Friends" or Loyalist "Foes"?

LINCOLN DIAMANT

It is never too late to correct a libel, even though, as Mark Twain joked, a lie is halfway around the world before the truth can pull on its pants. But to set the record straight for future lower Hudson Valley histories, pamphlets, and schoolbooks, the answer to the title question of this chapter is, simply, "loyalist foes."

For more than a century and a half, the patriot irregulars who fought British and German invaders in the "neutral ground" between royalists and patriots in Westchester County during the Revolutionary War have been slandered. Ignoring printed evidence 165 years old, too many authors and eminent historians have accused these patriotic citizens of war crimes equal to or worse than those committed by the British Army, its loyalist allies, and its German mercenaries. Unfortunately, the libel continues, telling us more about the ways mistakes are repeated in contemporary historical scholarship than we may wish to acknowledge. Correcting an error so long enshrined in the literature is no easy task.

Where to begin? Perhaps the best place is Merriam-Webster's Unabridged *Third New International Dictionary of the English Language*, which carries this definition: "Skinner: one of a band of guerrillas and irregular cavalry claiming attachment to either the British or American troops and operating in Westchester County in New York during the American Revolution."[1]

"*British* or *American*?" Even the simplest definition is ambiguous, and it ignores an important piece of evidence about the origin of the name. It did not come from any patriot guerrilla practice of "skinning" Hudson Valley farmers of their food or household goods. "Skinners" were simply the three battalions of British refugee volunteers raised by the fifty-year-old erstwhile attorney general of New Jersey, Brigadier General Cortlandt Skinner. Under his Tory leadership, Skinner's Skinners saw partisan service for King George III in and around New York City from 1778 to 1783.

The alternative nickname "Cowboys" was applied by the Continental soldiers, militia, and patriotic farmers to the provincial Westchester Light Horse battalion, another British loyalist corps raised in 1777 by loyalist Colonel James De Lancey. Distinctively uniformed in green jackets, the Light Horse cavalry were stationed in the Morrisania section of Westchester, near King's Bridge. The Cowboys raided regularly between the lines, rounding up food—especially cattle on the hoof, hence their sobriquet—for the British army and civilian population of lower Manhattan Island.

With the exception of a single diary entry to which we shall allude, one finds no mention of Skinners in any portion of the vast collection of Revolutionary daybooks, journals, orders and dispatches. On the other hand, references to De Lancey's Cowboys abound. One example of the latter is Joseph Plumb Martin's *Narrative of Some of the Adventures, Dangers and Sufferings of a Revolutionary Soldier.*[2] Martin, a private who fought through the entire Revolution from Massachusetts to Virginia, relates how an officer along the Hudson "had collected some stores of flour, port &c. for the use of the militia in his neighborhood. A part of the enemy," says Martin, "denominated 'Cowboys' (Refugees) destroyed his stores." There is no mention anywhere in Martin's autobiography of Skinners—just Cowboys. But when George F. Scheer edited the little book for publication in 1968 under the new title *Private Yankee Doodle*, Scheer found it necessary to add a footnote to supply what he considered important missing information: "The Tory sympathizers called themselves *Cowboys* or Refugees, and the rebel sympathizers called themselves *Skinners*."[3]

How and where did this myth about the Skinners arise?

It began in the imaginations of James Fenimore Cooper and Washington Irving—those wonderful spinners of tales of fearless Hudson River Americans who conquered adversity, slept for twenty years, and rode around with pumpkins on their heads. Early in both authors' careers, they sank their teeth into the exciting wartime history of the Valley, particularly of Westchester County.

Cooper was born in Burlington, New Jersey, six years after the end of the Revolution. Literary legend tells how, in 1820, he tossed aside an English novel he was reading aloud to his wife, Susan De Lancey Cooper, a direct descendant of the militant Tory family which included the commander of the Cowboys. "I could write a better one myself," said the thirty-year-old Cooper, a former naval officer, and proceeded to make the attempt.

His first effort was the novel *Precaution*, quickly forgotten on both sides of the Atlantic. Unfazed, Cooper continued his new career. The *Encyclopedia Britannica* says of his second book *The Spy: A Tale of the Neutral Ground*, published anonymously in Philadelphia in 1821: "Never was a work written with such contemptuous carelessness." Despite only rare flashes of dramatic narrative buried beneath a verbiage of exposition, Cooper's sprawling novel still commanded three printings in a single year, and quickly became the most successful book yet published in the infant United States. Unusual among contemporary novels, *The Spy* dealt with thinly disguised actual Revolutionary personages and events in the Hudson Valley, most of which held nostalgic appeal for readers in the forty-year-old nation. *The Spy* also proved to be of great interest abroad, where this country was still largely geographic and political terra incognita. Cooper's mannered, prolix prose may also have been improved by its translators—including one who rendered it in Russian.

In a special introduction written long after *The Spy*'s initial popularity, Cooper tells how the convoluted plot was derived principally from tales and anecdotes told him by a "Mr. —," now known to have been none other than his Westchester neighbor John Jay, then more than eighty years old. But the word "Skinner" is nowhere to be found in Jay's public or private correspondence. Jay, who appears in Cooper's novel as "Mr. Harper," was a key member of the Secret Committee of the New York State Convention controlling Hudson Valley espionage during the American Revolution. It was Jay who actually employed Enoch Crosby, a daring patriot secret agent—fictionalized as Cooper's country peddler, Harvey Birch.

With a bow towards his wife's forebears, Cooper inserted an exculpatory footnote in Chapter XVIII of *The Spy*, asserting that Colonel James De Lancey's hitherto undisputed wartime cruelty was only "fancied . . . there is no evidence of his being guilty of any acts unusual in this species of warfare."[4]

That brings us directly to Cooper's literary problem. His imaginary British and American officers were always patrician gentlemen. With such an enormous cast of unblemished heroes, the fictional villains necessary to make a good story were in short supply. Cooper's solution was to introduce the Skinners, a name he added—we hope not permanently—to the Hudson Valley lexicon as a synonym for American patriot irregulars. Cooper uses the word first on the final page of Chapter I of *The Spy*, as part of the incoherencies uttered by the faithful Black retainer Caesar: "I been to see—Massa Harper on he knee—pray to God—no gemman who pray to God tell of good son, come to see old fader—Skinner do that—no Christian!" Cooper explains Caesar's rather cryptic reference in the four paragraphs that follow and end the chapter:

> The convenience, and perhaps the necessities, of the leaders of the American arms, in the neighborhood of New York, had induced them to employ certain subordinate agents, of extremely irregular habits, in executing their lesser plans of annoying the enemy. It was not a moment for fastidious inquiries into abuses of any description, and oppression and injustice were the natural consequences of the possession of a military power that was uncurbed by the restraints of civil authority. In time, a distinct order of the community was formed, whose sole occupation appears to have been that of relieving their fellow citizens from any little excess of temporal prosperity they might be thought to enjoy, under the pretense of patriotism and the love of liberty.
>
> Occasionally, the aid of military authority was not wanting, in enforcing these arbitrary distributions of worldly goods: and a petty holder of a commission in the state militia was to be seen giving the sanction of something like legality to acts of the most unlicensed robbery, and, not infrequently, of bloodshed.
>
> On the part of the British, the stimulus of loyalty was by no means suffered to sleep, where so fruitful a field offered on which it might be expended. But their freebooters were enrolled, and their efforts more systematized. Long experience had taught their leaders the efficacy of concentrated force; and, unless tradition does great injustice to their exploits, the result did no little credit to their foresight. The corps—we presume, from their known affection to that useful animal—had received the quaint appellation of *Cowboys*.
>
> Caesar was, however, far too loyal to associate men who held the commission of George III with the irregular warriors, whose excesses he had so often witnessed, and from whose rapacity neither his poverty nor his bondage had suffered even him to escape uninjured. The *Cowboys*, therefore, did not receive their proper portion of the black's censure, when he said , no Christian, nothing but a *Skinner*, could betray a pious child, while honoring his father with a visit so full of peril.

Thus did Cooper move to establish villains to match his heroes—thereby creating the "Skinner myth." Cooper's patriot miscreants are subsequently allowed to wander in and out of the novel's remaining 170,000 words. Cooper's story ends with the death of the spy Harvey Birch on a Canadian battlefield—during the War of 1812! Fearing that the author would never complete his huge novel, Cooper's publisher had insisted on premature delivery of that final scene.

In Chapter X, Cooper describes the leader of the Skinners:

> A man still young in years, but his lineaments bespoke a mind long agitated by evil passions. His dress was of the meanest materials, and so ragged and unseemly, as to give him the appearance of studied poverty. His hair was prematurely whitened, and his sunken, lowering eye avoided the bold forward look of innocence. There was a restlessness in his manner, that proceeded from the workings of the foul spirit within him, and which was not less offensive to others than distressing to himself. This man was a well known leader of one of those gangs of marauders who infested the country with a semblance of patriotism, and who were guilty of every grade of offense, from simple theft to murder.

Having so established the imagined character of his Hudson Valley irregulars, Cooper, in Chapter XIV, has a Skinner party burn Birch's house. A Virginia cavalry troop horsewhips them in Chapter XVIII. The Skinners burn another home in Chapter XXII. And in Chapter XXXII, in one of the grimmest scenes in American literature, the turncoat Skinner leader is lynched by two Cowboy officers, but not before crying out:

> "Help! Cut the rope! captain!—Birch! good peddler! Down with the Congress!—sergeant! for God's sake, help! Hurrah for the King!—O God!—mercy, mercy—mercy!"

When Cooper published *The Spy* in 1821, no aging British military refugee volunteers came forward to comment on the author's application of a Tory nickname to a group of fictional patriot banditti. It was four decades after the Revolution had ended, and most members of General Skinner's corps had long since died or been evacuated to Nova Scotia. But a corrective description of Skinners—in the memoirs of Continental Army surgeon James Thacher—appeared in print almost immediately.

Dr. Thacher was not only an excellent medical man but an astute historical observer and writer. Born in 1754, he served the Revolution from the siege of Boston to the siege of Yorktown, and lived to be ninety. In his sixty-ninth year, Thacher saw through the press his voluminous two-volume manuscript *Military Journal During The American Revolutionary War, from 1775 to 1783, Describing Interesting Events and Transactions of This Period, with Numerous Historical Facts and Anecdotes.*[5] *The Military Journal* was only one of Thacher's many books; he also wrote an *American Medical Biography*, *American Orchardist*, *Management of Bees*, *Demonology*, *Ghosts and Apparitions*, and a *History of the Town of Plymouth* [MA]. In *The Spy*, Cooper's compassionate Continental Army dragoon surgeon-philosopher, Dr. Archibald Sitgreaves, may even have been modeled on the talented doctor. "It was a maxim with Dr. Sitgreaves," wrote Cooper, "that no species of knowledge was to be despised."

Thacher's memoirs, based on his wartime diary, recalled his long role in the American Revolution. It was quite a story. In the fall of 1780, Thacher was stationed in the lower Hudson Valley. His journal entry for November 24th reads:

> The country which we lately traversed, about fifty miles in extent, is called neutral ground, but the miserable inhabitants who remain are not much favored with the privileges which their neutrality ought to secure to them. They are continually exposed to the ravages and insults of infamous banditti, composed of royal refugees and Tories. The country is rich and fertile, and the farms appear to have been advantageously cultivated, but it now has the marks of a country in ruins. A large proportion having abandoned their farms, the few that remain find it impossible to harvest the produce. The meadows and pastures are covered with grass of a summer's growth, and thousands of bushels of apples and other fruit are rotting in the orchard. We brought off about two hundred loads of hay and grain, and ten times the amount might have been procured, if teams enough had been provided. Those of the inhabitants of the neutral ground who were Tories, have joined their friends in New York, and the Whigs have retired into the interior of our country. *Some of each side* [emphasis supplied] have taken up arms, and become the most cruel and deadly foes. There are—*within* the British lines—*banditti* [emphasis supplied] consisting of lawless villains, who devote themselves to the most cruel pillage and robbery among the defenceless inhabitants between the lines, many of whom they carry off to New York, after plundering their houses and farms. *These shameless marauders* have received the

> names of *Cow-boys* and *Skinners*. [emphasis supplied] By their atrocious deeds they have become a scourge and terror to the people.

Thacher's story is straightforward. It is reproduced unedited here only because his diary contains the sole firsthand reference to Skinners anywhere during the American Revolution. Everything else is later and secondhand. Even a casual reading of the above entry reveals that the antecedent of Thacher's nouns, "These shameless marauders . . . Cow-boys and Skinners," is not "Some of each side"—but "banditti . . . within the British lines." Skinners were British banditti, never Americans. After 1823, only the most inattentive historical reader could develop a contrary view.

But why did Cooper slip so easily into his unprecedented identification of the lower Hudson Valley's angry, impoverished patriot yeomen of 1780–1781—the period of *The Spy*—with the frightful depredations created by their opposite numbers, Brigadier General Skinner's loyalist volunteers? After all, two generations after the Revolution, printed descriptions of British devastation in the area were not uncommon. Chaplain Timothy Dwight's haunting eyewitness description of the Post Road from New York to Boston during the Revolution is just one example: "Where I had heretofore seen a continual succession of horses and carriages, and life and bustle lent a sprightliness to all the environing objects, not a single, solitary traveler was visible from week to week, or from month to month."[6]

In 1821 when Cooper wrote his novel, the United States was still slowly working its way towards what we now term "Jacksonian democracy"—through the Embargo Act of 1807, the 1814 separatist Hartford Convention, and the Panic (and first Immigration Law) of 1819. Disturbing memories of Shay's violent 1787 Massachusetts revolt and Pennsylvania's equally tumultuous 1794 Whisky Rebellion and 1799 Fries Uprising still lingered in the minds of the literate propertied classes that included most of Cooper's readers, and into which he—the eleventh of twelve children from a log cabin family—had successfully married. To that audience, the concept of patriot Hudson Valley Skinners was not unwelcome.

What happened thereafter? In 1855, after almost two generations of Americans had absorbed *The Spy*'s characterization of Skinners as marauding patriots, Washington Irving added new life to Cooper's myth in *A Chronicle of Wolfert's Roose*:

> Hence arose those two great orders of border chivalry, the *Skinners* and the *Cow-boys*, famous in the heroic annals of Westchester county. The former fought, or rather marauded, under the American, the latter under the British banner; but both, in the hurry of their military ardor, were apt to err on the safe side, and rob friend as well as foe. Neither of them stopped to ask the politics of a horse or cow, which they drove into captivity; nor, when they wrung the neck of a rooster, did they trouble their heads to ascertain whether he were crowing for Congress or King George.

Periods of social ferment lend explosive license to common criminality. There is no reason to assume that the Hudson Valley during the American Revolution offered an exception. But for Cooper to have buttressed a creaky plot by provocatively asserting that patriots operating under the sanction and protection of the Continental Army were freebooters is an unacceptable libel that places the founding fathers' Revolutionary purpose in an unfavorable light.

As an object lesson in the dissemination of incorrect information, it is therefore of some interest to see how many otherwise thoughtful and distinguished historical writers and researchers during the last century and a half have picked up and even embellished Cooper's fictional allegation.

First was Jared Sparks, the well-known American historian who spent four years as chaplain of the United States House of Representatives. Later he became president of Harvard. Sparks' biography of Benedict Arnold (1834) asserts:

> The *Skinner* and *Cow-boys* often leagued together. The former would sell their plunder to the latter, taking in exchange contraband articles brought from New York. It was not uncommon for the farce of a skirmish to be acted near the American lines, in which the *Skinners* never failed to come off victorious; and then they would go boldly to the interior with their booty, pretending it had been captured from the enemy while attempting to smuggle it across the lines.[7]

Sparks, also known to have bowdlerized Washington's collected letters, offers no source for the anecdote.

Robert P. Bolton's pioneer *History of the County of Westchester* (1848) brings additional flavor to Cooper's myth:

> There was another description of banditti, called Skinners who lived, for the most part, within the American lines, and professed attachment to the American cause; but, in reality, they were more unprincipled, perfidious and inhuman than the Cowboys themselves; for these latter exhibited some symptoms of fellow feeling for their friends, —whereas, the Skinner committed their depredations equally upon friends and foes.[8]

Nevertheless, only six years later John M. McDonald's paper, "The Neutral Ground of Westchester," delivered before the New York Historical Society in 1854 and based on 407 interviews with 241 different county residents born before the Revolution, makes no reference at all to Skinners. That dedicated antiquarian refers only to "lawless followers who hung loosely upon the skirts of either party," and "plunderers who huzzaed for 'God and Congress.'" Ignoring those firsthand McDonald interviews, Benson J. Lossing's *Pictorial Field Book of the American Revolution* (1860) further embroiders the Skinner myth: "The *Skinners* generally professed attachment to the American cause, and lived chiefly within the patriot lines; but they were of easy virtue . . . treacherous, rapacious, and often brutal."[9] Lossing also repeats Sparks's anecdote, by then twenty-six years old.

Moving into the present century, the pace of misinformation increases. Frederic Shonnard and W. W. Spooner's *History of Westchester County* (1900) claims that "In addition to the regular troopers on either side, there were unauthorized and wholly illegal bands, organized principally for plunder, called *Skinners* and *Cowboys*, the former being patriotic and the latter of Tory affiliation."[10] And again Benson J. Lossing, now editing *The Encyclopedia of United States History* (1902) inserts a Skinner entry: "A predatory band in the Revolutionary War whose members professed to be Whigs. They were not very scrupulous in their choice of victims, plunder being their chief aim."[11]

More recently, Nelson Greene's *Valley of the Hudson* (1931) says that the guerrilla bands "which lurked within or near the American posts were known as *Skinners*. The bandits frequently changed their 'loyalty' as the occasion required."[12] The authoritative *Dictionary of American History* uses "ironically" to iron out possible ambiguities: "The *Skinners*, ironically named after Gen. Cortland (*sic*) Skinner's Brigade of New Jersey volunteers . . . claimed attachment sometimes to the British and sometimes to the Americans."[13]

Even Carl Van Doren says in his *Secret History of the American Revolution* (1941): "But in that Neutral Ground between the armies, where the more or less loyalist *Cowboys* and the more or less patriot *Skinners* kept up a savage warfare of raid and retaliation and plunder. . . ."[14]

Occasionally there is a glimmer of the truth—as in Ernest Freeland Griffin's *Westchester County and Its People*: "The infamous *Cowboys* and *Skinners* robbed and murdered. These last were worse even than the irregular troops. They were as likely to be American as Tory."[15] But George F. Scheer and Hugh F. Rankin continue the original myth in *Rebels and Redcoats*: "In the 'Neutral Ground,' no stranger was safe. Allegedly patriotic *Skinners* fought as relentlessly as *Cowboys* for plunder more than for politics."[16]

In 1958, Allison Albee, writing in *The Westchester Historian*, makes an assertion that goes far beyond Cooper's invention. "The Patriot *Skinners*, he says, "worked under arrangement with the regular Continental Army command."[17]

Corey Ford in his *A Peculiar Service* relates: "Some bandits called themselves *Skinners* and leaned to the patriot cause."[18] Ford also refers to Major André's captors as "Three illiterate *Skinners*."

The *Oxford Companion to American History* puts it bluntly: "*Cowboys* . . . lawless Tory marauders. (Their patriot counterparts were *Skinners*.)"[19] In 1967, James H. Pickering writes in *The Westchester Historian*: "The *Skinners* seem to have been an anomalous group . . . what turned a 'patriot' into a *Skinner* apparently, was the failure to discriminate between friend and foe."[20]

In *The Price of Loyalty* (1973), Catherine S. Crary levels the strongest allegation of rapacity and cruelty: "The rebel counterpart of the *Cowboys* were the *Skinners*, so-called because they robbed and often murdered their victims. They were banditti . . . some of whom were simply bent on depredation and gainful plunder under the sinister guise of patriotism . . . committing inhuman acts of banditry on hapless Westchester farmers whenever convenient."[21] Crary follows that denunciation with a lengthy quotation from Thomas Jones's *History of New York During the Revolutionary War* which she captions: "The Skinners Plunder and Burn the Seat of General Oliver Delancey and Treat the Ladies of his Family Barbarously." But nowhere in Jones' writing does the word "Skinner" appear.[22]

Again in *The Loyalist Americans* (1975), a collection of scholarly essays edited by the respected historians Robert A. East and Jacob Judd, Crary considers British guerrilla activities in the lower Hudson Valley under the subtitle "Conventional Warfare or Self-Interested Freebooting?"—and follows the direction of Cooper's century-and-a-half-old *Spy*. She refers to the U.S. experience in Vietnam to illustrate the "hazy bounds of conventional warfare" and concludes analogously that "the opprobrium heaped on [the Cowboys] at the end of the war went to extremes and was not justified." At the same time, her observations on Skinners have softened: *Skinners*, "their rebel counterpart, skinned their victims of purses and clothes"; and the Skinners "in general supported the rebels."[23] Crary also repeats Pickering's 1967 comment from *The Westchester Historian*.

Even so thoroughly researched a work as Mark Mayo Boatner III's *Encyclopedia of the American Revolution* (1975) equivocates: "The *Cowboys* were generally concluded to be Tories and the *Skinners* patriots."[24]

The *Encyclopedia Americana* (1977) paraphrases the Skinner entry that appeared in the *Dictionary of American History*: "Skinners, bands of marauders during the American Revolution . . . regarded as supporters of the American cause . . . ironically named after Gen. Cortlandt Skinner's brigade of New Jersey volunteers."[25] But Michael Martin and Leonard Gelber in the *Dictionary of American History* (1978) remain foursquare: *Skinners* refers to irregular bands of colonial patriots in the American Revolution who harried the British in New York State.[26]

And as recently as 1986, Robert McConnell Hatch makes three separate references in his *Major John Andre: A Gallant in Spy's Clothing* to the mythical patriot guerrillas:

> The *Skinners* called themselves patriots, but this did not stop them from robbing anyone they came upon. John Paulding, Isaac van Wart and David Williams [Major André's captors] were three of eight local residents who had set forth that morning . . . Some, but not all, may have been *Skinners*. There

> was at least a fifty-fifty chance' that the three [captors] might have been *Skinners* and Andre should have instantly produced his [patriot] pass.[27]

Is it possible that Major André failed to produce his pass because he knew that one or more of his captors were indeed Skinners, and he knew that Skinners were loyalists?

Nevertheless, the myth endures. In the identically titled *Major John André* by the British novelist Anthony Bailey, published just last spring, André "reminisces" after his capture: "The militia Captain had warned us about Skinners, the rebel volunteers who served the Continental cause by . . . terrorizing the Westchester countryside . . . some of them moving back and forth, serving both armies as it suited their own interests."[28]

Putting all such questionable scholarship behind us, we conclude with a suggestion: Had James Fenimore Cooper not married into the aristocratic De Lancey family, the American patriot irregulars of the lower Hudson Valley could have gone down in history not as cutthroat "Skinners," but as true patriots—as effective, selfless, and dedicated as Leatherstocking himself.

Which, of course, they were.

This article originally appeared in the *Hudson Valley Regional Review*, Vol. 4.2, September 1987.

NOTES

1. Merriam-Webster's Unabridged *Third New International Dictionary of the English Language* (Springfield , MA, 1968), p. 2134.
2. Joseph Plumb Martin, *Narrative of Some of the Adventures, Dangers and Sufferings of a Revolutionary Soldier* (Hallowell, ME: Glazier, Masters, 1830).
3. George F. Scheer, ed., *Private Yankee Doodle* (Boston: Little, Brown, 1962), p. 138.
4. A century later, Otto Hufeland's authoritative study *Westchester County During the American Revolution* (White Plains, Westchester County Historical Society, 1926), p. 422, supplied missing evidence of some of De Lancey's "fancied" acts: "Abuse of women . . . clubbing and stabbing, repeated hanging up until nearly dead . . . applying hot coals to the soles of feet . . . tearing the seat from a chair, placing the naked victim on it, then kindling a fire under the chair."
5. James Thacher, *Military Journal During the American Revolutionary War, from 1775 to 1783, Describing Interesting Events and Transactions of This Period, with Numerous Historical Facts and Anecdotes* (Boston, Richardson & Lord, 1823).
6. Timothy Dwight, *Travels in New-England and New-York* (New Haven: Converse, 1821).
7. Jared Sparks, *Benedict Arnold* (Boston: "Library of American Biography," Little Brown, 1834), Vol. I, p. 258.
8. Robert P. Bolton, *History of the County of Westchester* (New York: Cass, 1848), Vol. I, p. 306.
9. Benson J. Lossing, *Pictorial Field-Book of the American Revolution* (New York, Harper and Brothers, 1860), Vol. I, p. 753.
10. Frederic Shonnard and W. W. Spooner, *History of Westchester County* (New York: New York History Company, 1900), p. 417.
11. Benson J. Lossing, *Encyclopedia of United States History* (New York and London: Harper and Brothers, 1902), Vol. 8, p. 202.
12. Nelson Greene, *Valley of the Hudson* (Chicago: S.J. Clarke, 1931), Vol. I, p. 38.
13. J.T. Adams, ed., *Dictionary of American History* (New York: Scribners, 1940), Vol. II, p. 81.
14. Carl Van Doren, *Secret History of the American Revolution* (New York, Viking Press, 1941), p. 340.
15. Ernest Freeland Griffin, *Westchester County and Its People* (New York: Lewis, 1946), p. 287.
16. George F. Scheer and Hugh F. Rankin,

Rebels and Redcoats (Cleveland and New York: The World Publishing Company, 1957), p. 381.

17. Allison Albee, *The Westchester Historian* (Westchester County Historical Society, White Plains), Vol. 34, No. 4, 1958.
18. Corey Ford, *Peculiar Service* (Boston: Little, Brown and Company, 1965), pp. 237–38.
19. *Oxford Companion to American History* (New York: Oxford University Press, 1966), p. 218.
20. James H. Pickering, *Westchester Historian*, Vol. 43, No. I, 1967.
21. Catherine S. Crary, *The Price of Loyalty* (New York: McGraw-Hill, 1973), p. 174.
22. Thomas Jones, *History of New York During the Revolutionary War*, ed. by Edward Floyd De Lancey (New York: The New-York Historical Society, 1879).
23. Catherine S. Crary, "Guerrilla Activities of James De Lancey's Cowboys in Westchester County" in Robert A. East and Jacob Judd, eds., *The Loyalist Americans* (Tarrytown: Sleepy Hollow Restorations, 1975), p. 16 and footnote no. 2, p. 153.
24. Mark Mayo Boatner, ed., *Encyclopedia of the American Revolution* (New York : David McKay, 1975), p. 291.
25. *Encyclopedia Americana* (New York: Americana Corporation, 1977), Vol. 25, p. 9.
26. Michael Martin and Leonard Gelber, *Dictionary of American History*, (Totowa, N.J.: Rowmand and Littlefield, 1978), p. 583.
27. Robert McConnell Hatch, *Major John Andre: A Gallant in Spy's Clothing* (Boston, Houghton Mifflin Company, 1986), pp. 2, 243, and 257.
28. Anthony Bailey, *Major John André* (New York, Farrar, Straus, and Giroux, 1987), p. 75.

7

The Central Hudson Valley and the American Revolution

THOMAS S. WERMUTH

THE CENTRAL HUDSON VALLEY was one of the most contested battlegrounds in the War for American Independence, for the Hudson River separated the ardently revolutionary New England from the rest of the states and also linked Canada to New York City. In 1777, the Burgoyne campaign, which began in Canada and was defeated in Saratoga, drew men and resources from the central Hudson Valley. The American victory at Saratoga has been recognized widely as the "turning point" of the Revolution. From 1782 to 1783, George Washington's headquarters at Newburgh and New Windsor were his last encampments, and at Newburgh Washington squashed the threatened military conspiracy against civilian government. Moreover, throughout the war the region was the "breadbasket" of George Washington's army, and the area's fields, flocks, and herds kept his troops, and, at times, the troops of his enemy, fed. In addition, several thousand valley men fought in the war, whether for the Continental Army, the New York militia, or, less frequently, for the King.

The military contest for control of the river valley continued for several years, affecting local society in the central Hudson Valley. Many of the region's residents initially saw the Revolution as a struggle against a tyrannical British government that was attempting to subvert traditional liberties and rights. As the Revolution dragged on, others concluded that the conflict meant something else as well. Indeed, various groups promoted their vision of what the Revolution was, or, more precisely, what they thought the Revolution *should* be. For some people, the war years brought the possibility of political empowerment, as many who had hitherto been denied access to power found in the revolutionary upheaval the opportunity for political advancement. Young, enterprising middle-class men, such as Dutchess County's Dirck Brinckerhoff and Jacobus Swarthout, who had enjoyed few political opportunities before the war, now emerged to challenge the power and prestige of the landed aristocracy that had dominated the Hudson's east bank. Modestly born Ulster lawyer George Clinton shocked New York's elite by being elected the first governor of New York State in 1777. For still others the Revolution represented an opportunity to challenge the existing social order. The War revived the tenant conflicts that had troubled the eastern bank of the Hudson in the years before 1774. Laboring men and women spearheaded boycotts against profiteering Patriot shopkeepers and seized staple products during periods of economic distress, demanding economic justice from local dignitaries. This article will examine the transformation that the military struggle caused in the central Hudson Valley counties of Orange, Ulster, and Dutchess.

THE MID-HUDSON VALLEY: THE SETTING

On the eve of the Revolution, the mid-Hudson Valley was one of the most fertile and productive farm regions in British North America. Its grain, flour, and dairy products were sent to the West Indies, Europe, and South America. The port towns of Poughkeepsie (in Dutchess County on the Hudson's east bank) and Kingston (in Ulster) were thriving little commercial entrepots that served as regional hubs in the vibrant agricultural trade with New York City. Nevertheless, the backcountry away from the river had much in common with Washington Irving's "Sleepy Hollow," small towns, where little happened, and change, when it occurred, happened slowly and imperceptibly.[1]

The mid-Hudson's west bank included the counties of Orange and Ulster, which the Dutch had settled in the mid-seventeenth century. The English followed soon thereafter, and many French Huguenots and some Germans also came to the area. Slavery took hold early, and by the Revolution some 15 percent of the population of the Hudson's west bank consisted of African-American slaves.[2] Despite this diversity, on the eve of the Revolution, much of the west bank remained ethnically and culturally Dutch, perhaps three generations removed from Europe. Dutch customs prevailed. The Dutch Reformed Church dominated. When the Second Continental Congress was approving the Declaration of Independence, Dutch was spoken more regularly than was English in many west bank towns. Indeed, as late as 1774, Kingston (a mere two years away from becoming the state capital) still kept its official town records in Dutch.[3]

Ulster and Orange Counties were populated by freehold farms. Although the "Great Hardenbergh Patent" comprised the western part of Ulster, it lay primarily in the Shawangunk Mountains and beyond and had few tenants. A few families, such as the Hasbroucks and Hardenberghs, dominated local politics and society, but the Hudson's west bank was a society of "roughly equal men," who owned their own land and marketed the produce of their farms and shops.[4]

THE CENTRAL HUDSON VALLEY

Dutchess County faced Orange and Ulster across the river on the Hudson's east bank. The Dutch and Germans populated the central and northern parts of the county, but the English predominated in the south. Many of these English settlers were recent eighteenth-century migrants from New England and northern Long Island. As did Ulster and Orange, Dutchess did have some small communities, thriving port towns, and also many freehold farm families. But what characterized the Hudson's east bank, from Westchester north to Rensselaerwyck, was the continued existence of a manorial system, in which landowners used their economic power to politically control the county.[5]

Such landlords as Robert R. Livingston, Beverly Robinson, and Roger Morris possessed leases for more than five hundred tenant families in Dutchess County, many of whom owed their manor lords traditional services and duties that were more characteristic of medieval England than eighteenth-century North America. For example, leases might run for several generations, demand that tenants grind their wheat at the landlord's mill, work several days a year for the lessor, and require symbolic payment of portions of rent in fowl and fruit.[6]

The usual tensions between landlords and tenants were exacerbated by this manorial system. Tenant uneasiness expressed itself in different ways: simple resentment, the nonpayment of rents, intimidation of the landlord's agents, and, at times, outright rebellion. In 1741 and again twenty-five years later, fighting broke out between tenants and landlords on several of the manorial estates.[7]

The Great Dutchess Tenant Uprising of 1766 was significant. Beverly Robinson's attempt to expel both New England squatters and tenants who were withholding rents caused the rebellion that included upward of one thousand participants (about 20 percent of the adult male population) and that resulted in pitched battles between forces of the landlords and rioters. Although this event was unrelated to the growing crisis with Britain, the mutual distrust that landlords and tenants had for each other only increased, and that helped shape the relationship of both groups to the Revolution as it unfolded.[8]

THE REVOLUTIONARY CRISIS BEGINS

Unlike in New England and New York City, there was little organized anti-British activity in the central valley before 1774. Indeed, there were few attempts to challenge British authority or policy. Much like the rest of the northern colonies, however, this changed rapidly with passage of the Coercive Acts in 1774. In communities throughout the midvalley—from bustling port towns like Poughkeepsie and Kingston, to smaller, sleepier villages like New Windsor and Amenia—committees of safety, observation, and inspection sprung into action. For example, the Kingston Committee of Safety expressed its dismay at Parliament's attempt in the Quebec Act (1774) to establish "the Romish Religion in America." This committee was equally shocked by the "avowed design of the ministry to raise a revenue in America." The New Windsor Committee of Observation objected to levying taxes "on us without our consent" and asserting absolute legislative authority over the colonies. The committee resolved that such efforts were "subversive of our natural and legal rights as British subjects, and that we would be deficient in point of duty to our King and the British Constitution were we to yield in tame submission to them."[9]

When the war began in 1775, the people of the Hudson Valley began to choose sides. From the start, both Ulster and Orange Counties enjoyed unusually high responses to Patriot "oath of allegiance" petitions. Indeed, throughout the course of the war, though Loyalism was present in both counties, devotion to the revolutionary cause was quite strong. Although several distinct ethnic groups—English, Dutch, German, and French Huguenots—lived in the region, there is no evidence that any group was more predisposed to Patriotism or Loyalism; indeed, the one clear fact is that there were few Loyalists in either county.[10]

Although Loyalism was weak in Dutchess as well (particularly when compared to nearby Westchester County), the situation was nonetheless more complicated than the one on the west bank. When war began, both landlord and tenant were wary about taking sides in the crisis. While the Livingstons and Beekmans, who owned much of the county's land, generally supported the new Patriot Provincial Congress and demanded compromises from Parliament, they also sought to control the protest movement, so that the social and political order, which they dominated, was not disturbed.[11]

For a variety of reasons, tenants viewed the Revolution even more warily. First, some Dutchess County tenants were chary about siding with landlords who had oppressed them before 1775, even though other landlords did convince their tenants to side with them. Second, there were rumors that British agents were promising tenants ownership of the land they presently held in leasehold if they fought with the British. Finally, many tenants in southern Dutchess were simply indifferent to the struggle. Possessing no political and relatively little economic power, they were absorbed in the daily toil of farming and expressed little interest in the conflict. Although William Smith thought that tenants in certain Dutchess towns were "forty to one" against independence, this was most certainly an exaggeration. Many were lukewarm Patriots, until New York State offered them the possibility of becoming landowners, when it confiscated and redistributed Loyalist property.[12]

RISE OF THE REVOLUTIONARY COALITION

Although the traditional leadership of the mid-valley was at the forefront of resistance to Parliament in 1774 and 1775, the beginning of the war opened new opportunities for ambitious men who had been for many years on the periphery of power. This process was most pronounced in Dutchess, where a powerful manorial landlord class still controlled most of the county-wide and town offices. Landlord Beverly Robinson, who purportedly owned one-third of southern Dutchess, was the first judge of the county and a member of the Provincial Congress; Philip Livingston was the county sheriff; and Robert R. Livingston Jr., was one of the county's representatives in the Provincial Assembly. By 1776, new faces began to join the customary leadership of Dutchess County: freehold farmers and tradesmen like Dirck Brinckerhoff and Jacobus Swarthout, as well as tenants like Henry Luddington, who had developed local power bases, were elected to the committees in the counties. Nonetheless, their renown had never approached the provincial-wide reputations of the Livingstons, Beekmans, or Robinsons. By 1777, with the traditional leadership moving somewhat hesitantly on wartime issues of importance to county residents, these new, middle-class leaders began to exert greater power first in local Dutchess politics and then in the New York State Assembly.[13]

In Ulster and Orange Counties, a similar challenge to the "old guard" took place. Although historian Edward Countryman is correct in his assertion that the Hudson's west bank was a "socicty of roughly cqual mcn," a handful of prominent and powerful families had exerted considerable social, political, and economic influence before the war. More often than not, members of the oldest, most prominent families, including the Coldens, Hardenberghs, and Ellisons, had held such prestigious political offices as sheriff and county supervisor and had been appointed commanders of the local militias. In this hierarchical, deferential society, family name, education, wealth, and prestige counted for much.[14]

As the Revolution unfolded, many of the west bank's old elite found themselves first sharing and then relinquishing their political and military power. Merchants William and John Hasbrouck, leading members of two of the most prominent families in the county, had been the commanders of Ulster's two militia regiments at the beginning of the war, but they were not reelected to commands they had held by appointment for twenty years. Neither received enough votes from their volunteer units to compete for leadership.[15]

Ulster County politics offers a glimpse of the political struggles that characterized this region as it entered the Revolution. On the eve of the conflict, New Paltz's Johannes Hardenbergh was a member of the Duzine (the governing board of the town) as well as the wealthiest man in the town and perhaps in all of Ulster County. A colonel in the Ulster militia for twenty years and a delegate to the Provincial Congress, Hardenbergh was the grandson of the original patentee of the "Great Hardenbergh" Patent, two million acres that sprawled across Western Ulster. In the elections for the county-wide Committee of Safety in 1775, Hardenbergh's neighbors deferentially selected him a member and immediately named him chair and treasurer. Although Abraham Hasbrouck, one of Ulster's prominent merchants was also on the committee, these two traditional leaders were joined by new men like Robert Boyd and Johannes Snyder, whose social standing had previously not given them access to county widc political power. Accustomed to being obeyed, Hardenbergh soon clashed with the more middling members of the committee. Eventually, after a series of squabbles, he realized he had to work with them if he wanted to remain in power.[16]

Although most disagreements between the Hardenberghs and the the Hasbroucks, on the one hand, and the rest of the committee, on the other, were generally procedural, they broke sharply on the issue of support for Ulster's George Clinton. The New York Assembly had recently appointed Clinton the general of the New York militia and put him in charge of Ulster's regiments. Members of the county's elite viewed him as an upstart; Col. John Hasbrouck (Abraham Hardenbergh's cousin and a substantial farmer) refused to serve in a regiment "commanded by Mr. Clinton." Johannes Hardenbergh went further and, abusing his authority as chair, refused to accept the Ulster Committee of Safety's resolution appointing Clinton one of Ulster's delegates to the Provincial Congress, where Clinton had much support among the delegates from Ulster, Orange, and Dutchess. The Provincial Congress reprimanded Hardenbergh, demanded an explanation for his refusal, and then appointed Clinton to the Ulster delegation in the Provincial Congress.[17]

Following continued disagreements with several other committee members, Hardenbergh was ousted from his position as treasurer of the committee. He complained about these political upstarts and refused to relinquish the £300 in the treasury. The committee threatened Hardenbergh with an "altercation" and ordered him to turn over the money. Hardenbergh not only relented, but he soon began cooperating in the new political environment, for which he and most other committee members had little training: democratic political discussion, debate, and compromise.[18]

Despite Hardenbergh's preference for deferential politics and his discomfort with popular decision-making, he was committed to the revolutionary cause. Other members of the colonial elite on the west bank were not so inclined, and they did not fare as well. Cadwallader Colden Jr., son of the lieutenant governor, made clear his disdain for democratic politics and his loyal support for the Crown. He suffered the consequences, when a delegation from the New Windsor Committee of Safety stormed his estate at midnight on 21 June 1776. The committee searched and ransacked his house and ordered him arrested. Colden hoped to remain under house arrest and even offered to pay for guards to stay at his home that night, but the committee refused. When Colden continued to insist upon house arrest, the committee threatened him with the humiliating alternative that he would "be rode upon a rail" to the local jail, if he did not accompany them willingly. This type of theatrical punishment had traditionally been reserved during the Colonial Period for prostitutes, wife-abusers, and other community miscreants, not for men of Colden's stature. To threaten one of the most substantial men in the midvalley with such a fate, and his apparent belief that the committee would make good on their threat, reveals the extent of the military conflict's challenge to the existing social and political order.[19]

In the place of this traditional elite there emerged in Ulster and Orange a group of talented, opportunistic men, such as Robert Boyd, Charles DeWitt, and Matthew Cantine, who had developed strong local support, but who lacked the wealth and pedigree of the prewar leadership. These newly elected officials in the midvalley were not simply new names; they were men who came from a lower socioeconomic status than the traditional elite. They held divergent views on political leadership and political participation and had a different understanding of the goals of the Revolution. For these men the Revolution offered the opportunity for political and social advancement, something that had been denied them before the war. These new political leaders now had the opportunity to assume political roles on the many committees of correspondence, safety, and inspection. Further, the dramatically increased size of the state legislature (the delegations from the mid-Hudson Valley doubled in size) opened up new opportunities at the state level.

The most dramatic example of the new political opportunities in the midvalley (or in any part of Revolutionary America, for that matter) was the meteoric rise of George Clinton.

Clinton was not new to political power, nor was he a simple farmer making his first foray into politics. Born to a "well-to-do" (though not prominent) family on the Ulster-Orange border, Clinton had practiced law in Ulster and New York City, and served as the Ulster representative to New York's Provincial Assembly from 1769 to 1771. He often spoke in the years before the war against British policy and had forged careful and practical alliances with such prominent provincial-wide leaders as Philip Schuyler and Robert Livingston.[20]

Clinton's rise was swift. In 1776, the New York Congress appointed him a brigadier general in the New York militia, an appointment that drew the scorn of Ulster's traditional aristocracy. Col. John Hasbrouck, commander of the Ulster militia, pointedly asked the New York Congress "how he [Clinton] comes to be promoted to so high a rank . . . and how it was brought about to supercede so many brave officers in the regiment." Clinton's unexpected triumph as New York's first governor in 1777 brought equally critical commentary from the New York elite. Clinton's former ally in the New York Assembly, Philip Schuyler, a losing candidate, claimed that Clinton's "family and connections do not entitle him to so distinguished a predominance."[21]

THE WAR IN THE MIDVALLEY: 1775–1783

Although no fighting took place in the region during the first year of the war, from 1776 through 1783, control of the Hudson River Valley remained one of the primary strategic objectives of the British high command, and the valley's defense was equally important to Gen. George Washington. American control of this region bottled up the British in New York City and kept other British forces far to the north in Canada. In 1776 Washington, whose army would spend more than one-third of the Revolutionary War in or in close proximity to the Hudson River Valley, stated that "the importance of the river in the present contest and the necessity of defending it, are so well understood that it is unnecessary to enlarge upon them." Washington nonetheless proceeded to do so, citing its strategic transportation and communications significance as well as the importance of its agricultural production.[22] His concern for the defense of this strategic region led the Americans to construct an "Iron Chain" and boom across the river at Forts Clinton and Montgomery near Popolopen Creek. This impediment was soon destroyed by Sir Henry Clinton's forces and rendered useless. In 1776 Washington had also ordered the construction of three forts along the Highlands: Forts Montgomery, Clinton, and Constitution. By the summer of 1777, these three forts were still unfinished and only lightly garrisoned.

The British in New York City engaged in several small raids in the midvalley in 1776 and 1777, including one on Peekskill in March 1777. The main force under General John Burgoyne was to depart from Canada in summer and push southward through the Adirondacks to Albany, where it was to meet up with a combined British-Indian force that had been pushing eastward along the Mohawk Valley. The third force was to be an expeditionary unit from New York City under the command of Sir Henry Clinton. Clinton's troops were to move up the Hudson and meet Burgoyne or at least give him support. The military's lack of proper planning, coordination, and execution of this major invasion led directly to the British defeat at Saratoga, the "turning point of the war."[23]

Instead of using all his military resources to support Burgoyne, Sir William Howe, commander in chief of the British army in America, took a large force to capture Philadelphia and left Sir Henry Clinton only a small contingent to support the invasion from Canada. About two thousand Continental soldiers and elements of the Ulster and Orange County militia garrisoned the Hudson Highlands. The state's new governor, General George Clinton, commanded the posts at Forts Clinton and

Montgomery. On the morning of 6 October, after a day of fierce fighting, British troops captured both forts and spent the next several days destroying the forts and the iron chain across the Hudson. The main part of the American force managed to escape northward.[24]

Although the British victory was complete, Henry Clinton's troops suffered almost two hundred casualties and were delayed by the military action. They finally resumed their slow movement upriver and stopped at a number of points along the way, where they landed several small units for limited forays against local militia units. British forces reached Kingston, the state capital, ten days later.

Advance British units entered Kingston before dawn on October 16. Many Kingstonians had already escaped, and local militia forces had stood ready to conduct a delaying action against enemy forces. However, a British raiding party of several hundred troops under Major General John Vaughan quickly drove these militia units west from the town in predawn fighting on the banks of Rondout Creek just a few hundred yards from the Hudson. Determined to punish the region, British troops burned most of the town before departing later that afternoon. Vaughan pushed ten miles upriver over the next few days, dropping landing parties at various points (including the Livingston estate at Clermont) before heading south to New York City. By this time, Burgoyne had already surrendered his army at Saratoga, and Clinton's slow northward movement was now irrelevant.[25]

Although the next year witnessed only limited military action in the midvalley, the Hudson remained a primary target of both British and American strategies for the remainder of the war. Sir Henry attempted a second invasion of the river valley in June 1779, seizing Stony Point in then Orange County. However, Washington kept his army between Henry Clinton and the northern river valley. In July "Mad" Anthony Wayne drove the British from Stony Point and by fall sent them retreating southward down the river.[26]

It was the importance of the Hudson that had led Washington in 1778 to order construction of fortress West Point, which overlooked the Hudson in Orange County. He also ordered that a heavy and formidable great iron chain, be erected to prevent any future British incursion up the river. The British did make one more attempt to gain control of the Hudson in 1780, when Henry Clinton opened secret negotiations with General Benedict Arnold, the recently appointed commander of the Hudson Highlands and West Point, to gain control of the fort. Arnold's plans were discovered, when Clinton's aide-de-camp John André was captured in Westchester County. André was hanged in Tappan as a spy, and Arnold was barely able to escape to safety in British-occupied New York City.[27]

In the last years of the war, the midvalley remained central to Washington's planning. Although the British were defeated at Yorktown in 1781, they continued to occupy New York City for two more years, and their continued threat to the river valley kept Washington and his army stationed nearby. The Continental army encamped in southern Ulster County, in and around the town of New Windsor, while Washington himself took up headquarters a few miles north on the Hudson at Newburgh.

POPULAR POLITICS AND THE COMMITTEE MOVEMENT

The years of military conflict had a significant impact on the mid-Hudson Valley. The gradual collapse of New York's colonial government throughout 1775 impelled extralegal committees of safety, observation, and inspection to fill the power vacuum. In most towns these committees developed alongside existing legally constituted town boards and governments. In many communities these committees exerted their influence not only in the political sphere, but also in the economic arena by regulating prices, controlling the importation and exportation of goods, and setting maximum and minimum wage rates for local labor.

The committees enjoyed formidable powers that grew increasingly broad over time in response to wartime needs. Initially, the committees' role was simply to organize and promote revolutionary support and to communicate with the populace about the latest developments in the imperial crisis. With the disintegration of the official provincial government in late 1775, however, the committees became quasi-legal institutions replacing the power of the crumbling old government. Although the committees' powers were curtailed with the creation of the New York State government in 1777, these bodies nonetheless enjoyed significant local authority throughout the late 1770s.

The various committees that emerged in the mid-Hudson Valley during the war were popularly elected and supported. Among the earliest committees of correspondence were those elected at the town meetings of the Kingston Corporation, Poughkeepsie town government, and the New Paltz Duzine. Participation in these meetings was not open to all residents; only freeholders could vote. The people initially elected to the committees tended to be chosen from the traditional community leaders, for the mid-Hudson Valley was still a hierarchical and deferential society. During the war, as old leaders moved up to state and continental positions or retired from active efforts, the social and economic status of committee members elected by freeholders changed substantially. A majority eventually came from the "middling-sorts." In this way, the freeholder-elected committees often served as avenues of advancement for aspiring political leaders, whose social background had heretofore denied them access to prominent elective office.[28]

The powers invested in the committees were often greater than those that town officials had possessed in the colonial period. In 1776, the Provincial Congress gave the committees the authority to tax and appoint tax collectors and assessors. During the war, the committees gradually gained additional political powers and became the governments of many midvalley towns. Besides control over local taxation and legislation, the committees also assumed judicial and police powers. Furthermore, committees employed local militia units as police to enforce their rulings.

Usually, the committees were able to employ community pressure against those suspected of unpatriotic actions or of any activity seen as threatening to the community. These punishments included public denunciations of those considered to be enemies of the cause, symbolic burnings of effigies, and boycotts of shopkeepers and tradesmen who were lukewarm to the Revolution. For example, the Kingston committee stated that if persons were guilty of actions endangering the community, "they should be punished in the public newspapers as enemies to the liberties and privileges of American subjects," and all residents should abstain from commerce with the offender.[29] The Ulster Association instructed county residents not to patronize establishments, businesses, or shops whose patriotism was suspect, because "every shilling of property we put in their hands . . . enable them to purchase the chains to bind us in slavery."[30]

Committees encouraged political action in other ways. At times they sponsored the public destruction of Loyalist assets in such places as the Kingston public market.[31] The committee also acted against members of the county's oldest and most prominent families, who seemed to impede the war effort. Leading members of valley towns came under public attack, were dislodged from political office, suffered riots or demonstrations at their homes or places of business, or, more ignobly, were arrested and charged with being "enemies of the cause." Some victims undoubtedly were Tories; others simply lacked enthusiasm for the cause, while still others had put self first and engaged in economic activities that residents felt compromised the integrity of the local economies that were already endangered by the extreme war-time dislocations. As a result, the Revolution successfully challenged the political and social order that had heretofore shaped life in small valley towns.

The issues upon which committees expended the most energy tended to be economic. On the eve of the war, the local committees of observation had supervised economic activities in their counties and towns and enforced the economic measures required by the Continental Association. During the war, when shortages and inflation had become rampant, the local committees scrutinized the trade and economic activities of local shopkeepers, to ensure that they engaged in business practices that promoted the war effort and supported a vibrant local economy.[32]

These activities included regulating prices, preventing hoarding and price-gouging, and forcing shopkeepers to sell necessary foodstuffs at affordable prices. As early as 1776, local committees had begun enacting price controls on variety of staple products, including wheat, flour, and salt. They also fined shopkeepers and merchants, who violated these price maximums, by confiscating their goods and foodstuffs. Finally, these committees forbade the exportation of certain staple products beyond town boundaries.[33]

As the military conflict dragged on, the committees heightened their efforts to control Loyalists, motivate neutrals, and prohibit economic activities that would weaken the American cause. In 1777 the Ulster Committee, which met regularly at Andrew Oliver's home, forbade the exportation of flour, meal, or grain outside of the county. In 1778, at the height of the wartime shortages, the town leaders of Marbletown gave permission to export flour, but "not more than four barrels" per person and only on the condition that an equal value of salt be brought into the town. By 1779 the situation had grown so desperate in several west bank communities, that the export of wheat or its use in distillation was forbidden.[34] Even though it is impossible to know today how much illegal trade there was, committees worked diligently to suppress it.

The state government, too, began regulating the prices of various goods once it was created in 1777. Each year from 1777 through 1780, it established various price controls in an unsuccessful attempt to halt hyperinflation. The state set the prices of all grains, flour, vegetables, leather, shoes, and a variety of other products. In addition, the state regulated wages and labor, ordering that "the various kinds of labour of farmers, mechanics and others, be set and affixed, at rates not exceeding seventy-five per centum" over the normal wages for a given locality. Moreover, in 1779 and 1780 and again in 1782, midvalley political officials requested that the State Assembly provide greater assistance in regulating prices. Specifically, the Ulster and Dutchess County committees asked the Assembly to introduce new, even stricter price controls to regulate the soaring price of grain and other staples.[35]

Legislation was passed not only to cap prices and control inflation but to regulate economic behavior within communities as well. Many believed, as did Dutchess County's Henry Ludington, that the scarcity of bread in that county in 1776 was not the result of natural forces but of the actions of the "wicked, mercenary intrigues of a number of ingrossing jockies." In order to set a proper example, committees of observation and safety made public examples throughout the war of those thwarting the committee's dictates.[36] For example, in 1777 New Windsor residents accused Mrs. Jonathan Lawrence of price-gouging and selling tea for two shillings a pound above the rate the committee had set. Mrs. Lawrence claimed that she only charged the committee set price of six shillings, "but will not let the purchaser have the tea unless he takes a paper bag to put it in at two shillings." When challenged by the local Committee of Inspection, she sent the tea to her husband, Jonathan, the commissary at nearby Fort Constitution. The committee consequently seized the tea, discharged Jonathan from his duties, rebuked the couple, and agreed to keep a careful eye on Mrs. Lawrence in the future.[37]

CROWDS, RIOTS & POPULAR REVOLUTION IN THE MID-HUDSON VALLEY

Even more significant than the actions taken by the committees in these years was the popular action that occurred throughout the midvalley in the 1770s and 1780s. As early as 1776, Kingston and New Windsor residents took matters into their own hands, for they thought that their elected officials were not going far enough in regulating the economy and prosecuting monopolizers and engrossers.[38] In response, the Ulster Committee reported in 1776 that "we are daily alarmed, and our streets filled with mobs." According to the Committee, the situation had grown so desperate in Ulster that if the legislature could not solve the economic woes affecting the central valley, local committees would have to assume authority in the name "of the People at Large."[39]

Between 1776 and 1779, popular action led to frequent boycotts, forced sales of necessary products, and riots in the mid-Hudson Valley. The first major riot occurred in Kingston in November 1776, when a crowd raided warehouses and stores seizing tea. Two weeks later, one of Ulster County's first families, the Ellisons of New Windsor, became victims when a large crowd came to William Ellison's store. After accusing him of price-gouging and engrossment, they seized all the salt "except one bushel," which they left for his family's use.

Even merchants who lived outside the three-county-area were not safe from this form of popular activity.[40] Two Albany merchants who had purchased tea in Philadelphia had the misfortune of sending it overland through New Windsor in 1777. A crowd of men and women besieged the transporters, seized the load, asserting that it was being marketed for more than the six-shilling limit the local committee had set, and sold it to themselves at that price. Crowds of local Dutchess women visited Poughkeepsie shopkeeper Peter Messier in the spring of 1777. Accusing him of selling tea above the Poughkeepsie Committee's imposed price-cap, the women used their own weights and measures to divide and distribute the tea among themselves. The women, accompanied by two Continental soldiers, offered Messier "their own price," one that was considerably lower than his selling price. The women returned twice more over the next several days to repeat these actions.[41]

The New Windsor and Poughkeepsie riots reveal that rioters often used the local committees' authority to justify their own actions. The rioters at Ellison's store reminded the shopkeeper of the committee's price regulations that he was allegedly breaking. The women who confiscated Messier's tea specifically stated that "they had orders from the Committee to search his house." However, it is essential to point out that in each of these activities, the rioters exceeded the committee's dictates. Neither riot was authorized by the local committee, and indeed, some committee members criticized the New Windsor riot.[42]

The activities of the committees in controlling prices and commerce, as well as in prosecuting hoarders, are clear indications of a public economic policy that aimed to regulate the workings of the free market and protect the community's interest. The importance of these activities was not the imposition of price controls, for many of the powers of market regulation and price-setting were already well accepted. However, while enforcing these regulations, the committees were functioning as local governments.[43]

The actions of the rioters in seizing foodstuffs were yet another matter. The rioters clearly held traditional economic beliefs that denied the role of an unregulated market in times of economic crisis. They questioned the unfettered use private property, when they seized goods, making clear their belief that a shopkeeper was not the only person to decide what to do with his or her merchandise and that the community had a legitimate voice in its distribution as well. During the Revolutionary War, these beliefs and activities became associated, even synonymous, with patriotic behavior and loyalty to the community. Those who participated in the riots were claiming that by their actions they were expressing their loyalty to the cause, while their targets, such as William Ellison, were exhibiting signs of diminished patriotic allegiance and even of Toryism.[44]

Also remarkable was that many of the rioters were ordinary women who had no public, political role, and who had limited control over property. During the Revolution, such women often took the lead in Hudson River Valley riots. It was a crowd of women, for example, who first confronted Mrs. Lawrence in 1777 for price-gouging and who by so doing forced the committee to act. Furthermore, the crowd that three times raided Peter Messier's store in Poughkeepsie comprised mainly women. At a riot in New Windsor, a local observer complained to a tea merchant that "the women! in this place have risen in a mob, and are now selling a box of tea of yours [the owner] at 6s per lb."[45]

The action of women regarding economic matters was not limited to seizures and crowd action. Women also used their power as wives and mothers to disrupt the war effort, if the committees failed to regulate the economy. In August 1776, the women of Kingston surrounded the meeting room of the Committee of Safety and declared that if the food shortages were not resolved, "their husbands and sons shall fight no more."[46] These riots were thus not only economic but also had clear political implications. The site of the women's protest was neither the Kingston public market nor a shopkeeper's warehouse, but the meeting-house where the town's political authorities conducted business. Finally, these women were not just making economic threats of boycotts or disruptions but promising political action if their demands were not satisfied.

Women, who had few political rights, were now exerting a public voice about those issues, in which the needs of the domestic sphere crossed those of the public sphere. Women's right to demand salt, tea, or flour at what they considered fair prices fell firmly within the socially and culturally constructed gender roles of eighteenth-century America. Like their counterparts in the French Revolution, women's political action usually formed around issues of family and domestic concerns (particularly food and supplies).[47]

Residents of the mid-Hudson Valley were divided over the best policy to follow in handling the economic dislocations created by the military conflict. Generally, price controls had been needed before the Revolution only in times of economic crisis and only on certain necessities. However, some farm families benefited from wartime inflation, since it increased the profits they earned on the sale of farm produce. Yet many other residents suffered from the depreciated currency and soaring prices changed at shopkeepers' stores. As a result, by the late 1770s, many midvalley residents led the state-wide battle to implement policies that would halt spiraling inflation. Indeed, from 1779 through 1782, calls from the populous midvalley, which did not face a direct military threat, became increasingly pronounced for government regulation of prices, quality, and distribution of various staple products.[48]

The movement for the community regulation of prices and wages and of the distribution of goods occurred because of wartime exigencies. Whether in the eighteenth or the twenty-first century, wars generally engender shortages of goods and demands for personal sacrifice and community-mindedness. As a result of revolutionary problems, both local and provincial authorities began regulating economic affairs. What is remarkable is not these practices per se, but the methods employed to implement them. Official town authorities who regulated prices also sponsored boycotts and denounced tepid Whigs who threatened the goals of the Revolution. The people out-of-doors also used extralegal popular action in the form of seizures, public denunciations, and riots that sometimes supported the local authorities but that also at times exceeded what officials thought necessary.

LAND CONFISCATION AND ITS EFFECTS IN DUTCHESS COUNTY

Although Dutchess County was beset by food and price rioting and by other popular demonstrations throughout the war, a revolution of even more far-reaching proportions was unfolding there. Indeed, Dutchess witnessed what was, arguably, one of the most dramatic episodes of the Revolution in New York: tenant unrest and the state's confiscation of landlord property.

The Revolution was not the first time that mid-Hudson valley tenants had resorted to mass violence. Serious conflict had occurred as early as the 1740s, and the Uprising of 1766 was the only time before the Battle of Lexington that British regulars were used in the North American colonies against provincials. This agrarian conflict had little to do with the imperial crisis but much to do with limited access to land and growing resentment among both long-time tenants and more recent settlers from New England.[49]

At the beginning of the war, both Dutchess County landlords and tenants were generally supportive of, but not enthusiastic about the Revolution. Although some contemporary observers believed that many tenants were Tories who hoped for a British victory that would lead to the confiscation of the large estates and the redistribution of this property among the tenants, there is no strong evidence to affirm that large numbers of tenants in Dutchess were Loyalists, although some undoubtedly were. Allegiances were unstable throughout the war, and Loyalism could also be found among the landlord class.[50]

In 1775, the traditional Dutchess elite continued to represent the county in colonial government. Indeed, landlords Beverly Robinson and Robert Livingston were elected to the New York Provincial Congress in both 1775 and 1776. Nevertheless, the landed aristocracy was no longer the only voice speaking for the county. The Dutchess delegation in Congress was now almost double the size of the county's representation in the prewar Provincial Assembly and included such middle-class representatives as Dirck Brinckerhoff and Jacobus Swarthout. Although neither Brinckerhoff nor Swarthout were tenants, they were middle-class men drawn from a very different class than the landlord elite and had been elected in the tenant-dominated region of southern Dutchess. Despite these differences, at the outset, both landlord and middle-class representatives shared the common goal of resisting British imperialism and generally worked together in the New York Congress. Once the war began to affect adversely the economy of the Hudson's east bank, however, this alliance weakened. In time, the military conflict and the negative economic consequences that flowed from it, sundered the fragile unity between the two groups.[51]

Some of the problems facing tenants on the Hudson's east bank were little different from those confronting freeholders who lived there or on the other side of the river. The economic problems created by the war and the British blockade of New York City had resulted in inflated prices for necessary goods, shortages of essential foodstuffs, and a state tax burden beyond the ability of many to pay. Because of the apparent failure of Dutchess County's traditional leadership to resolve these problems, the "old guard" was effectively pushed from power. In 1777 Robert Livingston lost his reelection bid to the State Assembly, and Beverly Robinson openly declared himself a Tory and fled his estate. Now that landlords had lost their monopolistic hold on political power or were exposed as Tories, the clamor for the confiscation of Loyalist property began to grow among the county's landless class.[52]

The war had so eroded the tenuous economic conditions that many Dutchess tenants now perceived that freehold ownership of land was their only economic hope. If many Patriot leaders supported the confiscation and sale of Tory property in order to raise money for the war effort, many tenants of southern Dutchess did so because they believed it would lead to their independence and freedom as landowners. As political pressure for land redistribution grew, so too did the possibility that the old, simmering tensions between landlord and tenant might revive, unless some sort of official action on this front was taken. The new state government first approached this problem by confiscating Loyalist-owned manors. In late 1778 a petition from "freeholders and others, inhabitants of the county of Dutchess" stated that unless Loyalist lands were confiscated and redistributed, "tumults and insurrections" might result.[53]

Dutchess County Assemblymen took the lead in calling for land confiscation. Although it was John Morin Scott of New York City who had proposed in the Assembly in 1778 the first serious plan for confiscating Loyalist land, the Dutchess County delegation of Henry Luddington, Jacobus Swarthout, and Dirck Brinkerhoff became the champions of land confiscation and redistribution. The statewide legislative battle over confiscation can be seen in microcosm in the Dutchess County delegation in the Assembly. Egbert Benson, a conservative revolutionary, who represented landlord interests in the new landscape of popular politics, fought against the confiscation and sale of land in the 1779–1780 Assembly debates. Dirck Brinckerhoff, representing Fishkill in southern Dutchess (where a majority of the householders were tenants) led the fight for confiscation and sale. The legislative battle resulted in a Brinckerhoff victory and the Confiscation Act, which allowed for the confiscation of Loyalist property throughout the state. Brinckerhoff emerged as a champion of tenant-claims for land; Benson, who had previously dominated the Dutchess delegation and had been an important provincial-wide voice in the Assembly, lost his bid for reelection.[54]

Ultimately, the Confiscation Act provided for the sale of 496 forfeited lots in Dutchess. Over 80 percent of this land had belonged to the once dominant Loyalist landlords Beverly Robinson and Roger Morris. The law required that lots be no more than 500 acres in size, and 401 separate buyers purchased this land in Dutchess. Although many of these purchasers were already freeholders, some of Robinson's former tenants also purchased the lots they had once worked under lease. In this way, land redistribution of substantial proportion had occurred in the mid-Hudson Valley. Some 150,000 acres of land once possessed by just two landlords had been divided among several hundred residents, including tenants who had not previously owned land.[55]

If tenants demanded land, slaves demanded freedom. Slavery had been an integral part of the economic and social life of the mid-Hudson Valley since the early eighteenth century. Approximately 6 percent of Dutchess County's population in the decade before the Revolution consisted of slaves, and the proportion of slaves on the west bank was probably twice as high. The overwhelming majority of slaves were owned by small freeholders, and very few slaveholders owned more than a handful. In Ulster County, most freeholders did not possess slaves, but those who did averaged about three slaves per household, which was about the same number that the typical Dutchess slaveholder owned.[56]

Although most slaves in the midvalley worked on farms, many were skilled tradesmen and artisans. Hudson Valley slaves worked in grain and flourmills, labored in warehouses on the river docks; and served as teamsters moving goods around the valley and along the river. For the most part, female slaves worked around their owner's home. Michael Groth, the foremost student of slavery in the Hudson Valley, has found that few owners freed their slaves before the Revolution, even though some European Americans were already criticizing the institution.[57]

The rhetoric of the Revolution, with its emphasis on freedom from tyranny and the British attempt to "enslave" North Americans, was surely not lost on African-Americans or on many whites. At the outset of the war, some New Yorkers were already questioning slavery. New York Quakers petitioned the State Assembly very early in the conflict for an end to slavery, and Governor George Clinton joined the New York Society for Promoting the Manumission of Slaves, which was established in 1785. Nevertheless, although the rhetoric of the Revolution emphasized personal liberty, the wartime need for labor and the heightened fear of slave insurrections overcame the arguments for manumission. Ultimately, the strongest opposition in the midvalley to abolition developed among slaveholding farmers who successfully resisted the ever-growing demand for emancipation for more than a decade after the Revolution.[58]

African-American slaves waged a most powerful battle against slavery in the midvalley, however. The number of slave runaways increased during the war, as slaves used the close proximity of the British army and the various wartime dislocations as their opportunity to flee. Newspaper advertisements seeking the return of runaway slaves reveal that at least sixty slaves escaped from owners in Dutchess County during the war, and the actual number was probably much higher. Some slaves even destroyed their owner's property before fleeing. "Rachel," a Dutchess County slave, fled her master in 1781 with stolen clothes and other belongings. She returned one week later, however, and set her owner's home on fire before escaping south behind British lines.[59]

Although slavery did not receive its death blow in the Revolution, the continued existence of the institution was debated often in the New York Assembly, which actually called for gradual emancipation as early as 1785. Although the Council of Revisions vetoed the bill, the emancipation of slaves in several other northern states, including the newly independent Vermont, kept the debate alive in the decade after the war. Slavery was gradually abolished in New York beginning in 1799 with the passage of an emancipation act. Farmers in Ulster, Orange, and Dutchess, however, remained opposed.[60]

WAR AND ECONOMIC OPPORTUNITY IN THE MID-HUDSON VALLEY

Even though the wartime midvalley economy was characterized by shortages of staple products, hyperinflation, and an increasingly devalued currency, it also offered economic opportunities that were not lost on enterprising farmers and artisans.[61] The enemy blockade halted the importation of British textiles and thereby encouraged increased domestic production of clothing and other manufactured goods. Perhaps most important for Hudson River Valley farmers between 1781 and 1783 was that the encampment of Gen. George Washington and his Continental army around New Windsor created a large market for agricultural produce. The number of the troops changed from year to year (from only a few hundred to several thousand), but there was, almost without interruption, a body of men and women who needed to be fed, clothed, and supplied on a daily basis.[62]

Although this situation was atypical, most people of the area participated in economic activities to support the war. For example, even before the troops were encamped around New Windsor, the farmers of the region had been brought into a production network that supplied the army wherever it was stationed. As part of this system, the Continental Commissary Department built a series of supply routes and depots throughout the northeastern states of New York, Pennsylvania, and Connecticut.[63]

The extent of wartime production in the mid-Hudson region can be examined through the Coenradt Elmendorph Account Book. Elmendorph was an army commissary, instructed to make purchases for the military throughout Orange and Ulster counties. He was a resident of Kingston, a lieutenant colonel in the Continental Line, and a person of some wartime prestige in the Hudson River Valley. Elmendorph directed purchases, hired laborers to move the produce, employed the butchers and bakers to service the army, and was one of the Continental government's representatives in determining the price of goods for a given locality.[64]

Elmendorph's "Invoice of Supplies, 1778–1779" records in detail the types of goods he purchased, the quantity, the unit cost, and total price. He also listed the farmers from whom he purchased goods, their towns, the date of the purchase, and the payment his customers were to receive. This ledger reveals the market opportunities that the military conflict created for west bank farmers and the extent to which they took advantage of the prospects.

Elmendorph transacted business with 440 customers. Production of alcohol (primarily in the form of distilled grain whiskey and rum) earned the highest profits for local farmers in their dealings with the commissary. Liquor was part of a soldier's daily ration and was used in surgery as an anesthetic. It consequently accounted for nearly 40 percent of local earnings, even though far more farmers engaged in the production of beef or grains than of whiskey. Beef and pork accounted for about 35 percent of Elmendorph's purchases. One hundred and eighty-three farmers produced meat products, but only forty produced alcohol. Elmendorph also purchased grain from local farmers. Two hundred and sixty-six farmers sold, on average, sixty bushels of grain to Elmendorph.[65]

This evidence suggests that a large number of midvalley farmers were engaged in substantial production for the war. Although Patriotism and devotion to the cause cannot be discounted as a possible motivation, economic self-interest induced many farmers to sell. However, if farmers refused to sell, the commissary would have requisitioned whatever it needed anyway, leaving the farmer no position to decide what he wanted to sell to the military and what he wanted to dispose of in other ways. The most significant aspect of this production, however, is the way it was marketed. Almost all of the produce was sold to an army agent who paid in cash or notes, an experience that was new to many mid-Hudson farmers, who were more accustomed to exchanging produce with neighbors or bartering with local shopkeepers.

The war years also witnessed an increase in domestic textile manufacturing. Before the Revolution, the North American colonies annually imported more than ten million yards of linen and cloth from England. The nonimportation movement and the Revolution changed that. Not only did the farmers of mid-Hudson communities agree not to import British manufactures, but they began wearing homespun and engaging in domestic manufacturing. To increase wool production, the Ulster County Committee of Safety voted in 1775 to "improve the breed, and increase the number of sheep," and tried to secure a pledge from local residents not to kill any "sheep under four years old, or procure them to be killed by others; neither will we sell the best of our sheep to butchers, or others employed by them to purchase, whereby the breed of Our sheep is so much injured." Anyone who sold or ate lambs or ewes was denounced as an enemy of the American cause.[66]

Furthermore, during the war, the Ulster Committee of Safety employed hundreds of women to sew stockings and blankets and to weave the fabric needed for military uniforms. The state government assessed local towns a quota of shirts, shoes, and other products, and it then sent to the towns the wool, cloth, or other raw products needed to produce these goods. The local committees distributed raw materials to local farm families, who spun and wove the finished products, which were then collected and sent to the army supplier. For example, in April 1777, the Provincial Congress paid £600 for stockings and blankets to the Ulster Committee, which then distributed the cloth and yarn to local farm families for production. Ulster also became a focal point for shoe manufacturing for the Continental army, as the various county committees collected and then sent hides to Marbletown, where the hides were tanned and then "put-out" to local cordwainers to manufacture shoes at eighteen to twenty shillings a pair.[67]

Even with these developments, the midvalley failed for several reasons to develop into an extensive postwar manufacturing region. First, the market for finished products was still small and dispersed, and after the war those urban areas, where the demand existed, could get their goods more cheaply from British producers. In addition, local merchants in the region (and elsewhere) favored investing in bonds, public certificates, real estate, and a variety of other areas but not in developing a rural outwork system of manufacturing. These other mediums of investment were potentially much more profitable in the post-war period than a large-scale network of outwork production.[68]

Nevertheless, the midvalley connection to commercial markets received a boost from the war, as military contractors and merchants actively sought farmers' goods and thereby opened up a variety of opportunities and a competitive market hitherto unknown to many yeoman farm families. After the war, speculators from New York City, recognizing the possibilities that lay in developing the Hudson River Valley into a sophisticated manufacturing region, made their way north to implement their ideas. Daniel Parker and William Duer won military contracts and opened a series of stores in Orange and Ulster to purchase local grain. Dutchess County's Melancton Smith opened a store in 1783 near the old main army camp in New Windsor with the plan of promoting a continued high level of market production in the area. In this way, the war impelled farmers to view their production and trade in market terms.[69]

The Revolutionary War had other profound effects on the mid-Hudson Valley economy. First, the valley, like much of the northeast, was flooded with a variety of paper currencies. Some small farmers had never used cash before, and most had never used it regularly. The war, therefore, helped produce a farm population increasingly astute in commercial matters. Before the war, many farmers had dealt only with neighbors or their local shopkeeper. These exchanges were primarily for obtaining goods; the farm produce they exchanged was a tool to help obtain the goods they needed.

Although these economic developments were significant for the war period, the increased production of agricultural goods and textiles was not sustained in the years following the war. Essentially, this enlarged production, much like the increased use of cash was a response to immediate wartime needs. The relatively limited market for manufactured goods, as well as the existence of alternative, and more profitable, investments for those with capital, restrained, at least temporarily, the region's long-term economic development.

THE AFTERMATH OF WAR: THE MID-HUDSON VALLEY AFTER 1783

How had the Revolution changed the mid-Hudson Valley? The most famous fictional character to live through the struggle, Washington Irving's Rip Van Winkle, found that the Revolution brought about dramatic changes to his community. After he returned to town from the Catskills and some twenty years of sleep, he was befuddled by the unfamiliar surroundings and was briefly mistaken for a Tory. Indeed, he found that the "very character of the people seemed changed. There was a busy, bustling, disputatious tone about it, instead of the accustomed phlegm and drowsy tranquility."[70]

What did Rip detect to be the big difference? Politics! A new democratic spirit of debate and discussion (indeed, he is not uncoincidentally returning to town on election day!). Instead of a small group of Dutch elders sitting on the porch of the local tavern dictating the activities of this fictionalized town, villagers are debating and arguing politics, "haranguing vehemently about the rights of citizens-elections-members of congress."[71] In essence, what Washington Irving described in a fictionalized form was a far more democratic, egalitarian society, which he believed, had emerged in the central Hudson in the years following the Revolution.

Much happened during the Revolution to support this fictionalized view. In the first place, the war created new opportunities for political advancement. Before the war, the political leadership in each of the three counties under analysis came from a small, socially and economically prominent part of the population. New leaders emerged in all three counties. Some had been wealthy and prominent before the war, but many had been modest in their backgrounds and experience, even if they had been ambitious in their goals. These men used the new town and county committees, the dramatically expanded state assembly, and the broader franchise offered by the Revolution to advance themselves and their own self-interest.

A new "class" of leadership, represented best by middle-class leaders like George Clinton and Dirck Brinckerhoff, emerged and replaced established families that had led their towns and villages for generations. Many of these new leaders began their political careers serving on local committees of safety and inspection and quickly graduated to representing their neighbors in the New York Provincial Congress and the State Assembly. Yet, many of the old families remained powerful and influential. The Hasbroucks and Hardenberghs continued to wield great economic power and remained important political leaders on the Hudson's west bank, but they now did so in a vastly different political and social environment, one in which power was competitively struggled for and, often, shared.

Some of the most prominent prewar leaders of the mid-Hudson did not survive the war with their power intact. Some, like Dutchess landlord Beverly Robinson became Tories, forfeiting their elite status. Nevertheless, most of the truly powerful families in the midvalley retained their status and property. Even though the Livingstons of Dutchess suffered politically during the war (Philip lost his reelection bid for county sheriff, and Judge Robert his seat in the Assembly), they reemerged in the years following the struggle as important political players in local, state, and national politics. The various branches of the Livingston family retained their large landholdings and tenants, and continued to enjoy enormous power through the nineteenth century.

Slavery in the mid-Hudson Valley survived the war virtually intact. Although the number of runaways increased, midvalley farmers were among the staunchest defenders of chattel slavery and resisted efforts to end the institution. Indeed, farmers in the three mid-Hudson counties were still fighting against the gradual emancipation bill in New York at the end of the eighteenth century.

Probably the most dramatic development of the Revolution in the mid-Hudson was the impact of the Loyalist land confiscation program. As described, hundreds of different buyers purchased lots carved from the estates of Roger Morris, Beverly Robinson, and others, many of the buyers being former tenants on these estates. Farmers, who once worked on land that had been leased for several generations and for which they were required to make improvements and perhaps work for several days for the lord, now owned their own five-hundred-acre lots with no obligations to former landlords. The fact that many of these new independent landholders lost title to their land over the next few years because of an inability to pay taxes or to meet loan payments does not detract from what had been one of the most important developments of the war and which surely was of great importance to these families. Although tenantry continued in Dutchess and the northern valley after the Revolution, the land redistribution of the 1780s opened opportunities for land ownership and free-hold status previously denied to hundreds of Dutchess farmers.

This article originally appeared in *The Other New York*, March 2005. Used by permission.

NOTES

1. Peter Kalm, *Travels in North America: The English Version of 1770*, ed. Adolph B.

Benson (New York, 1987), 335, 647, and Richard Smith, *Journal from New York to Albany*, reprinted in Nelson Greene, ed., *History of the Valley of the Hudson*, 2 vols. (Chicago, 1931), 1: 9, describe the midvalley in the eighteenth century. Economic life in the Hudson can best be viewed through town records and mercantile accounts. For the west bank, see "*Benjamin Snyder Account Book, 1765–1798*," New-York Historical Society, N.Y.C. (NYHS), and the "*Kingston Trustees Minutes, 1736–1783*," Ulster County Clerk's Office, Kingston, New York. For the valley's backcountry, see Martin Bruegel, *Farm, Shop, Landing: The Rise of a Market Society in the Hudson Valley, 1780–1860* (Durham, N.C., 2002), 13–31.

2. Nathaniel Bartlett Sylvester, *History of Ulster County* (New Philadelphia, 1880); Edward Ruttenber, *History of Orange County, New York* (New York, 1911). The best analysis of mid-Hudson Valley slavery is Michael Groth, "Slaveholders and Manumission in Dutchess County, New York," *New York History* 78 (1997): 33–50, and *idem*, "Forging Freedom in the Mid-Hudson Valley: The End of Slavery and the Formation of a Free African-American Community 1770–1850" (Ph.D. diss., Binghamton University, 1994).
3. Alice Kenney, *Stubborn for Liberty: The Dutch in New York* (Syracuse, 1975), 69–70, 88–89; Thomas S. Wermuth, *Rip Van Winkle's Neighbors: The Transformation of Rural Society in the Hudson River Valley* (Albany, 2001), 15–16.
4. Wermuth, *Rip Van Winkle's Neighbors*, 38–42. Edward Countryman, *A People in Revolution: The American Revolution and Political Society in New York, 1760–1790* (Baltimore, 1982), 26–27; the phrase is from Countryman and is particularly accurate when comparing the west bank to Dutchess County. Carl Nordstrom, *Frontier Elements in a Hudson River Village* (Port Washington, N.Y., 1973).
5. Patricia Bonomi, *A Factious People: Politics and Society in Colonial New York* (New York, 1971), 188–90; Staughton Lynd, "Who Should Rule at Home: Dutchess County in the American Revolution," in his *Class Conflict, Slavery and the United States Constitution* (Westport, Conn., 1980), 30–31; Henry Noble McCracken, *Old Dutchess Forever! The Story of an American County* (New York, 1956), 470–71.
6. Bonomi, *Factious People*, 180–96; Sung Bok Kim, *Landlord and Tenant in Colonial New York* (Chapel Hill, N.C., 1978), 235–80.
7. In Ulster County in 1790, 3,945 of 4,590 farmers owned their own freehold, Census for the State of New York for 1855 (Albany, 1857). For the east bank, see Kim, *Landlord and Tenant*, 39–40; 235–37.
8. Bonomi, *Factious People*, 220–23; Kim, *Landlord and Tenant*, 381–96.
9. "Letter from an Anonymous Kingston Farmer" in Peter Force, ed., *American Archives*, 4th Ser. (Washington, D.C., 1837–1853), 1: 1230, herein cited as *American Archives*; Resolves of New Windsor Committee, *American Archives*, 2: 131–33.
10. Countryman, *People in Revolution*, 104–05.
11. Lynd, "Who Should Rule at Home," 32–34; George Dangerfield, *Chancellor Robert Livingston of New York, 1746–1813* (New York, 1960), 60–62; and Philip L. White, *The Beekmans of New York in Politics and Commerce, 1647–1877* (New York, 1956).
12. *Historical Memoirs from July 12, 1776 to July 25, 1778 of William Smith*, ed. William Sabine (New York, 1958), 118; Lynd, "Who Should Rule at Home?," 34–35.
13. Countryman, *People in Revolution*, 313–16. For background on political divisions in Dutchess, including Brinckerhoff's rise to power, see Bonomi, *Factious People*, 245–46.
14. Wermuth, *Rip Van Winkle's Neighbors*, 38–40.
15. Robert Boyd to George Clinton, July 3, 1776, *Public and Private Papers of George Clinton*, 1:244–47; E. M. Ruttenber, *A*

History of New Windsor, Orange County (Newburgh, N. Y., 1911).

16. "Minutes of the Provincial Congress, May 25, 1776," *American Archives*, 6: 1333. Background on Hardenbergh can be found in Sylvester, *History of Ulster County*, 84–87, and Countryman, *People in Revolution*, 225.
17. This ongoing political intrigue can be followed in "Hasbrouck to New York Congress, Kingston, Mar. 8, 1776," *American Archives*, 4: 137–38; "Minutes of the Provincial Congress, May 31,1776," *American Archives*, 6: 1349; and "Ulster Committee to New York Congress, June 14, 1776," *American Archives*, 6: 898–900.
18. "Ulster Committee to New York Provincial Congress, July 4, 1776," *American Archives*, 6: 1273–74.
19. "Cadwallader Colden, Jr., to Ulster County Committee, June 27, 1776," *American Archives*, 6: 1112. See also, Eugene Fingerhut, *Survivor: Cadwallader Colden II in Revolutionary America* (Washington, D.C., 1983), 53–54.
20. E. Wilder Spaulding, *His Excellency George Clinton: Critic of the Constitution (*New York, 1938), 39–41; John P. Kaminski, *George Clinton: Yeoman Politician of the New Republic* (Madison, Wis., 1993).
21. "Col. John Hasbrouck to New York Congress, Mar. 18, 1776," *American Archives*, 5:138; Countryman, *People in Revolution*, 198.
22. Washington's quote is cited in Louis V. Mills, "Attack in the Highlands, the Battle of Ft. Montgomery," *Hudson Valley Regional Review* (Sept. 2000), 39–40.
23. Mark Lender and James Kirby Martin, *A Respectable Army: The Military Origins of the Republic* (New York, 1981), 83–87.
24. Mills, "Attack in the Highlands," 39–40.
25. "General John Vaughan to Sir William Howe, Oct. 17, 1777," *Dutchess County Historical Society Yearbook* 21 (1936), 118–19.
26. Lincoln Diamant, *The Chaining of the Hudson: The Fight for the River in the American Revolution* (New York, 1989), 156.
27. Diamant, *Chaining of the Hudson*, 158–74; William Sterne Randall, *Benedict Arnold: Patriot and Traitor* (New York, 1990), 526–37.
28. "Minutes of Mar. 14, 1775, New Windsor Town Meeting," *American Archives*, 2: 131–33. The resolves and proclamations of New Paltz are in *American Archives*, 2: 832–33, 1183–84.
29. "Ulster County Committee Minutes," Apr. 7, 1775, *American Archives*, 2: 298–99.
30. "Resolves of the Ulster Association, 1775," *American Archives*, 2: 132–33.
31. The pamphlets were also burned in Marbletown; see *American Archives*, 1: 1100, 1183–84; 1201.
32. For the "non-importation" agreements in Ulster, see Ulster County Association, Jan. 6, 1775, *American Archives*, 1: 1100–1101. For the general background and purpose behind the "non-importation" movement, see Pauline Maier, *From Resistance to Revolution* (New York, 1972), 137–38.
33. These activities were not unique to the Revolution. Midvalley communities had long history of regulating economic activities within their towns. See, for example, "Minutes of Corporation of the Town of Kingston," 12 Feb. 1748, Ulster County Clerk's Office.
34. Alphonse Clearwater, *History of Ulster County, N.Y.* (Kingston, N.Y., 1907), 281–82; Sylvester, *History of Ulster County*, 202.
35. Some of the prices were firmly set by the Congress, such as wheat at thirteen shillings per bushel, and "good merchantable wheat flour" at one pound sixteen shillings per hundred gross weight. Other prices, such as leather and various animal skins were set "in the proportion of the price they usually bore to raw hides." See *Journals of the Provincial Congress*, 1: 455–57, Apr. 3, 1778, for a full listing of the regulation of prices. Ulster County's call for new price controls can be found in "Ulster County

Association Instructions to Assemblymen, 1779" Matthew Visscher Folder, Albany Institute; "Ulster County to New York State Legislature, 1782," Box 4239, New York State Library, Albany; Dutchess County's requests can be found in "Jacob Heermane to Council of Safety, Nov. 1777," *Journals of the Provincial Congress*, 2: 457.

36. "Henry Luddington to New York Council of Safety, Dec. 3, 1776, *Journals of the Provincial Congress*, 2: 355.
37. *American Archives*, 5: 635, 638–39.
38. "Ulster County Committee to New York Convention," Nov. 18, 1776, *Journals of the Provincial Congress*, 2: 229–30.
39. Ibid.
40. Barbara Clark Smith, "Food Riots and the American Revolution," *William & Mary Quarterly*, 3rd Ser., 51 (Jan. 1994): 15.
41. Correspondence of John Hathorn, Dec. 2, 1776, Ruttenber, *History of New Windsor*, 67–68; and Countryman, *People in Revolution*, 183.
42. Correspondence of John Hathorn, Dec. 2, 1776, Ruttenber, *History of New Windsor*, 67.
43. For examples of prewar economic regulations see the "Minutes of Corporation of the Town of Kingston" Mar. 2, 1772, [for regulation of wheat prices], and Mar. 2, 1728, Nov. 8, 1752 [for regulations on other economic activities], Ulster County Clerk's Office.
44. For a discussion of the political implications of revolutionary rioting, see Smith, "Food Riots," *William & Mary Quarterly*, 5–12. For suspicions that Ellison was unpatriotic because of his economic dealings, see "Boyd to Clinton, July 3, 1776," *Clinton Papers*, 1: 244–47.
45. "James H. Kip to James Caldwell, New Windsor, July 14, 1777," *Journals of the Provincial Congress*, 506.
46. New York Convention Proceedings, Aug. 1776, *American Archives*, 5th Series, 1: 1542–43.
47. Linda Kerber, *Women of the Republic: Intellect and Ideology in Revolutionary America* (New York, 1980), 44.
48. For New York farming interests that supported both inflationary policies and paper currency, see Matson, "Liberty, Jealousy, and Union: The New York Economy in the 1780s," in Paul Gilje and William Pencak, eds., *New York in the Age of the Constitution* (New York, 1992), 114–15.
49. Kim, *Landlord and Tenant*, 367–415; Bonomi, *Factious People*, 218–24; Philip Schwarz, *The Jarring Interests: New York's Boundary Makers, 1664–1776* (Albany, 1979).
50. Lynd, "Who Should Rule at Home?" 34. Lynd's research on the Revolution in Dutchess County remains the standard interpretation. The following section on the debate over land confiscation in Dutchess is informed by Lynd's research.
51. Countryman, *People in Revolution*, 215–17; Lynd, "Who Should Rule at Home?," 34–36.
52. Lynd, "Who Should Rule at Home?," 42–43.
53. Ibid., 46.
54. Ibid., 51–53; Countryman, *People in Revolution*, 173–74.
55. Lynd, "Who Should Rule at Home?" 52–53; 59–60.
56. Groth, "Forging Freedom in the Mid-Hudson Valley," 75; Federal Manuscript Census for New York, Ulster County, 1800.
57. Michael Groth, "Laboring for Freedom in Dutchess County," 60–62, in Myra B. Young Armstead, ed., *Mighty Change, Tall Within: Black Identity in the Hudson Valley* (Albany, 2003). For slave life in the mid-Hudson River Valley in the eighteenth century, see Margaret Washington, ed., *Narrative of Sojourner Truth* (New York, 1993), 6–8. Truth spent the first thirty years of her life in Ulster County.
58. For an overview of the antislavery arguments during the Revolution, see Gary Nash, *Race*

and Revolution (Madison, Wis., 1990); Groth, "Forging Freedom in the Mid-Hudson Valley."

59. Groth, "Forging Freedom in the Mid-Hudson Valley," 85–86; and idem, "Laboring for Freedom," 70–71.
60. Countryman, *People in Revolution*, 284–85; Groth, "Slaveholders and Manumission," 35–36.
61. For new policies of taxation, see Robert Becker, *Revolution, Reform, and the Politics of Taxation in America: 1763–1783* (Baton Rouge, La., 1980).
62. The extent of Ulster's production for the war can be seen in George Clinton's report for 1778, where he argued that the entire west bank, "Having long been the seat of the war," had been "ravaged plundered and greatly exhausted." "Clinton to F. M. Dana, Feb. 17, 1778," *Clinton Papers*, 2:824–25. Indeed, in 1778, the Continental army was fed almost exclusively on Ulster wheat; see *Olde Ulster*, 3:365–69.
63. Louis C. Hatch, *The Administration of the American Revolutionary Army* (New York, 1904), 86–115; Flick, *Revolution in New York*, 179–202.
64. This and the next several paragraphs are based on an analysis of the "Coenradt Elmendorph Account Book, 1778–79," New York State Library, Albany, and Ulster County Wills and Inventories, 1760–1791, Ulster County Surrogate Court, Boxes 9–49.
65. "Coenradt Elmendorph Account Book, 1778–79."
66. James Shepherd and Gary M. Walton, *Shipping, Maritime Trade, and the Economic Development of Colonial North America* (New York, 1972), 110–13, 182; "Ulster County Committee Resolves," Mar. 14, 1775, *American Archives*, 4th Ser., 2: 132; and Alexander C. Flick, ed., *The American Revolution in New York* (New York, 1926), 184.
67. Flick, *American Revolution in New York*, 187. See also the reports of the commissaries of clothing in Clinton Papers. Commissary John Henry worked out of Shawangunk—see his report of Aug. 26, 1778, *Clinton Papers*, 3: 693; 4: 31–32. Commissary Peter Curtenius was in charge of the store in Wallkill. See his report in *Clinton Papers*, 3: 692.
68. James Henretta, "War for Independence and American Economic Development," in Ronald Hoffman, John McCusker, and Russell Menand, eds., *The Economy of Early America: The Revolutionary Period, 1763–1790* (Charlotteville, Va., 1988), 81–86; Virginia Harrington discusses New York merchants' fondness for provincial bonds and real estate, not manufacturing in her *The New York Merchant on the Eve of the Revolution* (New York, 1935), Chapter 4.
69. For the Duer and Parker plans, see Duer to William Alexander, June 15, 1781, Alexander Papers, NYHS; Daniel Parker to Duer, June 26,1781, Duer Papers, NYHS. For Smith's store, still in operation in 1785, see Duer Papers, Box 8, NYHS.
70. Washington Irving, *Sketch Book* (New York, 1915), 50–51.
71. Ibid., 51.

PART II

Suffrage and Society

8

Open to All Parties

Alexander and James Robertson, Albany Printers, 1771–1777

DENIS P. BRENNAN

In 1810, when Isaiah Thomas published the first edition of *The History of Printing in America*, information about the first newspaper in Albany, New York, was rather scarce. Thomas correctly identified the publishers as Alexander and James Robertson but called their paper *The Albany Post-Boy* while admitting, "At this period, very little intelligence respecting it can be obtained."[1] The 1874 edition of his book contained considerably more information about the Robertsons, but still referred to the *Post-Boy,* although it acknowledged in a footnote that all copies of the Robertsons' paper that had been found were titled *The Albany Gazette.* These changes can most likely be credited to Joel Munsell, an Albany printer and antiquarian who assisted in updating Isaiah Thomas's work. The resulting second edition, as well as Munsell's own *Typographical Miscellany,* have been the sources for most of what is known and written about the Robertsons and *The Albany Gazette.* Alexander and James Robertson's place in Albany history is generally fixed with a short reference to the fact that they published the city's first newspaper in 1771 and later supported the Loyalist position.

The Robertsons were born in Stonehaven, Scotland, and were taught the printing trade in Edinburgh by their father. James was five years younger than Alexander but came to America first. He arrived in Boston in 1766 at the age of nineteen, and completed his training as a journeyman printer under the tutelage of fellow Scotsmen John Mein and Thomas Fleeming, Boston printers and publishers of *The Boston Chronicle.*

James's service with Mein and Fleeming coincided with a critical period in American colonial history and a time of significant change in the printing industry. The Stamp Act of 1765 had altered the relationship of the colonies to the mother country and set them on a course that would eventually lead to independence. Newspapers would help to chart this course. The repeal of the Stamp Act was significantly aided by the efforts of printers and journalists. Prior to November 1, 1765, when the Stamp Act was scheduled to take effect, newspapers published many articles and resolutions outlining colonial opposition. No stamped newspapers were ever printed, and many either suspended publication or otherwise circumvented the letter of the law. The act was repealed on March 1, 1766; Sidney Kobre aptly describes what the confrontation meant to journalists: "The publishers of the press had been, generally, middlemen, who printed the news of interest to their readers. . . . Now the colonial newspapers began to develop strength, to exert a positive conscious influence. The publishers realized, perhaps for the first time, that their papers could be utilized to protest effectively."[2]

In Boston, John and Samuel Adams and many others recognized the potential of newspapers not only to educate but also to propagandize. According to Frank Luther Mott in his book, *American Journalism: A History 1690–1960,* Mein and Fleeming made an honest effort to be impartial and present both Patriot and Tory viewpoints. The Boston Committee of Safety, however, refused to accept neutrality. Eventually, Mein was assaulted, hanged in effigy, and had to seek protection with the British military.[3] Certainly, young James Robertson knew of the confrontation and it may well have been the first in a series of incidents that would lead him also to side with the British.

James Robertson completed his training with Mein and Fleeming and in late 1768 moved to New York City, where he was joined by his twenty-six-year-old brother. Alexander Robertson suffered from a disease which Isaiah Thomas explains left him "deprived of the use of his limbs, and incapacitated for labor."[4] Nevertheless, judging from Thomas's comments about the brothers, it would appear that between them they had the talents and potential to be successful in the printing business. He explains that James "was a worthy man and a very good printer" and that Alexander was "intelligent, well educated and possessed some abilities as a writer."[5] In 1769, they set up a printing company on the corner of Beaver Street and on May 8, 1769, published their first newspaper, *The New York Chronicle.*

The Robertsons did not enter unobserved into the company of printers in New York City. James Parker, a longtime New York publisher, kept an eye on them, and his observations can be found as part of his regular correspondence with his former partner, Benjamin Franklin. For instance, on November 22, 1768, he wrote, "A new printer from Scotland has set up here. . . . If he lives, he must have a better Faculty than ever I had, tho I think I live as soberly as he can." He goes on in the same letter to express frustration over economic conditions: "And I have not much hope of either Ease or Prosperity, till I rest in the Grave."[6] Parker's letter of February 17, 1769, reports to Franklin the death of William Weyman, Parker's former partner, who had published his own newspaper, *The New-York Gazette,* until December 1767. He continues, "a young Scotch man has got his [Weyman's] tools and set up here, and 'tis said, in the Spring will publish a News-paper."[7] It would appear that at this point, either Alexander Robertson had not yet arrived from Scotland, or Parker was not aware of his presence.

Parker's pessimism about business difficulties continues as a theme in his letters. Although he was printing and selling a large quantity of newspapers, he was unable to make ends meet because costs had increased so dramatically. To make matters worse, he was now faced with additional competition in the form of James and Alexander Robertson. By late March of 1769, Parker was aware of both of them and their plans for the *New York Chronicle.* Somewhat cynically he assessed their chances: "They are Scots Lads: and if they be fortunate Fools, they will have no Need of Wisdom, otherwise they will fall through."[8]

The first issue of the Robertsons' *Chronicle* appeared on May 8, 1769, and their apparent initial success seems to have stoked the fires of resentment. Parker's letter of May 30 to Franklin referred to "a Couple of smuggled Scots Men" who were, in Parker's opinion, "as bad Workmen as ever Bradford was, but from a large Portion of Impudence, and the National Biass [sic] of all Scotch Men in their favor, I am told they have more Subscribers already than I have."[9] The reference to "Bradford" is presumably William Bradford, under whom Parker had served as an apprentice and whose paper, *The New York Gazette,* was generally considered to be poorly printed and edited. The success of the *Chronicle,* if indeed it was a success, was short-lived. Publication ceased in early 1770; the last issue located is dated January 4, 1770. Parker probably felt some satisfaction as he gloated in a letter dated February 2, 1770, to Franklin that "they puffd and flourished away a While, but the paper is now dropd. They were ignorant Blockheads, but have Impudence enough. I hear they are now at work or going to work for Rivington."[10]

In 1769 the Robertsons also printed a document written by William Smith titled *Review of the Military Operations in North America.* The report takes the form of a letter—signed, in New York on September 9, 1765, "Your Lordship's most obliged and obedient servant"—but contains 170 pages. Among the *Review's* many references to activities in and around the Albany area we find the following: "Albany, my Lord, is an old compact city, consisting of 3 or 400 well-built houses . . . The inhabitants are far from being indigent: the adjacent country abounds with provisions . . . "[11] Smith, however, was not very complimentary to Sir William Johnson and military operations in northern New York. The significance of this particular work to the Robertsons may well be that it served as an introduction to the upstate New York area, which they would soon call home.

Exactly what it was that brought James and Alexander Robertson to Albany, New York, in 1771 is simply not yet known for certain. In the second edition of Thomas's *History of Printing* we are told, "They were patronized by Sir William Johnson, then superintendent of Indian affairs who advanced them money to purchase a press and types."[12] This statement has been generally accepted; yet I cannot find any reference in the collected volumes of Sir William Johnson's papers to support it. Furthermore, Isaiah Thomas's own records add to the confusion. Thomas's first edition, published in 1810, made no reference to Johnson's connection with the Robertsons. Thomas kept extensive notes in preparation for a second edition, which was finally published in 1874, more than thirty years after his death. Included in his handwritten notes are two statements which indicate that the Robertsons' patron was Sir John Johnson, Sir William's son. "John" is crossed out in the second statement and "William" is inserted above it in what appears to be a change made by Joel Munsell. It is more likely that Sir William rather than Sir John would have encouraged the establishment of a printing house in Albany, if indeed either of them were involved, but the connection is far from certain.[13]

The papers of Sir William Johnson do confirm Sir William's wide range of interests. His activities required that he stay aware of the news in the colonies as well as around the world. He corresponded regularly with many people, including General Thomas Gage, whose house was "nearly opposite" the Robertsons' printing business in New York, and James Rivington, whom Parker had suggested that the Robertsons may have worked for after the *Chronicle* ceased publication. Rivington's letters were usually accompanied by copies of recent newspapers, either English or colonial. His short letter of December 25, 1769, to Johnson enclosed a newspaper that contained the latest "intelligence" from Europe, and it is possible that the paper was Robertsons' *New York Chronicle*.[14] Other people also sent Johnson newspapers. Joseph Chew, Sir William's secretary, sent a Boston newspaper to Sir William on November 7, 1769, so that he might "be able to form some judgement of the spirit of the times."[15] Among the news Chew mentioned was a report on the assault against James Robertson's former master, John Mein.

The only clear indication that Sir William Johnson may have been actively looking to set up a printing business in Albany is found in a letter dated December 28, 1769, from Peter Silvester, Johnson's lawyer. Silvester wrote to introduce William Goddard, the printer and publisher of the *Pennsylvania Chronicle*, who came to Albany "with a View to enlarge his Business & to set up a printing office & publish a Weekly paper in this place if he can meet with proper Encouragement." Goddard came specifically to see Johnson and "to communicate this his design & to know your sentiments."[16] We do not know Goddard's plans, nor do we know Johnson's sentiments, but we do know for certain that Goddard's Pennsylvania printing house did not expand into Albany.

Alexander and James Robertson's printing office in Albany "is said to have been in Barrack, now Chapel Street."[17] It was from this office that on November 25,1771, Volume I, Number 1, of the *Albany Gazette*, the first newspaper in New York State outside of New York City, was issued. Alexander was not yet thirty years old, James not twenty-five; they were far from their place of birth, printing pioneers on the fringe of colonial society. They explained in the opening article of the first issue, certainly not without some measure of self-interest, the values they found in newspapers:

> . . . an impartial Paper, conducted with Judgement; is an Epitome of modern History: Brings Men of Merit into public View: promotes a Spirit of Enquiry: is favourable to Civil and Religious Liberty; a cheap vehicle of Knowledge and Instruction to the Indigent; and attended to numberless commercial Advantages.— The perusal requires but a short Recess from Business; and the annual Expense is so inconsiderable, that few can be deprived of enjoying it, through Apprehension of trespassing, either upon their Time or their Pockets.[18]

Newspapers did indeed epitomize the modern world of the eighteenth century in colonial America. Begun in Boston in 1704, journalism in America was an outgrowth of English press experience which, after a period marked by attempts at suppression or control, became identified with the right of the people to be informed and educated, and as a means of preserving liberty. Imbued with the philosophy of enlightenment and the spirit of Whig politics, the colonial newspaper industry was dynamic, but it developed slowly at first. Around the middle of the century, newspapers began a significant transformation that can be attributed to the changing social and political atmosphere in the colonies.

In the *Albany Gazette*, the Robertsons recognized the developing social and cultural aspects of colonial life. What appears to be missing is any sense of the political aspect. Each of the fifteen issues that are among the collection at the New York State Library follows a regular pattern that includes essays, letters to the printers, international and colonial news, a healthy amount of advertising, and, without fail, the "Poets Corner." There is limited sense of the political tensions that were about to erupt into revolution. Perhaps the Robertsons had come to Albany hoping to avoid those tensions and maintain the impartiality that had long been the hallmark of the printer. Perhaps they published during the calm before the storm of change struck Albany. In any case, the Robertsons, at least during their early years in Albany, appear to have been most interested in the newspaper as a tool of the enlightenment and not as a weapon of the political wars. This may be the result of an honest effort on their part to remain neutral and to serve in the more traditional role of impartial printer, or they may simply have known that making their true feelings known would destroy their business.

Unfortunately, as with the *Chronicle* in New York, the *Gazette* in Albany did not last one year. The exact date publication ceased is not known, but the last issue located is dated August 3, 1772. Also unknown is the reason why the paper failed. It may have been a lack of subscriptions or poor advertising revenue or even the difficulty of obtaining paper for printing. At least once the Robertsons apologized to their readers for missing a week's publication because they did not receive a shipment of paper from New York. The first paper mill in the northern part of New York State was built in Troy, but not until 1793.[19] Whatever the reason, the fact remains that over the thirty-seven-week period from November 25, 1771, to August 24, 1772, the Robertsons printed only twenty-four issues. During one stretch in March, April, and May of 1772, they managed to print only two issues in eleven. All this does not necessarily mean that they were poor journalists, but simply underscores the challenges they faced along with others who chose to settle on the frontier.

The Robertsons maintained a presence in Albany until 1777, well after they discontinued publication of the *Albany Gazette*. However, as of October 7, 1773, their involvement with newspapers shifted to Connecticut. In Norwich they established a partnership with John

Trumbell and began printing a newspaper with the grandiose name *The Norwich Packet and the Connecticut, New Hampshire, Massachusetts and Rhode Island Advertiser.*[20] More often known simply as the *Norwich Packet,* the name may point to a further connection with James Rivington, who, in April of 1773, had begun a similarly titled New York City paper called *Rivington's New-York Gazette; or the Connecticut, New Jersey, Hudson's River, and Quebec Weekly Advertiser.*[21] The partnership with Trumbell lasted until May of 1776, when the Robertsons sold their interest and Trumbell carried on alone. By this time, the Robertsons' Loyalist tendencies were more well defined and the split resulted, according to Isaiah Thomas, because Trumbell "differed in his politics with his partners."[22] Years later, James Robertson would explain that they left the paper because they realized that "they could no longer carry it on without making it subservient to the cause of Rebellion."[23] Trumbell continued to publish the paper until his death in 1803.

There is ample evidence of continued printing activity for the Robertson Printing Company in Albany. In 1772, they published, "By order of his excellency William Tryon, Esq; governor and commander in chief," a manual of exercises and maneuvers for the New York Provincial militia.[24] Among their work for 1773 was the *Law and Ordinances of the Mayor, Recorder, Alderman, and Commonalty, of the City of Albany.* This was a sixty-six-page document of regulations covering the local ferries, street paving and cleaning, storage of gunpowder, the marking of bread, "Negros, Mulattoes and other Slaves," and even the height of fences. It was well printed and easily readable, with an ornate descriptive banner across the top of each page.[25] In the same year, they also printed a five-act heroic play written by George Cockings titled, "The Conquest of Canada: or, The Siege of Quebec."[26]

Perhaps most interesting of all their work for 1773 were the confessions they printed for three men who were sentenced to death for counterfeiting the currency. John Smith, Joseph-Bill Packer, and John Wall were executed at Albany in February, March, and April of 1773, respectively, but only the statement of Packer is in the Early American Imprints collection published by the American Antiquarian Society. Packer's letter is fifteen pages long, addressed "To the Printers" and in it he vehemently protests his innocence. He accuses a man he calls "Doctor Smith," who may be the John Smith mentioned above, as well as other men, who remain unnamed, of causing his downfall. It may well be that Packer, Smith, and Wall were involved in one scheme. However, Packer indicates that he is alone in his punishment, for he states, "it seems that I must be an Escape Goat to bear their transgressions into the other world."[27] In any case, the confessions represent an interesting view of the variety of work that printers were engaged in.

During the time the Robertsons maintained printing offices in both Norwich and Albany, there are a number of examples of the same work printed in both places. In 1774, both offices printed "Extracts from the Votes and Proceedings of the American Continental Congress" in the form of an address to the people of Britain. The Norwich edition makes it clear that the radicals were not yet in control of the Congress. The document begins in part by "avowing our allegiance to his Majesty"[28] and concludes by pointing out that "we have chosen a method of opposition, that does not preclude a hearty reconciliation with our fellow citizens on the other side of the Atlantic."[29] The Albany copy also included a letter to the citizens of Albany City and County from the delegates who represented them at the Philadelphia Congress.[30] Also, the Robertsons printed with Trumbell in Norwich *Bickerstaff's New England Almanack, For the Year of Our Lord, 1776*[31] and, with little change, the same book in Albany under the name *Bickerstaff's Albany Almanack.*[32] There is evidence that, in addition to having the same document printed at both locations, printed material from one location was available for sale at the other.

The news of the Battle of Lexington, which took place on April 19, 1775, reached Albany on May 1, and the city authorities immediately formed Committees of Safety and Correspondence. Local patriots assembled shortly thereafter to form militia companies and prepare for what now seemed to be certain armed conflict.[33] The next two years would be difficult times for Alexander and James Robertson. If they had been inclined to support the British, they were, up to this time, able to keep their sentiments out of public scrutiny, but impartiality would no longer be tolerated.

Once again, the starting point for examining this period in the Robertsons' stay in Albany is the second edition of Isaiah Thomas's *History of Printing in America.*

There we find the following:

> They . . . continued their printing house in Albany until the commencement of the revolutionary war; when, being detected in publishing and circulating in a private manner, highly obnoxious handbills, etc., in support of the royal cause which they decidedly espoused, they judged it expedient hastily to leave the city, and went to Norwich.[34]

As with most of the information in Thomas about the Robertsons, the above comments were not found in the first edition and are not wholly accurate. *The Minutes of the Albany Committee of Correspondence 1775–1778* provide some additional information on the Robertsons' activities before 1777. Furthermore, in 1784, James Robertson presented a sworn statement to the British Commission of Enquiry into the Losses and Services of the American Loyalists. His statement, which is admittedly prejudiced, remains the only primary source of information on the Robertsons' final years in Albany.

James's statement before the British Commission starts at the beginning of the war. He explains that at that time they were settled in both the City of Albany and the Town of Norwich. The Norwich newspaper provided what he called "a very handsome profit," but he and his brother, as explained above, felt compelled to end their partnership with Trumbell.[35] They returned to Albany, where "they imagined they could be of more immediate Service to Government," which presumably means the British government.[36] By this account, then, sometime after May 1776, the Robertsons concentrated their printing activity in Albany. In 1776, Robertson continues, they were employed by a Colonel Edmeston, who was being held in jail in Albany, "to print and circulate such papers as might have tendency to promote the interests of Great Britain."[37] Robertson does not mention that during this period they also published as a broadside "The Tory Act," which was part of the resolves of the Continental Congress. The act alerted the patriots that "divers honest and well meaning, but uniformed people in these colonies . . ." do not fully understand the American cause and they were admonished to "treat all such persons with kindness and attention."[38] No doubt the Robertsons hoped for such understanding and consideration.

Robertson's admission would seem to confirm the charge that Isaiah Thomas said was placed against them, of publishing and distributing "highly obnoxious handbills, etc., in support of the royal cause." Furthermore, there was a resolution presented before the Committee of Correspondence on October 18, 1776, "That Major Edmunston be immediately taken into Custody."[39] This could very well be the officer that James Robertson named as "Colonel Edmeston." Whether the Robertsons were printing leaflets for the Loyalists or not, it is certain that they were doing printing for the Patriots. There are eight references in the committee's minutes to bills for printing done by the Robertsons which were all ordered paid. The first bill was in September 1775, followed in 1776 by two in June, one each in July, September, October, and November, with the final payment on June 7, 1777. If they were printing for both the British and the Americans, it is difficult to know whether they were serving in the role of impartial printer or were simply out for economic gain.

The confrontation over the printing and circulation of Loyalist handbills finally reached a climax in early February 1777. On February 3, the Committee of Correspondence appointed a committee "to examine the Printing Office in this City, and also to take & seize all such papers as they shall deem necessary."[40] They were looking for evidence of the printers' involvement with the distribution of pro-British literature. There is no mention in this account of the names of the printers, but the Robertsons ran the only printing office in Albany. Later the same day, Jacob Cuyler and Harmanus Wendell reported back to the committee that they could find no evidence and that the printers denied publishing the proclamations in question. The printers, however, would not declare their innocence under oath. It was then further resolved that if "the said Printers do not declare upon Oath whether the said proclamation &c. has been reprinted by them or in their office, and at whose request," their press, types, and other printing equipment could be taken and kept in custody. However, there is no indication that the Robertsons' equipment was confiscated at that time.[41]

The available records make it difficult to establish the exact sequence of events, especially since James Robertson's statement to the Board of Enquiry mentions few dates. However, he does state that he felt compelled to leave Albany, and it is reasonable to assume that the Committee of Correspondence's investigation may have given him adequate incentive. He claims to have gone into hiding at a settlement thirteen miles from the city and to have taken printing materials with him. He presumably intended to continue printing for the British. This was evidently not a very unusual practice for printers. Hugh Hastings wrote that during the Revolution, "The average printer maintained a portable shop, ready to be moved at a moment's warning . . . to reach a destination safe from the enemy."[42] Aware that he was being sought, Robertson returned one night to Albany to visit Colonel Edmeston and to arrange his escape to New York City, where he would be protected by the British military. Edmeston provided Robertson with a forged pass to help insure his safe passage, "a card recommending him to Capt. McKenzie, Sir Wm Howe's secretary," and some secret messages to deliver. James evidently made good his escape, trusting perhaps in the kindness suggested by the Tory Act to protect his handicapped brother, Alexander.[43]

According to James's account, Alexander did not receive very good treatment. Angered by James Robertson's escape, the committee "seized upon the Body of Alexander Robertson who for a Series of Years has been entirely deprived of the use of his Legs" and placed him in prison. Also imprisoned were William Lewis, an apprentice, and Patrick Kelly, a servant.[44] Exactly when this occurred is unclear, but Alexander Robertson was certainly in jail by June 11, 1777, because on that date he wrote a letter to the Albany Committee complaining about their violent treatment at the hands of the jailer, Stephen Bell. In a scuffle with Bell, Patrick Kelly was severely cut, almost lost his thumb and was left without medical treatment for hours.[45]

If we accept the timing of these events, then the payment to "A & J Robertson" for "printing Two Hundred Hand Bills," which was made on June 7, 1777, as referred to above, seems somewhat out of place.[46] James was clearly no longer in Albany, so Alexander Robertson and William Lewis may simply have been ordered to do the work. Because of his handicap, Alexander could not have operated a printing press alone. The records show that five days after this bill was paid, on June 12, 1777, William Lewis, the apprentice who was arrested with Robertson, was "ordered sent down to the Fleet prison at Kingston."[47] This transfer may thus mark the end of printing activity in Albany until after the war was over.

Alexander's ordeal was not yet ended. James Robertson explains that after about six months "confined in a most hideous Apartment in Albany Gaol [sic]," he was sent to prison in Kingston.[48] He was nearly trapped in that jail when Kingston was burned on October 16, 1777. With no one to help him, he managed to escape by crawling on his hands and knees to a cabbage patch outside his jail. He was found there three days later, burned and bruised, but was simply returned to another prison. Information contradicting this scenario is found in a November 18, 1777, letter from General Israel Putnam to New York State Governor George Clinton. Putnam wrote to recommend the exchange of Alexander Robertson for John Dennis of New Jersey. The exchange was the result of "repeated applications from James Robinson [sic] of N: York," and Putnam favored it because "Robinson [sic] is a Cripple (& I believe a worthless fellow)."[49] Putnam also states that Alexander was moved from the Kingston jail before it was burned. Clinton responded to Putnam on November 24, 1777, but objected to the exchange unless it was for "Mr Miller of West Chester County or any other Subject of this State."[50] Despite this objection, Major General Gates granted permission for the original exchange and Alexander was allowed to join his brother in New York City.[51] James then dramatically concluded his statement before the commission: "It is notorious that no Printers on the continent of America did more, or ran greater risks to serve their King and country than your Memorialists, and at a time when they were far from protection of a British Army."[52]

The final pages of the Robertsons' statement before the board includes a breakdown of the losses for which he was seeking reimbursement and sworn statements by others to help substantiate his claim. The items listed totaled £650 and included £311 for a printing office, £77 for salaries paid to Lewis and Kelly while they were in prison, and £135 for prison expenses. They eventually received £350.[53] Of further interest is the fact that one of those attesting to the Robertsons' claim was Joseph Chew, "late Secretary to Indian Affairs under Sir Wm Johnson."[54] Chew could not specifically confirm Robertson's claim but did state that he knew the Robertsons and had seen their newspaper.

For the next six years, as long as the British stayed in New York City, the Robertsons were busy publishing newspapers. In New York, they published the *Royal American Gazette* from January 16, 1777, until July 31, 1783. For a short period in 1778, James Robertson published the *Royal Pennsylvania Gazette* in Philadelphia. In 1780, James traveled to Charleston, South Carolina, and for about two years he published the *Royal South-Carolina Gazette*. When the British evacuated New York, the Robertsons moved, along with many other Loyalists, to Shelburne, Nova Scotia. There, in 1784, they restarted the *Royal American Gazette*. Later that year, Alexander died at the age of forty-two. James moved the paper to Charlottetown, Prince Edward Island, where he expected to be appointed the King's Printer. He was greatly disappointed when he received the appointment, but was granted no salary for the position. He returned to Edinburgh, Scotland, in 1789 and worked as a printer and bookseller until his death in 1816.[55]

The Robertsons' *Albany Gazette* remains isolated in area history, still a mystery. Today little more is known about the newspaper or the printers than Isaiah Thomas knew in 1810. No printing was done before they came to Albany, and after they left, the printing presses were silent until 1782. There is even an unconfirmed story, again found in Thomas's second edition, that the Robertsons gave their press to a friend for safekeeping, and the friend buried it. The press was dug up in 1782 and sold to Solomon Balantine, who then published Albany's second newspaper.[56] As with much of what is found about Albany in *The History of Printing*, the accuracy of the story is uncertain, but that does not mean it is untrue. Douglas McMurtrie at least confirms the printing hiatus in his book on Albany imprints, where he explains," . . . no imprints are recorded for the years 1777 to 1781, inclusive. No satisfactory evidence of printing in Albany during those five Revolutionary years has yet been found."[57]

Obviously, the information available at the present time leaves many unanswered questions about Alexander and James Robertson and their experiences in Albany. We cannot be certain who or what brought them to the city, but I believe that what they sought was simply the chance to practice their trade. Albany was an untouched market, an opportunity for literary and commercial success. They were young, enthusiastic, and truly convinced of the importance of "an impartial paper, conducted with judgment," as they wrote in the opening article of the first edition of the *Gazette.* There is no doubt that they were also interested in the financial benefits of a profitable printing house. Judging from James Parker's comments, they were not likely to find that in New York City. Their most critical error was in not recognizing the transformation that the press underwent during the Stamp Act crisis. The crisis enhanced the importance of the press but only at the price of its impartiality. Perhaps the Robertsons thought they could ride out the pendulum of change in a place like Albany, which was removed from the center of controversy. Notwithstanding James Robertson's dramatic remarks before the British Board of Enquiry, I believe they were carried, mostly by circumstance, to the Loyalist position and then to self-imposed exile in Canada. In any case, Alexander and James Robertson deserve more than a footnote in Albany's history. Whatever motives drove them, they brought to Albany "an Epitome of modern History" and, for better or worse, controversy and the press are inseparable. The city has not been the same since.

This article originally appeared in the *Hudson Valley Regional Review*, Volume 10.1, March, 1993.

NOTES

1. Isaiah Thomas, *The History of Printing in America* (Worcester: American Antiquarian Society, 1810), 318.
2. Sidney Kobre, *The Development of the Colonial Newspaper* (Gloucester: Peter Smith, 1960), 112.
3. Frank Luther Mott, *American Journalism: A History 1690–1960* (New York: The Macmillan Company, 1965), 79–80.
4. Isaiah Thomas, *The History of Printing in America,* 2nd ed. (New York: Burt Franklin, 1874), 1:193.
5. Ibid.
6. *The Papers of Benjamin Franklin,* ed. Leonard W. Labaree (New Haven: Yale University Press, 1970), 15:270.
7. Ibid., 19: 43.
8. Ibid., 17:75.
9. Ibid., 16:139–40.
10. Ibid., 17:56–57.
11. William Smith, *Review of the Military Operations in North America* (New York: Alexander and James Robertson, 1770), Evans Bibliography no. 11701, 105.
12. Thomas, *History of Printing,* 2nd ed., 1:313.
13. Isaiah Thomas, handwritten notes in first-edition copy of *History of Printing,* 118–19, Manuscript Collection of the American Antiquarian Society Library, Worcester, Mass.
14. *The Papers of Sir William Johnson*, ed. Alexander C. Flick (Albany: University of the State of New York, 1931), 7:381.
15. Ibid., 7:240.
16. Ibid., 7:322.
17. George R. Howell and Jonathan Tenney, eds., *Bicentennial History of the County of Albany, N.Y. From 1609 to 1886* (New York: W.W. Munsell, 1886), 699.
18. *The Albany Gazette* (Albany), vol. 1, no. 1, November 25, 1771, 1.
19. Joel Munsell, *Typographical Miscellany* (Albany: Joel Munsell Printing Co., 1850), 227.
20. F. Morgan, *Connecticut As A Colony and As A State, or One of the Original Thirteen* (Hartford: Publishing Society of Connecticut, 1904), 2:299.
21. Dumas Malone, ed., *Dictionary of American*

Biography (New York: Charles Scribner's Sons, 1960), 8:638.

22. Thomas, *History of Printing,* 2nd ed., 1:192.
23. *Transcript of the Manuscript Books and Papers of the Commission of Enquiry into the Losses and the Services of the American Loyalists* (Transcribed for the New York Public Library, 1900), 41:453.
24. Douglas C. McMurtrie, *A Check List of Eighteenth Century Albany Imprints* (Albany: University of the State of New York, Bibliography Bulletin 80, 1939), 15.
25. *Law and Ordinances* (Albany: Alexander and James Robertson, 1773), Evans Bibliography no. 12369.
26. McMurtrie, *Albany Imprints,* 15.
27. Joseph-Bill Packer, *A Journal of the Life and Travels of Joseph-Bill Packer* (Albany: Alexander and James Robertson, 1773), Evans Bibliography no. 12914.
28. "Extracts from the Votes and Proceedings of the American Continental Congress" (Albany: Alexander and James Robertson, 1774), Evans Bibliography no. 13723, 11.
29. Ibid., 40.
30. McMurtrie, *Albany Imprints,* 16.
31. *Bickerstaff's New England Almanack* (Norwich: Robertsons and Trumbell, 1775), Evans Bibliography no. 14618.
32. Ibid., Evans Bibliography no. 42771.
33. Cyler Reynolds, ed., *Albany Chronicles: A History of the City Arranged Chronologically* (Albany: J.B. Lyon Company, 1906), 273.
34. Thomas, *History of Printing,* 2nd ed., 1:313.
35. *Transcript of the American Loyalists,* 41:453.
36. Ibid.
37. Ibid., 454.
38. "Resolves of the Hon. Continental Congress" (Albany: Alexander and James Robertson, 1776), Evans Bibliography no. 15147.
39. *Minutes of the Albany Committee of Correspondence: 1775–1778,* by the Division of Archives and History, James Sullivan, Ph.D., Director and State Historian (Albany: University of the State of New York, 1923), 1:580.
40. Ibid., 672.
41. Ibid.
42. *Public Papers of George Clinton,* Published by the State of New York, with an Introduction by Hugh Hastings, State Historian (New York: Wynkoop Hallenbeck Crawford Co., 1899), vol. I, 64.
43. *Transcript of the American Loyalists,* 41: 455–56.
44. Ibid., 456.
45. *Journals of the Provincial Congress, Provincial Convention, Committee of Safety and Council of Safety of the State of New York: 1775–1776–1777* (Albany: Thurlow Weed, 1842), 2:469.
46. *Albany Minutes,* 1:787.
47. Ibid., 792.
48. *Transcript of the American Loyalists,* 41:457.
49. *Clinton Papers,* 2:528.
50. Ibid., 547.
51. Ibid., 525.
52. *Transcript of the American Loyalists,* 41:461.
53. Arthur M. Schlesinger, *Prelude to Independence, The Newspaper War on Britain* (New York: Alfred A. Knopf, 1958), 259.
54. *Transcript of the American Loyalists,* 41:468.
55. Marion Robertson, "The Loyalist Printers: James and Alexander Robertson," *The Nova Scotia Historical Review,* vol. 3, no. 1 (1983): 92–93.
56. Thomas, *History of Printing,* 2nd ed., 1:313.
57. McMurtrie, *Albany Imprints,* 11.

9

Taxation and Suffrage in Revolutionary New York

JONATHAN CLARK

THE AIMS OF THIS ARTICLE are rather more modest than the imposing title I gave the piece would suggest. More accurately, the title would read, "A Re-examination of a Few Issues Having to Do with the Relationship between Taxation and Suffrage in Revolutionary New York Based on Evidence Available for Dutchess County." In this instance, it seemed appropriate to sacrifice clarity for brevity. Besides, even the long title failed to mention the New York Constitution of 1777, the document that established a relationship between taxation and the franchise in revolutionary New York.

Each draft of that Constitution, including the final version proclaimed at Kingston, limited the franchise for the assembly to men who paid taxes. The final version, of course, listed other criteria as well. Qualified voters would include only those men who owned a freehold worth at least £20, or who rented a farm valued at forty shillings a year, or who enjoyed the status of freeman in Albany or New York City.[1]

Historians have usually viewed these additional requirements as part of a larger conservative victory. Had "the more democratic elements gotten their way," wrote Alfred F. Young, "taxpayer suffrage" would have prevailed.[2] Only it did not prevail and, according to Bernard Mason, even moderates in the Convention of Representatives "gave up substantial ground when they dropped the universal male suffrage proviso [i.e. taxpayer suffrage] for the assembly. . . ."[3] Presumably, taxpayer suffrage would have expanded the franchise to include most of those men (an estimated one-third of the free adult male population) denied the vote by the Constitution.[4]

Such conclusions rest on a perfectly reasonable assumption. Taxpayer suffrage, it goes, pretty closely approximated universal male suffrage because most free males must have paid taxes. Had taxpayer suffrage survived the conservative onslaught, it should have resulted in a clear and simple relationship between taxation and suffrage: one man equaled one taxpayer equaled one qualified voter. Since that possible relationship also depends on the validity of the original assumption, the assumption itself bears looking into.

The draft of the constitution written by John Jay offers the first clue that something may be amiss. Following Bernard Mason's reconstruction of the drafting process, Jay authored the fourth draft, and in the main "contributed clarity and economy of language."[5] Jay, though reputedly conservative on many political issues, supported a provision, in the words of Richard B. Morris, "very close to universal manhood suffrage."[6] Jay, in short, advocated taxpayer suffrage for the assembly. The pertinent portion of his draft gave the vote to any man over twenty-one, "Provided that he is a Freeholder in the County, or that he has resided therein for one year immediately preceding the said election and has been rated and actually paid public or county taxes."[7] Curiously, Jay's draft separated eligible voters into two distinct categories, freeholders and taxpayers, and he did so when a taxpaying proviso alone should have sufficed. Highly skilled in the law and with words, Jay appears unaccountably to have thrown economy of language to the winds. Unless, of course, he thought he knew something historians may have missed: namely, that not all freeholders paid taxes.

Jay's draft, as well as the Constitution finally adopted, explicitly limited the right to vote to men who had been rated for purposes of direct taxation, and subsequently paid the taxes assessed. Local assessors normally made their ratings but once a year, and any non-freeholder they neglected to rate automatically became disenfranchised. Put simply, even Jay's version of taxpayer suffrage would have extended the right to vote only to those men whose names appeared on a local tax list in a given year.

In laying direct taxes, the legislature left the issue of how much each man paid largely in the hands of local authorities. The Assembly simply voted to raise a certain amount of money and then made each county responsible for a specific portion of the total. Subsequently (Dutchess County provides a typical example), the Board of Supervisors would meet and further apportion the county's share of taxes among the precincts.[8] Each precinct supervisor would report back to the locally elected assessors, who would then "make Assessments on the several Inhabitants, Residents, and Persons holding Real or Personal Estate . . . according to the Estate, and other Circumstances and Ability of each respective Person, to pay Taxes, collectively considered."[9] The tax laws—maybe deliberately—left much to the discretion of local assessors.

On paper, despite the discretionary power given to assessors, most free men should have paid direct taxes. In New York City, as late as 1769, the Common Council supposedly raised taxes upon "the Estates real and personal, of the freeholders, freemen, Inhabitants, Residents, and Sojourners."[10] Earlier, in Dutchess County, where no freemen as such lived, the assessors had the job of rating all "freeholders, inhabitants and Residents."[11] By the rules then, any adult who owned anything should have received an assessment.

But it did not work out that way in Poughkeepsie or in the other precincts of Dutchess. While the first accurate census of the precinct was not taken until 1790, and the last complete tax list that survives is for 1778, it is possible to reconstruct fairly accurately the adult male population for 1775. Along with other evidence that helps verify residency, both the tax lists and the New York Association lists for that year have survived. In 1775 at least 329 free males resided in town, but the names of only 256 of them appear on the tax list for that year.[12] Either seventy-three men in town owned nothing worth taxing or else—no matter how rigid the rules—the assessors simply did not bother to rate certain kinds or amounts of property. In either case, had taxpayer suffrage prevailed, it would have served to exclude upwards of twenty percent of the adult males in Poughkeepsie from the franchise.

In Rombout Precinct, adjacent to Poughkeepsie, taxpayer suffrage would have served to disenfranchise men of eminent status and prominent wealth. John Jay, along with his father, brother Frederick, and their families moved to Rombout in the fall of 1776. They arrived with more than sixty sheep, twenty-odd cows and five horses, all of which represented a sizeable—and taxable—amount of property.[13] Yet no member of the Jay family appears on any surviving tax list for Dutchess County. The assessors did rate the Van Wyck farm—in Van Wyck's name—on which the Jays lived, but did not assess any of the personal property the well-to-do tenants brought with them.[14] In sum, taxpayer suffrage alone would have disenfranchised the Jay menfolk from voting as Dutchess County residents.

Poughkeepsie assessors, like their colleagues in Rombout, also appear by and large to have overlooked changes in personal estate. True, while a few men like Matthew Van Keuren (rated at £6 in 1757, but at only £1 in 1779) either lost or gave away appreciable quantities of their estates and while a few others, like Richard Snedeker, a locally well-known Tory, amassed taxable property (hopping from £10 in 1765 to £30 in 1779), the assessments made on most men varied little over the years.[15] Henry Livingston, who paid more taxes than anyone else in Poughkeepsie, possessed an estate rated at £34 in 1757. Twenty years later his assessment had only risen to £38. Jeremiah Dubois owned an estate worth £2 in 1765, and at £2 he stayed through 1778. Representing more the rule than the exception, Myndert Rynders and Peter Van Vliet each owned property assessed at £1 in every year between 1765 and 1778.[16] The very stability of assessments suggests that when assessors made their annual ratings they looked to lands and buildings, not to personal assets.

Other evidence from the tax lists enhances the likelihood that direct taxes in Revolutionary New York corresponded to what Americans today call property taxes. The estates of freeholders who left town temporarily received the same assessment in their absence as in their residency. When, for example, Hugh Van Kleeck left Poughkeepsie for a year or so in 1775 his estate was assessed at the same £2 he had been rated and would again receive after his return. Similarly, Bernardus Swartwout owned property rated at £3 in 1775, and the same evaluation on the worth of his "place" had been made in 1774. Either Van Kleeck and Swartwout left all their personal property behind when they departed, or else the assessors cared little about personal property.[17]

It is not likely that the "places" of those two men remained vacant during their absence. Temporary tenants probably lived in their houses, but, just as in the case with the Jays on the Van Wyck farm, the owners and not the tenants paid the taxes. When renters paid the taxes, assessors took note of it, as they did in the case of the "minister's house" where Ezekial Cooper lived in 1770 and 1771.[18] During those two years, he appeared on the tax lists as both tenant and taxpayer, though the assessment was made on the house itself. If taxpayer suffrage had prevailed in 1777 a man in the situation of an Ezekial Cooper would qualify to vote while a John Jay would not. In Dutchess County, then, taxpayer suffrage would have proven exclusionary. The seemingly simple relationship between direct taxation and the suffrage was complicated by a singular obstacle: any man who did not own a freehold had to make the tax list before he could vote.

Nor was that the only complication. Read literally, the tax lists indicate that only two men in Poughkeepsie had the wherewithal to meet the £20 freehold requirement. The ranks of the newly disenfranchised would include Zephaniah Platt and Gilbert Livingston, delegates to the Convention from Dutchess County (Platt was assessed at £18, Gilbert Livingston at £6). Both men, incidentally, voted for every amendment that supposedly restricted the franchise.[19] Again, on the face of it, Livingston and Platt actually voted to deny themselves the right to vote.

They had, of course, no such intention. And a poll list from 1783 containing the names of 92 voters, including those of Platt and Livingston, makes clear that what was not intended did not occur.[20] Since some men voted in Poughkeepsie, the assessed value of taxable property that appears on the tax lists must have represented some amount less than the full value of an estate. How much less presents something of a problem: the oath taken by the locally elected assessors required them only to make an assessment "according to the Same Equitable Rate and Proportion as hath hitherto been the Custom in said County according to the best of your Skill and Knowledge."[21] But indirect evidence strongly suggests that, at *most,* the assessment which appears on the tax list reflected only one percent of the full value of the estate. As an example, proceeds from Henry Livingston's estate, sold in 1801, brought in more than £7,000. About half that figure came from the sale of his home in Poughkeepsie.[22] Barring any great change in prices since the 1770's, one percent of that amount accords well with the £38 value placed on Livingston's estate in 1778.

Local deeds tend to verify the 1-to-100 ratio, and also to suggest that the market value of an estate usually exceeded the full value from which the assessors must have worked. A weaver named John McBride was rated on the 1773 tax list at £2. In January 1774, he sold his small farm to Simon Noxon for £380. Noxon appeared on the tax list for the first time in 1774, rated at £1. In 1775 his assessment rose to £2, and in 1777 and 1778 (no list survives for 1776) he was assessed at £3.[23] Despite his low assessment, Simon Noxon could vote for governor and senators if he wished, owning as he did an estate worth almost £400.

The relationship between taxes assessed on—and prices paid for—real property, comes through most clearly in the cases of Lewis Dubois and Thomas Poole. Dubois, a successful tavern keeper (and future regimental commander in the New York Line), had received an assessment of £5 in 1772.[24] At that point he decided to change careers and become a gentleman farmer. He sold his tavern and bought a farm, along with several parcels of land, for the sum of £1,445.[25] The assessors kept up with Dubois and rated his estate at £11 in 1773, the amount at which it remained through 1778.[26] Thomas Poole, who had been annually assessed at £2 between 1765 and 1772 (apparently divesting himself of his land)[27], became the new tavern keeper. He paid Dubois £685 for the tavern, and in 1773 his estate was assessed at £5, precisely the amount at which the assessors had rated Dubois when he had owned the place a year earlier.[28]

Had the tax list for 1783 survived, it would be a simple matter of checking it against the poll list for that year in order to make a compelling case regarding the relationship between taxation and suffrage in Poughkeepsie. Even so, an indication of the probable relationship can be gained by noting the assessments given in 1778 to men who voted in 1783. Fully 51 of the 87 men who voted in 1783 for governor, senators *and* assemblymen—thus meeting the £100 freehold qualification—had resided in Poughkeepsie since at least 1775.[29] As of 1778, only three of those men, Henry Livingston, Zephaniah Platt, and Richard Snedeker, had been rated at £20 or higher. A further six had been assessed between £10 and £20; another eleven had been rated between £5 and £10; five at either £3 or £4; 14 at £2 and six at £1. Finally, six of the men who had lived in Poughkeepsie since 1775 and voted for governor in 1783 had been assessed no taxes whatsoever in 1778.[30] Either each of the twelve men assessed nothing or rated at £1 in 1778 enjoyed a remarkable change of fortune during the next five years or, which seems far more likely, an assessment of £1 indicated possession of an estate worth £100.

Five of the men whose names appear on the poll list of 1783 did not meet the £100 freehold qualification, but did qualify to vote for members of the Assembly. One of their number, David Barclay, a barber and part-time express rider for Governor George Clinton during the war, lived in Poughkeepsie, but does not appear on any surviving tax list.[31] Stephen Harris, a cordwainer, did not pay taxes until 1779. The name Simon Schermerhorn also appears for the first time on the partial list of 1779, but the assessment was on property belonging to a man named Bussing: Schermerhorn just happened to reside there. Malcolm McEwen's sole appearance on the surviving tax lists occurred in 1778.[32] James Douglass, another barber and a long-time resident of Poughkeepsie, paid taxes only from 1774 to 1777, after which his name disappears.[33] It is thus well within the realm of possibility that, while each of these men, except Schermerhorn, may have been a freeholder, not one of them paid direct taxes in 1783.

The available evidence does not constitute an open and shut case. But the preponderance of evidence does indicate that a man who owned an estate assessed at £1 in fact owned an estate worth £100. It also indicates that the bulk of the property taxed was real property (every lot with a house on it in the village of Poughkeepsie received a minimal £1 assessment).[34] Ezekial Cooper's move from tenant to freeholder offers a typical example. In 1771, while living in the minister's house (assessed at £2), he purchased an unimproved lot in the village for £50 and apparently proceeded to build a house on it.[35] The next year he was, according to the tax list, living in his own house, and his assessment had abruptly risen to £4. In 1773, the assessed value of his property dropped to £3 where it remained through 1778.[36] Owning a home in Poughkeepsie, it would seem, minimally put a man in possession of a £100 freehold.

That last figure suggests another tantalizing possibility. The first two drafts of the constitution opened the franchise for higher offices to all men who owned a £40 freehold, thus liberalizing the suffrage by making provincial requirements for the assembly the new requirements for the governor and senate of an independent state. The third draft upped the ante to a £100 freehold. Jay kept the higher figure, and it ultimately became part of New York's highest law.[37] Historians have offered no explanation why the delegates settled on £100, a figure which appears to have only its roundness going for it. If, however, the convention was aware of the method of tax assessment in Dutchess County, the £100 restriction would make eminent sense. It would extend the franchise to all men who owned real property of sufficient value to be taxed.

The £100 freehold requirement, it has been estimated, excluded two out of every three men in New York from having a say in the election of a senator or governor.[38] Those offices supposedly became the private preserve of what George Dangerfield has called the "landed interest."[39] But, if the voting list from Poughkeepsie offers any indication, that landed interest consisted of a pretty diverse crowd of partisans, farmers, lawyers, and barkeeps.[40]

The additional, though undetermined, number of men who could vote for assemblymen only, would not have needed to own much or have much to lose. In a deed recorded in 1766, John Romer sold an eight-acre lot to John Hunt, a "Laborer" living in Poughkeepsie, for the sum of £20.[41] John Hunt was not assessed taxes in 1766 or in 1767. His name appears on the tax list for the first time in 1768, presumably after he had built a house on his lot. Had Hunt made the same purchase in 1777 he would have qualified to vote for assemblymen. As it was, his £1 assessment that year in all probability qualified him to vote for senators and governor as well.[42] Similarly, had John Sedaw, a free black, invested into real estate the £25 he had received for binding himself out as a servant for life, he too would have met the constitutional requirement for the franchise.[43]

Evidence for Dutchess County in general, and for Poughkeepsie in particular, cannot serve as a test-case for the extent of suffrage in revolutionary New York. But the evidence does suggest that some revisions of current wisdom may be in order. In the first place, taxpayer suffrage differed measurably from universal manhood suffrage. The relationship between paying taxes and voting was far more complicated. In the second place, as Sun Bok Kim's analysis of tax lists from Livingston Manor also indicates, the suffrage requirements may not have excluded as many men as currently accepted estimates would have it.[44]

The men who debated New York's first Constitution were no Levellers. But those who prevailed may have held somewhat more democratic leanings than we have given them credit for. Maybe, just maybe, they only wished for voters to demonstrate a state in society. In order to vote for governor or senator, that demonstration consisted of both owning land and paying taxes. In order to vote for an assemblyman though, a man had only to own a bit of land *or* pay taxes. Such a reading of the Constitution, as it relates to Jay's draft, is far more compatible with what is known about Jay's other political ideas than is the notion that in 1777, for some unexplainable reason, he climbed on a radical bandwagon for the next best thing to universal manhood suffrage. Such a reading, as it relates to the Constitution finally adopted, might also just be more

Table 9.1. Value of Estate in Comparison to the Number of Sons with British

Name	*Number of Sons with British*	*Value of Estate 1780*	*Assessed Value of Estate—1778 Tax List*
John Miller	1	£380	£3
William Low	1	£200	£2
John Palmatier	1	£300	£2
Francis Jacocks	1	£133.6.8	£2
Samuel Smith*	2	£920(460)	£4
Peter Laroy	1	£1120	£9
Caleb Carmen, Jr.	1	£600	£4
Abraham Ferdon	1	£133.6.8	£1
Magdalene Westerfelt, widow	1	£133.6.8	£1
George Sands*	2	£1253(626.10)	£7
Andrew Lawson	1	£133.6.8	£3
John Midler*	2	£2200(1100)	£5
Zachariah Ferdon*	2	£1880(940)	£5
Margaret Utt, widow	1	£133.6.8	£0
Joseph Scott	1	£650	£4
Lancaster Burling	1	£133.6.8	£0
James Compton	1	£133.6.8	£0

* Value of estate doubled because of having two sons with the British.
The above table is based upon one printed in Hastings, ed., *Papers of Clinton*, IV, 586, used in conjunction with the *Poughkeepsie Tax List* for 1778.

compatible with the realities of who did and did not have to pay direct taxes in New York a century and a half before the invention of Form 1040. But only further research, especially at the local level, can let us know for sure.

APPENDIX

Further confirmation that the assessed value of an estate in all likelihood represented only one percent of the "real" value of an estate—and less than one percent of its market value—comes from the results of a special tax levied by the state in late 1780. The law applied to any parent whose son or sons had gone off to join the British. Local assessors were to rate the personal and real estate of each person with a wayward son at its "Value in Specie." If a person had the misfortune of being a parent of two Loyalist sons, his or her assessment got doubled. Once the assessors had completed their work, the Supervisor would levy a tax on those persons at the rate of nine pence per pound, the only provision being that "each person to be assessed as aforesaid, shall be assessed in such Sum, as that his or her Tax shall amount to at least Five Pounds.[45]

Seventeen residents of Poughkeepsie felt the bite of that particular tax.[46] A comparison between the assessed value of these persons' estates in 1781 and the amounts they were assessed for tax purposes in 1778 tends, in a majority of the cases, to verify the proposition that assessments for normal tax purposes represented about one per cent of full value (see Table). Plausible explanations exist for a couple of the exceptions. Lancaster Burling (who left New York City sometime after the British occupied the place) and George Compton were recent arrivals to Poughkeepsie.[47] Since anyone assessed at £100 would pay a tax of only £3.6.8, the minimum assessment had to be fixed at £133.6.8 in order to yield a tax of £5. The available evidence does not shed light on the difference in the assessments of 1778 and 1781 for Andrew Lawson and Zachariah Ferdon (though possibly in the wake of a special tax, assessors took a more rigorous accounting of personal property).

This article originally appeared in the *Hudson Valley Regional Review*, Volume 1.1, March 1984.

NOTES

1. Bernard Mason, *The Road to Independence: The Revolutionary Movement in New York,* 1773–1777 (Lexington. 1966), 241–42, and Charles Z. Lincoln, *The Constitutional History of New York* (Rochester, 1906), I, 514–15.
2. Alfred F. Young, *The Democratic Republicans of New York: The Origins, 1763–1797* (Chapel Hill. 1967), p. 19.
3. Mason, *Road to Independence, 244.*
4. The most recent estimate, offered by Bernard Mason, concludes that the final property qualifications (£20 freehold or £2 per-year-tenement) for the assembly meant that only 60% of the men qualified to vote for any state office. Bernard Mason, "New York State's First Constitution," in *Essays on the Genesis of the Empire State* (Albany, 1979), 20, 23.
5. Mason, *Road to Independence, 228.*
6. Richard B. Morris, *Seven Who Shaped Our Destiny* (New York. 1973), 186.
7. Lincoln, *Constitutional History, 514.*
8. Because precinct supervisors in the county met periodically to apportion the amount of taxes to be raised by each precinct, the method of assessment used in any one precinct applied to the rest of Dutchess as well. Staughton Lynd, *Antifederalism in Dutchess County, New York* (Chicago, 1962), 27, also took note of that fact. See the Dutchess County Tax Lists, 1757–1779, Microfilm No. 925055, Adriance Memorial Library, Poughkeepsie, New York (hereafter cited as Tax Lists).
9. *Laws of the State of New York, Commencing with the First Session of the Senate Assembly* . . . (Poughkeepsie, 1782), 94.
10. Herbert L. Osgood, et. al., eds., *Minutes of the Common Council of the City of New York* (New York, 1903), VII, 42.
11. *Old Miscellaneous Records of Dutchess County* (Poughkeepsie, 1909), 131.
12. The Association lists, though available in Peter Force, *American Archives.* 4th Series, III, 597–608, are most accurately transcribed in *Calendar of Historical Manuscripts Relating to the War of the Revolution* (Albany. 1868), I, 77–79.
13. See Charlotte C. Finkel. *The Jay Family in Fishkill (Now East Fishkill) 1776–1781,* Fishkill Historical Society (1967), 1–19.
14. Tax Lists, 1777–1779.
15. Tax Lists, 1757 through 1779; for Snedeker's Loyalism see Hugh Hastings, ed., *The Public Papers of George Clinton. First Governor of New York* (Albany, 1899), I, 849.
16. Tax Lists, 1757–1779.
17. Tax Lists, 1774–1777.
18. Tax Lists, 1770–1771.
19. *Journals of the Provincial Congress, Provincial Convention, Committees of New York* (Albany, 1842), I, 866–67.
20. *New York Historical and Genealogical Register,* II (January, 1871), 150.
21. The oaths appear at the beginning of the microfilm reel of Tax Lists, 1757–1779.
22. See Joan Gordon, "Kinship and Class: The Livingstons of New York, 1675–1860," unpublished doctoral thesis, Columbia University (1959), 199.
23. Tax Lists, 1773–1778; Dutchess County Clerk's Office, *Deeds,* Liber 6, 406.
24. Tax Lists, 1772.
25. *Deeds,* Liber 7, 305.
26. Tax Lists, 1773–1778.

27. Ibid., 1765–1772.
28. *Deeds,* Liber 7, 30.
29. Limiting the sample to those who lived in Poughkeepsie since at least 1775 allows a glimpse at possible leaps in wealth between 1775–1778, of which none of consequence appear.
30. Tax List, 1778.
31. *New York Historical and Genealogical Register,* 150; Chilton Williamson, *American Suffrage: From Property to Democracy* (New York, 1960), 161; Hastings, ed., *Papers of Clinton,* III, 245; VII, 533.
32. Tax Lists, 1778, 1779; *New York Historical and Genealogical Register, 150.*
33. Ibid., Tax Lists. 1774–1777.
34. Edmund Platt. *The Eagle's History of Poughkeepsie from the Earliest Settlement, 1683–1905* (Poughkeepsie, 1905), 33.
35. Tax Lists, 1771–1772; *Deeds,* Liber 7, 258.
36. Tax Lists, 1772–1778.
37. Mason, *Road to Independence,* 224–28.
38. The potential size of the electorate qualified to vote might have been reduced by the proviso in the Constitution that freeholds had to be worth £100 "over and above all debts charged thereon." But the first act to regulate elections, passed in 1778, stipulated that every mortgagor and every mortgagee was deemed a freeholder. In theory, at least, one freehold could thus qualify two men to vote. Lincoln, *Constitutional History,* 514; *Laws of the State of New York* (First Session), 19, estimated that only half the voters could vote for the higher offices; Bernard Mason has estimated that the £100 qualification excluded 70% of the white males: *Genesis of the Empire State,* 20, 23.
39. George Dangerfield, *Chancellor Robert R. Livingston of New York 1746–1813* (New York, 1960), 90.
40. *New York Historical and Genealogical Register,* II, 150.
41. *Deeds,* Liber 5, 43.
42. Tax Lists, 1768, 1777.
43. *Deeds,* Liber 4, 260.
44. Sun Bok Kim, *Landlord and Tenant in Colonial New York: Manorial Society, 1664–1775* (Chapel Hill, 1978), 272–73.
45. *Laws of the State of New York* (4th Session) 160–62; this law was also printed in *The New York Journal and the General Advertiser,* October 1 and October 8, 1781.
46. Hastings, ed., *Papers of Clinton,* VI, 586.
47. Frederic G. Mather, ed., *New York in the Revolution as Colony and State; Supplement* (Albany, 1901), 66.

10

The Right to Choose

Suffrage During the Revolutionary Era in Charlotte Precinct

WILLIAM P. McDERMOTT

"AYE," ANSWERED ABEL PETERS, when asked if he would post a bond for Enoch Lester, midway through the annual meeting held in the newly established Town of Clinton. On that day, April 1, 1788, he agreed to guarantee Lester's performance as a newly elected town constable, a post Lester had held for five years immediately before the American Revolution.[1] This was not the first time the paths of these two very different men had crossed. In 1776 both men had been arrested by the Committee for Detecting and Defeating Conspiracies, then a newly organized committee empowered by the New York Provincial Congress to incarcerate any individual who subverted the American cause.[2] Even then Lester and Peters had been neighbors. Peters, an affluent member of the community in 1788, had opened the first general store in Clinton Corners shortly before the Revolution. Lester, probably a patron in Peter's store, seems to have lived an undistinguished life, moving from one property owned by members of the Lester family to another.[3] Both of these men came from affluent families. The Lester family, as partners in the Nine Partners Company, owned part of the approximately 140,000-acre Nine Partners Patent which included Clinton. Abel Peters had come to Dutchess County only a decade before the Revolution as the fifteen-year-old son of George, who soon became a successful storekeeper in Pleasant Valley.

Although released shortly after his arrest, Lester's provocative description of himself as "a true subject to George the third . . . [who] meant to live and die so" resulted in a second arrest. Paroled a few months later, he returned home in October 1777 and maintained a low profile for the duration of the war.[4] Peters, too, had been released. He reopened his store and conducted business in Clinton Corners during the Revolution. No doubt his pledge to support the Revolution and his service in the militia had redeemed his earlier transgression. Also his neighbors and patrons, almost exclusively Quakers who objected to armed conflict of any sort, had little quarrel with him for his support of the "old" order.

These arrests, not particularly significant against the larger tapestry of the American Revolution, and Lester's reelection to public office in 1788 raise a curious and interesting question. Was the Revolution and the events which followed, such as the Constitutional Convention held at Poughkeepsie in 1788, treated as a significant social movement by the average individual in the agricultural communities of Dutchess County? Obviously by 1788, if Lester's election to public office is any barometer, memories regarding his earlier behavior had faded. However, could it be that the inhabitants of Clinton did not regard the events of the previous dozen years as matters central to day-to-day living, regardless of their political, social, or economic significance? Perhaps, as Edward Countryman concluded about New Yorkers at the outset of the Revolution, "a great number . . . tried desperately just to keep out of it."[5]

Staughton Lynd in his analysis of the Revolutionary era in Dutchess County observed that, "Contemporaries had no doubt that the War for Independence was accompanied by a struggle over who should rule at home." And this struggle, Lynd believed, was "a conflict between economic classes," which was a principal "factor in shaping the politics of the seventeen-eighties." He concluded that newly emerging popular leaders in the county, in contrast to those of the privileged class, "developed a democratic philosophy of politics which called for the election to office of men of the 'middling sort,' frequent elections, rotation of office. . . ."[6] But Robert Brown, in his often cited study of Massachusetts, argued that colonial society even before the Revolution had already become "a relatively egalitarian middle class society in which there was a great deal of economic opportunity."[7] Therefore, Brown infers, the American Revolution primarily reflected a dissatisfaction with British policies regarded by all the colonists as oppressive rather than a clash between classes within the colonies.[8] And yet a third point of view argues that while there were wide economic differences between classes before and after the Revolution, the behavior of the people of New York regarding the American Revolution and the events which followed cannot be explained only in terms of class differences. Patriots and loyalists, and Federalists and Anti-Federalists were found at the top of the economic ladder as well as on its lower rungs.[9]

Studying "the way government worked at the local level" to determine whether the earlier interpretations, social and economic, accurately portray the Revolutionary period is an important, but often overlooked approach.[10] Two questions deserve attention if one is to understand the reaction of ordinary people to the important events which transpired between the years 1775 and 1788: 1) How responsive was the ordinary citizen to these events? and 2) Was there a struggle between the more affluent and those of lesser means at the local level? The purpose of this article is to examine these questions as they are reflected in the voting behavior of citizens in the town of Clinton and its predecessor, Charlotte Precinct, during the Revolutionary era.

This area of Dutchess County is particularly well suited for study. Clinton, when established as a town in 1786, had been part of a larger geographical unit called Charlotte Precinct from 1762. This precinct encompassed the present towns of Clinton, Hyde Park, Pleasant Valley, Stanford, and Washington. In 1786, Charlotte was divided into Clinton (Hyde Park and Pleasant Valley included) and Washington (Stanford included). Combined, they covered 22 percent of the land mass of Dutchess County at that time and represented about 17 percent of the county's population in 1775. Charlotte, in many ways, was representative of Dutchess County as a whole. Its location, its ethnic composition, and its agricultural economy reflected much of Dutchess County's makeup during the Revolutionary era. Its location in the middle and northwest section of the county with two principal roads, the present Routes 9 and 44, and its shoreline along the Hudson River planted it firmly in the stream of Dutchess County's commercial activity. Most of its land was owned and farmed by its residents, although there appear to have been pockets of land rented to tenants. Additionally, its population, largely English by the time of the Revolution, included substantial groups of Germans and Dutch. This mix was representative of Dutchess County as a whole during this era. Using the 1775 tax lists as a measure of personal wealth, although comparability between precincts has yet to be studied, Charlotte Precinct was representative of the economic condition of Dutchess County citizens in 1775.[11]

The attitudes of Charlotte's inhabitants to the politics of the Revolutionary era could be understood best if a record of their thoughts and actions had been left. But the inarticulate neither chronicle their lives, nor leave memoirs of it; nevertheless, they can be heard. A glimpse of their points of view regarding politics is reflected in the surviving minutes of "town" meetings held in Charlotte and, later, Clinton. Skimpy though they are, these records at least noted who was elected to public office at the annual meetings held each April. In addition, tax lists and other records can be used to ferret out clues regarding elected officials, the "class" to which they belonged, and other pertinent information about them.[12]

In February 1775, after the New York Assembly failed to support the First Continental Congress, its supporters in New York City appealed to all New York counties to send delegates to a provincial convention, convening on April 20, to elect delegates to the Second Continental Congress. In a sense each county and town was being asked to choose between loyalty to the Crown and the more radical policy of revolution and independence.[13] In Dutchess County, only the vote on this issue taken in Charlotte and Poughkeepsie precincts have survived. At its annual meeting, April 7, 1775, this vote was supervised by Cornelius Humphrey, Esq., who favored sending delegates, and Enos Northrup who was opposed. The resolution to send delegates was defeated soundly, 250 to 35.[14] But the outcome in Charlotte was not unique; only four of eleven precincts in Dutchess County, Amenia, Northeast, Rhinebeck, and Rumbout, voted to send delegates. At a meeting of those four precincts, Egbert Benson, Morris Graham, and Robert R. Livingston were chosen to represent Dutchess County. This questionable decision did not go unnoticed. One angry Dutchess County freeholder, noting Charlotte's rejection and referring to Poughkeepsie's vote of 110 to 77 against the resolution, questioned in his letter to a New York City newspaper the right of this minority to represent all of Dutchess County. Nevertheless, Dutchess County was represented.[15]

The vote in Charlotte is particularly interesting. The tax list compiled in 1775 lists 658 taxpayers. Individuals who didn't own taxable property were not recorded so the actual number of "freeholders and inhabitants" eligible to vote exceeds this number by as much as 30 percent.[16] Based on this, fewer than 40 percent of eligible voters made their point of view known by voting. What is important here is that about 60 percent of Charlotte's residents remained uncommitted. While some may have been lackadaisical, a great many others were simply neutral, defined by Edward Countryman as those "who avoided being mentioned in any of the political sources."[17] And in Poughkeepsie, despite its higher percentage of voters, at least four of ten chose to remain uncommitted. These findings and the fact that only four of eleven precincts voted in favor of sending representatives indicates that, like Charlotte, a great majority of individuals in Dutchess County were opposed, neutral, or simply unwilling to commit themselves. This conclusion is consistent with the outcome of the same vote on the same proposal taken at the same time in Queens County. There, only 12 percent supported the American cause, while fully 60 percent chose to remain neutral.[18] Incidentally in 1788, the delegations sent by both of these counties to Poughkeepsie were opposed to a federal constitution.

The election of town officials in Charlotte in April 1775 reflected an attitude of "business as usual." Despite Humphrey's obvious support of the American cause, he was elected town supervisor, a position he had held in 1773. Northrup, apparently loyal to Britain, was elected one of two assessors. He was also elected highway commissioner. Before the year closed Humphrey, becoming more deeply immersed in the revolutionary movement, prepared his mill for sale, and was elected to represent Dutchess County at the Provincial Congress in New York. At the town elections the following year Northrup was elected again as assessor.

In 1776, James Smith, Esq., was elected Town Supervisor. His three years experience in that position, 1768–1770, would serve him well during this period of tension. But a few months later, he was tarred and feathered for sentencing to jail a member of the Revolutionary Committee of Safety.[19] This followed on the heels of an armed skirmish in Charlotte between 150 Tories and a number of Dutchess County patriots, strengthened by 500 Connecticut militia.[20] Smith and other public officials from Charlotte, some of whom had been involved in the armed skirmish, did not serve their full term in office. They had been arrested by the patriots and sent to jail.[21] This incident stimulated the citizens of the precinct to take action at the next annual meeting held in April 1777. Incidentally, Enos Northrup, perhaps a loyalist but an inactive one, remained in town but never again held public office. His opponent, then Colonel Humphrey, served the town in several significant capacities after the war wound down in 1781, including town supervisor in 1786.[22]

The 1777 election saw the most dramatic change in government since Charlotte Precinct was established in 1762 or for that matter until well into the nineteenth century. The voters swept out of office every public official who served in 1776. The completely new slate was led by the newly elected supervisor, Ezra Thompson, a prosperous farmer who had held only one other public office previously, but in subsequent years became prominent in precinct politics. A decade later in 1788, he would be elected an Anti-Federalist delegate to the Constitutional Convention. The magnitude of the change in those who served in public office in Charlotte in 1777 is startling. All but two or three of the newly elected individuals were political newcomers, never having held a precinct office before. Even more significant is the fact that typically individuals, once elected, were likely to be reelected in the following year. Obviously, this was not the case in 1777. Also, 8 or 38 percent of the newly elected individuals or their sons were officers in one of the nine militia companies reported by Charlotte's Committee of Safety in September 1775, yet not one had been elected in 1776.[23] Not only had the voting inhabitants of Charlotte become politicized, but the events of 1776 seem to have swung their allegiance to one favorable to the Revolution. Unfortunately, how large was the group of inhabitants who continued to remain neutral is not known, the number of votes at annual meetings were never recorded. The following year, 1778, voters returned to office the highest percentage of public officials ever reelected; twenty of twenty-one incumbents were reelected.

In a span of just two years, the inhabitants of Charlotte had twice used their right to vote to affect the policy making body in the precinct—its public officials. While neutrality was an option chosen by about 60 percent of the inhabitants in 1775 and continued to be an option, presumably chosen by fewer people in 1777, voters had had it their way. They exercised their right to disagree. Even a particularly well-respected leader like Cornelius Humphrey could not persuade them. Nor were these important decisions reserved only for those who had "a stake in society," i.e., those who owned property of a certain minimum value or leaseholders who met a similar property test.[24] Property qualifications required to vote in colony-wide elections were, as Williamson pointed out, "seldom if ever the same as those for voting in local elections in Town."[25] All of Charlotte's "freeholders and inhabitants" were permitted to vote in town elections.

It was local conditions rather than colony-wide issues related to broad principles, such as universal suffrage or other related issues, which determined how people voted at the local level. What was important was maintaining a certain orderliness in the community. Incidents, such as the skirmish with the Tories in 1776, or issues, such as the vote in 1775 which might have led to a sudden decision to separate from Great Britain, threatened the sense of order and therefore were quickly defused when ordinary people raised their voices at the annual meetings. Following the dramatic results of the 1777 election and the equally dramatic reelection of 95 percent of the incumbents in 1778, Charlotte inhabitants returned to their more usual voting behavior. Except for electing new assessors, reflecting the new law which required nine instead of the usual two or three, about 60 percent of the incumbents were reelected in 1779. In subsequent years this percentage was even higher. Apparently, an acceptable order had returned to the community in 1778 and continued thereafter. Perhaps as Joseph Tiedemann so aptly put it, "traditional agricultural people . . . were more concerned with the soil, the weather, and the prospects for the next crop than debating the merits of Britain's imperial administration."[26]

If the voters in Charlotte were able to impose their will as effectively as they did in 1775, 1776, and 1777, would this access to power affect whom they would elect in subsequent years? More specifically, did the democratic principles which were central to the Revolutionary movement become manifest in town politics, i.e., did voters elect a greater number of individuals who were less affluent? To study this question, the tax lists were divided into five categories representing different levels of wealth based on the assessed value recorded therein. The percentage of individuals in each of five wealth categories is listed in Table 10.1. As one might expect there was an inverse relationship between assessed value and the number of individuals in each category. Next, the men who held public office and the assessed value of each during three periods, 1765–1768, 1775–1778, and 1786–1789, were examined. The assessed value in the first year of each of these periods was used to determine the relationship between wealth and the probability of holding public office and the relationship between wealth and the importance of the office held.

Additionally, public offices were divided in this study into two categories based on the degree of responsibility. In Category I were the supervisor, assessors (usually two or three, but in 1778 there were nine), commissioners of highways (usually three), and the town clerk. All of these officeholders, except the town clerk, were policy makers whose decisions affected the town at large and most of the individuals in it. The town clerk, primarily an administrative position, was included because of his close working relationship with this group and the likelihood he influenced their decisions. In Category II were the following lesser officeholders: a tax collector, four or five constables, two appraisers of interstate estates, two fenceviewers, two pound keepers, and two overseers of the poor.

Table 10.1. Percent of Taxpayers at Each Assessed Value

Assessed value (in pounds)	*1765*	*1775*	*1786*
1	32.9%	30.1%	31.0%
2	26.0	27.2	24.0
3-4	19.0	24.0	28.6
5-6	8.7	9.4	10.9
7+	13.5	9.3	4.8
	100.1%	100.0%	100.2%

As one might have expected, wealth in Charlotte and later in Clinton was not distributed evenly. Briefly stated, during the twenty-five-year period studied only about a quarter of the town's wealth, as reflected in the assessment rolls, was controlled by those on the lower half of the economic ladder, i.e., those assessed at £2 or under. In contrast, about 40 percent of the town's wealth was controlled by men in the upper 10–12 percent of the economic scale. The remaining one third of the town's wealth was held by the middle group, i.e., those assessed at £3 to £5. If representation in public office had been "democratic," it should have been apportioned in a similar manner. This, in fact, was not the case.

Even before discussing the issue of representation, it is important to note that public office was typically held by a very small number of individuals. As Table 10.2 shows, twenty-seven men were elected to the seventy-two town offices during the period 1765–1768. Many were reelected, and a few held several offices. Twenty years later, at the end of the Revolutionary period, the picture was essentially the same.

Table. 10.2. Officeholders Partitioned by Value of Assessment and Category of Office Held

Assessed value (in pounds)	*1765–1768* I	*1765–1768* II	*1775–1778* I	*1775–1778* II	*1786–1789* I	*1786–1789* II
1	0	1	0	7	0	4
2	0	2	0	1	1	4
3-4	0	3	7	6	3	3
5-6	2	2	11	2	3	3
7+	3	14	3	7	2	3
Unknown	0	0	0	3	0	3
	5	22	21	26	9	20
Number of offices in each category	16	56	35	55	33	56

NOTE: a) when two or more offices were held by the same man, only the principal office was placed in the category.
b) The names of Commissioners of Highways were not recorded until 1774.

But during the 1775–1778 period, this pattern was interrupted when forty-seven men were elected to ninety offices. Had public office become more accessible to a broader segment of the population during the early years of the Revolution? Actually not; it was the dramatic discharge from office in 1777 of every incumbent that accounted for almost all of the change during that period. In the following year and the subsequent years voters returned to their old habits. A few men were elected to all the public offices, many were reelected, and several were elected to two or more offices each year.

Regarding the issue of distribution of public office among the economic classes, the findings are clear. Table 10.3 shows that wealthy men in the community held a large number of the public offices throughout the entire 25-year period studied. Although there was a marked decline in their numbers over the years, the wealthy continued to be elected in numbers which far exceeded their numbers in town. However, despite an apparent trend towards more equitable distribution of public offices, substantial underrepresentation of those from the lower socio-economic group continued. This underrepresentation was even more pronounced when the importance of the office is taken into consideration. In the 1765–1768 period, three of the five men who held the sixteen most important offices in town (reelections included) were from the wealthy group. Twenty years later, this condition had not changed: nine men held the thirty-three most important offices during the 1786–1789 period and five of them were from the wealthiest group. Even more striking is the fact that during the entire twenty-five-year period only one man, Hugh Wildey, an ordinary farmer and veteran of the Revolution, served in an important office. Elected assessor in 1786, he was reelected each of the following three years.

Yet, one cannot overlook the gradual trend toward more egalitarian representation; a greater number of individuals from the middle and lower economic groups were able to attain public office after 1775. This trend, imperceptible in the most important offices, is apparent in the secondary offices. About 20 percent of these offices were held by men from the "lower order" after 1775 compared to ten percent during the earlier period. However, half of these men were elected to the office of town constable, probably regarded as the least prestigious office. But can even this change be attributed to newly developed interest in democracy brought about during the Revolution and the years which followed? Probably not. The trend toward broader representation had already begun in the late 1760s and it crystallized in the early 1770s. For example, during the period 1772–1775 37 men

Table 10.3. Percent of Public Offices Held by Wealthy Men

Period	*Number of Offices*	*Number of Men Elected*	*Percent Held by the Wealthiest 15 Percent*
1765-1768	72	27	63%
1772-1775	79	37	48
1775-1778	90	47	34
1786-1789	89	29	38

were elected to seventy-nine offices. Of these only half were men from the wealthier group compared to 63 percent during the 1765–1768 period.

As Table 10.3 shows, a greater number of men were elected to public office during the 1770s than had been elected during the 1760s or the 1780s. Clearly, during the 1770s there was dissatisfaction. In 1773, four years before the clean sweep in 1777, three of every four incumbents were not reelected. Although the extant records shed no qualitative light on this election, the matter, whatever it was, also colored elections in 1774 and 1775. In those elections only about 45 percent of the incumbents were reelected. While it would be some time before a consistent reelection rate of about 75 percent evident from 1765 to 1772 would return, the election in 1776 returned 62 percent of the incumbents to office. Except for the debacle in 1777 and its reversal in 1778, reelection rates were closer to 65 to 75 percent in the years which followed than to the 27 percent noted in 1773. While these years were marked by high inflation, call to duty of men in the militia, profiteering by a few, and other such wartime ills, elections in Charlotte were uneventful. Men who served in local office were not seen as responsible for these conditions, nor did the inhabitants choose to vent their frustrations about the war and its effects at their public officials.

Thirteen years after the issue of independence was initially considered in 1775, the people of Charlotte and Dutchess County were again presented with a broad issue to vote on, the ratification of the Constitution. And once again voters were neutral or indifferent, though those who did vote strongly opposed ratification. In Dutchess County fewer than 2,700 votes were cast, about one third of the total electorate of 8,000.[27] Nor was this unenthusiastic response unique to Dutchess County. Alfred Young, comparing the number of voters in 1775 and in 1788, demonstrated voting turnout in New York was lighter than one might have expected.[28]

Again in 1788 and 1789 inhabitants in Clinton focused more on conditions immediately relevant to their lives. Because local controversy was absent, these elections, contrary to those in 1776 and 1777, were uneventful. The reelection rate was 75 percent, and men were elected to town offices regardless of their obvious differences about the Constitution. Anti-Federalist Cornelius Humphrey was elected to the position of inspector (overseer of the town meeting) in 1788 at the same time that Federalist Richard D'Cantilion was elected town supervisor. At the state level Clinton resident John De Witt, an Anti-Federalist, served in the New York Assembly in that year and the next. And during this time Cornelius Humphrey served his Dutchess County constituency as state senator.

What conclusions can be drawn? There are several:

1. Many voters in Charlotte and Dutchess County chose to remain uncommitted regarding significant issues in 1775 and again in 1788.
2. Voters in Charlotte were not adverse to discharging incumbents from office when a significant issue of local importance stirred them.
3. Contrary to general belief, the change to broader or more democratic representation in public office had already begun to evolve prior to the Revolution.
4. Men of wealth were favored with elective office significantly more frequently than

those of lesser means before, during, and after the Revolution.

5. Elected office did become more available to men from the lowest economic group during the 1770s, but it was primarily secondary offices which were attainable.
6. The number of different individuals elected to public office increased during the Revolutionary era during periods of dissatisfaction, but when dissatisfaction was not evident the electorate typically elected men from a small pool of individuals.
7. And finally, in Charlotte/Clinton it was local conditions which appear to have affected elections rather than issues of general political, social, or economic magnitude.

Was the struggle between classes a principal issue at the polls during the Revolutionary era? To be sure, antagonism did exist between the classes, and between some tenants and landlords, it was intense. The tenant uprising on Livingston Manor in 1777 is a good example of dissatisfaction which festered well before the Revolution.[29] But this struggle was not necessarily representative of all of the mid-Hudson Valley. Nor did it necessarily intrude in local politics. In fact, it may not have characterized the politics of freehold settlements at all. Charlotte Precinct is a case in point. Primarily a freehold, its political atmosphere, if its elections are a credible measure, was often indifferent, focused on local conditions, and interested in maintaining the status quo locally.

That is not to say in Charlotte or in the rest of Dutchess County there was no interest in broader political issues during the Revolutionary era. Both sides of issues such as independence at the start of the Revolutionary period, and the ratification of the constitution at its end were represented when county-wide votes were taken. But on home ground inhabitants were essentially satisfied to vote for men they had always elected regardless of their stand on the broader issues: men who had achieved status in the community. Many of the men elected to public office in Charlotte were successful merchants or large landowners who operated farms worked, one might assume, by "hired men." But these men, although wealthy relative to the rest of the inhabitants, were not, nor had they ever been, nor were they likely to join the ranks of the super-rich of the sort spoken of in discussions regarding the land rich aristocracy in the mid-Hudson Valley. In fact, in all of Dutchess County only twenty-eight men were assessed at £20 or higher, and fewer than 100 were assessed more than £12 in 1775. Of the 3,950 individuals whose names appeared on the tax lists only Henry Beekman of Rhinebeck, assessed at £265; Beverly Robinson of Philipstown, assessed at £70; David Johnson of Charlotte, assessed at £50; and perhaps a dozen others assessed at £35 or higher could be considered super-rich. Typically, these men did not hold local office.

Struggle for control based on class conflict was not evident at the ballot box in local elections. Certainly, men of wealth were elected to local office considerably more frequently than those of lesser means, not only in Charlotte Precinct but in other precincts in Dutchess County. This was also the case in similar towns in Massachusetts. Towns like Amherst and Weston elected men of wealth more frequently, particularly to the principal town offices. It was "proper" to elect this kind of men, and as Patricia Bonomi observed, the "better sort" continued to be chosen for political office forty years after the Revolutionary period. Ordinary people believed elective office had been earned by and was reserved for men of status and dignity. Seeing through our 20th-century eyes and minds it is difficult to conceive this was the prevailing attitude. But the concept of equality at that time was still only a fresh breeze, yet to be appreciated. As J.R. Pole so aptly put it, "Deference, it does not seem, in retrospect, is a very secure cement to the union of social orders. Yet to those who live under its sway it can be almost irresistible." Even Melancton Smith, regarded at the Constitutional Convention as the spokesman for the common man, acknowledged the power of deference. "Will anyone say that there does not exist in this country the pride of family, of wealth, of talents, and that they do not command respect among the common people." But as Pole further points out, men were willing to accept their lot, even when it meant accepting less than universal suffrage, because they, too, expected to advance to loftier heights one day.[30]

This article originally appeared in the *Hudson Valley Regional Review*, Volume 6.2, September 1989.

NOTES

1. Franklin D. Roosevelt, ed., *Records of Crum Elbow Precinct, Dutchess County, New York. . . . Town of Clinton, 1738–1799, Collections of the Dutchess County Historical Society* (Poughkeepsie: D.C.H.S. 1940), Vol. 7 (1940), 73, 74, 76, 77, 120.
2. *Minutes of the Committee and of the First Commission for Detecting and Defeating Conspiracies in the State of New York, 1776–1778, Collections of the New York Historical Society* (New York: N.Y.H.S. 1924–25), Vol. 1 (1924), 3–4.
3. Robert Livingston to Gilbert Livingston, November 22, 1786, cited in Staughton Lynd, *Anti-Federalism in Dutchess County, New York: A Study of democracy and class conflict in the Revolutionary Era* (Chicago: Loyola University Press, 1962), 106.
4. *Commission for Detecting Conspiracies,* Vol. 1, (1924), p. 228 and 291; Vol. 2 (1925), 392.
5. Edward Countryman, *A People in Revolution: The American Revolution and Political Society in New York, 1760–1790,* (Baltimore: Johns Hopkins University Press, 1981), 103.
6. Staughton Lynd, "Who Should Rule at Home? Dutchess County New York, in the American Revolution," *William & Mary Quarterly*, Ser. 3, Vol. 18 (1961), p. 331 and 356; Lynd, *Anti-Federalism,* 3.
7. Robert E. Brown, *Middle-Class Democracy and the Revolution in Massachusetts, 1691–1780* (Ithaca: Cornell University Press, 1955), 19.
8. A review of these policies can be found in Edmund S. Morgan, *The Birth of the Republic, 1763–1789* (Chicago: University, 1956), chapters 2, 3, and 4.
9. Countryman, *A People in Revolution,* chapter 4.
10. Edmund S. Morgan, "The American Revolution: Revisions in Need of Revising," *William & Mary Quarterly*, 3rd Ser., 14 (1957), 14 and 15.
11. Dutchess County Tax Lists, 1757–1779, 1786, Adriance Memorial Library, Poughkeepsie.
12. *Records of Crum Elbow*, 67–124.
13. Carl Becker, *The History of Political Parties in the Province of New York, 1760–1766* (Madison: University of Wisconsin Press, 1909, reprint 1960), 176–87.
14. The vote was actually 140–35, but another 110 inhabitants who intended to vote against the resolution arrived at the polls too late to vote. Peter Force, *American Archives: A Documentary History of the English Colonies in North America* (Washington: M. St. Clair and Peter Force, 1839), Fourth Series, Vol. II, 304.
15. "Protest of the Freeholders of Seven Precincts in Dutchess County, New York." Shortly thereafter on May 1, 1775, the validity of this protest was questioned by another Dutchess County freeholder, who challenged the initial letter writer to obtain 600 signatures to support his protest. He indicated that of the 1,800 freeholders in Dutchess County, he could obtain 1,200 signatures from those who would agree to send delegates. Force, Fourth Series, Vol. II, p. 304; *Calendar of Historical Manuscripts relating to the War of the Revolution,* 2 vols. (Albany: Weed, Parsons and Co., 1868), Vol. 1, 41.
16. William P. McDermott, "Settlement and

Settlers," in William P. McDermott, ed., *Clinton, Dutchess County, N. Y.: A History of a Town* (Clinton Corners, New York: Clinton Historical Society, 1987), 31–32.

17. Countryman, *A People in Revolution,* 118.
18. Joseph S. Tiedemann, "Communities in the Midst of the American Revolution: Queens County, New York, 1774–1775," *Journal of Social History,* 18 (1984), 58.
19. Force, *American Archives,* Fifth Series, Vol. III, 457–58.
20. Philip Ranlet, *The New York Loyalists* (Knoxville: University of Tennessee, 1986), 143; Force Fifth Series, Vol. I, 1408n, 360.
21. *Commission for Detecting Conspiracies,* Vol. I, 3 and 4.
22. *Records of Crum Elbow,* passim.
23. Force, Fourth Series, Vol. III, 653.
24. *The Colonial Laws of New York from the Year 1664 to the Revolution,* 5 vols. (Albany: James B. Lyon, 1894–1896), Vol. I, Chap. 74 and 94, 407 and 453.
25. Chilton Williamson, *American Suffrage from Property to Democracy, 1760–1860* (Princeton: Princeton University Press, 1960), 16; see also 26–29.
26. Tiedemann, "Communities in the Midst," 69.
27. *Country Journal,* June 3, 1788. In 1790 there were 10,968 males over 16 years of age in Dutchess County. Using the 75 percent to 80 percent rule regarding ratio of males over 21 years to total number of males produces an electorate of over 8,000. Also it should be noted that shortly before the election, provisions had been made for universal male suffrage on this issue. Furthermore, a secret ballot and voting places located in each precinct provided the broadest opportunity to vote. *Heads of Families at the First Census of the United States in the Year 1790* (Washington: Government Printing Office, 1909); Lynd, *Anti-Federalism,* 18.
28. Alfred Young, *The Democratic Republicans of New York: The Origins, 1763–1797* (Chapel Hill: University of North Carolina Press, 1967), 92.
29. Staughton Lynd, "The Tenant Rising at Livingston Manor, May, 1777," *New York Historical Society Quarterly,* Vol. 48 (1964), 163–77.
30. Dirk Hoerder, "Society and Government 1760–1780: The Power Structure in Massachusetts Townships," John F. Kennedy Institute, Free University, Berlin, FRG, 1972), 23–31; J.R. Pole, "Historians and the Problem of Early American Democracy," *American Historical Review,* vol. 67 (1962), pp. 642 and 646; Jonathan Elliot, ed. *The Debates in the Several State Conventions, on the Adoption of the Federal Constitution . . .* 5 Vols. (Washington: 1854), II, 245 and 246, as cited in Young, *The Democratic Republicans,* p. 96; Patricia U. Bonomi, "Revisiting The American Revolution as a Social Movement," *Reviews in American History,* Vol. 10, (1982), 339.

11

"The women! in this place have risen in a mob"

Women Rioters and the American Revolution in the Hudson River Valley

THOMAS S. WERMUTH

HISTORIANS HAVE LONG ASSESSED the role of women as participants in pre-industrial riots. One of the most famous of these, of course, was the 1789 "March of the Fishwives" at the beginning of the French Revolution. The 1863 Confederate Bread Riots are another example. Less attention has been given to the role of women in American Revolutionary riots.[1] This chapter examines the important role of Hudson Valley women in the crowd actions that characterized that era.

From the beginning of the war through the late 1770s, popular disturbances and crowd actions became a part of the social landscape in the Hudson Valley. Usually aimed at Tories, many of these actions were sanctioned, or at least tolerated, by the local governments or the popular committees that directed Revolutionary activities.

Crowd actions were not peculiar to the Revolutionary period, nor were they specific to this region. Indeed, as historians like Natalie Davis, George Rude, and E.P. Thompson have pointed out, mass disturbances and riots were seen as acceptable resolutions to a community's social or economic problems in the early modern period.[2] Throughout the eighteenth century, crowds engaged in popular action served as quasi-official forces, sometimes with authority delegated by local governments, sometimes without. For example, in 1740, a Kingston "delegation" investigating an ongoing boundary dispute between Johannis Wynkoop and Christian Nedick was given the authority to "pull down his Fence" if "Wynkoop did not comply w/the proposition they make to him." Others who threatened community standards, such as monopolizers or prostitutes, were threatened with "skimmington rides" and "charivaris" in Poughkeepsie, while residents representing more dangerous threats in Kingston and Saugerties witnessed the destruction of their property.[3]

These actions conform to the model described by historians of popular protest: a group of community residents act with "quasi-official" authority to address and redress a problem threatening their town or village. Classic examples of this in early America include crowds harassing price-gouging merchants, press gangs, or prostitutes.[4]

The number of such crowd actions increased substantially during the American Revolutionary period. This was true for several reasons. First, the official government was in disarray, leading townsfolk to take matters into their own hands more frequently than would have been the case under normal conditions. Second, the Revolution created a series of problems and threats—political, social, and economic—that had not existed earlier and that needed speedy resolution, and which official authorities seemed unable to resolve.

Some of the crowd actions were clearly political, as with the arrest of Loyalist Cadwallader Colden Jr., son of the former acting governor, at his home near Newburgh. Acting on the

Fig. 11.1. William Hogarth's depiction of a riot in eighteenth-century England.

authority of the local Committee of Safety, a "delegation" stormed his estate at midnight on June 21, 1776. The group searched and ransacked his house and ordered him arrested. Although the raiding party threatened him with the humiliating possibility that he would "be rode upon a rail" to the local jail if he did not accompany them willingly (a punishment traditionally reserved for prostitutes, wife abusers, or other community miscreants), he was ultimately arrested far less dramatically. Nevertheless, to threaten one of the most substantial men in the mid-Valley with such a fate—and Colden's apparent belief that the committee would make good on their threat—reveals the extent of the challenge to the existing social and political order.[5]

Shortly before the British invasion of New York City, crowds there seized Tories, rode them on rails, and stripped them of their clothes. In Albany, crowds made suspected Loyalists run a gauntlet, beating them as they ran.[6] Riots of this nature, aimed primarily at Tories, continued throughout the war.

Many other popular disturbances were not so well coordinated with local authorities and were aimed, not at Loyalists, but at resolving social and economic threats to the community. It is important to keep in mind the social and economic context in which these riots occurred. The day-to-day workings of village economies in the Hudson Valley were not left to the vagaries of the free market. Local town governments, as well as New York provincial authorities, enforced formal legislation or exerted informal community pressures that sought to encourage neighborly behavior and discourage any economic actions that might threaten the corporate body of the community. Old medieval injunctions against forestalling (withholding goods from the market in order to drive up prices) and engrossment (the monopolization of products destined for markets) remained on the law books throughout New York, although before the American Revolution they were irregularly enforced.[7]

Regulation of the local economy relied heavily on the force of community tradition. Where informal means proved insufficient, responsibility for balancing competing economic interests fell to the local governing boards. These policies generally reflected the communities' consensus of the primary importance of fostering a healthy agricultural trade. Nevertheless, local regulations—whether of prices, trading practices, or quality standards—were shaped as much by broad community concerns as by a desire to protect the interests of producers.

The government regulation that began with the original acts of incorporation in the seventeenth century carried into the early nineteenth. The charter of Kingston called for a public market, eventually located at Hendrick Sleght's, where the weights and measures were inspected, sellers and butchers licensed, financial exchanges supervised, flour and meat routinely inspected, and prices on various goods capped.[8] The towns of New Paltz and New Windsor set maximum prices on bread and salt, among other goods, and scrutinized wages as well. The regulation of prices and quality of goods continued well into the early nineteenth century in Kingston and Poughkeepsie, where the "assize of bread" was regularly posted. The assize listed the price and size of the normal loaf, and set these prices according to the price of local flour. It also ordered that "each loaf shall be marked with the initials of the Christian and surname of the baker."[9]

The Corporation of Kingston also kept wheat on hand in the common store for local use, with limits on the amount one could purchase, a ceiling on prices, and instructions for its use. This wheat, rye, and "indian corn" was sold at a further reduced rate to poorer residents, so long as it was to be used "for Bread" and not sold.[10] The trustees also regulated interest rates for money put out on loan, with six percent the maximum allowed to be charged within the town. Additionally, no more than five percent could be charged to the town's poor or to freeholders, but seven percent could be "Lett out upon Interest out of the Corporation." The trustees also lent money, usually to the poor or freeholders. However, the corporation mandated that "such persons as are able to let money out themselves, shall not have it unless they pay 8%."[11]

Thus social settings, personal relations, family and personal reputation, and even economic needs and demands that could not be met through commercial markets helped determine proper economic behavior.

During the economic crisis of the Revolution, shortages of necessary items (particularly bread and salt) were blamed on "ingrossing jockies," and high prices were believed to be the work of price-gouging merchants. As early as 1776, residents of Kingston and New Windsor took matters into their own hands when they felt that their elected officials were not going far enough in regulating the economy and prosecuting monopolizers.[12] The Ulster County Committee reported in 1776 that "we are daily alarmed, and our streets filled with mobs." According to the committee, the situation had grown so desperate in Ulster that if the legislature could not solve the economic woes affecting the central valley, local committees would have to assume authority in the name "of the People at Large."[13] Kingston's Johannes Sleght appealed to the Provincial Congress for help, declaring that "mobs" were "breaking of doors, and committing of outrages."[14]

The years 1776 through 1779 witnessed regular boycotts, forced sales of necessary products, and riots in the mid-Hudson Valley. Many of the participants in these riots were women. The first of these occurred in Kingston in November 1776, when a crowd raided warehouses and stores, seizing tea. Two weeks later, one of Orange county's first families, the Ellisons of New Windsor, were the victims of a riot. A large crowd, composed of both men and women, came to William Ellison's store, and after accusing him of price-gouging and engrossment, it seized all the salt "except one bushel," which it left for the use of his family.[15]

Poughkeepsie-area shopkeeper Peter Messier suffered a crowd action in early 1777. Claiming that he was selling tea above the Poughkeepsie Committee's imposed price-cap, a crowd of women used their own weights and measures to weigh and distribute the tea among themselves. The women, accompanied by two Continental soldiers, offered Messier "their own price," which was considerably lower than his selling price.[16] The women returned twice more over the next several days to repeat these actions.

Two Albany merchants who had purchased tea in Philadelphia had the misfortune of sending it overland through New Windsor in 1777. A crowd of both "men and women" besieged the transporters and seized the load, asserting that it was being marketed at a higher price than the six-shilling limit set by the local committee. They then sold it to themselves at that price.

The New Windsor and Poughkeepsie riots reveal that the rioters drew upon the legitimacy of the local government in order to explain their own activities. The rioters at Ellison's store reminded the shopkeeper of the committee's price regulations, which he was allegedly breaking. The women who confiscated Messier's tea specifically stated that "they had orders from the Committee to search his house." However, it is important to point out that in each of these actions, the rioters exceeded the committee's dictates. Neither riot was authorized by the local authorities.[17]

The actions of the rioters in seizing foodstuffs reveal traditional economic beliefs that denied the role of an unregulated market during times of economic crisis. Further, these rioters questioned the very essence of private property when they seized goods, making clear their belief that a shopkeeper was not the only person who could decide what to do with his or her merchandise, and that the community had a legitimate voice in its distribution. What is remarkable is that during the Revolutionary War, these beliefs and activities became associated, even synonymous, with patriotic behavior. Those who participated in the riots claimed that by their actions they were revealing their loyalty to the cause, while their targets, such as William Ellison, were exhibiting signs of Toryism.[18]

Also remarkable is that many of the rioters were women, who had no public or political role in the mid-Valley at this time, for voting, jury duty, and even unlimited control over property were denied to them. However, during the Revolution, women often took the lead in Hudson Valley riots. It was a crowd of women, for example, who first confronted New Windsor shopkeeper Mrs. Lawrence in 1777 for price-gouging, and by so doing forced the committee to act. At another riot in New Windsor, a local observer complained to a tea merchant that "the women! in this place have risen in a mob, and are now selling a box of tea of yours [the owner] at 6s per lb." A store in Fishkill was raided by female relatives of the owner.[19]

The action of women in relation to economic controls was not limited only to seizures and crowd action. Women also made it clear that they would use their power as wives and mothers to halt the war effort if certain measures were not taken to regulate the economy. In August 1776, the women of Kingston surrounded the chambers of the Committee of Safety and demanded that if the food shortages were not resolved, "their husbands and sons shall fight no more."[20] In this way, these riots were not only protests against the economy; they had clear political implications as well. The site of the women's action was not the Kingston public market, nor a shopkeeper's warehouse, but the meeting house of the town's political authorities. It was not simply a symbolic location for the women to make their statement: it was the place where policy-makers met. And far from making threats of boycotts or disruptions, these women were warning of political action if their demands were not met.

Women tended to exert a public voice around those issues in which the needs of the domestic sphere crossed those of the public. The ability to get salt, tea, or flour at good prices fell firmly within the socially and culturally constructed gender roles of eighteenth-century America. Like their counterparts in the French Revolution, women's political action usually formed around issues of family and domestic concerns, particularly food and supplies.[21]

Generally, historians have agreed that women's participation in bread and food riots was based on their socially constructed gender roles as being responsible for providing food for their children. Also, as Natalie Davis has suggested for early modern France, women's participation could be excused by the fact that they were not viewed as responsible for their actions, and therefore could not be held accountable for their behavior. Since a riot was, at best, of questionable legality, those with limited legal and political roles could not be held fully responsible. English officials complained during the 1605 enclosure riots that women were "hiding behind their sex."[22]

Nevertheless, as E.P. Thompson has pointed out, women were primarily responsible for marketing, most sensitive to price fluctuations, and more likely to detect irregularities in sales or inferior products.[23] Women, therefore, would probably detect subtle price changes or questionable marketing practices and were more likely to act on them.

The involvement of women in food riots reveals a level of public participation often overlooked by traditional histories of the American Revolution. Although women did not actively take part on the battlefield, they were involved in important economic decisions concerning the just allocation and availability of goods at affordable prices. Further, their actions had clear political significance: when they could not obtain the necessary goods and items for the home, they threatened the ability of authorities to wage war. In this way, the actions of women-led crowds were not peripheral to the Revolution, but must be seen as an important component of wartime activities.

This article originally appeared in *The Hudson River Valley Review*, Volume 20.1, summer, 2003.

NOTES

1. For a useful corrective, see Barbara Clark Smith, "Food Riots and the American Revolution," *William & Mary Quarterly* (1994), 3–30.
2. Natalie Davis, *Society and Culture in Early Modern France* (Stanford, 1975), 102–05; George Rude, *Ideology and Popular Protest* (New York, 1980), 27–37; E.P. Thompson, *Customs in Common* (New York, 1993), 185–89.
3. "Kingston Trustees Minutes," May 14, 1740; 1721.
4. Gary Nash, *The Urban Crucible: Social Change, Political Consciousness, and the Origins of the American Revolution* (Cambridge, Mass., 1979), 77–78; Edward Countryman, *A People in Revolution: The American Revolution and Political Society in New York, 1760–1790* (Baltimore, 1981), 37–45.
5. Cadwallader Colden Jr. to Ulster County Committee, June 27, 1776, in Force, *American Archives* 6:1112
6. Countryman, 170.
7. Ibid., 56–59.
8. "Kingston Trustees Minutes," July 27, 1753, describes the market at Hendrick Sleght's. Petrus Smedes was appointed the "first manager of the market." See "Kingston Trustees Minutes," Oct. 19, 1753 and Jan. 29, 1790, Ulster County Clerk's Office, for various aspects of market supervision.
9. "Kingston Trustees Minutes," Apr. 12, 1779, U.C.C.O.; "Kingston Directors Minutes," Apr. 20, 1807, and May 14, 1819, Kingston City Hall; Edmund Platt, *The Eagle's History of Poughkeepsie, 1683–1905* (Republished by Dutchess County Historical Society, Poughkeepsie, N.Y., 1987), 75.
10. For price ceilings on corporation wheat, see "Kingston Trustees Minutes," Mar. 22, 1772; Feb. 6, 1785; Jan. 29, 1790. For restrictions on its use, see Feb. 19, 1790, U.C.C.O.
11. For regulation of usury see "Kingston Trustees Minutes," Mar. 2, 1728, New-York Historical Society. This rate was reduced to five percent in 1750, but raised back to six percent in 1752. "Kingston Trustees Minutes," Dec. 10, 1750; Nov. 8, 1752, U.C.C.O. "Trustees Minutes," Mar. 2, 1728, NYHS.

12. Henry Ludington to New York Council of Safety, Dec. 3, 1776, *Journals of the Provincial Congress*, 2:355.
13. "Ulster County Committee to New York Convention," Nov. 18, 1776, *Journals of the Provincial Congress*, 2:229–30.
14. Clark Smith, "Food Riots and the American Revolution," *William & Mary Quarterly*, 15.
15. Ibid.
16. Correspondence of John Hathorn, Dec. 2, 1776 in Ruttenber, *History of New Windsor*, 67–68; Countryman, 183.
17. Correspondence of John Hathorn, Dec. 2, 1776 in Ruttenber, *History of New Windsor*, 67.
18. For a discussion of the political implications of Revolutionary rioting, see Clark Smith, 5–12. For suspicions that Ellison was unpatriotic because of his economic dealings, see "Boyd to Clinton, July 3, 1776," *Public Papers of George Clinton*, 10 vols. (Albany, 1899–1914), 1:244–47.
19. James H. Kip to James Caldwell, New Windsor, July 14, 1777, *Journals of the Provincial Congress*, 506; Clark Smith.
20. New York Convention Proceedings, Aug. 1776, in *American Archives*, 5th Series, 1:1542–43.
21. Linda Kerber, *Women of the Republic: Intellect and Ideology in Revolutionary America* (New York, 1980), 44.
22. Davis, 146.
23. Thompson, 234.

12

Three Officers and a Lady

The Hudson Highlands and Georgia During the Revolution

EDWARD J. CASHIN

THE THREE OFFICERS in our title are General Nathanael Greene, General Anthony Wayne, and Lieutenant Colonel Henry "Light-Horse Harry" Lee. The lady is the beautiful and charming Catherine Greene, known to her friends as Caty (which we shall call her). A proper drama has a stage setting, and for the first act, the stage is the majestic Hudson River Valley, the historic pathway of nations, acknowledged by everyone as the key to the continent. For the second act, the stage is messy rather than majestic—the southern backcountry, ignored by many historians and a puzzle to most.

To give away the ending, the plot is that the campaign to win control of the Hudson Valley was determined in the southern backcountry.

By 1779, the British thrust aimed at the Hudson Valley had been frustrated at Saratoga, and a British expeditionary force had overrun Georgia and restored royal rule to that state, the only state to revert to colonial status. General Sir Henry Clinton's army occupied New York and continued to have designs on the great waterway. In order to sever Washington's lifeline across the Hudson at King's Ferry, the British occupied and fortified Stony Point and Verplanck's Point—at either side of the crossing—on June 1, 1779.

Washington hurried from his camp at Middlebrook, New Jersey, to meet the threat, moving by way of Smith's Clove. Nathanael Greene, Washington's trusted Quartermaster General, wrote to Caty on June 9: "We were yesterday down to West Point through all the Highlands. A rougher country nature never formed." Washington made his headquarters at New Windsor and immediately began to plan an attack on Stony Point. He commissioned Major Henry Lee, with his mounted troop, to reconnoiter. Lee's troops secured the area, and Lee himself crept so close to the British fortifications that he could hear the sentries pacing along the stone ramparts. Lee employed a civilian spy to get inside the fort and count the garrison. He reported 772 soldiers and eleven pieces of artillery.

On June 15, Washington ordered Anthony Wayne to march with his light infantry under absolute secrecy. The men had no idea of their destination as they marched from Fort Montgomery, around Bear Mountain, and through the ravines of the Dunderberg.

On the evening of June 17, Wayne halted at the Springsteel farm, two miles west of Stony Point, and gave strict orders that the fort would be taken by surprise and by bayonet, no shots fired. At 11 p.m., the men swarmed up both sides of the steep slopes and gained a quick victory. Wayne sent the message to Washington, "The fort and garrison with Col. Johnson are ours. Our officers and men behaved like men who are determined to be free."

Greene wrote to Caty, "Never did men or officers behave with more spirit. They deserve immortal honor." It did not matter that the Americans abandoned Stony Point two days

GENERAL WAYNE.[1]

after taking it. The victory was a great boost to morale, and Congress voted medals for Wayne and his principal officers.

On July 26, Washington called a council of officers to West Point to tell them that the enemy had reoccupied Stony Point and reinforced Verplanck's Point. He asked for advice on strategy. Greene wrote his opinion, "The North River I consider as the first object upon the Continent and the communication between the Eastern and Western States essential to the Independence of America." He cautioned against a risky offensive against New York.

Although Congress had overlooked Light-Horse Harry's role at Stony Point, Washington did not. He unleashed Lee's mounted troop to do whatever damage they could. On the Hudson across from Staten Island, a British garrison occupied a narrow finger of land called Paulus Hook. British warships anchored in the bay provided protection. On August 18, Lee staged a risky night assault on Paulus Hook and took the fort without firing a shot. Greene enthused to Caty, "Major Lee has performed a most gallant affair. He has surprised and taken the greater part of the garrison at Paulus Hook. The expedition is thought to be more gallant than Stony Point."

Fig. 12.1. Nathanael Greene, Anthony Wayne, and Henry "Light-Horse Harry" Lee. Pen and ink drawings reproduced from *Pictorial Field Book of the Revolution*, in Two Volumes; Benson J. Lossing, Harper & Brothers, New York, 1850.

Fig. 12.2. Map of Stony Point and Verplank's Point Fortifications.

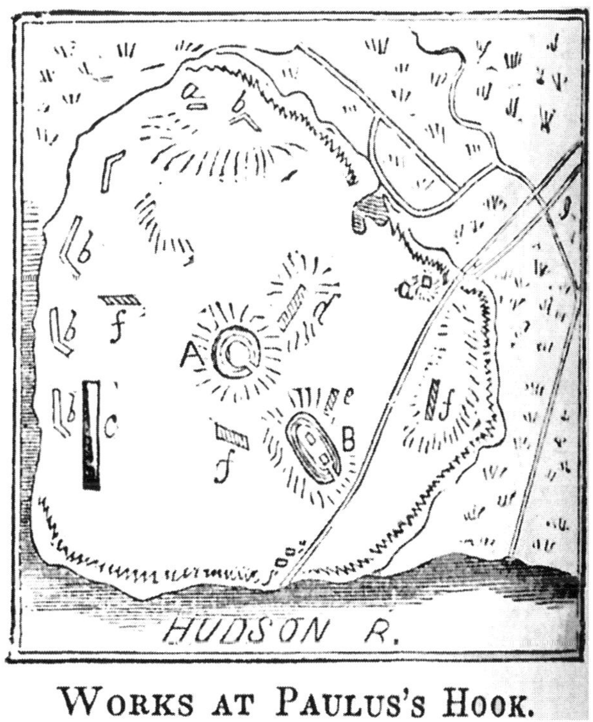

Fig. 12.3. The Works at Paulus Hook.

On September 26, Washington at New Windsor informed Greene at West Point that a French army under Count d'Estaing approached. Greene should prepare barges for a joint attack on New York. Greene engaged carpenters at Fishkill to begin building boats. He wrote Caty on October 15, "We are in daily expectation of the arrival of Count d'Estaing and the moment he arrives offensive operations will commence against New York." Unknown to Greene—and to Washington—d'Estaing had decided to attack British-held Savannah rather than New York. After a prolonged siege, d'Estaing's French forces and General Benjamin Lincoln's Americans staged a grand assault on the British lines on October 8 but failed to break the lines. Polish volunteer Count Casimir Pulaski was among the dead. The battered French army could do no fighting in New York.

The British success in Georgia caused Sir Henry Clinton in New York to shift the focus of his operations from the Hudson Valley to the South. He recalled the garrisons from Stony Point and Verplanck's Point for a major expedition against Charleston, South Carolina. Washington learned of the French defeat at Savannah only on November 15, more than a month after the battle. But not until Clinton's transports left New York on December 26 did he abandon his planned attack on New York, and only then did Greene stop building boats. While the British landed in Georgia and proceeded to besiege Charleston, Washington's army went into winter quarters at Morristown, New Jersey, leaving a strong garrison at West Point.

Caty Greene joined her husband at West Point and went with him to Morristown. (Winter encampments were notoriously miserable for the foot soldiers, but the best times of the war for officers' wives.) Caty was especially close to Martha Washington and Lucy Knox, the vivacious wife of Major General Henry Knox, commander of the Continental Army's artillery. She had met both at the first winter encampment, at Valley Forge, in 1777. There, Caty and Nathanael had occupied a large house that quickly became a social rendezvous. She had learned French well enough to charm and make a lasting friend of Lafayette. She would later send her first son, George Washington Greene, to be educated in France under his care. Anthony Wayne was so smitten with Caty that he seemed to forget that he had a wife back in Philadelphia.

The second camp, at Middlebrook, in the winter of 1778 followed the example of the first. Washington had insisted that Caty join them and bring her three children. (She had intended to do so, anyhow.) She came by way of Peekskill and King's Ferry. The Greene's house again became an oasis of cheer in an otherwise grim winter. Wayne put in an early appearance, bringing his friend, Henry Lee. Caty's biographer wrote that "'Light-Horse Harry' was a man of such dash and verve, and so splendidly uniformed—that Caty had picked him out as the kind of soldier little girls dream of." Caty, a consummate flirt, charmed him, too.

Greene's twenty-five-year-old wife loved dancing. As it happened, so did George Washington. And they particularly enjoyed dancing with each other. While encamped at Middlebrook, Washington bet Caty that he could outlast her on the dance floor. She took the bet. The good-natured Nathanael reported to a friend, "They danced upward of three hours without once sitting down."

So it is understandable that Caty wanted to accompany her husband to the camp at Morristown in 1779, even though she was seven months pregnant. The solicitous Nathanael ordered a quarter cask of Madeira "as Mrs. Greene has nothing to drink." In the midst of his demanding duties as quartermaster, he found time to ask a subordinate to trace some of Caty's belongings that had gotten lost along the way: "Mrs. Greene is anxious about her bandbox." Caty gave birth to Nathanael Ray Greene on January 31 and quickly recovered her health, her figure, and her role as social arbiter.

Since we are not above indulging in gossip, we will mention a scene Caty thought scandalous at one of her Morristown parties. It seemed that George Olney, a relative of Nathanael's, disapproved of drinking. He withdrew from the men's company and joined the ladies, showing his displeasure. The men took notice and suggested that they capture Olney away from the women and make him take a drink. Washington entered into the spirit of the moment and led the charge into the ladies' chambers. Olney, who seemed not to have had much of a sense of humor, resisted. His wife, with even less of a sense of humor, clung desperately to him. Washington playfully took her hand away from her husband. In a rage she screamed, "Let go of my hand, or I'll pull every hair out of your head!" That ended the gaiety. Caty was furious at Mrs. Olney for insulting her friend the commander and for ruining the party.

The return of Clinton's army from the South prompted a return of Washington's army to the Hudson Highlands. The British had taken Charleston, and resistance collapsed all over the Carolinas and Georgia. Leaving Lieutenant General Charles Cornwallis in command of an army of occupation, Clinton returned to New York. He had not abandoned his designs on West Point, even though in June 1780 he staged a diversionary raid into New Jersey that was repulsed by Greene and Wayne. Clinton's real strategy would soon become evident.

On August 14, Greene wrote Caty that he had resigned his commission as quartermaster. Since he was out of a job, he added: "let me conjure you by the bonds of affection—to contract your expenses as much as possible." He confessed that he was discouraged by his critics in Congress. He received a sympathetic letter from General Benedict Arnold, then in command of West Point, who nursed his own grievances against Congress. Greene responded with the news that Horatio Gates, Arnold's old rival at Saratoga, had been disastrously defeated by Cornwallis at Camden, South Carolina, on August 16. It was "a deadly wound to his glory," he wrote. At the time, Greene did not guess how Gates' defeat would affect him.

From September 17 to the 28th, Washington left the Highlands to confer with the Count de Rochambeau, who had landed in Rhode Island with 6,000 French reinforcements, about a joint attack on New York. Greene assumed command of the American army camped at Tappan. On September 25, Greene received a shocking report from Alexander Hamilton at Verplanck's Point: "There has just unfolded at this place a scene of the blackest treason." British Major John André had been captured in civilian clothes with proof of Arnold's treason found on him. Arnold managed to escape aboard a British vessel. While Wayne's troops guarded André at Tappan, Greene presided over his trial and conviction. André died bravely by hanging on October 2.

Three days later, Greene applied to Washington for command of West Point. Washington obliged. Greene made his lodgings at the Beverly Robinson house in Garrison and immediately sent for Caty to join him. He looked forward to a comfortable winter there.

He had just settled down to his new command when Washington named him to succeed Gates as Continental commander in the South. He could not even wait for the arrival of his wife. "My dear angel what I had been dreading has come to pass," he wrote to her. "I had been pleasing myself with the prospect of spending the winter here with you." He went as far as Fishkill hoping to meet her. "My longing eyes looked for you in all directions." he wrote again. She did not come, and he left West Point on October 21.

Greene asked for Lee's mounted troops (now referred to as Lee's Legion) and Wayne's Pennsylvania Light Infantry to go south with him. Washington agreed that Lee could go, but he could not spare Wayne. Greene made his way southward from Philadelphia by way of Annapolis, Mount Vernon (where he was entertained by Martha Washington), Richmond, Hillsborough, and Salisbury, finally reaching Gates' camp at Charlotte, North Carolina, on December 2, 1780. Greene expressed shock at the condition of the troops in a letter to Caty. "I arrived on the 2nd of this month and been in search of the army I am to command, but without success, having found nothing but a few half-starved soldiers who are remarkable for nothing but poverty and distress." He cautioned Caty not even to think of coming to join him.

The only organized body of troops between Greene and Cornwallis's victorious army at Winnsboro, in the center of the South Carolina upcountry, was that of veteran Daniel Morgan, who had come out of retirement after Gates' defeat at Camden. The British held the South with Cornwallis's formidable army, and with a string of garrisons stretching from the coast to Augusta, Georgia. Greene had little confidence in his decimated army, but hoped to rely on partisan bands that acted independently of each other. Many of the partisans lived by indiscriminate plundering, and had formed the habit—distressing to Greene—of killing their prisoners.

Facing insurmountable odds, Greene searched for a strategy. A letter from one of the partisan leaders gave him his plan. Benjamin Few of Georgia asked for help from the Continentals. He believed that the people of the Georgia backcountry would resist the British if encouraged by the approach of an American

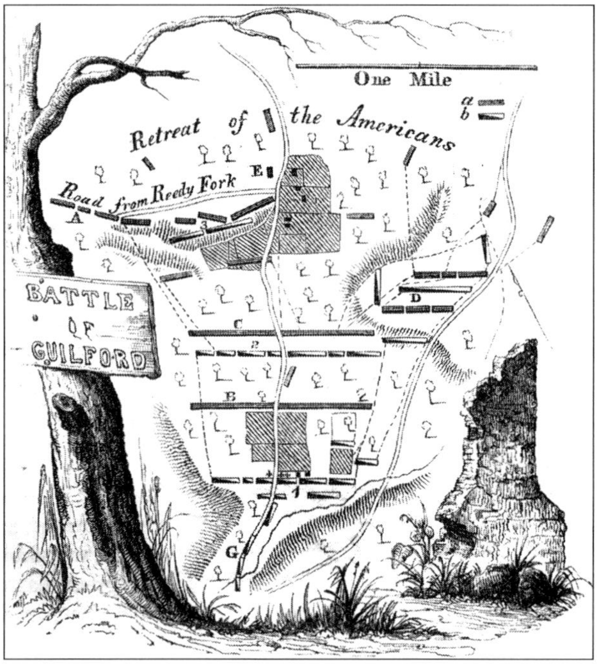

Fig. 12.4. The Plan of the Battle of Guilford.

army. Greene immediately seized upon the idea. On December 16, he wrote to Few: "In order to give support to your exertions and spirit up the people in that quarter I propose to send General Morgan with a large detachment from this army to act on the west side of the Catawba."

On the same day, Greene ordered Morgan to march into western South Carolina: "The object of this detachment is to give protection to that part of the country and spirit up the people." Morgan commanded 320 infantry from Maryland and Delaware, 200 Virginia militia, and 90 dragoons. Greene expected him to be joined by Georgia and South Carolina partisans, but a leading partisan, Thomas Sumter, felt slighted by not getting the command and refused to cooperate.

Greene's decision to send his only fighting force to the west, leaving no protection between him and Cornwallis, has been called "the most audacious and ingenious piece of military strategy of the war." Greene explained in a letter to Washington that "Cornwallis could not come at me or his posts at Ninety-Six and Augusta would be exposed."

Morgan accepted the assignment with relish. In his reply he suggested, "Could a diversion be made in my favour by the main army I should wish to march into Georgia." Greene encouraged him to move toward Augusta if he could do it. But Greene could not put on a diversion because his main army was a fiction.

Morgan's unexpected march west took Cornwallis by surprise. He countered by dispatching his best fighter, Lieutenant-Colonel Banastre Tarleton, to oppose Morgan. The result was a smashing victory for the Americans at Cowpens on January 19, 1781. Morgan wrote Greene, "I should be exceedingly fond to make a descent into Georgia, but am so emaciated that I can't undertake it." He thought Andrew Pickens of South Carolina could do the job. In fact, Pickens would do just that, but not yet. Georgia had to wait because Cornwallis meant to destroy Greene's little army, and Greene needed all the help he could get.

Greene sent out calls for the militia of North Carolina and lower Virginia to join him as he retreated before Cornwallis. Fortunately, Harry Lee's Legion had arrived to act as a rear guard, burning bridges and delaying the enemy. Nearing the Virginia state line, Greene's army had swelled by the addition of 2,000 militia. He had 1,600 regulars, only 300 of whom were veterans. He finally turned to fight Cornwallis at Guilford Courthouse. After two hours of the hardest fighting in the Revolution, Greene withdrew from the field in good order.

Greene lost the battle, but won the campaign. Cornwallis had to withdraw to the sea for supplies. When Cornwallis then turned to Virginia, Greene made another crucial decision. Instead of opposing the enemy, he would let him go, then turn his attention to the British outposts. He told Harry Lee, "Cornwallis has gone North and the rest will be a war of posts." He knew it would not be easy. In a letter to Congress he told how the outposts at Camden, Ninety-Six, and Augusta controlled the countryside around them, writing, "The enemy have got a firmer footing than is generally accepted."

With Morgan incapacitated by rheumatism, Greene sent Andrew Pickens and Georgian Elijah Clarke to lay siege to Augusta. (Again, Thomas Sumter refused to have anything to do with the operation.) On May 12, Pickens wrote Greene that the Augusta garrison was too strong and could not be taken without the help of regulars. Greene turned to Lee: "You will march immediately for Augusta. Cooperate with Pickens." Lee covered seventy-five miles in two days. Greene complimented him: "For rapid marches, you exceed Lord Cornwallis and everybody else."

Lee, Andrew Pickens, and Elijah Clarke conducted a hard-fought two-week battle for the town of Augusta. Even hard-bitten fighter Harry Lee expressed amazement at the savagery of fighting. "They exceed the Goths and the Vandals in their schemes of plunder, murder and iniquity, all this under the pretense of supporting the virtuous cause of America." He warned Greene, "If you do not take on yourself to govern this state til civil government can be introduced, you will lose all the benefit from it."

Greene accepted the responsibility. While the battle for Augusta was in progress, he wrote to Pickens, "The idea of exterminating Tories is not less barbarous than impolitick, and if persisted in, will keep this country in the greatest confusion and distress." He warned that he would administer capital punishment to anyone guilty of "private murders."

On June 5, a triumphant Lee notified Greene that "the capital of Georgia with a large extent of territory is recovered." Greene had heard that peace negotiations had begun in Paris and that there was a possibility of losing Georgia to the negotiators. He sent one of his aides, Georgian Joseph Clay, to Augusta with orders to hold elections for a new government. "A legislature is necessary to give you existence not only in America, but in Europe much more than here," he stated. He also wrote the Georgia delegates in Congress: "Georgia has been an object of my attention and I hope to afford her in future all the support that the peculiar situation in this department will admit."

Meanwhile, Greene's army had fought at Camden and Ninety-Six and lost both engagements, but in both cases the British abandoned their posts and withdrew from the backcountry. While Georgia was being restored to the union, Washington remained at Newburgh, planning to attack New York. He dutifully forwarded letters from Greene to Caty. Despite Greene's protestations that the southern battlefields were no place for a lady, Caty decided to go south anyhow. The journey took two months, including a long visit to Martha Washington at Mount Vernon and balls in her honor in Fredericksburg and elsewhere.

One of the first actions of the newly elected governor of Georgia was to ask Greene, by now Georgia's godfather, for troops to drive the British out of Savannah. Greene responded by sending the newly arrived Anthony Wayne. "General Wayne marches tomorrow with a considerable body of horse to take command in your state," he told the governor. Greene urged Wayne to "put a stop to that cruel custom of putting people to death after they have surrendered."

A month later, Wayne reported, "The duty we have performed in Georgia was much more difficult than that of the children of Israel. They had only to make bricks without straw. We had to make Whigs out of Tories." Wayne's campaign to drive the British out of Savannah succeeded despite all odds. His victorious troops marched into the city on July 12, 1782.

So between the two of them, Harry Lee and Anthony Wayne had rescued Georgia. With a touch of satisfaction, Greene wrote Georgia's governor, "Be assured I shall always be happy to afford Georgia every aid in my power. Her interest has always been near my heart and I shall be attentive to her future safety."

With the British evacuation of Charleston on December 14, 1782, the Revolution in the South ended. It is fitting for our story that Anthony Wayne first marched into the port at the head of Lee's Legion. (Lee was away in Virginia.)

The last months of the war were relieved for Nathanael Greene—and for a number of other officers—by the presence of Caty. "I am now under petticoat government," Greene wrote a friend. Caty organized a gala ball to celebrate the liberation of Charleston; then she and Nathanael went to Savannah to receive the grateful plaudits of Georgians. Even better than plaudits, the state gave them the state's largest and richest confiscated plantation, Mulberry Grove. For good measure, the state presented Wayne with the neighboring plantation, Richmond.

Washington's long-planned attack on New York proved unnecessary because Cornwallis's army in Virginia proved a better objective for an allied operation. Washington won New York at Yorktown. Greene's campaign in the South won the war.

And so Nathanael Greene became a Georgia planter and Anthony Wayne a Georgia Congressman. Wayne's wife never joined him, and Savannah gossips whispered about Wayne's frequent visits to Mulberry Grove.

Our story should conclude with that happy ending, but a few postscripts must be added. First: Nathanael Greene did not long enjoy his family and new life. He died in 1786 at the age of forty-four.

Second: Anthony Wayne, in his short term in Congress, managed to secure a handsome pension for Caty—over the objections of South Carolina Congressman Thomas Sumter.

Third: When Washington made his southern tour in 1791, he made a point never to stay at a private residence, but he stayed two days at Mulberry Grove with Caty Greene.

Fourth: Caty and a guest named Eli Whitney invented the cotton gin at Mulberry Grove in 1793. That invention fastened slavery upon the South and foreshadowed another war.

Fifth, and finally: Light-Horse Harry Lee died in 1818 and was buried at Caty Greene's plantation in Georgia.

The exploits of Nathanael Greene, Anthony Wayne, Harry Lee—and especially those of George Washington—made Georgia more inclined to join with her sister states in a stronger federal union, and made New York more accepting of Georgia. It is ironic that Caty Greene's cotton gin nearly tore that union apart.

This article was first a lecture, delivered by Dr. Cashin at Overlook Lodge, in Bear Mountain State Park as a part of Patriots' Weekend 2004, which commemorated the 225th anniversary of the Battle of Stony Point. It originally appeared in *The Hudson River Valley Review*, Volume 21.2, spring, 2005.

WORKS CONSULTED

Noel B. Gerson, *Light-Horse Harry: A Biography of Washington's Great Cavalryman General Henry Lee* (New York: Doubleday and Company, 1966)

Francis Vinton Greene, *General Greene* (New York: D. Appleton, 1863).

William Johnson, *Sketches of the Life and Correspondence of Nathanael Greene* (New York: Da Capo Press, 1973).

Henry Lee, *The Campaign of 1781 in the Carolinas* (Chicago: Quadrangle Books, 1962).

Paul David Nelson, *Anthony Wayne, Soldier of the Early Republic* (Bloomington: Indiana University Press, 1985).

Richard Showman, ed. *The Papers of Nathanael Greene*, 12 vols. (Chapel Hill: Published for the Rhode Island Historical Society by the University of North Carolina Press, 1976–2002).

John F. Stegeman and Janet A. Stegeman, *Caty* (Athens: University of Georgia Press, 1977).

Michael Frank Treacy, *Prelude to Yorktown, the Southern Campaign of Nathanael Greene* (Chapel Hill: University of North Carolina Press, 1963).

Harry Emerson Wildes, *Anthony Wayne, Trouble Shooter of the American Revolution* (NewYork: Harcourt Brace and Company, 1941).

PART III

Fortresses, Prisons, and Huts

13

Lewis Graham's House in Pine Plains

A Revolutionary Log Building

NEIL LARSON

AT FIRST GLANCE, the Lewis Graham house in Pine Plains is an extremely rare and significant example of eighteenth-century log architecture in the Hudson Valley. It is one of only three intact log buildings built before 1800 that are known to exist in the region. Although these dwellings have virtually disappeared from the region's landscape, they were once a prolific house type appearing during a major settlement period between 1750 and 1800. This paradox underscores the importance of the surviving relics and makes them invaluable resources for the study and interpretation of New York's architectural heritage, as well as the history of the people who occupied them. The exotic historic value of Lewis Graham's log house was recognized over 100 years ago, but the antiquarian preciousness of this house has belied an even more remarkable significance. Lewis Graham's house appears to be the only example of a log building built to military specifications during the Revolutionary War that retains sufficient architectural integrity accurately to represent the character of the hundreds of log huts constructed by the Continental Army to house troops and refugees from Virginia to Maine temporarily, including the major encampments at New Windsor, Morristown, and Valley Forge.

Lewis Graham built the house to accommodate himself and his family when they were exiled from their home in Morrisania, located in southern Westchester County (now the Bronx), by the British invasion of New York in 1776. Lewis Graham was a scion of a wealthy and influential New York family. He was a grandson and heir of Augustine Graham, a patentee in both the Great Nine Partners Patent and Little Nine Partners Patent, two land grants made in central Dutchess County at the end of the seventeenth century that were pivotal in the settlement history of the Hudson Valley. The log house was built on a lot deeded to the Grahams when the Little Nine Partners Patent was partitioned in 1744.

SITE

The Graham-Brush Log House is located near the principal crossroads of the hamlet of Pine Plains in northeastern Dutchess County, New York. The east-west axis of this intersection originated in the early eighteenth century as part of a regional route linking the Hudson River and Connecticut later known as the Dutchess and Ulster Turnpike. This highway is now identified as NYS Route 199 and is called Church Street in Pine Plains. The north-south axis Main Street is also an old road that links the hamlet with associated rural town in Columbia County to the north and with the central part of Dutchess County (and the county seat at Poughkeepsie) to the south. The southerly leg of this axis is now part of NYS Route 82.

The Graham-Brush Log House occupies a 0.4-acre lot in the midst of the northeast quadrant of this crossroads. The house was

Fig. 13.1. View of exterior from northeast. Photo by Neil Larson, 2012.

constructed sometime after 1773 when Lewis Graham assumed ownership of a 259-acre parcel that extended more than a mile north of the house. It originally fronted on Church Street, but the road was realigned farther south when it became part of the Dutchess and Ulster Turnpike in 1802. Small commercial and residential lots were gradually subdivided on Church and Main Streets, leaving the log house and its associated acreage isolated within. In 1829, the house was sold to Alfred Brush with approximately one acre of land. In three transactions over the next twenty-one years, Brush expanded the size of the lot to roughly three acres, which has been gradually reduced over the past one hundred years as the hamlet has grown and consolidated. The house was situated on a 1.3-acre parcel until it was conveyed with 0.4 acres to the Little Nine Partners Historical Society in 1997.[1]

GENERAL DESCRIPTION

The Graham-Brush Log House is a two-room log structure with a woodframe lean-to on its rear elevation. The log section roughly measures 39 feet long and 18 feet wide and one-and-one-half stories in height; it has a gable roof oriented with its ridge parallel to the long side. The one-story lean-to adds approximately 10 feet to the width and has a flatter, single-pitch roof that joins the log-house roof at the eave line. The exterior log walls are covered with "German" or novelty siding with two horizontal gouges planed out of each board creating an appearance of siding with a more narrow exposure. The lean-to is sided with wider boards with only one gouge per board. The roof of the log portion is covered with wood shingles; the lean-to has a raised-seam metal roof; both were added in a recent restoration. Large brick chimneys protrude through the roof ridge of the log house at the gable ends. A stone-walled basement exists under the east end of the log house. All other sections are built on stone foundations over crawl spaces.

A door is centrally located on the front facade and is flanked by pairs of windows containing six-over-six sashes. The stone back of the fireplace on the west end of the house protrudes through the log wall and is exposed on the exterior elevation. Two nine-pane casement windows flank the chimney on the second story. There is no masonry exposed on the east end of the log house. A window is located near the southeast corner of the ground floor with six-over-six sashes consistent with those in the front. An entrance to the basement and its bulkhead doors are located under this window. Two four-over-four sash windows flank the chimney on the second story, being different in type, dimension, and pane configuration from those on the west elevation.

Fig. 13.2. View of exterior from southwest. Original one-room log hut (c. 1776) left of door; log addition (c. 1776–1778) on right; window sash installed c. 1820, front wall rebuilt with wood frame and siding added c. 1888; rear lean-to added c. 1910. Photo by Neil Larson, 2012.

Before restoration, the lean-to contained a variety of window types and sizes, a number of them are older than those in the log house. There is one window on each end: one with twelve-over-twelve sashes on the west and one with twelve-over-eight sashes on the east. The north elevation has been renovated with four windows and one door opening fairly evenly spaced. The windows contain eight-over-eight sashes.

Fig. 13.4. View of west room from east. Photo by Neil Larson, 1999.

LOG HOUSE, PHASE I: 1776

It is apparent that the log house was erected in two sections, and the lean-to was added at a still later phase; other alterations occurred over the long history of the house. The western front room represents the original one-story, one-room log building erected on the site when Lewis Graham and his family fled their home in Morrisania, Westchester County, following the British invasion of New York. Measuring nearly square, 18 feet on a side, the building was constructed of pine logs hewn on four sides to the dimensions in the wall of six inches wide and eleven inches high. Corners were made by sawing six-inch square notches halfway into the ends of the logs and lapping the front and rear wall logs over the side wall logs. The sill logs were raised slightly on a stone foundation. They were wider than the wall logs leaving an inside ledge to support the floorboard ends. Pine logs hewn only on their top face were mortised into notches cut into the top of front and rear sill logs at about three-foot intervals to support floorboards. About six feet higher on the wall, hewn beams were similarly installed and floored over. At this initial stage, the log wall would have terminated at or just above the ceiling of the room. Rafters, hewn on four sides, likely the present rafters later raised above this section, would have been notched and pegged or spiked to the wall plates and lap-jointed and pegged together at the ridge as they are in the existing roof. The original roof would have been fabricated with wood shingles. Lewis Graham was operating a saw mill on his property by this time.[2]

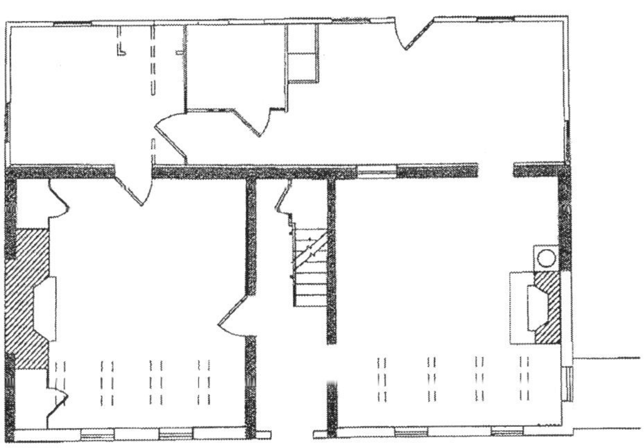

Fig. 13.3. First-story floor plan (north at top). Field measurements by Neil Larson & Michael Devonshire, drawing by JHP Associates, 1999.

A stone fireplace was constructed on the west end of the house. The chimney and hearth are supported by a shallow stone footing in the ground beneath the floor, and the log walls are built around the back of the firebox exposing the stonework on the exterior of the building. A stone or brick chimney was built inside the wall and exited through the roof. The existing fireplace contains elements of the original one; the firebox was reduced in size in a subsequent stage. The entrance to the original house would have been on the south side of the house where two later windows are framed into a void in the log wall. A nine foot-long notch is cut in the underside of the log serving as the header of this opening and appears to exist from the initial construction of the house. This indicates that the entrance would have been paired with a window to create the facade of the house. A patch in the east wall identifies where another window was located in the 1776 house. The present door connecting this room to the center passage was later inserted in its place. A similar notch in the header log above the existing door in the rear wall of the room indicates that a door or window was built into the north elevation of the building, but perhaps at a later period. The garret windows in place in the west end of the house would not have existed in the shorter original house and were added in a later phase.

The one-room-plan house would have been Spartan in its level of finishes. Log walls where they are visible in the room are whitewashed indicating that they were not plastered originally. The ceiling retains evidence of having been painted as well. The beams and boards were planed somewhat smooth to create a finished appearance, and the beams have been chamfered in a rough fashion. They may have been unpainted originally, which was the norm in eighteenth-century English houses. The fireplace was wider than it is in its current altered condition. A stone hearth extended into the room. The cabinets that fill the spaces on either side of the chimney if not original were added in Phase II. Placing the doorway and a window on the southern exposure would have been a practical arrangement for both warming and illuminating the interior of the house. The door would have been constructed simply with boards and battens like the door now in the opening to the passage; this door is probably the original exterior door.

The windows would have been sash units by this time, and the opening is large enough for a sash the size of the 12-over-12 or 12-over-8 units placed anachronistically in the lean-to. Trim around these and the other window or windows would have been minimal. The low, dark garret would have been unfinished and unlighted. Access to the space would have been made either from a trap door in the ceiling or an exterior hatch. Eighteenth-century log houses in other regions left a portion of the ceiling open and used the upper level as a loft, but for this to have been the case here, since there are no cuts or patches in the ceiling, the loft would have had to have been refloored during later renovations.

LOG HOUSE, PHASE II: C.1776–1780

Very shortly after the original one-room house was erected, a second log crib was constructed off its east side. The new section was built in essentially the same dimensions and manner as the existing house, except that a basement was dug beneath it and the ceiling height was increased. The four-walled log structure defining the new room was separated from the old house by a space five feet wide that was enclosed by extending the logs on the front and rear walls to create a center passage. The three spaces were further joined together by new courses of logs above them that raised the second floor to a half-story. Hewn pine logs 36 feet long spanned the entire distance between corners on the long elevations. As in the original room, widely spaced beams in the addition were saddled into front and rear wall logs to support the floor above. Ceiling height in the addition was increased by one log over that in the old section, or about twelve inches. A new roof was constructed to cover the enlarged building using hewn rafters and collars. Rafters and collars numbered I to IV from the west were reused from the Phase I roof and elevated into new positions; new rafters and collars numbered I to V from the east provided structural support for the roof of the Phase II addition.

The facade of the house changed dramatically after the addition. With a new entrance built into the center passage between the cribs, the entrance into the original room was relocated from the south to the east side, taking its present place in the former window position. The space left on the facade was probably filled with two windows as it is now. There

Fig. 13.5. View of center hall with stairs looking north from entrance. Photo by Neil Larson, 1999.

would have been enough room in the original opening for this using the existing window and adding another in the door space. A similar hole or holes were built into the front wall of the new section of the house as it was being built, and two windows were inserted there to achieve an axial symmetry on the expanded facade. The doorway in the north wall of the old room was probably cut through at this time providing access to the back of the house. At some point, possibly at this phase, a detached or attached kitchen would have likely existed, and the old room would have been the logical point of connection. Also, the passage was built without a rear door so an exit here would have been practical. At least one opening in the rear wall of the new room was original, used for a doorway or a window. The window located on the east wall of the new room was added during later renovation efforts in the house. There is evidence in what remains of the log wall on the east end of the building for a stone fireplace with an exposed back like that which remains in view on the west end. At a later time, a small, cast-iron fireplace was inserted, and a new brick hearth installed. More recently, the chimney enclosure was widened on the north side when a furnace flue was brought up through the floor and broken into the chimney above the mantel. All these Phase II enlargements and alterations were concealed by weatherboards nailed on the outside of the log walls.

Stairs to the second floor were built at the time the passage was constructed. The existing staircase is the result of a late-nineteenth-century alteration that lengthened and flattened the run of stairs. Cruder, steeper stairs descending to the basement are enclosed beneath with an intact old door with iron strap hinges and a wooden latch closing off the space. Log walls are exposed on all four sides of the passage. A void was left under the header log in the front wall for the entrance; the rear wall is solid with no evidence (or space) for a doorway. Each side wall has a single doorway entering the flanking rooms. The doorway into the old house section is roughly centered on the wall. A patch is evident to the right of the door trim where an earlier window existed. The doorway into the new room of the house is positioned closer to the front of the house to allow adequate space for the stairs, which make a straight run to a landing two steps below the upper floor level. Boards span the five-foot-wide gap between cribs to create the passage floor and ceiling.

With its whitewashed log walls, board ceiling, doors and stair, the passage provides a fairly accurate representation of the historic appearance of the rest of the ground floor of the house. Although the east room was plastered and covered with recent applications of manufactured materials, it is evident that in the beginning it was as roughly finished as the original house. As in the old room of the house, the log walls

Fig. 13.6. View of east room from west. Photo by Neil Larson, 2009.

and ceiling bear traces of heavy layers of whitewash and paint. Lath nail holes in the beams document that the ceiling was plastered at some interim date. With alterations to the ceiling, fireplace, fenestration, and finishes, it is evident that an extensive updating of this space occurred in the early nineteenth century.

A second floor was created in the second phase of construction. Raising the roof created headroom for living space. Because of the higher ceiling level in the added section, floor levels are uneven. A room was created over the old room where the floor was lower, and there was more headroom added by erecting the board partition that still exists west of the stairs and laying a board ceiling above the rafter collars. An elegantly shaped horizontal batten on the room side of the partition also serves as a decorative chair rail. In a remarkable display of the economical use of materials and craftsmanship typical in log houses, the ceiling boards are pegged to the collars rather than nailed. The remaining portion of rafters and roofing between the collars and the plate was left exposed. The first floor center passage with stairs, looking north from the entrance, plank wall, ceiling and roof surfaces, and the exposed logs have been painted and/or whitewashed many times. The original Phase II finish has not been determined. The chimney was extended through the new space, and the small fireplace was constructed to heat the room. These, too, have thick coatings of paint. Two end-wall casement windows were installed at the time the roof was raised, and the room created. Surviving boards behind the chimney indicate that the gable end walls above the log were constructed with vertical planks.

A second board partition dividing this room is a later alteration, as is the slim doorway cut into the Phase II board wall to provide access into the second room the partition created. In this second phase of construction, the garret above the new section of the house was left unpartitioned and open to the rafters. A board wall was erected to partition off the space over the east room in a later phase. Like the room on the west side of the garret, this room was, still later, bisected by a plaster partition to create two sleeping rooms. There were likely windows on the east end of the house to light the garret space, but the discrepancy in the types that survive on opposite ends suggests that the sash units in the east end are later additions made when rooms were created in the space.

In the garret space, the stairway turned on a landing two steps below floor level. As built, this platform was shallower. (The rafters were not yet plastered over so there would have been more headroom.) The stair hole was cut back about twelve inches when the stairs were shifted back from the wall, and the railings were extended to enclose the void. Otherwise the stair arrangement at this level is intact and perhaps the house's most remarkable example of

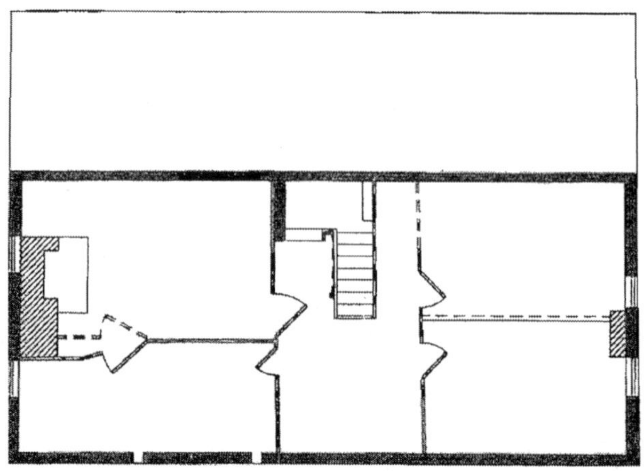

Fig. 13.7. Second-story floor plan (north at top). Field measurements by Neil Larson & Michael Devonshire, drawing by JHP Associates, 1999.

craftsmanship. At the landing, the stairs turned left around a shaved and carved (not turned) post with a pyramidal finial. The smaller stair hole was fenced off using a hierarchy of decoration that reinforces the distinction between the finished and unfinished sides of the house. On the west side, a fancy balustrade with chamfered spindles made a short run up the final two steps and across the hole. It cornered at a plainer post with the same finial and traversed the south side of the hole with a simpler rail. The rail was neatly mortised into the post at the fancy corner but was nailed to a tapered board that served as the post at the plain corner. (Marks under the rail indicate that there were balusters beneath the rail, but none survive to show if they were scaled back from the decorative level of the others.) From here a rail fence extended to the back wall, closing off direct access to the unfinished side of the house. On this side, corner and medial posts were cleated to the log wall supporting the floor along that side. The rails were planed and beaded and nailed at the top end of the posts.

In the basement, the joint between the Phase I and Phase II sections of the house is evident where a new sill is butted against an earlier sill and by a comparison of floor joists side to side. As noted above, the sleepers under the floor of the old house are hewn only on the side that meets the floorboards; the rest of the joists are unhewn with their bark intact. In the addition, floor joists are hewn on four sides. The original Phase II set of stairs to the passage are located in the northwest corner of the space. The stairs are hung from a beam embedded under and cantilevered from the paired sills on the west side of the basement. The only other structural feature in the basement is the chimney and hearth support on the east end of the house. A narrow stone base was built out from the basement wall to carry the chimney. When the fireplace was altered in the early nineteenth century, a heavy frame crib was built to support the brick hearth in the floor overhead. Its small scale and sawn components correspond with the early nineteenth-century characteristics of the iron fireplace and other alterations and small chimney in the room above.

LOG ARCHITECTURE

Log construction was introduced into Hudson Valley domestic architecture as a lesser alternative to frame and masonry construction and required only basic tools and experience. This excessive use of wood at the bottom of the architectural hierarchy signifies that raw materials were cheap, and skilled labor was expensive. As settlement in the region finally began to progress in the second half of the eighteenth century, log houses became the affordable housing of people at the lower end of the economic scale. The pioneer image of the homesteader cutting down trees, chopping notches in the ends of logs, and building his own crude abode is not far from the truth. How, from where, or by whom log construction was introduced cannot be determined. By this time, architectural ideas were freely circulating. Immigrants were arriving from all areas of Europe and the American colonies; through inter-colonial trade and travel, people were aware of the different ways of building in other places. Log construction should not have been a mystery to anyone, and it would have been a near intuitive solution for a settler in a forest, with an axe and the desire for shelter.

TEMPORARY LOG HOUSING DURING THE REVOLUTIONARY WAR

While there are no personal accounts, the documentary record convincingly supports the conclusion that Lewis Graham moved his family into the log house in Pine Plains as a temporary refuge from the enemy occupation of their home in Morrisania, Westchester County. Following the British invasion of New York in August 1776, New York City and lower Westchester County (now the Bronx), where Morrisania was located, were controlled by the British military until peace was declared in 1783. British troops were billeted at the Graham home, and it eventually burned due to their negligence. Morrisania became the headquarters of James Delancey's Loyalist marauders and a camp of Tory refugee huts was built there. Farms were raided by both sides for cattle, wheat, and other foodstuffs; this area was quickly abandoned by virtually all civilians and remained a wasteland through the entire rebellion. Diarist Timothy Dwight made the following observations during the autumn of 1777:

> The unhappy inhabitants . . . houses . . . were in a great measure scenes of desolation. Their furniture was extensively plundered or broken to pieces. The walls, floors and windows were injured, both by violence and decay, and were not repaired because they had no means to repair them, and because they were exposed to the repetition of the same injuries. Their cattle were gone. Their enclosures were burnt when they were capable of becoming fuel, and in many cases thrown down when they were not. Their fields were covered with a rank growth of weeds and wild grass.[3]

Lewis Graham was active in the rebellion, and he and his family would have been in jeopardy had they stayed at Morrisania. His role was recorded by historian Isaac Huntting as follows:

> Lewis Graham was elected to the first Provincial Congress of the Colony of New York, May 8, 1775, from Westchester County. November 7th following, he was re-elected to the second Provincial Congress, which convened in New York November 14th following, which continued without dissolution—having several sessions—until the second Tuesday of May, 1776. Mr. Graham was an associate from Westchester County, and a member of the sub-committee of the "borough and town of Westchester" in '75 and '76, and in the latter year was a member of the committee to detect conspiracies, in which he took an active part. He held a commission as Colonel and was also Judge. . . . He signed the "association" when members of the first Provincial Congress of New York, held in New York, May 26, 1775, when all the members signed the same.

His intimate involvement with the war effort and military action made him and his family a target of violent reprisals. Thus, Lewis Graham, as well as his brothers and sisters, set up temporary households (some turned out to be permanent) in the safe and protective community of Pine Plains for the entire period of the war.[4]

Lewis Graham's role in the leadership of the American war effort would have introduced him to temporary military housing, which was being built throughout the lower Hudson River Valley as the Continental Army was bringing in increasing numbers of troops into the region to relieve the New York militia regiments. This housing was built of logs, and the army developed a standardized method of construction to direct soldiers in their fabrication at encampments in New York, New Jersey, and Pennsylvania. There are also accounts of log huts, as these one- and two-room buildings were commonly called at the time, being built by refugees or by Committees for the Poor in New York counties inundated with homeless exiles. Because of his familiarity with this housing option, and likely because he considered his habitation in Pine Plains to be temporary, Lewis Graham opted to build a log hut and followed a military prototype. Graham's original one-room house has a remarkable similarity to huts described in Revolutionary War records. Built without a basement on a trenched foundation, square in plan, seven feet tall, and with its hearth and chimney resting on the ground, the house is consistent with Revolutionary era descriptions. It utilizes the half-lapped corner method favored by the military, and following all accounts, it was built with few tools and metal parts. When Lewis

Graham decided shortly thereafter to enlarge the house, he amended the specifications to create a more comfortable residence for his family.[5]

Archeological investigations at the New Windsor Cantonment unearthed a continuous stone-wall foundation built in a trench for a regiment commander's hut, and evidence was discovered for stone fireplaces with flared wing walls and hearthstones that extended two feet beyond the firebox. Both of these are features found in Lewis Graham's log house. Detached kitchens were also common. At Newburgh in 1782, Quartermaster Thomas Pickering issued the following specifications for erecting kitchens: "The field officers will build kitchens of 14 feet by 14 from outside to outside—the captains and subalterns, kitchens of 12 feet by 12 feet, from outside to outside: All kitchens to be placed endwise behind the center of the huts to which they belong with an interval of eight feet between. The square of the kitchens is to be seven feet high." Kitchens were considered to be unhealthy in small, one-room living quarters. On April 22, 1783, the Second Massachusetts Regiment, which was camped at New Windsor, received the following directive: "The warm season being so far advanced that cooking in the huts makes them not only uncomfortable, but will destroy that health which is so remarkable in the Regiment, therefore in future (when the weather is dry) all cooking will be done in the kitchens made in front of the parade for that purpose. No fires are to be made in the huts but the ashes be taken from the hearths the hearths swept clean, and green brush put in the chimnies [sic]." The standard practice of defining kitchens separate from huts further supports the theory that the Graham-Brush Log House had an exterior kitchen in the eighteenth century and perhaps until the lean-to was added in the early twentieth century.[6]

THE GRAHAM FAMILY

The Graham family figures prominently in the political and land history of New York. Lewis's great-grandfather, James Graham, arrived in New York in 1678. He had emigrated from Scotland where his grandfather, the Marquis of Montrose had been executed as a leader in a nationalist uprising. James Graham was wealthy and well-positioned in the merchant class of the colony, and he was a confidant of Governor Thomas Dongan. Through this association, he was active in acquiring land in Ulster County, Staten Island, and New Jersey. In 1685, Dongan appointed him "Attorney General and Supervisor of all Patents" for the Province. He served through two turbulent terms, once during Dongan's ill-fated attempt to consolidate the New York and New England colonies (for which Graham was briefly imprisoned and exiled to England) and again in the midst of the Leisler Rebellion. Graham also acted as Speaker of the Colonial Assembly for three different terms between 1691 and 1699 before dying in 1701 at his home in Morrisania, Westchester County.[7]

James Graham willed his property undivided to his children. His eldest son, Augustine, following in his footsteps, became Surveyor General of the colony and positioned himself favorably in numerous land deals in the Hudson River Valley as the seventeenth century came to a close. In 1697, he became one of the proprietors of the Great Nine Partners Patent in central Dutchess County. Soon after, in 1706, he joined another group of nine partners in a smaller patent in northern Dutchess County that became known as the Little Nine Partners Patent. One of the drawbacks of large frontier patents like the Great and Little Nine Partners Patents was that surveying and dividing the grants into lots was costly and proprietors took years to complete the task, especially when demand for lots was so unpredictable. For many years, the only inhabitants on these patents were random tenants and squatters. When Augustine died in Morrisania in 1718, neither Dutchess County patent had been partitioned, and his eldest son James Graham became proprietor of his property in Dutchess County and elsewhere.[8]

EVIDENCE OF LEWIS GRAHAM'S PRESENCE IN PINE PLAINS

There is documentary evidence that associates Lewis Graham with Pine Plains during the late 1700s and with the property on which the log house was constructed. While there is no deed record of his ownership of the property which contains the house (Dutchess County land records are quite incomplete for this period), there is a reliable explanation in Huntting's *History of Little Nine Partners* based on records of which the author was aware in 1897. According to this account, Lewis Graham received title to the land where the Graham-Brush Log House was built in the distribution of his father James Graham's lands in the Little Nine Partners Patent. The Grahams owned two adjacent lots, identified as No. 29 and No. 48, which are of particular interest because they include much of the land that went into creating the Pine Plains hamlet. Lot No. 48 was bisected east-west by the Sharon Road (the Dutchess and Ulster turnpike), and this road intersected with a north-south route aligned with the lot's western boundary. Lot No. 29 abutted Lot No. 48, its northeast corner overlapping its neighbor's southwest corner. The south leg of the crossroads bisected Lot No. 29 on its course to Poughkeepsie. According to Huntting, both these lots were subdivided by the heirs in an unrecorded survey dated 1773. In the distribution of the land, Lewis Graham received approximately 259 acres of land on the west side of Lot No. 48 with its southwest corner aligned with the intersection.[9]

Following the Revolution, Lewis turned his attention to land matters in Pine Plains. A few local documents and public records place him in the town from just after the war until 1794 when he contributed timber to build a bridge across the Shekomeko Creek. Like his brothers Morris and Charles before him, Lewis Graham served in positions of local government, and his terms as supervisor of the Northeast Precinct occurred during this period from 1779 to 1781 and again in 1784. Huntting also reports that Lewis Graham married Margaret Walton of Pine Plains and fathered a daughter before they returned to Westchester, where he died around 1795. Pine Plains would have offered many opportunities to a landholder in the period following the Revolutionary War. It can be assumed that Lewis Graham was speculating with lands he and his siblings had inherited. For property of which he had obtained title, he was either seeking buyers or harvesting timber and other available natural resources. He and the others would have been managing leaseholds on lands not yet sold. On his own land, Lewis Graham operated a mill and supported a farm, using the log house as a headquarters for his business and political endeavors.[10]

When Lewis Graham died, his estate conveyed the 257 acres in Lot No. 48 of the Little Nine Partners Patent with its "mill & farm" to Cornelius Willett Van Ranst, the stepson of his brother Augustine. Both the Willett and Van Ranst families had been neighbors of the Grahams in Morrisania and had intermarried. Van Ranst owned the property for only a short time. The land records are incomplete, but by 1801 he had divided the parcel into three parts, selling the northern 105 acres and the mill to Matthias and Henry Hoffman and at least 100 acres of what remained to Stephen Leggett, scion of another prominent Morrisania family. The remaining 54 acres, including the log house were conveyed to Moses and Amy Barlow who in turn sold the property to Peter Husted in 1805. Husted subdivided three lots from this parcel, one at the north end for the burying ground and two along the turnpike (Church Street), one for the Meeting House and a house lot sold to Tyler Dibblee. The remaining 49.5 acres was tied up in Husted's estate from when he died in 1808 to 1825 when Dr. Cornelius Allerton, his son-in-law, obtained a deed for it. Four years later, Allerton sold the log house and one acre to Alfred Brush. Who was living in the house in the period of years between the end of Van Ranst's occupancy in 1801 to Brush's in 1829 is unclear. It was likely tenanted for a significant portion of the time, and with this transition into a more conventional domestic building, the log house's association with the Grahams and other elite families as a refuge became history. From that point, the log house began a renewed existence as component of the vernacular architecture of the rural hamlet of Pine Plains.[11]

ALFRED BRUSH AND THE REDEFINITION OF THE LOG HOUSE

Alfred Brush occupied the log house from 1829 until his death in 1872. Brush's occupancy is significant for making the log house into a permanent abode. At this time, significant changes were made to the house to restore its failing condition, improve some of its cruder elements, and make it more livable as a nineteenth-century dwelling. This work was either done by Brush or by Allerton in preparation for selling the house. The most evident alterations occurred on the facade of the house, where new six-over-six sash windows replaced eighteenth-century fenestration. By this point, the log walls would have also required some repair. On the interior, the east room was updated as a fancy parlor. The fireplace in this room was reduced in size, and an elegant iron firebox was inserted. A delicate mantel shelf was installed, and a closet enclosed the space between the chimney and rear wall (since removed). The walls and ceiling were plastered creating a low but stylish room. The older, west room was also plastered, but the wooden ceiling was left exposed. The fireplace in this room was also reduced in size and plastered. The old paneled cupboards flanking the hearth remained intact. The old-fashioned space clearly became secondary in the spatial hierarchy of the house. The reduction of the size of the fireplace in this room provides further support for the theory that a kitchen existed somewhere in the rear of the house at this time. Upstairs, both the board wall dividing the existing chamber and the plank partition enclosing the east side of the garret were built during Brush's occupancy, although probably at different times (with the room divider occurring first). Few other changes were made to the house at this time or during Brush's lifetime.

Little is known about Alfred Brush. He was born in Danbury, Connecticut in 1814, moving with his family to Dutchess County as a child. Brush was a tailor and probably operated his business out of his home, so some of the interior space, perhaps on the second floor, would have been devoted to a workroom. His property never extended to Church Street, so it is unlikely he had a shop in the midst of other commercial enterprises at the crossroads. He was independent but was of a "middling sort" or lower. In 1826, before he purchased the house (but perhaps was living there), he was assessed $0.51 of tax by the town. More than half the assessments were less than one dollar; however, his neighbors were much better off. Cornelius Allerton, from whom he bought the house, was assessed at $4.25, Stephen Eno at $6.29, Isaiah Dibblee at $ 10.64. Walter Reynolds, another neighbor, owed $0.85, and Henry Hoffman, who owned Lewis Graham's old mill site, led the town with an assessment of $23.25. In 1836, Alfred Brush hosted a meeting to incorporate the Baptist Society of Pine Plains. He and many of his neighbors had been baptized in the Shekomeko Creek in Hammertown the year before. The church was built in 1837. Over the years, he purchased three more small pieces of land from his neighbors, assembling nearly three acres total. One source notes that Alfred Brush was an invalid by 1852 and "helpless" from 1867 until he died in 1872. Brush and his wife were childless; Sophia Brush died in 1875. His estate held the title until 1881 when the property and the house were sold to Phebe Thompson.[12]

THE DIBBLEE ERA: GRAHAM-BRUSH HOUSE AS A HISTORIC RELIC

Phebe Thompson was a distant relative of Alfred Brush, as well as the granddaughter of

Lewis Graham's brother, Augustine. She sold it in 1890 to another cousin, Isaiah Dibblee. Huntting's otherwise reliable accounting of local history contradicts the deed history and raises a question about occupancy at this stage. It would not be necessarily critical except that the historian makes this reference in relation to the appearance of siding on the log house. The Huntting entry is as follows:

> Pine Plains village is indebted to the Grahams for its site, and to Lewis Graham in person. He built the log block house in 1773 or '74, known later as the "Brush House," now [1897] owned by Mr. Isaiah Dibblee who in 1881 put on siding and other repairs as it now appears. The frame and main portion were made from oak logs hewn square, and the house had a large entry and hall way in the center and a large room on each side of the hall. Mr. Isaac Huntting has an arm chair made by Henry Englekee from an oak log taken from the house when the repairs were made in 1881.

The above reveals the historic status the house had achieved, at least locally, by 1897, much of it probably the result of Huntting's newspaper articles on local history and his book. It is this history that created and then sustained people's historic interest in the house. However, this account is at odds with the interpretation presented here on a number of points. Huntting described the house accurately enough, but it is curious that in a place whose name and history revolve around the pine forest early settlers found there, he would refer to the logs used in the house as oak. (Did Mr. Englekee deceive Huntting about the wood he used in that chair?)[13]

Also, the present novelty siding was not the first layer of siding put on the building as Huntting asserted, although the existing siding appears to be the material put on by Isaiah Dibblee in 1881. There is physical evidence of older nails used to attach siding to the logs, probably weatherboard applied when Lewis Graham expanded the house. Perhaps this siding had deteriorated and come off during Alfred Brush's occupancy. Huntting was fairly fastidious about accuracy, and for a nineteenth-century historian, avoids many of the usual Romantic pitfalls. (In fact, Huntting was a genealogist and erred on the side of detail, especially when it came to listing names.) He was also related to Mr. Dibblee, which was probably how he became so intimate with the house. So in addition to using this account to document the age of the siding, it would appear that Isaiah Dibblee succeeded the Brush family as the occupant of the house, even though Phebe Thompson owned it for a time. The Dibblee family lived in the house longer than any other occupant. When Isaiah Dibblee's granddaughter, Gladys Dibblee Greene, who grew up in the house, sold the place in 1946 after her mother died, it ended 56 years of ownership and probably 65 years of living there. As a result, any of the significant alterations—the building of the lean-to, making rooms and plastering on the second floor, and as Huntting records, repairing and re-siding the log building—can be attributed to the Dibblees. And although there was no organized preservation effort in Pine Plains at that time, the house emerged as a local historic site during that time.

RECENT HISTORY

In 1946, the "Brush House" was purchased by George Sanford, who had recently moved to town to run a local grocery. When an old Pine Plains landmark just east of the house was torn down for a new Grand Union Supermarket in 1950, George Sanford became the store manager. Considering the Sanfords' economic and social position in the community, it appears that the Brush House had been elevated in image to an antiquarian object because of its age and reputation. During their twenty-two years in the house, the Sanfords made sensitive improvements. They modernized the lean-to kitchen and may have been the owners who built the first bathroom in the house. They also stripped layers of plaster and paint from the wooden ceilings to enhance the historic appearance that earlier occupants worked hard to cover up. The last family to occupy the house, the Shooks, purchased the house from the Sanfords in 1968. They continued to maintain and repair the decaying log structure, but few changes in the old section of the house are noticeable. When the Shooks moved out in 1989, the house was bought by a local construction company as an investment property. When their plans to renovate the house did not materialize, the Graham-Brush Log House was sold to the Little Nine Partners Historical Society. The building will now continue its long journey as a historic artifact as a museum.

The passage of time inevitably obscured and generalized the history of the house. Inaccuracies in written histories, such as Huntting's assumption that the house was built of oak logs instead of pine (which is all the more ironic having been built in Pine Plains) and the tradition of the building having been a block house, even though Pine Plains was well removed from the front, have continued to inform preservationists and local historians. While implausible, the legend of the house's association with the Revolution reflects the fact from which it originated.

This article originally appeared in *The Hudson River Regional Review*, Volume 17.1, March, 2000.

NOTES

1. Isaac Huntting's *History of Little Nine Partners of North East Precinct and Pine Plains, New York, Dutchess County* (1897; rpt. Rhinebeck, NY: Arthur C.M. Kelly, 1974) is the principal source of the history of the partition of Graham lands in Pine Plains. The earliest description of Lewis Graham's property is in a 1795 mortgage granted by the executors of his estate to his nephew, Cornelius Willett Van Ranst (Dutchess County Mortgages, Lieber 7, 63–64), and it contradicts Huntting's account, which he must have learned secondhand. The transactions by which Alfred Brush purchased the house and adjoining acreage are documented in county deed records, as are all the subsequent transfers.
2. Huntting dates the origins of the house to the undocumented 1773 partition of Lots No. 29 Lewis Graham's House in Pine Plains, New York and No. 48 in the Little Nine Partners Patent by the heirs of James Graham (347–49), but it more likely was built while the Grahams were living as refugees in Pine Plains during the Revolutionary War. The Grahams' property and family home in Morrisania was occupied by British and Loyalist troops throughout the war, beginning when the British landed at Throg's Neck in September, 1776. See accounts in the Rev. Robert Bolton's *The History of the Several Towns, Manors and Patents of the County of Westchester . . .* Third Edition (NY, 1905) and Otto Hufeland's *Westchester County during the American Revolution, 1775–1783* (White Plains, NY: Westchester Historical Society, 1926). The mill is referenced in the 1795 mortgage between Lewis Graham's estate and Cornelius Willett Van Ranst; it was located on the Shekomeko Creek on the northern edge of his property where Hoffman's or Patchin's Mill currently exists.
3. Timothy Dwight's *Travels in New England and New York* (New Haven, 1821).
4. Huntting, 69. This entire history is comprehensively covered in Hufeland's *Westchester County during the American Revolution, 1775–1783*, although there are few direct references to Lewis Graham. Also see appropriate sections in Bolton's *The History of the Several Towns, Manors and Patents of the County of Westchester*, as well as Huntting's chapters on the Revolutionary period.
5. There is a small repository of copies of documents relating to log huts at the New

Windsor Cantonment State Historic Site in New Windsor, Orange County, New York, where all the following references were collected. The National Archives is the source of most of the material, although the most explicit specifications for huts built at the cantonment, written by Quartermaster Timothy Pickering in 1782, are in the collection of the Massachusetts Historical Society. Charles Fisher's archeological report on one hut site in New Windsor, "A [draft] Management Plan for Archeological Resources at the Town of New Windsor Parkland" (Albany: New York State Office of Parks, Recreation and Historic Preservation, 1985), provides information on foundations, chimney bases and other material history regarding log huts. The New Windsor Cantonment State Historic Site also maintains a log-hut structure that the National Temple Hill Association had purchased in the 1920's understanding it to be a surviving hut that had been moved and adapted into a kitchen wing on a nearby farmhouse. In recent years, site managers began collecting physical and archival evidence for constructing huts to document this building only to find it quite inconsistent with eighteenth-century specifications. The Graham-Brush Log House may provide new information for this analysis and the accurate representation of log architecture on this and other Revolutionary War encampment sites such as Morristown, New Jersey, and Valley Forge, Pennsylvania, where no original buildings survive and reconstructions are of questionable authenticity. There is an account in Bolton's *History of... County of Westchester* regarding a member of the Leggett family, who were neighbors of the Grahams in Morrisania, who after the British invasion fled to Saratoga "cleared a small piece of land, erected a log house, and prepared to spend the winter," 447.

6. All these references are located in the New Windsor Cantonment State Historic Site's research files: Charles Fisher, "A Management Plan for Archeological Resources at the Town of New Windsor Parkland" (draft), 1985, NYSOPRH, 29; Pickering Letterbooks, Letter dated Nov 4th, 1782; Regimental Orders, 2nd Mass. Regiment, April 22, 1783.
7. Huntting, 343–44. James Graham's close association with the well-known Morris family of that place is indicated by his daughter Isabella's marriage to Lewis Morris; she was the mother of Gouverneur Morris and Lewis Morris, the signer of the Declaration of Independence.
8. Huntting, 345.
9. Huntting, 347; a mortgage issued in 1795 by Lewis Graham's estate for land sold in Lot 48 identifies that parcel as containing 259 acres, Dutchess County Mortgages, Book 7, 63–64. A "mill & farm" are referenced in the document.
10. Huntting, 346. Other than what Huntting has recorded and scant references to Revolutionary Era activities, no record has been located concerning Lewis Graham's personal life.
11. A deed for Van Ranst's transaction with the Hoffmans is recorded in the Dutchess County Clerk's Office (Lieber 178, 549, April 1, 1801). The Leggett transaction is referenced in a later deed for the sale of 100 acres immediately south of the Hoffman purchase as occurring on April 18, 1801 (Lieber 41, 282). The deed where the Barlows transferred the log house to Peter Husted, as well as the three exceptions, are referenced in an 1825 deed conveying the property from Husted's estate to Cornelius Allerton (Lieber 34, 28). Alfred Brush's purchase of the house and one acre is documented in a deed found in Lieber 42, 339.
12. Alfred Brush and his parents are buried in the Evergreen Cemetery in Pine Plains. His will (Dutchess County Wills Book 2, 315, dated: January 17, 1844) left his brother, Robert Starr Brush "all the tools Rule books

and measuring implements used by me in the Tailoring business." The tax assessments are in the Stephen Eno Papers at the New York State Library, Albany, New York (Box 2, Folder 85). The background of the Baptist Society is recorded in Huntting, 211–12. Additional information about Alfred Brush's health came from the name files in the library of the Dutchess County Historical Society; the notes were compiled by genealogist Rosemary Lyons O'Mara of Pine Plains. The sale to Phebe Thompson is recorded in Dutchess County Deeds, Lieber 252, 426.

13. Huntting, 349.

14

Revolutionary War Fleet Prison at Esopus, NY

FRANK DOHERTY

PRISONERS OF WAR have always been problematic, and during the Revolutionary War both the British and the Patriots found their land-based prisons inadequate and maintained "Fleet Prisons" to house those captured in battle or imprisoned for questionable loyalty.

The British had prisons on ships in Wallabout Bay, a small body of water in Upper New York Bay along the Brooklyn shore. These ships, including the *Jersey* and the *Judith*,[1] are well-known and deservedly detested. Less is known of similar prisons established by the New York Provincial Convention by resolution of 2 May 1777.[2] Our main subject is the Fleet Prison on Rondout Creek at Esopus established by the patriots, but a brief overview of the British prison ships offers perspective on the great suffering these hulks caused both sides in the conflict.

The Americans were taken prisoner during the Battle of Long Island, the retreat from New York, and especially at the fall of Fort Washington. Others were captured on ships. With the available buildings on land overflowing with prisoners, the British anchored old ships in the bay to serve as prisons. The *Jersey*, the most notorious ship, housed up to 1,000 men, and as many as 8,000 at one time or another.[3] The starving and freezing men suffered from smallpox and many other diseases. Estimates of the dead from the prison ships exceed 11,000—nearly triple the 4,400 Americans who died in all the battles of the Revolution.[4] As late as 5 June 1782 General Washington, trying to improve the conditions of the prisoners, complained to British Admiral Robert Digby:

> I am informed that the principal complaint is that of their being crowded, especially at this season [July] in great numbers on board of foul and infectious Prison ships, where disease and death are almost inevitable; . . . it is preposterously cruel to confine 800 men in one ship at this sultry season. We have the means of retaliation in our hands, which we should not hesitate to use, by confining the land prisoners with as much severity as our seamen are held.[5]

Prominent merchant Lewis Pintard was appointed to look after the welfare of the prisoners, Congress furnishing him with some funds to which he added money of his own. His work was continued by his nephew, John Pintard. The British blamed some of the deaths on the Americans themselves: Loyalist author Judge Thomas Jones blames Joshua Loring, the American Commissary of Prisoners, for the deaths of many American prisoners, saying that he appropriated two-thirds of the rations, actually starving 300 men before an exchange took place in February 1777. Hundreds were so enfeebled that many died shortly after their release.[6]

The patriots were wary of many "disaffected" residents, who were either willing to support the crown or unwilling to support the American cause. As early as 21 December 1775, the

Fig 14.1. Prisoners aboard the prison ship *Jersey* in New York Harbor. The History Project U.C. Davis: http://historyproject.ucdavis.edu/, Fordham University Library, Charles Allen Munn Collection.

Provincial Congress of New York "Resolved that Ulster County jail, or such part thereof as may be necessary, be used and taken as the jail of this Congress, and or the confinement of any such prisoners as may be ordered to be confined by this Congress, or their Committee of Safety." The prisoners were to pay all of their expenses while in jail, unless they were indigent; in that case, the colony would foot the expense. John Blackner was the first prisoner sent to the jail, on the same day it was established. By 18 March 1777 the jail in Kingston was so full that the Provincial Convention passed a resolution to permit smoking in the convention chamber, which was above the jail, because "the same is supposed to have become unwholesome, and very nauseous and disagreeable effluvia arises, which may endanger the health of the members of the Convention."[7]

However, John Jay insisted that some other remedy had to be devised. As a partial solution, fourteen prisoners were discharged four days later on taking the Oath of Allegiance, but the rest were kept in the prison. A final solution was reached by a resolution of the Provincial Convention on 2 May 1777:

> *Whereas*, A number of artful and designing persons in every county within this State are daily endeavoring by exaggerating accounts of the power of the enemy, and other wicked and criminal practices,

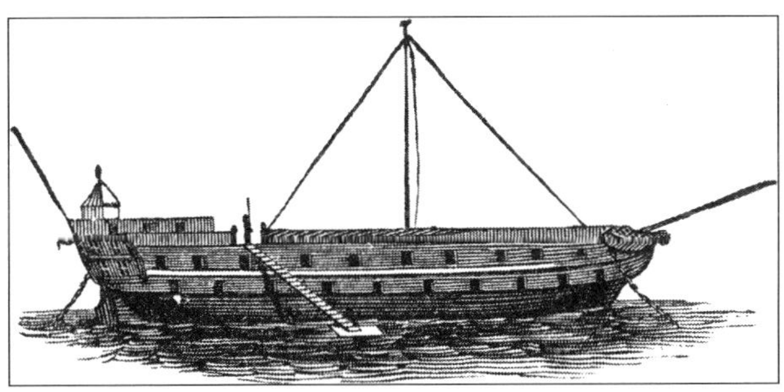

Fig 14.2. The *Jersey*, one of the prisons used by the British at New York during the American Revolutionary War, from Benson Lossing in *Harper's Encyclopedia of United States History* (New York: Harper & Brothers Publishers, 1912). Florida Center for Instructional Technology; http://etc.usf.edu.

to work upon the fears of weak and timid persons, and to betray the liberty of this country; therefore:

Resolved, That a committee be appointed to prepare any two or more of the vessels now lying in Hudson's River, for the reception of such persons as may be sent thereto, and that Captains Benson and Castle, or either of them, be directed to see the said vessels properly guarded by the privateers, of which they have the command, and that they suffer no person to go on board said vessels who is not properly authorized thereto.

Resolved, That the Commissioners for detecting and defeating conspiracies, etc., be directed to cause to be apprehended such of the persons in each county whose characters are suspicious, and who, by their influence in the county in which they reside, may be supposed dangerous to this State, and send them on board the said vessels, appointing a commissary to supply them with provisions at their own expense.

Resolved, That every person who shall be found on shore, after having been confined on board of the said vessels, or either of them, without being properly discharged, shall be deemed guilty of felony without benefit of clergy, and on conviction before the said commissioners, who are hereby directed and empowered to issue a summons to the sheriff or other officer to empanel a jury for their trial, shall be *immediately executed.*[8]

Several days later the Albany Committee of Correspondence reported to the Provincial Convention that its jails were full. On 12 May 1777, John Jay and Gouverneur Morris authorized the committee to "Prepare any two or more vessel[s] in Hudson's River, near the said city, for the reception of all such persons as they may think proper to confine on board the same." No other records on this subject have been found. It is doubtful ships were ever used as prisons at Albany, although the Albany committee did eventually send prisoners to Esopus.

The Fleet Prison was originally anchored along Rondout Creek in Esopus, near the creek's mouth. It consisted of several ships, one of which was the *Camden*. This ship had seen service as a privateer, but its munitions had been removed when it entered prison service. Other vessels like the *Hudson*, the flagship of the Fleet Prison's warden, Captain Robert Benson, were armed and served to police the prison ships.

Once established, the Fleet Prison received many men in a short period of time. On 19 May 1777, less than three weeks after authorization, Ulster County Sheriff Egbert Dumond reported that 175 persons were on board the vessels. Like their American counterparts, the Loyalist prisoners complained loudly about their poor conditions. On 21 June 1777, a committee of the Provincial Convention drafted a set of rules for the care and custody of the prisoners, set their rations, and appointed Captain Henry Benson as warden. Captain Charles Giles was appointed victualler at £9 per month, Cornelius Elmendorph commissary of provisions at £18 per month, and Henry Benson clerk. (He was to be paid a fee of six shillings sixpence from each prisoner when released.) Daily rations were fixed at three-quarters of a pound of beef, pork, or mutton, and one pound of bread, with a reasonable allowance of salt and vinegar to be served out three times a week in summer and twice in winter, all to be paid for by the prisoners. On 27 August this was deemed too great, and the allowance was reduced to a quarter-pound of meat, a quarter-pound of fish, and 1.5 pounds of flour daily, one ounce of salt and two quarts of peas every two days, and half a pint of vinegar every ten days. On 1 September the commissary was ordered to supply the jail in Kingston with 1.5 pounds of bread per day, and Dr. Luke Kiersted was authorized and requested by the Provincial Convention to visit the Fleet Prison and Kingston jail at least twice a week, as well as whenever called on by the warden or the jailor. On 3 September, Elmendorph:

> Having neglected to supply the State prisoners in jail with bread, agreeable to the order of the 1st instant, was peremptorily ordered to do so and informed that he could not resign his office until a replacement was found.[9]

Many, if not most, of the prisoners on the ships in Rondout Creek were sent there by the *Committee and the First Commission for Detecting and Defeating Conspiracies in the State of New York*,[10] which met in Dutchess, Ulster, and Columbia counties. The names of the majority of the men sent to the ships by this committee can be found on the tax rolls for Dutchess County. Other committees, including Albany County's, also sent prisoners; on 6 July 1777 the Albany Committee of Correspondence ordered that all 80 prisoners in the Albany jail be sent to the Fleet Prison. Prisoners also were brought in from out of state. The minutes of the local committee meeting held 28 June 1777 include:

> A Resolution from the Council of Safety directing this Board to send for all the Prisoners of this State now confined in the Gaols of the New England States, and cause them to be transported thence to the Fleet Prison at Esopus Landing in such manner as this Board shall think proper.[11]

The minutes of the Albany Committee of Correspondence meeting held 13 June 1777 include the following:

> Sir, Capt Swits sails this Day with a number of prisoners for Esopus, we would request you to proceed with your Privateer as a Convoy to said Sloop and afford him such assistance as he may want in order effectually to Guard & Secure the Prisoners on Board his Vessell.
>
> *Resolved*, That the following Instructions be given to the Officer Guarding the Prisoners to Esopus Vizt
>
> Sir You will receive in your Custody the Persons whose Names are herewith delivered you, with whom on Board of Capt Cornelius Swit's Sloop you will proceed to Esopus Landing. You are to wait on the Council of Safety at Kingston and delivered the inclosed Letter and receive their farther directions, you are to keep William Pemberton in Irons while in your custody we have to recommend to you to be extremely Vigilant to prevent any of the Prisoners making their escape.[12]

The Albany Committee of Correspondence at their meeting of 8 July 1777:

> Ordered that the Sheriff be requested to deliver immediately to the Secretary a list of the Names of the Prisoners confined in his Custody and that he make out the Crimes alledged against them. Resolved That two sloops be prepared to carry said Prisoners to the Fleet Prison.[13]

On Tuesday 7 Oct. 1777, the Commission for Detecting and Defeating Conspiracies, meeting on board the *Hudson* at Kingston, ordered:

> that Cornelius C. Elmendorph, late Commissary to the Prisoners confined on Board the Fleet Prison, Deliver unto Harman Knicker-Baker, Commissary appointed by this Board, all such quantity of Flour, Salt & other provisions purchased by him for the use of Prisoners, as remains now in his possession.

The commission also ordered

> that Capt Henry Benson be directed to Issue One Pound of Bread, Three Quarters of a pound of Beef per Day, one Pint

> of Peas per Week, with such proportion of Salt as he shall think necessary, to Each Prisoner on Board the Fleet.[14]

These provisions never reached the prisoners because, after Sir Henry Clinton captured Forts Montgomery and Clinton on 6 October, the Provincial Convention ordered the fleet prisoners to march to Hartford, Connecticut. Peter Cantine led about 150 prisoners on the trip; they arrived in Hartford on 20 October, minus a few who managed to escape. On 16 October Kingston was burned by British General John Vaughan, and the Fleet Prison ships were run up Rondout Creek and burned. It is unknown if any prisoners remained in the vessels at the time.[15] *The New York Journal and General Advertiser* newspaper, last published in Esopus on 13 October 1777 by John Holt, was printed prior to the prisoners' transport and the burning of the Fleet Prison's vessels, so it made no mention of either. Holt moved to Poughkeepsie and didn't resume publication until the following year. The *New York Packet and American Advertiser*, published at Fishkill by Samuel Louden, contained an article about the burning of Kingston, but nothing about the prisoners.

The vast majority of information available on the prisoners sent to the Fleet Prison is found in the "Minutes" of the Committee and of the First Commission for Detecting and Defeating Conspiracies in the State of New York,[16] which was charged with monitoring and suppressing all Loyalist activity in the state. A large part of that effort was keeping the disaffected away from the British lines, particularly after the British captured New York City in August 1776.[17] In addition to the commission minutes, which were later published by the New-York Historical Society, there is information in the *Public Papers of George Clinton.*[18] Many men were ambivalent in their feelings about the war; accounts of their dealings with various committees and commissions are helpful in understanding the conflict in the Hudson River Valley.

The reader will note the several times Esopus Creek is named in the minutes when Rondout Creek is where the prison ships were anchored. The British apparently never correctly identified the creek in their records. Rondout Creek empties into the Hudson River in the present town of Esopus, more specifically at the hamlet of Port Ewen, site of the Fleet Prison. Esopus Creek, which empties into the Hudson River at Saugerties, is about a dozen miles north of Port Ewen.

The following extracts from the commission's minutes from May through October 1777, as well as related correspondence, provide an excellent account of who was confined to the Fleet Prison and why. They also illustrate the research process whereby historic inaccuracies, such as the location on these prisons on the Rondout Creek, are corrected.

Minutes 15 May:

> Resolved that the following persons be sent up to Esopus, to be confined on Board the Vessells Station'd there for that purpose, Vizt[19]
>
> Samuel Wood — Robert McEndew
> Nathaniel Akerley — Charles Traver
> George Aims — Jacob Bush
> Benjamin Burrows — Thomas Lawrence
> William Yates — Anthony Breamer
> Elisha Powell — John Medlar
> Edward Howard — Dominicus Montfort
> John Cummins — Johannis Laroy
> John White — William Wilsey
> Philip Sisco — Barent A. Van Kleek
> James Goslin — Enoch Lester
> Jonathan Thorne[20] — Jacob Backer
> Michael Vincent — Francis Laroy
> Griffin Corey — Coonradt Smith
> Simon Knoxon — Lewis Shear
> James Smith Esq — Stephen Thorne.

Minutes 16 May:

> Resolved that Philip Sisco be permitted

to Inlist into the Continental Forces, & inlisted with Lieut Mott accordingly. James Smith Esqr, (one of the prisoners sent to Esopus), & John Cook are permitted to go home on their parole, to deliver themselves in five days from this Date, to the officer having the Charge & Custody of the prisoners at Esopus Creek. The committee also resolved "that Josiah Disbrow and Edward Henderson be sent to Kingston to be delivered to John McKesson & Robert Benson Esqr Commissaries of Prisoners of War in this State."[21]

Minutes 21 May:

The Committee: Permitted Roeliff J. Ellinge [*sic*] to go to his place of abode in the New Paltz to deliver himself in six days from this date to the officer having the charge and custody of the Prisoners confined on board the Vessels at Esopus Creek. John Cook appeared at this meeting and was permitted to return to his place of abode. The committee further resolved: that Hendrick Younkhance be permitted to pass from this to his place of abode in the little Nine Partners on his parole to surrender himself within Ten Days from the date hereof to Capt Castles to be confined on Board the Vessels in Esopus Creek, unless he shall previously appear before Major Landon, or Mr. James Winchell (either of whom are hereby authorized to administer the same to him) and take the Oath of Allegiance to this State.[22]

Minutes 9 June:

Resolved, that the Committee of Orange County be authorized to send such Prisoners as now are, or hereafter shall be committed to the Goal [jail] at Goshen, according to their discretion to be confined on board the Vessels at Esopus Landing, there to remain during the pleasure of the Legislature of this State, of this Board, or of the said Committee or until they shall be otherways delivered by Due Course of Law, And the person having Charge & Custody of Prisoners on Board the said Vessells, is hereby required to receive the said Persons that shall be so sent, and confine them accordingly.[23]

Minutes 10 June:

The Board ordered Henry S. Peltz to deliver to Simon Noxon all the Wheat & Flour & Flour casks in his possession & lately seized by order of this Board, as belonging to the said Simon Noxon.[24]

Elisha Powell (one of the persons confined on Board the Ships at Esopus) by this Board, having appear'd before Mr. Cantine one of the members of this Board and taken the Oath . . . he was thereupon discharged.[25]

Minutes 19 June:

William Bishop, Jacob Funck & Peter Showerman all of the Manor of Livingston, & were confin'd on Board the Ships at Esopus Creek, & since Employ'd on Board the Ship Montgomery, appeared, & having Voluntarily taken the Oath of Allegiance to this State. Ordered, that they be discharged.[26]

Minutes 23 June:

Doctr Nathaniel Worden (of Pawling) one of the Persons confined on Board the fleet prison, appearing before this Board and having Voluntarily taken the Oath of Allegiance to this State— Ordered that he be discharged.[27]

Minutes 29 June:

Griffin Cory & William Yates (two of the persons who were confined on board the fleet prison) appeared & having Voluntarily taken the Oath of Allegiance— Ordered that they be discharged.[28]

Minutes 1 July:
Resolved, that Henry Vanderburgh Esq[r] & Obadiah Griffin be conveyed to Esopus to be confined on Board the Fleet Prison there 'till the further Order of this Board or until they shall be thence otherwise delivered by due Course of Law. Johannis Shear, appeared, and having Voluntarily taken the Oath of Allegiance—Ordered that he be discharged.[29]

Minutes 9 July:
Resolved, that Capt Henry Benson deliver Paul Upton, now confined on Board the Fleet Prison at Esopus Creek, to Mr. Increase Carpenter in order to be conducted before this Board.[30]

Minutes 17 July:
Johannis Medlar and Thomas Lawrence having returned to this place by permission of this Board, from on Board the Fleet Prison at Esopus. Resolved that they be permitted to go and remain at home upon their finding Sureties, Each in the Sum of One Hundred fifty Pounds, so that they will appear again and Surrender themselves to this Board in three Weeks from this date. Messrs Gilyon Ackerman & Matthew Van Bunschoten appeared, and became sureties for the said Thomas Lawrence & Johannis Medlar agreeable to the terms of the above resolution . . .[31]

Minutes 23 July:
Resolved, that the sum of Three Pounds four Shillings be paid to Gerardus Smith, for his Services in Transporting Prisoners twice to Esopus Creek.[32]

Minutes 26 July:
Resolved, that Cap[t] Henry Benson deliver Silas Deuel now confined on Board the Fleet Prison, to John Macomber, who has stipulated to bring him before this Board within One Week from Monday next.[33]

Minutes 9 August:
Resolved that George Hughson, John Casewell, Elisha Hoag, Peleg Scissell, Thomas Williamson, Thomas Butler, Jacob Straat Jun., Peter De Pew 3rd & Corns John Blau Velt & John Mosher, & Joseph Holloway be sent to Esopus to be confined on Board the Fleet Prison there and Capt Henry Benson, Warden thereof, be required to receive & detain them in Custody 'till the further Order of this Board, or otherwise delivered by a due Course of Law.[34]

Minutes 12 August:
Two persons of known Integrity and approved attachment to the American Cause, appeared before the Board & Informed, that a Certain Henning Nichs Kister, Clark to the Lutheran Church at Rhinebeck was a person of a very dangerous & suspicious Character Violently opposed to the Measures pursuing by these States, and therefore advised, that he ought to be apprehended at this Critical Time, and that in their opinion, the safety and security of the State require it. Ordered that the said Kister be apprehended.[35]

Minutes 13 August:
Henning Nichs Kister, having been apprehended and brot before this Board, & Examined. Resolved, that he be sent on board the fleet prison at Esopus Creek.[36]

Minutes 18 August:
Samuel Titus appearing before the Board, and being Examined touching the Matters charged against him & offering in Excuse for his calling the Militia Officers Robbers, that he alluded to their not having returned to him the overplus of the Money which remain'd in their hands upon Sale of Cattle that were some time since taken from him & Sold in Order to Levy a fine, and refusing to affirm his allegiance to this State.

Ordered that he be committed to the Fleet Prison at Esopus Creek, till the further order of this Board.

Silas Deuel (a Prisoner on board the Fleet Prison) who had been permitted to return home for a few Days, to Visit his Son, appearing again before the Board, and still persisting in his refusal to affirm his Allegiance to this State, Ordered that he be recommitted to the Fleet Prison till the further order of this Board.

Resolved, that Lieut Reyher Heermanse provide two Men as a Guard to conduct Silas Deuel and Samuel Titus on board the Fleet Prison, and that this Board will defray the expence thereof.[37]

Minutes 22 August:

Whereas this Board has great reason to believe that Isaac Diamond, Absalom Creamer, Henry Dusenberry, Joseph Marks & Corn: McHagg, now prisoners at this place had Inlisted under a certain Andrew Palmerton in the Service of the Enemy.

Resolved that the said Prisoners be conveyed to Esopus, to be confined on Board the Fleet Prison there. Whereas it appears to this Board from the Best Information and Evidence that can now be obtained, that the following Persons, Prisoners at this place, to wit,

James Lester	Abra: Filkins
Henry Filkins	Ebenezer Marks
John O Niel	John Backus Jun[r]
Luke Schermerhorne	Jacob Diamond
John Filkins	Caleb White
Frederick Rous	Joseph Marks [Jun.]
Hugh O Niel	John Bain
John Marks	Ebenezer Knapp

Are Dangerous Enemies to the American Cause, and that the Safety and Security of these State required that the said Persons be closely confined, Resolved therefore that they be Committed to the Fleet Prison at Esopus.[38]

Minutes 23 August:

Capt. George White appeared before the Board and informed that he had apprehended and brought Prisoners to this Place, the following persons, Vizt.

Elisha Rogers	David H Wyatt
Isaac Austin	John Bratt
David Pearce	Peter I. Lampman
Timothy Biggs	Jacob Litcher
Caleb Carr	Daniel Munrow
Zebulon Jones	John Munrow
Samuel Brittan	Samuel Munrow
Amos Sweet	Elisha Sly
John Moon	Mills Sly
Cary Clark	Richard Turner
Abra: Bovee	Frederick Kalder
[Isaac Rogers]	William Kalder
John Drott	

That the said persons were taken in and about Hoosick, and that some of them had been with the Enemy when they were taken in that Quarter, & that the rest had very probably, either been with the Enemy, or had undoubtedly neglected or refused to turn out & oppose them.[39]

Resolved, that they be sent to Esopus to be confined on Board the Fleet Prison there.

Resolved, that Samuel Ingerson, & John Riley apprehended with Forged Passes from General Schuyler be sent to Esopus, to be confined on board the fleet Prison there.[40]

Minutes 3 September:

The Board with the assistance of Robert Harpur & Peter Van Zandt Esq[rs] Two of the Members of the Council of Safety, who attended for that purpose, proceeded to the Examination of the several cases of the following Seventeen Persons, now Prisoners on Board the Fleet Prison by order of this Board, whereupon, with the approbation of the above Two Gentn it was Resolved that,

William Kelder	David Pearce
Frederick Kelder	Timothy Biggs
Henry Filkins	Abraham Bovee
Frederick Rous	Jacob Letcher
John Marks	Zebulon Jones
Joseph Marks	Amos Sweet
Ebenezer Marks	John Moon
Isaac Austin	Cary Clark
Caleb Carr	

Be discharged.[41]

Minutes 12 September:

Ordered, that Luke Schermerhorne be discharged from his Confinement on Board the Fleet Prison, & permitted to return to his place of abode, on his paying the Expenses attending his Imprisonment.

David Wyatt, having voluntarily taken the Oath of Allegiance to this State. Ordered that he be discharged.

Mills Sly having voluntarily taken the Oath of Allegiance to this State. Ordered that he be discharged.[42]

Minutes 4 October:

Haning Nicholas Keister appeared, & having Voluntarily taken the Oath of Allegiance to this State, Ordered that he be discharged,

John Mosher, having Voluntarily taken the Oath of Allegiance to this State,

Ordered that he be discharged,

Edward Bumpas appeared before the Board, & stipulated with them upon Oath, that he will proceed from this forthwith to the House of Major Robert Hoffman near Poughkeepsie, and there remain within the limits of his Farm & not depart thence without the leave of the said Robt Hoffman or this board. Ordered that he be dismissed from his Confinement on Board the Fleet Prison accordingly.

Richard Turner appeared, & having Voluntarily taken the Oath of Allegiance to this State, Ordered that he be discharged.[43]

Abraham Miller appearing before the Board produced a Pass from Daniel Drummond, Aid De Camp to Lieu^t Genl Clinton purporting that he is permitted on his Parol to return from New York to Rye to be Exchanged for Thomas Butler now a Prisoner on Board the Fleet at Esopus Creek, (*sic*) or otherwise to return immediately.[44] Ordered that the said Thomas Butler be discharged accordingly.

Moses Wooster, Asa Beebe & Benj Ingrum having Voluntarily taken the Oath of Allegiance to this State, Ordered that they be discharged.

Josiah Dean, & Daniel Dean, Voluntarily taken the Oath of Allegiance to this State, Ordered that they be discharged.

James Mather, Voluntarily taken the Oath of Allegiance to this State, Ordered that he be discharged.

William Mash [Marsh?] appeared before the Board, and engaged with them upon Oath that he will proceed forthwith to the House of Melancton Smith in Charlotte Precinct and to remain there until the further order of this Board, or permission of the said Melancton Smith.[45] Ordered that he be discharged accordingly.

Nehemiah Gates, appeared before the Board, & engaged with them upon Oath that he will immediately proceed to the House of Henry Den Mark at Esopus, & be under his direction until further Order of this Board, or other proper Authority of this State. Ordered that he be discharged accordingly.[46]

The commission discharged twenty-nine prisoners between 4 and 6 October. These include Benjamin Spendelow, who was permitted to go to Rhinebeck and was recommended to the care of Dr. Annanias Cooper[47] to act in the capacity of a schoolmaster on his parole.

John Caswell was released to return home. He had been accused of murdering Captain Ephraim Nichols of Pawling in late June 1777 and was imprisoned after being brought before the commission on 3 July.[48]

Minutes 6 October:

> Resolved, That Harmen Knickerbocker be appointed Commissary to provide Capt Cooper's Compy of Rangers and the Prisoners Confined on Board the Fleet, with provisions & Necessaries (Beef Excepted) That he be allowed Twelve Shillings per Day for his Services: and that he observe such Directions & Instructions as he shall from Time to Time receive from Capt Henry Benson.
>
> Resolved that Capt Henry Benson be authorized to permit Robert Burdick, Joseph Holloway, Ebenezer Hurd and Joseph Mabbett to return home on their Parol.[49]
>
> Ebenezer Washburn is permitted to repair to the house of his father Simeon Washburn living in Keen, in the State of New Hampshire.
>
> Ephraim Mallery, (one of the People called Quakers) affirmed his allegiance to the State and is discharged. William Lewis is released from prison on the condition that he remain in Kingston in the service of Mr. Holt, the Printer.[50]
>
> On 7 Oct. 1777 Smith Simmons appeared before the Committee and posted an appearance bond of £100 in favor of his brother Edward Simmons.[51]

The Provincial Convention became concerned as early as 8 October about keeping prisoners near or on the Hudson River because of the advancing British Navy. On that date, William Floyd, President Pro Tem of the Provincial Convention, issued an order, which is reflected in the commission minutes:

> Resolved that the Commissioners for Detecting & Defeating all Conspiracies formed in this State or any one of them be Authorized and required to Superintend the removal of the Prisoners from this place to Hartford in Connecticut, to call out Detachments of the Militia of this State to Guard the said Prisoners; to impress such teams and Provisions as may be necessary for the said Prisoners and the Guard conducting them.
>
> In Consequence of the above Resolution, the Superintendence of the Removal of the Prisoners of this State was committed unto Peter Cantine, Esqr with full Power from this Board to Act therein as he should think most prudent & conductive to the safety of this State, & whose Proceedings are as follows, Vizt.[52]

William Floyd sent a letter to Governor Trumbull of Connecticut on 8 October:

> To His Excellency Governor Trumbull;
>
> [First few lines are illegible] Forts Montgomery & Clinton & Constitution. While assiduously employed in strengthening General Gates and the Northern Army from an opinion that the Fate of America would greatly depend upon our Exertions in that Quarter, the bases in the Highlands have been of necessity neglected. Add to this that General Washington hath called away almost all the continental troops which were in these Posts and you will readily perceive that we are entirely exposed. In this situation it would be impudent to keep a number of prisoners in the State[;] We have therefore sent by the bearer hereof, Peter Cantine Esquire, to your care the several persons mentioned in the list that Gentleman will deliver you and we pray your Excellency to take the most effectual Measures for securing them until this State can receive them with safety or make further Order for their safe Custody.
>
> I have the honor to be
> your most obedt servt
> Wlm Floyd, President Pro Tem[53]

Governor Trumbull replied from Hartford on 20 October:

> Sir, Your Letter of the 8th instant by Peter Contine, Esq. was duly received, who hath brought hither the prisoners therein mentioned, Excepting such as made their escape by the way. It seems there is a diversity of Circumstances among these people as to their criminality, some are said to be under sentence of death, the Case of others more or less aggravated & which may require different treatment and care in their confinement, which makes a further determination of their circumstances necessary, which you are desired to communicate to Ezekiel Williams, Esq. of Wethersfield, Commissary of Prisoners, a correspondence with him on the Subject of those prisoners will be sufficient.
>
> There are such numbers of prisoners in this state, as renders the reception and security of those you have now sent difficult, am therefore to desire your state would take further order for their safe custody as soon as circumstances will permit.
>
> It is said by the Commissary of prisoners that he cannot obtain provisions of Commissary for state prisoners, a distinction being made between them and prisoners of war, and that he might be under a necessity of sending to your state for the article of flour which he cannot otherwise obtain. I presume his Request for that purpose will be complied with.[54]

A subsequent letter to Governor Trumbull from members of the New York Committee, who were appointed to move the Fleet prisoners to Hartford, is dated 22 January 1778:

> Sir, We the Subscribers being appointed by the Commissioners & the Council of Safety of the State of New York, Commissioners to Superintend the return of the Prisoners removed from said state to this place soon after the reduction of the Fortresses in the Highlands on Hudsons River, upon application to Ezekiel Williams, Esqr Commissary of Prisoners for this State, into whose care they were delivered, Understand, that numbers of said Prisoners are confined in the gaols and in the Towns of Windham and Norwich and as our guard are exceedingly fatigued by the length of the Journey hither, We beg your Excellency will be pleased to order that a guard consisting of a Sergeant and Eight privates may be furnished from each of said Towns to conduct the prisoners to this place with all convenient speed, the necessary charges of which we will readily defray, we have the honor to be
>
> Your Excellenceys Most Obedt
> & very Hmble Servts
> Jer VRenselaer
> Melancton Smith
> Peter Cantine, Jr.[55]

Meeting of the Council of Safety, 11 October 1777:

> Resolved that the Commissioner for Conspiracies &c Superintending the Removal of the Prisoners from this Place to Hartford in Connecticut is authorized to discharge such Individuals of the said Prisoners as he may think proper.
>
> Resolved that it is inexpedient that the said Commissioner should exercise such Power in future.
>
> Resolved that the said Commissioner be authorized to discharge such of the said Prisoners only as have been Confined upon a General Charge of Disaffection,
>
> Extract from the Minutes
> Robert Benson, Secy[56]

Extracts from the log of *Dependence Galley*, (British) Lieut. James Clark, Commander, detail military action that took place at Poughkeepsie and Esopus shortly after the prisoners were evacuated:

Wednesday 15 [Oct. 1777] Pokeepsey Landg NNE 3 or 4 miles, Mod. and Hazy Weather these 24 Hours at 4 p. m. Cast off from the Hulk and made Sail in Compy 13 Transports at 10 p. m. Anch'd with the small Bower in 6 Fm Water in Cmpy His Majesties Brig DILIGENT SPITFIRE and CRANE Galley and 13 Transports Polleppers Isld NW Butter hill south 1 mile at 9 a. m. Weigh'd per signal in Compy as before at ½ past Passed the Chiveoux de frize brought too to wait for the Transports at 11 made sail at Pokeepsy Landg NNE 3 or 4 miles in Compy the Fleet.

Thursday 16 Esopus [Rondout] Creek W b. S. 1 Mile
Mod. Beezes and fair Weather these 24 Hours in Compy the Fleet at 4 p. m. burnt 3 Reble sloops at 8 p. m. Anchor'd per signal in 16 Fm Water Esopas Meaddow North 2 Miles at 9 a. m. Weigh'd per Signal in Company the Fleet at ½ past 10 a. m. the Rebles begun to Cannonade us from their Battery at the mouth of Esopas Creek fired 9 twenty four lbrs round shot at the Battery and Reble Galley that were playing on us at 11 Pass'd the Enemies Batters brought too for the Transports at Noon the Enemies Batteries at the Entrance of Esopus Creek W. b S. 1 Miles Fir'd 24 four pounders with Round and Grape to scour the Woods.[57]

After the prisoners were marched off to Hartford, the first information about them locally appears in the commission minutes of 8 November 1777:

Peter Cantine paid into the Board, the Sum of One hundred Pounds, which he drew from the Treasury of this State, by an Order from the Council of Safety for the Sum, which Order he filed with the Treasurer.

Peter Cantine, Jun. Esqr having returned from Hartford, reported to the Board, that agreeable to the foregoing Resolutions of the Council of Safety he had delivered into the Care of His Excellency Governor Trumbull, the Residue of such of the Prisoners as were not by him discharged, or Escaped, & delivered into the Board a List of their Names with a Rec^{t} for the same, and Ezekiel Williams Esqr Commr of Prisoners for the State of Connecticut, also a receipt from said Commissary for the remainder of such provisions which remained on hand at his arrival at that place, Vizt 385 lb. hard Bread, 357 lb, Loaf d^{o} & 50 lb. Boiled Beef. Also another rect from Lynde Lord, Esqr Sheriff of the County of Litchfield in said State, for Augur Hawley, a Prisoner confined at his own expense in the Goal of said County.[58]

Harman Knickerbaker produced his Accot & Vouchers for his Services & Money expended as Commissary to the Prisoners & Guard in removing them to Hartford, amountg to £166, the same being Examined & audited, was paid as per his rect of the 25th Oct. last.

Mr. Peter Cantine also produced the following Accots & Receipts, for Money Expended in Removing the Prisoners, &c.

To Smith Simmonds for 1,175 lb. Beef	£44 1 3
To Joel Sutherland, as per rect	3 11 -
To Lieut. Samuel Crandle as per Acct	9 15 -
To John Pinnier Jun. as per rect	1 8 -
To Lieut Halstead as per Acct	8 9 -
To John Marsh 3rd as per rect	6 16 -
Carried Forward	£74 0 3
Brought Forward	£74 0 3
To Lieut Barce as per rect	5 11 4
To Joshua Pierce Jun. per d^{o}	6 13 4
To Peter Cantine Jun. Esqr per Acct & rect	32 0 9
	£118 5 8

(*sic*)[59]

The receipts containing the names of the prisoners who arrived in Hartford or when they were released have not been located. There are several articles that discuss the subject but they do not include names of Dutchess County men. At least two prisoners escaped on the march, as recorded at the 2 October 1778 meeting of the Albany Committee of Correspondence:

> Daniel Dobs was ordered to be apprehended and brought before Col. (Cornelius) Humphrey, who on examining him he found that he was last year a Prisoner on Board the Fleet Prison and that he made his escape from the Guard who conducted him to Hartford last fall. Dobs was bound in £20.[60]

Ezekiel Bishop also escaped on the march to Hartford, per an account in the *Clinton Papers*.[61]

The minutes of the Albany Committee of Correspondence meeting on 4 November 1777 also note:

> Rec'd a letter from Jesse Root Esqr Chairman of Prisoners at Hartford informing that Abraham C. Cuyler Esqr and Mr. Benjamin Hilton had broke their paroles and were run away inclosing a copy of their paroles.[62]

Several prisoners died at Hartford, including Jonathan Thorne, who passed away about 12 November 1777 and was buried two days later in Hartford's Center Church Burying Ground. On 5 Nov. 1777 there was another death: "Cannon, the prisoner; Internment Charg'd William Hosmer, aged 32."[63]

The prison fleet at Esopus served their purpose, but for a relatively short period of time—just under six months. They relieved the crowded jails in surrounding counties and reduced the Loyalist threat. Many, if not most, of the prisoners were not punished severely, other than having to suffer the uncomfortable life aboard the ships. They were released after signing the Oath of Allegiance or put on parole to a known patriot. A number of them joined patriot militia companies, including at least eighteen of the first thirty-two prisoners sent to the ships on 15 May.[64] The records of the local committee show that it sent ninety-six men to the Fleet prison and the Albany Committee of Correspondence sent eighty men, for a total of 176. Twenty-one men took the Oath of Allegiance, twenty-eight were placed on parole, and twenty-nine were discharged and free to go home. At least one of these men enlisted in the militia as a reason for discharge. Since seventy-nine were released, leaving a balance of ninety-three men, and 150 men marched to Hartford, there were at least another fifty-seven men who were in the prison when they began the march.

This article originally appeared in *The Hudson River Valley Review*, Volume 28.1, autumn, 2011.

NOTES

1. George Clinton, *Public Papers of George Clinton, First Governor of New York 1777–1795—1801–1804*, ed. Hugh Hastings, 10 vols. (New York and Albany: State printers, 1899–1914), 2:830.
2. New York, *Provincial Congress, Provincial Convention, Committee of Safety and Council of Safety of the State of New-York. 1775–1776–1777*, 2 vols. (Albany: Thorlow Weed, Printer to the State, 1842), 1:908.
3. Danske Dandridge, *American Prisoners of the Revolution* (Michie Company, Printers, 1911).
4. Eugene L. Armbruster, *The Wallabout Prison Ships, 1776–1783* (New York, 1920). Other writers estimate 7,000 died in the British prison ships in the Hudson. See Henry S. Commager and Richard B. Morris, *The Spirit of Seventy Six*, 1958 and the most recent treatment, Edwin G. Burrows, *Forgotten Patriots: The Untold Story of American Prisoners During the American Revolutionary*

War (New York: Basic Books, 2008).

5. General George Washington to Admiral Robert Digby, 5 June 1782, quoted in Armbruster, 9.
6. Thomas Jones, *History of New York During the Revolution* (New York: New York Historical Society, 1879), 1:351. See *The Settlers of the Beekman Patent*, 1: 558–61, for a Dutchess County soldier who came down with smallpox on the ship and died soon after returning to the county.
7. *NY Provincial Convention*, 1: 842.
8. Ibid., 1: 908.
9. *NY Council of Safety*, 1:1055.
10. *Minutes of the Committee and the First Commission for Detecting and Defeating Conspiracies in the State of New York, December 11, 1776–September 23, 1778, with collateral documents: to which is added Minutes of the Council of Appointment, State of New York, April 2, 1778–May 3, 1779* (New York: New York Historical-Society, 1924), hereinafter cites as *ConC*.
11. *ConC*, 325.
12. *Albany Committee of Correspondence, 1775–1778* (Albany: University of the State of New York, 1923), 93, hereinafter cited as *AConC*.
13. *AConC*, 809.
14. *ConC*, 396.
15. Jones, *History of New York*, 710.
16. It is interesting to note that the first meeting of the Commission for Detecting and Defeating Conspiracies was held 17 Oct. 1776 in Fishkill, Dutchess County, and the first name in the minutes is Col. Henry Ludington of the present town of Kent, then in Dutchess County but now part of Putnam County, *ConC*, 1. Col. Ludington's daughter, Sybil Ludington, the "Paul Revere" of New York State, is almost as well known as her father and is remembered with a statue on the shore of Lake Gleneida in Carmel, NY; she became famous for her night ride on 26 April 1777 alerting her father's regiment about the British raid on Danbury, CT.
17. As much as possible these are the exact minutes of the meetings, including the odd capitalization, abbreviations, etc.
18. *Public Papers of George Clinton*.
19. *ConC*, 291. It would appear that a number of prisoners currently in jails were moved to the Fleet Prison at this time. They accounted for the 175 prisoners on the vessels as of 19 May 1777.
20. Jonathan Thorne lived on the farm adjacent to that of the compiler of these records and was married to Catherine Livingston, daughter of Gilbert and Cornelia (Beekman) Livingston. Because of his marriage, he was one of the very few living in the Beekman Patent who owned his farm. Like the rest of the Fleet prisoners, he was sent to Hartford, CT, in October 1777, where he died. Almost all these prisoners were living in Dutchess County and about half in Beekman Precinct.
21. *ConC*, 293
22. *ConC*, 299. Many of the prisoners sent to the Fleet Prison spent very little time there—some as little as a day—before they agreed to sign the Oath of Allegiance. Some enlisted in the militia and were probably able to spend time on their farms, while others deserted and joined the British. Still others, like Jonathan Thorne, remained on the vessels from the first day to the last, and then marched to Hartford.
23. Ibid., 316–17.
24. *ConC*, 317. Simon Noxon was son of Bartholomew Noxon who operated a grist mill in Poughquag, Dutchess County.
25. *ConC*, 318.
26. Ibid., 321.
27. Ibid., 322.
28. Ibid., 326.
29. Ibid., 327.
30. Ibid., 331.
31. Ibid., 337.
32. Ibid., 341.
33. Ibid., 342.

34. Ibid., 354.
35. Ibid., 357.
36. Ibid. At least two members of the clergy were sent to the Fleet Prison: Kister and Rev. John Beardsley, the pastor of Christ Church in Poughkeepsie. Rev. Beardsley is first mentioned at the meeting of the commission held 2 June 1777: "John Beardsley, is permitted to return to his place of abode, & to remain there on Parol, to appear before this Board in five Days from this date. Resolved, that this Board doth consent that there be a Meeting of the Vestry of Christs Church held at the Rev[d] M[r] Beardsley on any Day during the course of this week." On 7 June, after Beardsley refused to take the oath, the commission "Ordered that he return home & remain on his farm until the further order of this Board, with permission to go and Visit the sick & Baptize Infants where requested." On 22 June a resolution of the Council of Safety required the commission "to cause the Rev. Mr. Beardsley and all those of the People called Quakers, who have lately been to Long Island and are returned to be apprehended, and sent under guard to the fleet prison at Esopus Creek." Yet two days later, the minutes record: "Resolved that the 9 Dollars in Silver taken from John Miller be transmitted by the Rev[d] M[r]. Beardsley to New York to be delivered to Major Paine in order to be distributed among the Prisoners of this State in the hands of the enemy." On 3 July John Miller enlisted in the Continental Service and the commission "Resolved that the residue of the money detained from John Miller, (being 9 dollars in specie sent down to New York by M. Beardsley to be distributed to the prisoners there), be repaid to the said John Miller in paper currency." On 5 September 1777 the commission was informed that Rev. Beardsley had returned from New York and they "resolved that he appear before this Board at this place on Monday next. Resolved, that if the said Rev[d] M[r]. Beardsley should in any wise appear reluctant to obey the above Summons, that Mr. Stephen Hendrickson be authorized to take him into Custody, and convey him on Board the Fleet Prison at this Place, and that this Board will defray the Expence thereof." Eventually Rev. Beardsley was considered a loyalist and ordered to New York City with his family. He was denied his request to take any personal property, including items that had been gifted to his children. [*ConC*, 313, 315, 321–23, 328–29, 373–74, 441, 444–45, 447–48].
37. Ibid., 359.
38. Ibid., 364.
39. About half of these men were from Beekman or Pawling, Dutchess County.
40. Ibid., 364–65.
41. Ibid., 373. This is another instance where most of these men spent only a little more than a week on the ships.
42. Ibid., 386.
43. Ibid., 390.
44. *ConC*, 391. In this instance the commission again erred in the location of the prison ships.
45. Melancton Smith of New York and Dutchess County is credited by many with being a primary force behind the inclusion of a Bill of Rights in the U.S. Constitution. See *New York History*, vol. 72, October 1991, 407–20; Betsy L. Rosenblatt, *New York State's Role in the Creation and Adoption of the Bill of Rights.*
46. *ConC*, 391.
47. Dr. Annanias Cooper had been of Fishkill and married into the Palmatier family.
48. See *Settlers of the Beekman Patent*, 7:485–87 for this event.
49. These men, except for Mabbett, were all of Pawling.
50. Holt printed his last edition 13 October 1777 and left Kingston soon after it was burned by the British. He set up shop in Poughkeepsie, where he resumed printing

The New-York Journal and General Advertiser on 25 May 1778.

51. Ibid., 393.
52. *ConC*, 397. The "Proceedings" are not given.
53. "Governor Trumbull Papers," Connecticut State Library, Hartford, CT, 7: 99a.
54. "Trumbull Papers", 7:99ab.
55. Ibid.
56. Ibid., 401.
57. Extract from the log of the *Dependence* Galley, 15 October 1777, *Year Book*, 1935, Dutchess County Historical Society, 99.
58. "Trumbull Papers," 7: 401.
59. Ibid., 402.
60. *AConC*, 249.
61. *Public Papers of George Clinton*, 2:466, 472, 476.
62. *AConC*, 597.
63. See Herbert H. White, *British Prisoners of War in Hartford During the Revolution* (Connecticut Historical Society Bulletin, 19, July 1954), 65–81. Also *The Connecticut Quarterly*, Vol. IV, #4, (1898), 417–18 for burials.
64. From research in *History of New York*. It's possible some of the more common names may be for a different soldier, but many served in local companies.

15

The Flawed Works of Fort Constitution

JAMES M. JOHNSON

THE HUDSON RIVER and West Point played a significant role in the outcome of the American Revolution.[1] This article will critique the work of Bernard Romans, the first military engineer at Constitution Island.

American and British political and military leaders considered the Hudson River militarily significant throughout the American Revolution. George Washington had recognized the value of the Hudson River at least as early as May 1775, when he had served on a committee of the Continental Congress that had recommended fortifying both its sides in the Hudson Highlands.[2] His later view, in 1783 in his "Sentiments on a Peace Establishment," was that the fortifications at West Point had been the "key of America." This had influenced his thinking throughout the war.

Units of the Continental Army generally garrisoned in the Hudson Highlands, and Washington concerned himself personally with the construction of the works along Popolopen Creek and at Constitution Island, Pollepel Island, and West Point.[3]

The British made the "line of the Hudson" the centerpiece of their strategies to take New York City in 1776, Albany in the Saratoga campaign of 1777, and West Point in 1780 (with the assistance of its commander, Benedict Arnold). The British Commander in Chief, General Sir Henry Clinton, who was involved in all three of these plans and the capture of Stony Point in 1779 later wrote that "the River Hudson naturally presents itself as a very important object."[4]

Washington, Clinton, and their respective political leaders were convinced that the British could bisect the colonial rebellion economically and politically by controlling this major river.[5] The New York Provincial Convention and Committee of Safety repeatedly reminded the Continental Congress of the Hudson's importance "for the defense of the United American States, and keeping up a communication between the eastern and southern states," as it solicited funds for its defense.[6] British subjects and Americans would forfeit their lives and national treasure as they tried to maintain control of this vital artery.

The initial requirements for fortifying the Hudson at West Point had been clear from the very first reports rendered on May 19 by Washington's committee and on June 13, 1775, by James Clinton and Christopher Tappen. Both of these men, sent by the Provincial Congress to determine the best location to block the river, were New York delegates and residents of the Hudson River Valley. Additionally, Clinton, a surveyor, had served as a captain of militia in the French and Indian War.

The Continental Congress and the two New Yorkers had agreed that both sides of the river required posts and garrisons. After surveying other sites, such as Popolopen Creek and Con Hook, Clinton and Tappen chose the difficult, "S-shaped" curve at West Point. They believed the narrowness of the channel here—500 yards—and the effects of tide (3–5 feet high) and current made this the most appropriate spot. Their report included a description and drawing of a post on Martelaer's Rock with a garrison of 300 men and another at West Point with 200 men. They had also recommended stretching booms across the Hudson between the two posts.[7]

Fig. 15.2. *Chevaux-de-frise.*

Why did a venture that began with such insight and energy result in failure? Why were the works in the Hudson Highlands so flawed that they failed to stop the British in October 1777?

The failure was at two levels. First, the engineer hired by the New York Committee of Safety, Dutch-born surveyor, cartographer, and botanist Bernard Romans, failed as a military engineer at Martelaer's Rock. He did not locate the fortifications there properly. Second, he failed to develop them effectively, expeditiously, and economically. On August 29, 1775, Romans began work on a "Grand Bastion," dubbed Constitution Fort.

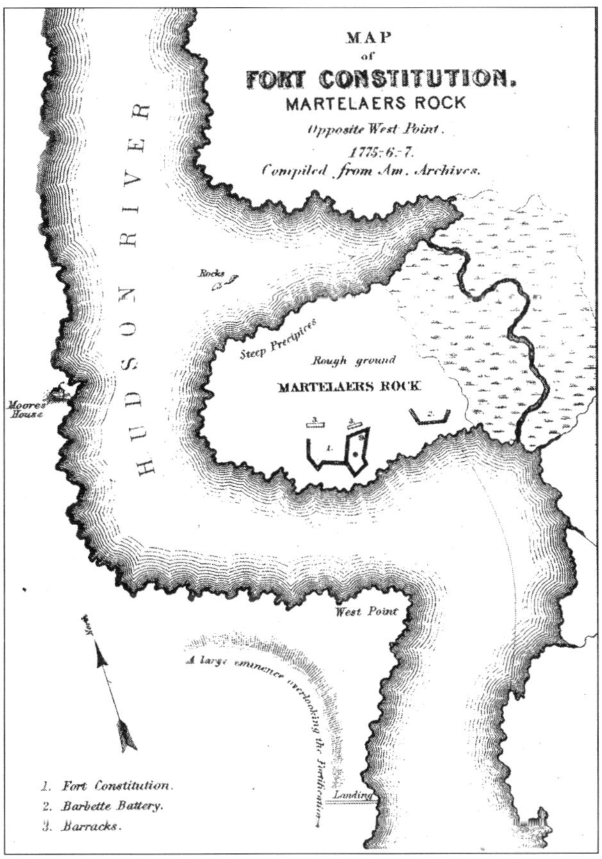

Fig. 15.1. Map of Fort Constitution. Images are from Peter Force, Ed. *American Archives*, 4th series, on microfilm at Special Collections, U.S. Military Academy Library, West Point, New York.

By February 9, 1776, when the Continental and Provincial Congress dismissed him, Romans had completed only an octagonal, wooden blockhouse with eight four-pounder cannons, barracks, a storehouse, and a curtain or wall mounting a battery of fourteen cannons.[8] Romans' failure at Martelaer's Rock led colonial leaders, who still accepted parts of his general plan for Fort Constitution, to seek alternative sites for fortifications and obstacles. Congressional leaders heard from visiting committees that Fort Constitution was inadequate, and that Popolopen Creek, more than four miles downriver, had off-setting advantages.

Beginning in January 1776, precious manpower and materials were diverted to two forts (Montgomery and Clinton), along with a chain and boom. A *chevaux-de-frise* (iron-tipped, wooden stakes protruding from sunken log cribs filled with rocks) was to be emplaced between Pollepel's Island, across the river to Plum Point on its west bank.[9]

These works and the *chevaux-de-frise* at Pollopel's Island would divert effort and manpower from Fort Constitution, as it was now called. Consequently, the patriots had incomplete fortifications or barriers at three places and too few soldiers to man them. The end result was failure when success might have been possible.

Fig. 15.3. Romans' Plan #1 indicated the terrain seen by Romans on Martelaer's Rock.

Romans failed at Martelaer's Rock because he did not follow the basic rules of military engineering as they were understood at the time. This is not surprising, because he apparently had little or no practical experience as a military engineer. His biographer cites some training in England prior to 1756, but this presumably was in civil engineering.[10] Romans had a working knowledge of military terms and structures, which he revealed in his observations of Fort St. Augustine, Florida.[11] He had also assessed the cost of repairing Fort Ticonderoga for Benedict Arnold in May 1775, after that once formidable work was captured.

Since his arrival in North America, however, Romans earned his livelihood as a surveyor, cartographer, and botanist. In fact, while he was in the pay of the New York Provincial Congress, the King of England was paying him a 50-pound annual stipend as the botanist for the Floridas.

To his credit, Romans purchased a copy of Roger Stevenson's *Military Instructions for Officers Detached in the Field* in Philadelphia before travelling to New York.[12] He may have learned something about fortifications from John William Gerard de Brahm, a military engineer and his original superior as Surveyor General of the Southern District. However, there is no evidence that he consulted or owned other treatises about military engineering.

Romans would have served himself and his adopted country better had he followed the maxims of acknowledged, published engineers, particularly those of Stevenson. He might then have first built field fortifications of earth and wood that commanded the river rather than starting a bastioned fort of masonry. A committee of the Continental Congress observed on November 23, 1775, that as the southwest curtain was the "least useful, we think it should have been last finished. . . ."[13] Without doubt, Romans was very skillful with a pen, as his drawings and plan of work for Fort Constitution reveal. His approach to his craft as a cartographer and even, perhaps, as a civil engineer are evident in the introduction to his book, *A Concise Natural History of East and West Florida*:

> A describer of countries, ought in a great measure, to imitate a building Engineer, in first laying before those, whom he will employ, accurate and distinct plans of his intended work, thereby enabling them more distinctly of the execution thereof. . . .[14]

Unfortunately for Romans, there was and is more to military engineering than a well-drawn plan, a point that John Muller made directly at the time to all who read his treatise on fortifications.[15] The flawed execution of Romans' plan would be his undoing and, ultimately, the Highlands' as well.

Because of his apparent inexperience as a military engineer, Romans chose poor locations for his major works. Had he consulted or remembered the contents of prominent published treatises on fortifications, such as those of Muller, Vauban, or Pleydell, he would have noted their caution to practitioners to be careful about their "choice of situation" and "to make use of every advantage of ground. . . ." Muller even thought that leaders should not trust the judgment of a single engineer, even one "so well qualified" but rather should seek other opinions.[16] Unfortunately for the colonies, engineers were in short supply. New York and the Continental Congress had little recourse at the time but to rely upon the careful drawings and detailed estimates of Bernard Romans.

In "his choice of situation," Romans accepted too literally the location on Martelaer's Rock proposed by Tappen and Clinton rather than surveying and tracing out the best site himself. His initial proposal proved that he was not totally bound by the opinion of "Some gentlemen, not well enough versed in the sience [sic] . . ." because he had himself found a spot a short distance to the east of the one selected by the committee.[17] Furthermore, after sketching a blockhouse and battery for a site that Clinton and Tappen had chosen at West Point, he had then ignored these dominating heights across the river less than one-half mile away. Stevenson pointedly warned against allowing such a thing to happen with terrain in the very book that Romans owned and presumably had read.[18]

Although most observers, like Clinton and Tappen, recognized the value of the higher ground at West Point, it would continue to be ignored until 1778. In June 1776, for example, Lord Stirling, General William Alexander, noted that "every work on the island is commanded by the hill on the West Point. . . ."[19] The reason for this crucial oversight may have simply been that Fort Constitution had now become an auxiliary to Forts Montgomery and Clinton. Cannons emplaced at Romans Battery would be unable to take an enemy ship under fire until it was broadside, more than halfway through the "S"-curve. Field works, made from fascines

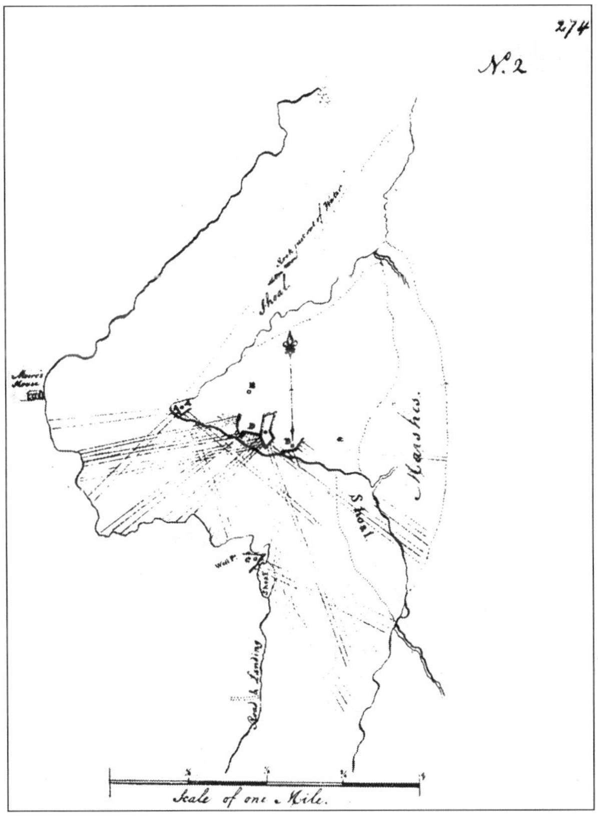

Fig. 15.4. Romans' Plan #2 shows his original scheme for batteries and blockhouses.

(bundles of sticks), timber, dirt, and sod—and located farther to the east at the future site of the Gravel Hill Battery where Romans himself had drawn a blockhouse and a battery—would have at least confronted both problems. Romans would have done well to have remembered or read Pleydell's admonition in 1768 "That an hundred men properly posted, and entrenched according to rule, can affect more than a thousand, who have taken up a wrong position."[20]

Having chosen the wrong place to begin his work, Romans next ignored or misunderstood the command relationship established by the New York Provincial Congress when it appointed the commissioners for the fortifications in the Highlands. As a result, there was no unity of command. The famous French engineer, Vauban, had made clear in his writings that members of his profession were "often forced to follow someone else's opinions and work at strange notions."[21]

To his ultimate regret, Romans stubbornly or pridefully viewed himself as the sole director of construction. He did not show his original plan to, or coordinate it with the commissioners, who then criticized it without offering an alternative. The plan was delivered directly to the New York Committee of Safety, which forwarded the impressive drawings and estimates to the Continental Congress.[22] This initial action led to increasing animosity and a paper war between the principals of the project—Romans writing from his blockhouse and the commissioners from their office in the storehouse a short walk to the rear.[23] This was not the first time, nor would it be the last, that Romans would show his difficult personality.[24]

Embroiled in controversy first with the commissioners and later with the respective Congresses, Romans proceeded to build a blockhouse and a battery too slowly and at too great expense. Muller had pointed out that a major consideration in planning a fortress must be "The expence necessary in the building of it" to avoid the possibility that "instead of being an advantage, it becomes a burthen to the nation."[25] Tappen and Clinton had originally estimated that the cost of their two proposed posts would be about 1,500 pounds; Romans' initial estimate was 4,645 pounds, 4 shillings, 4 pence, excluding ropes, iron stoves, and artillery. The minutes of the New York governing bodies indicate the routine disbursement of funds to support the construction to the north.[26]

Had the results of Romans' labor been more evident to the many observers sent to evaluate progress, the expense might not have been a major factor. Lord Stirling summarized the issue very succinctly in his report of June 1, 1776: "Mr. Romans has displayed his genius at a very great expence and to very little publik advantage."[27]

Cost became a consideration precisely because, even by the time of Lord Stirling's visit, Romans, the commissioners, and their laborers had accomplished so little of consequence. The commissioners completed a second curtain, to be called Marine Battery, mounting eight cannons.

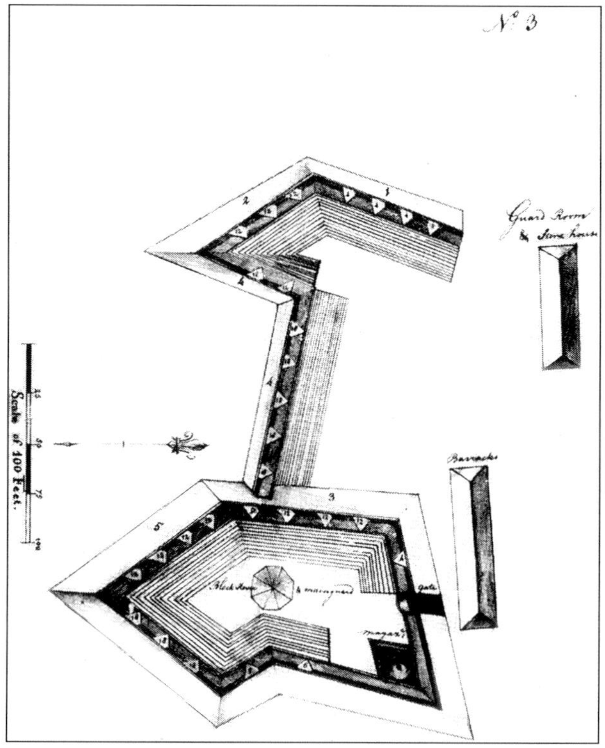

Fig. 15.5. Romans' Plan #3 of the "Grand Bastion," Romans completed only the center curtain and the octagonal blockhouse.

Investigating committees, influenced by their reports to the Provincial Congress, further added two batteries of fascines, planks, and earth (Gravel Hill—eight cannons, and Hill Cliff—three cannons) on the eastern end of the island. Here, the cannon could fire on British ships long before they reached Martelaer's Rock.

The British, upon their arrival in October 1777, faced a Fort Constitution that comprised Romans' Battery and Blockhouse, Marine Battery, and Hill Cliff and Gravel Hill Batteries.[28] Even these works, such as they were, would not be tested. The small detachment of militia and Continentals was demoralized by the British victories downriver at Forts Montgomery and Clinton. They would flee these works, third in priority at the time for resources behind the projects at Popolopen Creek and Pollepel Island, after firing only one shot at a British flag of truce.[29]

Forts Montgomery and Clinton fell quickly and tragically for reasons that parallel those that led to the ignominious demise of Fort Constitution. Started in the fall of 1775 as an alternative to Fort Constitution, these works nonetheless competed for men and materials, and later with the *chevaux-de-frise* at the northern gate of the Highlands. Patriot laborers had not completed either of the forts by the time of the British attack.

Generals George and James Clinton found that the forts were too large for the few Continentals and militia they were able to muster. Disregarding Washington's warnings, these inexperienced leaders and General Israel Putnam, the overall commander, failed to guard critical passes to the south and west. That allowed the British to attack the landward side of forts, which were tragically and ineffectually oriented on the river.

A chain, boom, row galleys, and Continental frigate served little useful purpose as Loyalist Colonel (and local resident) Beverly Robinson led British Regulars and provincials through Timp Pass and Doodletown. They attacked the rear of the two American works in a final assault that lasted only about thirty minutes. After occupying Constitution Island, the British naval squadron made equally short work of the inadequately defended *chevaux-de-frise* at Pollepel's Island and roamed as far north as Kingston, New York.

The Provincial Convention fled as the British first took and then burned the capital. Unable to save "Gentleman Johnny" Burgoyne at Saratoga, Clinton's soldiers and Commodore Hotham's sailors destroyed two years' futile efforts by Americans to prevent just such an outrage as they fell back downriver to New York City.[30]

The story loops full circle back to the post proposed for Martelaer's Rock, and the one at West Point—and to Bernard Romans' flawed interpretation of his assignment.

The New York Provincial Congress had hired Romans as a military engineer to block the Hudson River at a point that would begin to prove decisive in early 1778. As his "imagination took wing," Romans squandered time and money trying to build a "Grand Bastion" rather than field fortifications better suited to the needs of the moment.[31] Of even greater significance, he chose to build the fort where it commanded little and could be dominated from almost every direction.

Romans' initial failure led his political and military masters to fortify Popolopen Creek and Pollepel Island even as they continued some efforts at Fort Constitution. The patriots had too few men, too little time and money, and too little experience to do all of these tasks effectively at the same time.

It is most unfortunate that the reasoning of Silas Deane, of Connecticut, did not prevail in October 1775, as he and fellow delegates to the Continental Congress debated the future of Fort Constitution: "they have employed an engineer. The people and he agree in the spot and the plan. Unless we rescind the whole we should go on; it ought to be done."[32] The second generation of fortifications at West Point was true to Tappen's and Clinton's original conception. More competent engineers blocked the Hudson with a mighty chain and covered it with the fires of forts, batteries, and redoubts on both sides. Perhaps the words of engineer Pleydell best indicate why success could be achieved at West Point in four short months in 1778, when failure had plagued the work of the previous two years:

> It is very certain, that many, after throwing away great part of their lives in handling the scale and compass, have yet been unable, on service, to fortify posts as they ought to be; that is to say, they have not known how to take every advantage of the ground, and judge of its strengths and defects.[33]

Bernard Romans' failure as a military engineer set in motion a chain of events that proved disastrous but not fatal in 1777. Victory would come, and Fortress West Point would play a major role.

Paradoxically, the United States Military Academy later arose at the same site. Its mission was, and still is, to train military leaders to do their job better than Romans did his.

All art, except where indicated, courtesy of Special Collections, U.S. Military Academy Library, West Point, New York.

This article originally appeared in *Engineer*, Volume 20, October 1990. Used by permission.

NOTES

1. Lincoln Diamant, *Chaining the Hudson: The Fight for the River in the American Revolution* (New York: Carol Publishing Group, 1989).
2. Worthington Chauncy Ford, ed. *Journals of the Continental Congress, 1774–1789* (Washington: Government Printing Office, 1905) 2:52–53, 57, 59–60; Peter Force, ed., *American Archives*, 4th ser., 6 (Washington: M. St. Clair Clark and Peter Force, 1837–1853), 2: 844–45; George Washington, *The Diaries of George Washington*, ed. Donald Jackson (Charlottesville: University Press of Virginia, 1978), 3:330–31.
3. George Washington, *The Writings of George Washington from the Original Manuscript Sources 1745–1799*, ed. John C. Fitzpatrick (Washington: United States Government Printing Office, 1938), 26:382.
4. Sir Henry Clinton, *The American Rebellion*, ed. William B. Willcox (New Haven: Yale University Press, 1954), 11.
5. Dave Richard Palmer, *The River and the Rock* (New York: Greenwood Publishing Corporation, 1969), chap. 21; Charles E. Miller, Jr. et al., eds., *Highland Fortress: The Fortification of West Point During the American Revolution, 1775–1783*, 2d ed. (West Point: USMA Department of History, 1988), 5–8.
6. New York, *The Journal of the Committee of Safety*, 25 November 1776, Library of Congress, *Records of the States of the United States*, Reel 1, 718, microfilm. (Hereinafter cited by page number from the respective New York governing body).
7. Report of James Clinton and Christopher Tappen to the New York Provincial Congress, June 13, 1775, Force, 4th ser., 2:1296, map, 736. New York *Journal of the Provincial Congress*, 20, 40–41; *Papers of the Continental Congress, 1774–1789* (New York State Papers, 1775–1788), National Archives, Record Group 360, Roll 81, pp. 286, 288–90, microfilm (M247), hereinafter cited as Papers, Continental Congress. Lincoln Diamant's poor copy of the map unfortunately obscures the letter "B" used to mark the "post" at West Point, leading him to conclude in both books that the committee had only meant to fortify Martelaer's Rock. *Chaining the Hudson*, 4, and *Bernard Romans*, 60.
8. Lincoln Diamant, *Bernard Romans: Forgotten Patriot of the American Revolution* (Harrison, N.Y.: Harbor Hill Books, 1985); New York Provincial Congress, August 18, 1775, Force, 4th ser., 3:535; Romans to New York Committee of Safety, September 14, 1775; Commissioners to NewYork Provincial Congress, November 11, 1775, Force, 4th ser., 3:733–36, maps between 736–37, 1891–92; also in Papers, Continental Congress, 55–58, 272, 274, 276, 278–79; Romans, "Plan of a Part of Hudson's River Near & About the Fortifications Now Erecting in the Highlands," undated (probably late fall, 1775), USMA Special Collections.
9. Report of Nicoll, Drake, and Palmer, December 14, 1775, ibid., 312–19; the Continental Congress had asked the New York Provincial Congress to determine if there were other places "where small batteries might be erected," and Romans had highly recommended "Pooploop's Kill," minutes,

October 7, 12 and 17, 1775, Romans, Samuel Bayard and William Bedlow to Nathaniel Woodhull, President of the New York Provincial Congress, October 16, 1775, New York, *Journal of the Provincial Congress*, 172, 174, 177, 179–80.

10. Diamant, *Bernard Romans*, 15, 71, 132.
11. Bernard Romans, *A Concise Natural History of East and West Florida* (New York: Bernard Romans, 1775; repr., New Orleans: Pelican Publishing Company, 1961), 174–75.
12. P. Lee Phillips, *Notes On the Life and Works of Bernard Romans* (Deland, Fla.: The Florida State Historical Society, 1924), 47, 54; Diamant, *Bernard Romans*, 70.
13. Roger Stevenson, *Instructions for Officers Detached to the Field: Containing a Scheme for Forming a Corps of a Partisan* (Philadelphia: R. Aitken, 1775); Robert R. Livingston, Robert Treat Paine, and John Langdon to John Hancock, November 23, 1775, Force, 4th ser., 3:1657–58.
14. Romans, *Natural History*, 1.
15. John Muller, *A Treatise Containing the Practical Art of Fortification in Four Parts*, 3d ed. (London: W. Strahan et al., 1774), 123–24.
16. J.C. Pleydell, *An Essay on Field Fortifications* (London: J. Nourse, 1768), vi–vii; John Muller, *A Treatise Containing the Elementary Part of Fortification, Regular and Irregular* (London: J. Nourse, 1746; repr., Ottawa: Museum Restoration Service, 1968); Sebastien LePrestre de Vauban, *A Manual of Siegecraft and Fortification*, trans., George A. Rothrock (Ann Arbor: The University of Michigan Press, 1968), 157; Stevenson, 9; Muller, *Practical Art*, 124, 128–29.
17. Romans to the New York Committee of Safety, September 14, 1775, Force, 4th ser., 735–36.
18. Marked "C" on Plan No.2, September 14, 1775, *Papers, Continental Congress*, 274. No blockhouse or battery appeared at West Point in his "plan" done in late fall; he seems to have substituted instead a battery at present-day Garrison on the eastern side of the river. The sketch accompanying the report of Nicoll, Drake, and Palmer does not indicate any fortification at West Point, December 14, 1775, *Papers, Continental Congress*, and 280–83. "He must take care not to be commanded by any neighboring heights, . . ." Stevenson, 10.
19. Lord Stirling to General George Washington, June 1, 1776, Force, 4th ser., 6:672–78.
20. Pleydell, ix.
21. Vauban, 168.
22. Minutes, August 18, 22, 30, September 6, October 16, 18, 23, 1775, New York Provincial Congress and Committee of Safety, Force, 4th ser., 3:535, 541, 567, 571, 880, 1290, 1295–96, 1301, 1363–64; only Samuel Bayard had accompanied Clinton and Tappen on the original survey, ibid., 2:1296; commissioners would continue to supervise construction at Fort Constitution and Popolopen Creek until June 13, 1776 when the Commander in Chief assumed control, New York, *Journal of the Provincial Congress*, 493; minutes, September 25, 1775, ibid., 158–59; New York Committee of Safety to the Continental Congress, September 19, 1775, *Papers, Continental Congress*, 41; John Berrien to the New York Committee of Safety, September 21, 1775, Phillips, 112.
23. The correspondence exchange between the commissioners and Romans may be found in Force, 4th ser., 1355–67 and in Merle G. Sheffield, *The Fort That Never Was: A Discussion of the Revolutionary War Fortifications Built on Constitution Island, 1775–1783* (West Point: Constitution Island Association, 1969), 13, C-1-C-12.
24. Captain Mott of the Connecticut militia had commented on this in his journal while en route to Fort Ticonderoga in May 1775: "Mr. Romans left us and joined us no more; we were all glad, as he had been a trouble to us, all the time he was with us." General Philip Schuyler would later prefer

court-martial charges against Romans, now the commander of a Pennsylvanian company of matrosses, in April 1776, during his march to the Canadian Department, Diamant, *Bernard Romans*, 52, 123–26.

25. Muller, *Practical Art*, 130.
26. Report of Clinton and Tappen, June 13, 1775, Force, 4th ser., 2:1296; Romans' estimate, September 18, 1775, *Papers, Continental Congress*, 55–58.
27. Lord Stirling to General Washington, June 1, 1776, Force, 4th ser., 6:672–78.
28. Ibid., 6:678.
29. Sir Henry Clinton to Sir William Howe, October 9, 1777, and Commodore William Hotham to Lord Viscount Howe, October 9, 1777, Donald F. Clark, ed., *Fort Montgomery and Fort Clinton* (Fort Montgomery, NY: Town of Highlands, 1952), 12, 14.
30. For the most complete story of the state of the forts and their fall, see ibid., 3–16; William H. Carr and Richard J. Koke, *Twin Forts of the Popolopen: Forts Clinton and Montgomery, New York 1775–1777*, Historical Bulletin Number 1 (Bear Mountain, NY: Commissioners of the Palisades Interstate Park and the American Scenic and Historic Preservation Society, July 1937); report of Court of Inquiry to His Excellency George Washington, April 5, 1778, and Alexander McDougall to Washington, May 21, 1778, Alexander McDougall Papers, New York Historical Society, microfilm.
31. Diamant, *Bernard Romans*, 72. Report of Francis Nicoll, Joseph Drake, and Thomas Palmer to the New York Provincial Congress, December 14, 1775, Papers, Continental Congress, 312–19; report, 4:420–22, Lord Stirling to General Washington, June 1, 1776, 6:672–78, Force, 4th ser.; New York, *Journal of the Provincial Congress*, 322, 330; minutes, February 1776, Ford, 4:133–34. (In a 2-day visit to the Highlands, Captain William Smith, the engineer of General Charles Lee, traced out the former on Gravel Hill on a site identified but not fortified by Romans because the Continental and Provincial Congresses had dismissed him as of February 9, 1776. Smith would also propose a trace for Fort Montgomery).
32. Notes of debate, October 6, 1775, Ford, 3:485.
33. Pleydell, xii–xiii.

PART IV

Battles and Warfare

16

A Warm Reception in the Hudson Highlands

JAMES M. JOHNSON

AMERICAN FORCES in New York essentially won the war against Great Britian by preventing British forces in New York City and Canada from meeting in the Hudson Valley and thereby cutting off communications, supply, and military movement between New England and the rest of the rebelling colonies.

Most American schoolchildren learn that the Battle of Saratoga in October 1777, in which General John Burgoyne surrendered his army—one quarter of the British troops in North America—to General Horatio Gates, was the turning point in the American Revolution. Few know, however, that American warships on the Hudson River contributed to Gates's victory in the north country of New York. The two key ships in the small flotilla that opposed the British in October 1777 were the American frigates *Congress* and *Montgomery*, built at the Continental Shipyard in Poughkeepsie, New York. Their quest for glory would be brief, ending when their crews scuttled them to keep them out of the enemy's hands.

On 13 December 1775, Congress passed a resolution authorizing the construction of a fleet of thirteen frigates to challenge the Royal Navy, to be built at a cost of $66,666.67 each. New York would build and outfit two of the thirteen, *Congress* and *Montgomery*. The 682-ton *Congress* was rated at twenty-eight guns and had a deck length of 126 feet and a beam of thirty-four feet; the 563-ton *Montgomery* was rated at twenty-four guns with a deck length of 119 feet and a beam of thirty-two feet. Superintendents Jacobus Van Zandt, Augustus Lawrence, and Samuel Tudor would oversee the work in Poughkeepsie, on the eastern shore of the Hudson, north of the City of New York.[1]

Despite Congress's deadline of March 1776 for the ships to put to sea, the superintendents did not launch *Montgomery* and *Congress* until November of that year. Delayed by work stoppages, material shortages, and the diversion of naval stores to Brigadier General Benedict Arnold's fleet on Lake Champlain, the shipyard worked to complete and outfit the frigates even as the British landed at Staten Island and HMS *Phoenix* and HMS *Rose* ranged north as far as Peekskill Bay in July, ostensibly in search of the warships. When they were finally launched, the two new frigates spent the winter on Rondout Creek near Kingston.[2]

THE DEFENSE OF THE HIGHLANDS

On paper, General Israel Putnam, the commander of the Hudson Highlands, had enough forces to give British commander Sir Henry Clinton a fight and well-placed fortifications substantial enough to make any expedition against them difficult should Clinton venture north from New York City. Fort Montgomery on the west side of the Hudson, just north of Popolopen Creek, had been established in 1776. The heart of its defenses against an attack from the river was the 100-foot-long Grand

Fig. 16.1. The American Naval Flotilla, led by the frigate *Montgomery*, guards the chain and engages the British fleet, October 6, 1777. Painting by Dahl Taylor; courtesy of NYS Office of Parks, Recreation, and Historic Preservation.

Battery with walls eighteen feet thick. According to First Lieutenant William A. Patterson of the 15th Regiment, the battery with its six 32-pounders, "Rakes the River Pretty Well For Three Miles." The landward ramparts were "comparatively open with the works poorly situated and incomplete."[3]

On higher ground to protect Fort Montgomery's southern approach, and connected to it by a bridge across Popolopen Creek, was Fort Clinton. While the rear of the fort facing its sister was incomplete, this circular work was anchored by two star-redoubts, one of four points or bastions and the other of eight. Fifteen cannon, manned by forty artillerymen, protected the fort itself, including the eight-pointed redoubt; the four-pointed redoubt to the southwest had three 6-pounders fired by nine men. Colonel Lewis Dubois estimated that a garrison of 2,000 men was needed to defend both forts properly; unfortunately, on the day the British attacked fewer than 700 were present.[4]

A chain, designed to stop or to damage any English warships that attempted to barrel through it, had been put in place across the Hudson River at this point in March 1777. Stretching 1,700 feet from a cove just north of Popolopen Creek to the base of a rocky promontory called Anthony's Nose on the eastern shore of the Hudson, it was guarded by the sprawling Fort Montgomery.[5]

As early as 12 May 1777, Washington had personally taken steps to increase the odds against the British when he sent Major General Nathanael Greene to the Highlands to inspect the defenses and correct any errors he might find. He charged Greene with insuring that the defenses were ready to defeat an attack from either land or water and guard against a "coup de main" from the west.

Fig. 16.2. Awaiting the British at the entrance to the Hudson Highlands were Forts Montgomery (at right), on the north side of Popolopen Creek, and Clinton (at left), the chain (bottom, center) that was intended to bar a British fleet from the upper Hudson, and a small flotilla. Painting by Jack Mead; courtesy of NYS Office of Parks, Recreation, and Historic Preservation.

Greene and his committee—Brigadier Generals Alexander McDougall, Henry Knox, George Clinton, and Anthony Wayne—reported that additional water obstacles were all that was needed to complete the defenses. In their collective judgment, the addition of a boom and cables to bolster the chain and the presence of two armed galleys and the two New York frigates would combine with the batteries of the forts to "render it impossible for the Shipping to operate there." If the river remained blocked and if "the Passes into the Highlands be properly guarded, which can be done with about four or five thousand troops, the rest of the Army will be at liberty to operate elsewhere."[6]

The Continental Marine Committee acted almost immediately on Greene's recommendations by ordering *Montgomery* and *Congress* southward from Poughkeepsie in June. And, in July, absent a boom to protect the chain, General (and New York Governor) George Clinton, in command of the fort, placed a large cable south of the chain spliced from three smaller cables from the frigate *Montgomery* in July. By the end of July, the frigates, the New York sloop *Camden*, and the Continental row galleys *Shark* and *Lady Washington* were anchored near Popolopen Creek. By scouring the region for armament, each of the ships had acquired some cannons: *Montgomery*, with a crew of thirty-six, had eight 12-pounders; *Congress* had at least nine 9-pounders from Fort Constitution, farther north across from West Point; *Camden*, with a crew of eighteen, had six 6-pounders, four 4-pounders, and twelve swivel guns; *Shark*, with a crew of eighteen, had four 9-pounders; and *Lady Washington*, with a crew of 20, had one 32-pounder and eight 3-pounders. Captain John Hodge of *Montgomery* and Captain Thomas Grennell of *Congress* had scraped together crews from experienced sailors, soldiers, and even "Deserters, Boys, &ca."[7]

PUT TO THE TEST

Undermanned and undergunned, the Hudson's navy suffered from its organization and the mission that senior leaders had assigned it. The Continental Marine Committee had established a workable command relationship that linked its ships with the ground force: Grennell and Hodge were "to follow and obey such orders as they may receive from General Washington or the Commanding officer who may direct the operations in that quarter." Because the mission of the ships was to protect the chain, they had

Fig. 16.3. *"Attack!"* The Battles of Forts Clinton and Montgomery. Painting by Jack Mead; courtesy of NYS Office of Parks, Recreation, and Historic Preservation.

"become a part of the work itself." This meant that General George Clinton, rather than General Israel Putnam, exercised authority over the ships. One other twist complicated the issue: *Congress* had been ordered by Clinton to sail north on 5 October to Fort Constitution "lest she should meet with a Disaster."

Although Hodge rated the galleys "manned and in a proper state of defence" and his own ship "in great forwardness," he would find that his inflexible mission and the actual state of his small force limited the contribution he would be able to make to the outcome of the upcoming battle. Nonetheless he predicted that "we shall be able to give the enemy (when they approach) a warm reception."[8]

Sir Henry Clinton set the Hudson River Campaign of 1777 in motion on 2 October when he and Commodore William Hotham transported 3,000 men aboard some 56 warships, transports, and flatboats, landing first at Tarrytown on 4 October, at Verplanck's Point the next day, and finally at Stony Point on the 6th. Some 700 Continental infantrymen, artillerymen, and militiamen opposed the two-pronged attack from the south and west. By nightfall, however, following violent assaults on Forts Montgomery and Clinton after a twelve-hour march overland, Sir Henry occupied both fortifications. The march through the mountainous terrain had prevented the use of artillery, so this British attack was made by the infantry and what cannon fire Captain Sir James Wallace (formerly of HMS *Rose*) could bring to bear from his row galleys. In the face of a fierce cannonade from the American row galleys, frigates, and the sloop north of the chain, HMS *Dependence* fired ninety-five 24-pound shot and six 4-pounders against the vessels and the forts. Despite inadequate crews and too few guns, *Montgomery* and her consorts made a gallant if futile fight of it.

By 8 PM Henry Clinton knew that he owned the two forts. At the cost of some seventy killed, forty wounded, and 240 taken prisoner, the Americans had exacted a substantial price,

Fig. 16.4. The frigate *Montgomery* was burned by her own crew the night of October 6, 1777. Painting by Jack Mead; courtesy of NYS Office of Parks, Recreation, and Historic Preservation.

killing forty and wounding 150 of the attackers. While British forces won the battle, these fortifications and their ships disrupted Clinton's timetable, complicating any attempts to relieve Burgoyne's trapped army. At 10 PM, Clinton and Hotham nonetheless had the pleasure of observing the blazing *Montgomery*.

George Clinton reported to George Washington on 9 October that:

> by some Fatality the two Continental Frigates were lost . . . being badly manned they could not be got off in Time, though I ordered the Ship *Congress* to proceed to Fort Constitution the Day before the Attack, lest she should meet with a Disaster; and the Ship *Montgomery*, which lay near the Chain, having neither Anchors nor Cable to secure her, it being the Tide of ebb, and the Wind failing, she fell down so near the Chain, that Captn Hodge was constrained to set her on Fire to prevent her falling into the Hands of the Enemy, and the *Congress* unfortunately getting aground on a Flat near Fort Constitution shared the same Fate.[9]

Congress's acting commander, First Lieutenant Daniel Shaw, with the assistance of some sixteen artillerymen from Fort Constitution, burned her on 7 October. *Camden* ran aground and became a British prize. The American crews set fire to *Shark* as well. (*Lady Washington* later sailed up to Kingston, where she helped in the defense of the city but was scuttled during the attack.) With the forts reduced, the ships dispersed, and Putnam's forces withdrawing northward to protect the pass to Fishkill, Henry Clinton completed his control of the Highlands.

With the river clear of enemy ships and the shores barren of organized troops, by 8 October Clinton had taken Fort Independence on Peekskill bay, broken the chain across the river, occupied Fort Constitution to the north, and passed the *chevaux de frise* anchored on Pollepel's Island. Hotham's advance squadron, under Wallace, ranged the river unimpeded as far north as Poughkeepsie. From 16–26 October Major

General John Vaughan and Wallace sailed even farther to the north in a vain attempt to link up with Burgoyne's ill-fated army. The highlight of this expedition was a naval landing at Rondout Creek that culminated in Vaughan's burning of Kingston, the capital of New York.[10]

George Clinton's forces resisted this attack to no avail. Putnam, however, finally massed enough forces on the west bank of the Hudson to give Vaughan pause. This fact plus the knowledge that Burgoyne had surrendered and orders from Sir Henry made up Vaughan's mind, and he and his force slipped back down the river on 26 October. With no navy left, American forces could only harass the departing flotilla with cannon fire and musketry from the shore as it withdrew.

Despite their successful attack on American forces in the Highlands, Clinton's half-hearted efforts to save Burgoyne's army had been in vain. The sacrifice of American sailors and soldiers at Popolopen Creek had helped to turn the war around. The British would now have to confront French armies and navies in a world war that they ultimately could not win.

This article originally appeared in *Sea History*, Vol. 98, Autumn 2001. Used by permission.

NOTES

1. William Bell Clark, William James Morgan, and Michael J. Crawford, eds. *Naval Documents of the American Revolution*, 11 vols. to date (Washington: U. S. Government Printing Office, 1964), 3: 90; 6: 1201; John Fitzhugh Millar, *Building Early American Warships: The Journal of the Rhode Island Committee for Constructing the Continental Frigates Providence & Warren, 1775–1777* (Williamsburg, Va.: Thirteen Colonies Press; Providence, R.I.: Rhode Island Publications Society, 1988), 27.
2. Memoirs of William Smith, 5 November 1776, *Naval Documents*, 7: 47; Francis Lewis, 27 November 1776, and Samuel Tuter, 2 December 1776, to the New York Committee of Safety and Tuder to New York Convention, 12 December 1776, ibid., 7: 307, 350, 460.
3. Wm A. Patterson to Hon. &c, "22 April 1776," Merle Gardner Sheffield Research Files, Special Collections, USMA Library, West Point, NY, from originals in the Mass. HS.
4. "Capt. Moody's of Col. Lambs Redgment Testimony" and "Genl. Putnam, N°. 25," "Report of the Court of Inquiry on the Loss of Fort Montgomery" to Washington, 5 April 1778, McDougall Papers, United States Military Philosophical Society Records, 1789–1813, microfilmed by the New York Historical Society, Reel 2, USMA Library, West Point, NY, hereinafter cited as "Court of Inquiry"; George Clinton to Washington, 9 Oct. 1777, *Naval Documents*, 10: 94.
5. 150 white pine logs were originally ordered to a boom, 21 July 1776; theoretically, thirty-two rafts could have been constructed from the 150 logs; assuming each raft to be fifty feet wide with fifteen feet separation, twenty-seven rafts would span the 1,800 feet of river. Contract, Christopher Tappen, 26 July, Tappen to Gilbert Livingston, 27 July, James Clinton to John Jay, 12 Aug., minutes, Secret Committee, Papers of the Secret Committee, 1, 13 Aug., Tappen and Livingston to Johannis Sleght, 21 Aug., Sleght to Committee, 22 Aug., bill for 160 logs, 14 Sep., receipt for "Superintending the Fixing of the Chain," Ebenezer Young, 10 Aug. to 25 Dec., Papers of the Secret Committee; as of 11 Oct. Peter Tappen wrote that "I hope we shall now in a few Days git the Chain acrosst the River here as it is almost Done," Tappen to George Clinton, 11 Oct., John McKesson to Clinton, 31 Oct., 3 Nov., George Clinton, *Public Papers of George Clinton, First Governor of New York 1777–1795—1801–1804*, ed. Hugh Hastings, 10 vols. (New York and Albany: State

printers, 1899–1914), 1: 378, 404, 412.

6. "Continental Army Generals to General Washington," 17 May 1777, *Naval Documents*, 8: 987.
7. 14 Aug. 1776, "Memorandum of Stores Necessary for the Sloop Hudson & . . . Camden," Papers of the Secret Committee; George Clinton to Putnam, 15 June 1777, Captain John Hodge to the New York Council of Safety, 13 July 1777, ibid., 9: 118, 281; "Capt Hodge's Evidence, N 7," "Court of Inquiry."
8. Continental Marine Committee to the New York Council of Safety and to Captains Grennell and John Hodge, 26 June 1777, *Naval Documents*, 9: 176–77; Putnam to the New York Council of Safety, 5 June 1777, Phil. Livingston and Wm. Duer to Pierre Van Cortlandt, President of the New York Council of Safety, 31 May 1777, Hodge to Council of Safety, 13 Jul. 1777, and Cortlandt to the President of Congress, 11 June 1777, ibid., 9: 24, 42, 90, 281.
9. Ibid., 9: 838–43; Commodore William Hotham to Vice Admiral Viscount Howe, 1 Oct. 1777, Clinton to Hotham, 2 Oct. 1777, Hotham to Admiral Howe, 9 Oct. 1777, Clinton to General Howe, 9 Oct. 1777, journals, 3 Oct. 1777, of *Tartar, Diligent, Apollo, Experiment, and Mercury* and journals, 4 Oct. 1777, of *Dependence, Experiment, and Preston*, ibid., 10: 12, 16, 96–100; Hotham to Admiral Howe, 9 Oct. 1777, and journal of *Dependence*, 6 Oct. 1777, George Clinton to New York Council of Safety, 8 Oct. 1777, ibid., 10: 42–43, 47, 70, 96, 98–99; George Clinton to George Washington, 9 Oct. 1777, *Public Papers of George Clinton*, 2: 394; "Capt. Hodge's Evidence," "Court of Inquiry"; Stephen Kemble, "Kemble's Journal, 1777," *Collections of the New-York Historical Society for the Year 1883* (New York: New-York Historical Society, 1884), 132–33; extract from the log of the *Dependence Galley, 15 October 1777, Year Book*, 1935, Dutchess County Historical Society, 96.
10. Vaughan to Clinton, 17 Oct. 1777, Wallace to Hotham, 17 Oct. 1777, journals of the *Dependence* and the *Diligent*, 16 Oct. 1777, *Naval Documents*, 10: 183–84, 192–93.

17

Civil War in Schaghticoke

A Footnote to the Revolution in Upstate New York

R. BETH KLOPOTT

"NOTICE IS HEREBY GIVEN to the Inhabitants of the Town of Schorticoke to meet at the House of Henry Jackson, in Tomhanock on Tuesday the 4th day of September . . . to Elect a Governor, Lieutenant Governor and twelve Counsellors and two Representatives for the year ensuing, also a States Treasurer by order of the Selectmen [of Vermont]."[1] So read the notice from Jonathan Hobbart, Constable from Vermont, and signed by William Sheperd and "one Doty," both of Schaghticoke, to that community in New York in 1781.[2] How was it that such a notice was posted? Why would men in New York be voting for government officers in Vermont? Was the northeast section of Albany County seceding from New York to join Vermont? Did the majority of residents of the region approve of this possibility, or did the idea incite a situation of civil war?

The farmers of Schaghticoke and neighboring communities lying between the future state of Vermont and the Hudson River during the American Revolution had concerns that went beyond the conflict with Britain. The incursions against them committed by General John Burgoyne's troops and allied Indian forces as they approached Saratoga were only part of the difficulties facing the inhabitants of Schaghticoke. Caught in the middle of an ancient controversy between New York and New Hampshire over territory that lay between the two colonies (later Vermont), Schaghticoke residents split over support for Vermont or New York.

The original boundaries that were established by the colonial charters creating New York and New Hampshire were typically inaccurate and vague. New York claimed the Connecticut River as its eastern boundary. By 1750 both Connecticut and Massachusetts residents had purchased land west of the Connecticut River. The governor of New Hampshire, Benning Wentworth, wanted a settlement of the western boundary of his colony, which was supposed to run directly north from the Massachusetts line between New York and New Hampshire. The dispute was referred to the Crown, and in 1764 an Order in Council created the western bank of the Connecticut River, from Massachusetts to the 45° northern latitude, as the line between New York and New Hampshire.[3]

This should have ended the argument, but the battle had only just begun. By this date both colonies had granted land to numerous settlers, and neither government was willing to recognize outright the grants of the other. New York demanded that the New Hampshire settlers pay a second set of title fees to the New York government as well as additional fees for having their titles validated. Few people had the cash or the inclination to do so.

The area, referred to as the New Hampshire Grants, became the scene of endless lawsuits, accusations, and riots. Ethan Allen formed the Green Mountain Boys in response to the attempts by New York authorities to establish their jurisdiction over the territory. Part of the issue lay in the fact that many men, including

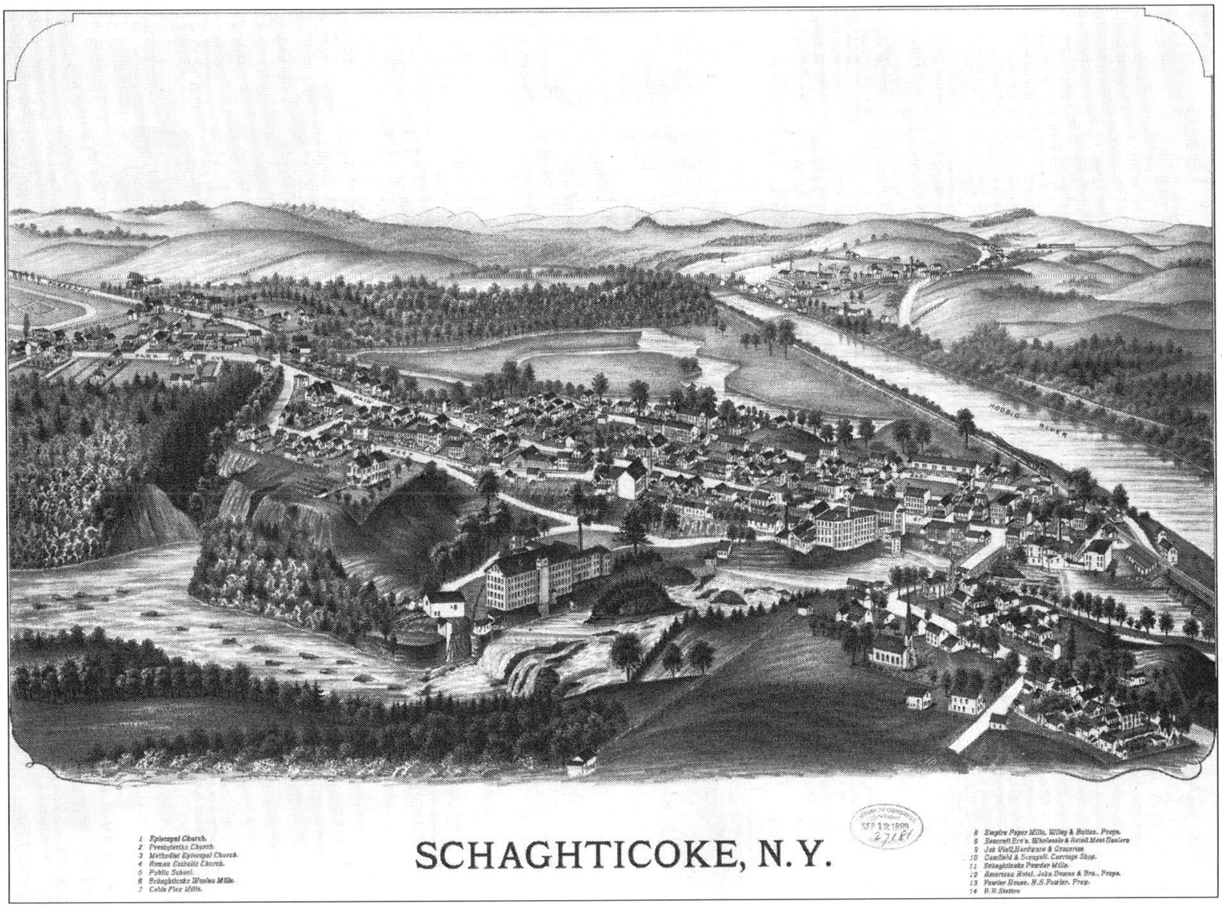

Fig. 17.1. Aerial View of Schaghticoke, N.Y. c. 1889. Library of Congress.

Allen, held title from New Hampshire to large quantities of unsettled territory in the Grants. The New York colonial government was willing to acknowledge settled land titles but not titles for unsettled land. New Yorkers were land speculators par excellence, and they were reluctant to pass up the chance for speculation and profit in the Grants.[4] By May 1771 affidavits were being sworn before Sheriff Samuel Monro testifying to harassment and riotous behavior on the part of people from the Grants against New Yorkers west of Bennington. By 1774 the disturbances had spread to Charlotte County and the northeast district of Albany County, and warrants were issued by the New York Assembly for the arrests of Ethan Allen, Seth Warner, Remember Baker, and others.[5]

At a convention held at Dorset in the Grants in September 1775, fifty-six delegates from thirty-six towns declared themselves the new state of Vermont, claiming all territory west to the Hudson River, which included Schaghticoke. Complicating matters even further, the Continental Congress authorized Allen to raise a regiment separate from New York. Outraged New Yorkers believed that this encouraged Allen in his behavior toward New York and his demand for a separate state.[6] Incursions into New York increased as Allen took advantage of the revolutionary situation to gain his objective. New York militia officers were arrested when the Green Mountain Boys attempted to force submission to Vermont authority. After 1780 raids into New York became more numerous and began to penetrate as far west and south as Schaghticoke. It was reported later by many residents that the Vermonters destroyed their forts and left them open to enemy attack. In addition, many of their relatives were taken to Vermont as captives.[7]

In May 1781 a convention held in Cambridge, New York, was attended by representatives from Hoosick, Schaghticoke, Cambridge, Saratoga, Upper White Creek, Black Creek, Skeinsborough, Kingsbury, Fort Edward, and Little Hoosick. Except for John Rodgers and Moses Robinson, who were the chairmen of the meeting, the identity of the representatives is unknown. The convention reiterated Vermont's claim to all land west to the Hudson River, stated "that the whole of the Military force of the State of Vermont shall be excerted in our defence as free Citizens against any Insurrection, Incursion whatsoever but especially against the Common Enemy," and recognized Vermont as a legitimate state and pledged allegiance to it.[8]

Ten months later, after the surrender of General Cornwallis at Yorktown, a number of Cambridge men, perhaps to save their own necks and property, renounced their part in the convention, stating that they collaborated with the ringleaders out of fear of arrest by Vermont authorities, loss of their property, and destruction of their forts, which left them open to enemy attack. The notice to the New York government was signed "Cambridge, 1st March, 1782."[9] But no one from Schaghticoke repudiated participation in the convention.

In the summer of 1781 Colonel Peter Yates and eighty members of the Fourteenth Militia Regiment, originally a Schaghticoke unit, were stationed in Schaghticoke for the purpose of suppressing the insurrection against New York and quelling riots incited by the Vermonters. In response to a request for reinforcements from Colonel Yates, General Stark, based at Saratoga, wrote to Yates stating that "the Insurrection you mention must be the result of folly and madness you will be very cautious not to begin hostilities with them but stand your Ground and Act defensively till reinforced. Genl's Gansevoort and V. Resselaer are raising their Brigades with the utmost dispatch for your Assistance."[10]

In October a notice arrived in Schaghticoke ordering the residents of the community to "Cease from all Seditious, factious conduct . . ." and commanding "all the inhabitants of this said Scortocook, by the authority invested in us by . . . the free men of Vermont, that they leave off their advising the people and trying to Disafect them, and spreading Evil Reports and Raising Seditiom among the people of this Town. . . ."[11] By this time some residents of Schaghticoke had been to the Cambridge Convention to announce their support for Vermont. Others were not partial to this arrangement and the community became divided over the issue.

In December Yates's troops were reinforced by General Gansevoort, who reported to Governor Clinton that there were insurgents in Schaghticoke, encouraged or threatened by men from Vermont. Schaghticoke residents were "in a very precarious Situation, Numbers have complained . . . they say that they daily expect to be taken by the people of the Grants and that they will be reduced to the alternative of either swearing allegiance to the state of Vermont or abandoning their Habitations, and that several of them have been already reduced to that Delemma."[12] Gansevoort notified the Vermonters that he had been sent to Schaghticoke to suppress an "Insurrection of some of the Subjects of this State residing in the district of Schachtikoke and Hoseck."[13]

But not all the "rioters" were from Vermont. In an affidavit sworn out by Casper Rouse of Schaghticoke, he stated that quite a number of people involved in the riots were from Schaghticoke themselves and acted on behalf of Vermont. He reported that in the summer of 1781 sixty inhabitants of the district of Schaghticoke met at the "House of Henry Jackson, also of Schaghticoke for the purpose of electing a governor and Representatives of Assembly for Vermont." The advertisement for the meeting, mentioned earlier, was signed by William Sheperd and "one Doty," both of Schaghticoke. At the meeting were Schadrick Phelps, Henry

Jackson, Jurry Wetzel, Peter Crawberger, David Smith, Edward Henderson, Jacob Van Wormer, Hendrick Van Der Hoof, Thomas Benedict, and Edward Jewitt, all of the district of Schaghticoke. Thomas Benedict and Edward Jewitt were, according to Rouse, acting as Justices of the Peace for Vermont.[14]

Lines were not clearly drawn. There was enough verbal and military harassment of the residents of Schaghticoke to convince some of them to cooperate with the Vermont invasion. Others chose to resist the pressure, provoking the authorities from Vermont to issue cease and desist orders. However, according to the affidavit of Casper Rouse, there were Schaghticoke people who willingly joined the Vermonters. Although probably small in number, these men attempted to bring the northeastern section of New York, including Schaghticoke, under the jurisdiction of Vermont. Yates and Gansevoort had a small civil war on their hands.

Early in 1782 a band of two hundred men from Bennington descended upon Schaghticoke. A deposition from Abraham Van Vechten reported that Albany County Sheriff John Ten Broeck, with part of Colonel Yates's and Colonel Henry Van Rensselaer's regiments, took several of the "rioters" prisoner and sent them to the Albany City jail. Because the disturbances had been quelled, along with the end of the Revolution, violence was eliminated as a course of action for the Vermonters. The case was finally settled by Congress in 1790, when New York ceded part of the disputed land to Vermont for $30,000 and Vermont became the fourteenth state.[15] Schaghticoke, Cambridge, and the other communities whose representatives partook in the Cambridge Convention remained under New York jurisdiction.

At the outset of the Revolution the community of Schaghticoke enlisted on the side of the patriots. The Fourteenth Militia Regiment formed by the community's leading figure, Johannes Knickerbacker II, fought at Saratoga and was subsequently sent to subdue the disturbances in Schaghticoke. At least a portion of the community favored aligning with Vermont. None of the men who went to Henry Jackson's home in the summer of 1781 were tenants on the land in Schaghticoke owned by the City of Albany. Their surnames indicate that many of them were originally from New England rather than from Dutch Albany. This accounts for their willingness to support Ethan Allen and his designs. These men did not represent a majority in the community, but the numbers were enough to encourage the Vermonters to continue their raids into northeastern New York and to create civil war conditions in Schaghticoke.

This article originally appeared in the *Hudson Valley Regional Review*, Volume 10, No. 1, March 1993.

NOTES

1. A Notice for the Call of a Vermont State Election, Jona. Hobbart, Constable, August 27, 1781, in Hugh Hastings et al., *The Public Papers of George Clinton, 1777–1795, 1801–1804,* 10 vols. (Albany, 1900), 7:302.
2. Affidavit of Casper Rouse, in Hastings et al., *Papers of George Clinton*, 7:302, 609–10.
3. Hastings et al., *Papers of George Clinton,* 7:591; E. B. O'Callaghan, ed., *Documentary History of the State of New York* (Albany, 1845–1851), 4:331–33, 335 (hereafter cited as *DHNY*).
4. O'Callaghan, *DHNY*, 4:356, 363–78, 380–412; Charles A. Jellison, *Ethan Allen: Frontier Rebel* (Syracuse, 1969), 39–83; Rowland E. Robinson, *Vermont: A Study of Independence* (Boston: Mifflin & Co., 1894). *Civil War in Schaghticoke: A Footnote to the Revolution in Upstate New York*, 45
5. O'Callaghan, ed., *DHNY,* 4:325–27, 412–34.
6. Ibid., 554, 556–58.
7. Ibid., 564, 575–77, 581, 604.

8. Ibid., 603–04.
9. Ibid., 604.
10. General Stark to Colonel Yates, Saratoga, December 8, 1781, in Hastings et al., *Papers of George Clinton,* 7:569.
11. Notice to inhabitants of Schaghticoke from Edward Jewitt and Thomas Benedict, Justices of the Peace, October 15, 1781, ibid., 591.
12. Hastings et al., ibid., 7:609–10, 615–18.
13. Peter Gansevoort, B. Genl. to Officer in Command of Body of Vermonters for Invading New York State, Headquarters, Schachtikoke, December 18, 1781, ibid., 602.
14. Peter Gansevoort to George Clinton, December 21, 1781, ibid., 615–18; affidavit of Casper Rouse, ibid., 302, 609–10.
15. *Calendar of Historical Manuscripts Relating to the War of the Revolution,* 2 vols., Office of the Secretary of State (Albany, 1868), 2:364–65; Jellison, *Ethan Allen,* Chaps. 14 and 15.

18

Interpreting the Battle for the Hudson River Valley

The Battle of Fort Montgomery

JAMES M. JOHNSON AND GREGORY SMITH

THE REMAINS OF Fort Montgomery are situated in the Hudson Highlands, the most dramatic stretch of the Hudson River Valley National Heritage Area. They sit 120 feet above the Hudson River on the west bank of Popolopen Creek and are surrounded by Bear Mountain Bridge, Anthony's Nose, and Bear Mountain State Park. With Fort Clinton, its sister work to the south, Fort Montgomery played a decisive role in the Saratoga campaign of 1777, "the turning point of the American Revolution."

When Governor George E. Pataki dedicated the Fort Montgomery State Historic Site on October 6, 2002, he guaranteed that the ruins of one of the nation's important Revolutionary War battlegrounds would be forever preserved. This article will explain how the Fort Montgomery Plan Team approached the challenge of interpreting this National Historic Landmark.

Two hundred twenty-five years to the day of the governor's dedication, Forts Montgomery and Clinton earned their place in history. On October 6, 1777, 1,500 Continental soldiers and New York militiamen confronted 3,000 British soldiers, sailors, and marines under Major General Sir Henry Clinton, in what was the beginning of the British attack against the fortifications of the Hudson Highlands. Sir Henry had designed his plan to support Major General John Burgoyne's expedition into New York from Canada. He began the operation with a feint against Verplanck's Point at King's Ferry, twelve miles south of the forts. His goal was to keep the forces of General Israel Putnam, commander in the Highlands, on the east side of the Hudson. The ruse was a success: American Brigadier Generals George and James Clinton would wind up defending the twin forts of the Popolopen, Clinton's main objective, with only 700 men.

Fort Montgomery was a sprawling work overlooking an iron chain that stretched 1,700 feet across the river, from a cove below its Grand Battery to the base of Anthony's Nose. Until he could place booms in the river to protect the chain, George Clinton, the state's governor and Fort Montgomery's commander, had substituted a cable made by splicing together three smaller cables from the Continental frigate *Montgomery*.[1] The length of the fort itself, from the tip of "Round Hill" redoubt on the northwest to the Grand Battery on the southeast, was over 1,400 feet. The heart of these defenses against an expected attack from the river was the 100-foot-long Grand Battery, with walls eighteen feet thick. According to first Lieutenant William A. Patterson of the 15th Regiment, its line of five 32-pounders "Rakes the River Pretty Well For Three Miles."[2] The rest of the fort had one more 32-pounder, ten 12-pounders, fourteen 6-pounders, and two 3-pounders. The landward ramparts were "comparatively open with the works poorly situated and incomplete."[3]

On higher ground to protect its southern approach, and connected to Fort Montgomery by a pontoon bridge across Popolopen Creek,

Fig. 18.1. The naval battle during the attack on Forts Montgomery and Clinton. Painting by Dahl Taylor; courtesy of NYS Office of Parks, Recreation, and Historic Preservation.

was Fort Clinton. Two star-shaped redoubts were the key defensive works in what could only loosely be called a fort. Colonel Lewis Dubois, commander of the 5th New York Regiment, estimated that a garrison of 2,000 men was needed to defend both forts properly.[4]

General Putnam did have one other trump card to play: a naval flotilla was present north of the chain to provide firepower and support in case of attack. A committee of Continental generals had recommended this step in its report in May, and the Continental Marine Committee had acted almost immediately, ordering two frigates—the *Montgomery* and the *Congress*—south from Poughkeepsie.[5] By July 13, they had been joined by the New York sloop *Camden* and Continental row galleys *Shark* and *Lady Washington*. Captain John Hodge of the *Montgomery* and Captain Thomas Grennell of the *Congress* had scraped together crews from experienced sailors, soldiers, and even "Deserters, Boys, &ca."[6]

Undermanned and under-gunned, this small navy suffered from its organization and the mission that senior leaders had assigned it. The Continental Marine Committee had established a workable command relationship that linked its ships with the ground force: Grennell and Hodge (who was in overall charge of the flotilla) were "to follow and obey such orders as they may receive from General [George] Washington or the Commanding officer who may direct the operations in that quarter."[7] Because the mission of the ships was to protect the chain, they had "become a part of the work itself." This meant that it was not Putnam but George Clinton, as overall commander of Forts Clinton and Montgomery, who exercised authority over them.

One other twist complicated the issue of authority: Hodge did not assume command over the *Congress*, which was ordered by General Clinton to sail on October 5 to Fort Constitution, near West Point, "lest she should meet with a Disaster." Although Hodge rated the galleys "manned and in a proper state of defence" and his own ship "in great forwardness," he would find that his inflexible mission and the actual state of his small force would limit the contribution he would be able to make to the outcome of the upcoming battle. Nonetheless he predicted that "we shall be able to give the enemy (when they approach) a warm reception."[8]

At dawn on October 6, under cover of fog, Henry Clinton began his overland attack against the two forts by landing all but 400 of his troops at Stony Point. (The British ships and transports anchored off Peekskill so they would be in position to support the final assaults.)[9] His plan of attack, designed with the assistance of Loyalist Colonel Beverly Robinson—who had lived nearby prior to the war—involved a two-prong advance over some twelve miles on Fort Montgomery from the west and Fort Clinton from the south. Lieutenant Colonel Mungo Campbell led an advance guard of 500 regulars from the 52d and 57th regiments and 400 provincials under Colonel Robinson from the Loyal Americans, New York Volunteers, and Emmerich's Chaussers. He was to seize the pass through the Dunderberg, march behind Bear Mountain, and attack Fort Montgomery. Major General John Vaughan, with 1,200 soldiers, led the main attack through the Dunderberg Pass and Doodletown against Fort Clinton.

Colonel Campbell had a difficult task. After taking the morning and part of the afternoon to complete the long march, he and his troops had to fight their way past a fieldpiece and 70 militiamen that George Clinton had sent out at about 1 or 2 p.m. Around 4 p.m., Campbell triggered the main offensive. According to Captain-Lieutenant Thomas Machin, who had commanded the fieldpiece, the Americans were deployed "in three redoubts formed by three bastions of the fort—the men were in a single rank behind the parapet and were not sufficient in number to occupy those lines of the redoubts from whence opposition might have been made to the assailants—the garrison at first gave the assailants a regular fire by platoons or divisions—but soon run into a promiscuous fire as did the enemy—the assailants frequently changed their ground, but still continued their approach." In fact, "the enemy came up several times—within 80 paces of the fort and were broke and repulsed, finally they formed a solid column from the center by files under cover of a rock at about 100 paces from the fort and in that form run up the parapet. . . ." Although Campbell was killed leading his 52d Foot into the works, the momentum of his assault carried Fort Montgomery in about forty-five minutes. Still, the firing of "the artillery and small arms continued until dark."[10] Henry Clinton waited "a favorable Moment" following the start of Campbell's fight at Fort Montgomery and then ordered Vaughan to launch his attack against Fort Clinton—using the bayonet only—across an open area of 400 yards filled with abbatis and covered by the fire of ten cannons.[11]

The mountainous terrain had prevented the British from using artillery, so the attacks were supported by what cannon fire could be brought to bear from row galleys. In the face of a fierce cannonade from the American ships, the H.M.S. *Dependence* fired ninety-five 24-pound shot and six 4-pounders against these vessels and the forts. Despite inadequate crews and too few guns, the Montgomery and her consorts made a gallant if futile fight of it.

Despite the determined efforts of the American Clintons, the unfinished twin forts fell to overwhelming British attack by nightfall. By 10 p.m. the victors had the pleasure of observing the blazing *Montgomery*, which had been torched by its crew to prevent it from falling into British hands. The *Shark* and the *Congress* would suffer similar fates near Fort Constitution. Only the *Lady Washington* escaped; it would oppose the British at Rondout Creek two weeks later. With the forts reduced, the ships dispersed, and Putnam and his forces withdrawing northward to protect the pass to Fishkill, Sir Henry would complete his control of the Highlands in a matter of days.[12]

At the cost of some 70 killed, 40 wounded, and 240 taken prisoner, the Americans nonetheless exacted a substantial price, killing 40 and wounding 150 of the attackers. While the

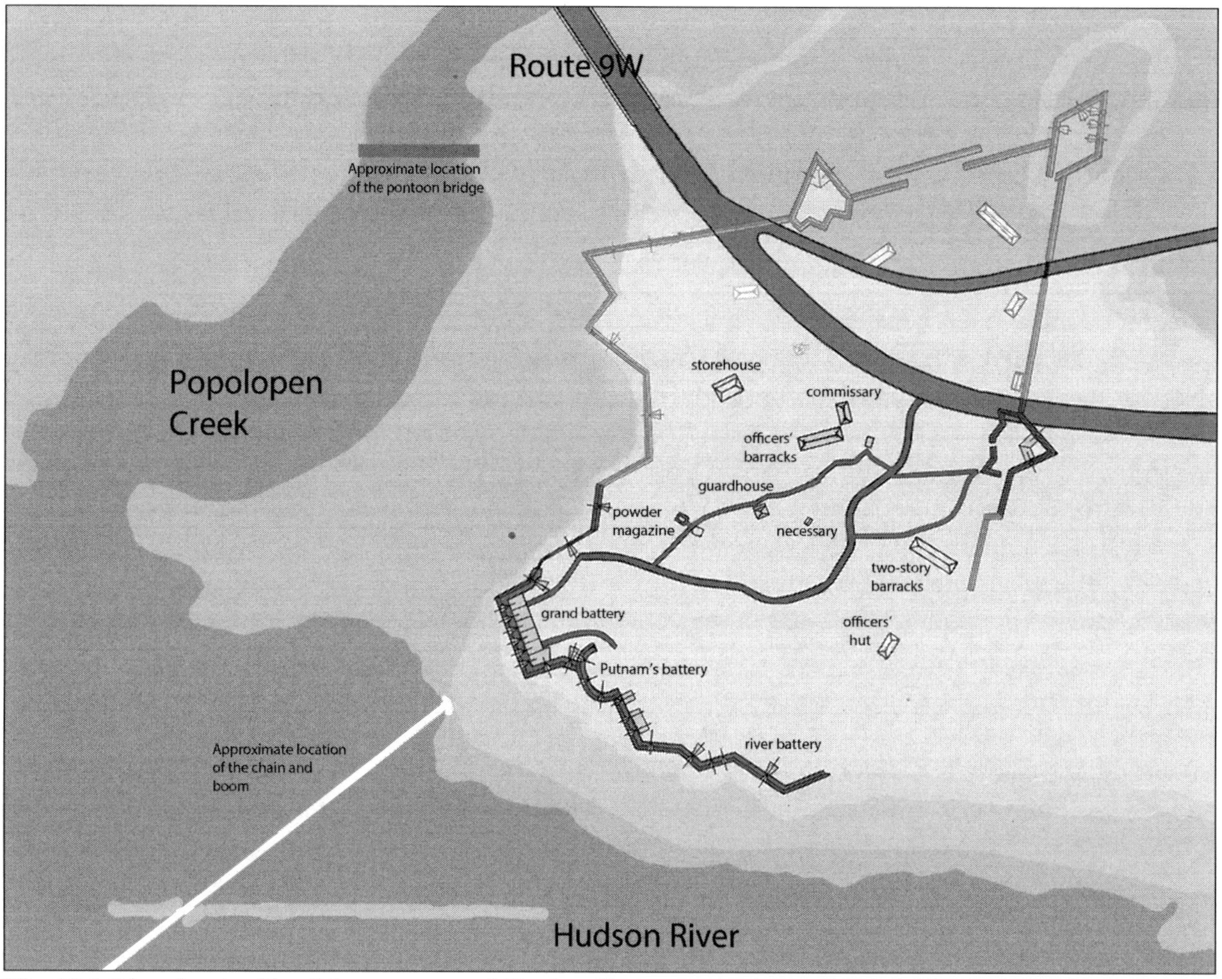

Fig. 18.2. Map showing Fort Montgomery; stabilized and interpreted ruins are labeled. Map by Jack Mead; courtesy of NYS Office of Parks, Recreation, and Historic Preservation.

British won the battles of Forts Clinton and Montgomery, the stubborn defense put up by the Americans caused the British to delay their northward thrust to join General John Burgoyne, who surrendered at Saratoga less than two weeks later. The results might have been different had Henry Clinton's substantial forces arrived in time. Most historians credit the American victory at Saratoga as being the turning point of the war: the French recognized that Washington's army possessed the ability and the desire to win a major engagement.

Since the historic battle in the autumn of 1777, Fort Montgomery has lain in ruins, awaiting the proper recognition of its contribution to victory. For five years, then Governor George Pataki, the Hudson River Valley Greenway, the Palisades Interstate Park Commission (PIPC), the New York State Office of Parks, Recreation and Historic Preservation (OPRHP), and the Fort Montgomery Battle Site Association worked to preserve, stabilize, and interpret the fort that helped change the course of American history. Their efforts made it possible for New York to open the site to the public on October 6th, 2002.

Visitors now have a remarkable opportunity to tour the fort, whose stone foundations have survived largely intact. Fort Montgomery comprises some twenty-five archaeologically significant features on 14.42 acres of land owned since 1914 by the PIPC. As shown on the map, (fig. 2) the ramparts of the irregularly shaped fortification follow the contours of the bluffs overlooking the Hudson River and Popolopen Creek and connect three landward redoubts (South, Round Hill, and North) and three river batteries (Grand, Putnam's, and River). Thomas Machin constructed gun batteries on the lower riverbank to protect the chain and boom. A stone wharf on the north bank of Popolopen Creek provided access to the fort and to the pontoon bridge connecting the twin forts. Within the fort itself, soldiers built structures to support the outer works and its garrison, including the guardhouse, powder magazine, main barracks, officers' commissary, a second barracks, storehouse, bake house, soldiers' necessary, provision stores, soldiers' hut, a "spring head," and four additional barracks. The remains of almost all of these structures are clearly visible and are in the process of being stabilized.

Interpreting a fort with the foundations of almost all of its features preserved proved challenging. Fortunately, the team had a wealth of archaeological data to rely upon. In 1916, archaeologists working for the New-York Historical Society began the first excavations at Fort Montgomery. More excavations were conducted in the 1930s, 1950s, and in the late 1960s/early 1970s by staff at Trailside Museums, located where Fort Clinton once stood. Much of what we know about the fort comes from the work done by these dedicated "diggers," particularly by the late Jack Mead, who supervised the last of these excavations. Although not formally trained as an archaeologist, Mead kept meticulous records of all of the excavations, which yielded well over 100,000 artifacts. (In 2002, archaeologists from the state's Peebles Island Resource Center conducted some additional, limited explorations in conjunction with the development of the site.)

Why did Mead and his predecessors do so much work? Their vision was one that many people in the 1960s and 1970s shared: they wanted to reconstruct the fort. It was not a new idea; in fact, it dates to at least 1930, when Arthur P. Abbott, a local author and friend of the PIPC, wrote the commission expressing his thoughts regarding reconstructions.[13] Even then, reconstructing Revolutionary War forts was an old concept; the rebuilding of Fort Ticonderoga dates to 1908. So when the Fort Montgomery Plan Team began meeting in the late 1990s, it had to address whether or not to reconstruct the fort.

Fig. 18.3. Artifacts unearthed during archaeological digs at Fort Montgomery. Courtesy of NYS Office of Parks, Recreation, and Historic Preservation.

The idea appealed to some members of the team. A reconstruction would help visitors envision and appreciate structures that no longer existed. Reconstructions set the scene for the imagination to take over. They have their place, but they are problematic. It is almost never possible to know all of the details of a building, a fort, or a hut. This is certainly true for eighteenth-century buildings for which there are no photographs or neat blueprints.

Although historians know a great deal about Fort Montgomery, both from a wealth of documentary sources and from the archaeological excavations, they know precious little about the buildings themselves. Because reconstructed buildings tend to be permanent, they cannot be changed easily to reflect advances in scholarship. And no matter how clear the interpretation that a building or a feature is a reconstruction, there are always visitors who either believe it to be the real thing or come away with the mistaken impression that the reconstruction is based on specific knowledge of the original structure.

Weighing the pros and cons of reconstruction, the Fort Montgomery Plan Team decided not to rebuild Fort Montgomery, but it recognized the need to help visitors imagine and appreciate those parts of the fort that no longer exist. The challenge, therefore, was to help present the story of the fort and the battle so visitors can imagine what took place, but in a manner that is flexible enough to address new information that may come to light. The team chose to tell the story of Fort Montgomery through a variety of media, including interpretive signs, commissioned artwork, an audio tour, three-dimensional exhibits, and, most important, professional interpretive staff.

Interpretive signs are used effectively at many parks and historic sites. Computer design and advances in printing processes have made it possible to create full-color panels that can withstand weather, ultraviolet fading, and moderate attempts at vandalism for at least a decade. Signs are made of phenolic resin in which a computer-generated image is embedded. At Fort Montgomery, there are twenty interpretive panels, in kiosks and adjacent to foundations, earthworks, and other features. Each sign includes color images and concise, descriptive text that explains not only what the visitor is viewing but also the story of the construction of the fort, significant archaeological discoveries, the battle, etc. The first phase of these signs was installed in October 2001. The second phase was added in September 2002, just in time for the site's grand opening.

Many of the signs incorporate interesting, high-quality images. In addition to being an archaeologist, Jack Mead was a talented artist. He left numerous sketches and paintings of the fort's buildings and scenes from the battle. To those, the plan team added other artwork and historic images to create visually engaging panels.

In cases where no images were obtainable, the OPRHP commissioned local artist Dahl Taylor to paint four scenes that highlight certain details of each feature but leave others to the imagination. For example, his painting of the guardhouse leaves a clear impression that this was a place where soldiers who had done something wrong were brought. It suggests that there was a building there, but its details are intentionally sketchy. Taylor's painting of the North Redoubt depicts this feature during the early part of the battle. It suggests what the redoubt looked like, but it does not make a definitive statement about the details of its construction. Visitors are left with an impression—a "mental snapshot"—of what happened there, yet it is clear that there is no definitive record of what the actual scene looked like.

The "one-story" barracks, another of Taylor's illustrations, is a perfect example of why reconstructions are problematic. When Jack Mead excavated this building in the late 1960s, he concluded, based on the chimney found by his excavation team, that this building was one story tall. However, while Taylor was working on preliminary sketches of the building for his painting, he forced a re-examination of the documentary evidence relating to the forts' barracks. In the past, historians had been guided by Colonel Thomas Palmer's description of "... one barrack, eighty feet by twenty, two stories high, with a cellar under half of it."[14] Like Mead, they assumed that Palmer's letter referred to the other 80 x 20 barracks building, located just to the north of this one.

But just as Taylor was about to begin painting the "one-story" barracks, a colleague made a crucial observation—that the key documents correspond with two historic maps of the fort

Fig. 18.4. Soldiers manning a redoubt at Fort Montgomery. Painting by Dahl Taylor; courtesy of NYS Office of Parks, Recreation, and Historic Preservation.

drawn contemporaneously with Palmer's letters.[15] When the documents are put together with the maps, it becomes very clear that the "one-story" barracks was actually described by Colonel Thomas Palmer and others as a two-story building. In the first of two maps drawn by Colonel Palmer, there is only one 80 x 20 barracks shown. This map was drawn in April or May of 1776. Palmer's letter, describing a "barrack, eighty feet by twenty, two stories high," dates to April 27, 1776. Palmer's letter goes on to say that this two-story barracks was completed, and that another barracks was planned. Furthermore, the dotted outline of another barracks different from the "one-story barracks" is faintly visible on this map, as if to indicate that this is the barracks to be built next.

Palmer's second map of Fort Montgomery, which accompanied advice written by Lord Stirling and incorporated in instructions issued by George Washington on June 10, shows a second 80 x 20 barracks.[16] Conveniently, the "new" building is labeled "E." In his instructions, Stirling writes that "The barracks E, which are begun and considerably advanced, should also be finished." Clearly, this cannot be the same building that Palmer had previously described as two stories high and completed.

The connection made between the documents and the maps caused a flurry of activity at the Peebles Island Resource Center, as archaeologists and architectural historians carefully examined all of the documents and Mead's field notes and debated whether the barracks was the "one story" or "two-story" building. In the end, they agreed that the documents in hand painted a convincing picture that this barracks had, in fact, been two stories tall. However, since all of the information that Mead left behind has not been examined, they may yet discover in his voluminous notes something that convinces them that he was right. So, Taylor reoriented his final artwork of the barracks from one story to two. This is a good example of how information and interpretations can change over time. Fortunately, the Fort Montgomery Plan Team has chosen interpretive methods that can change as new information is discovered.

The third form of interpretation is a visitors' center that exhibits many of the archaeological artifacts recovered from the fort. These treasures tell the story in a way that no media can. What kind of people garrisoned the fort? Based on the many ornate buckles and buttons recovered from the enlisted men's barracks, we get the sense that many of the common soldiers were comfortably well off. Are there items that we can connect with specific people? Nearly all of the spoons recovered from the fort bear the initials of their owners. Why were these men here? The inscription "Liberty" on a pair of cufflinks is certainly part of the answer. Because so many artifacts were excavated from the fort, there is a large pool from which to choose. The New York State Museum completed a report on these items to interpret them.

Interpretive signs and exhibits will go a long way toward helping visitors appreciate what the men who built and defended the fort experienced. However, there is no substitute for knowledgeable interpreters who can interact with visitors, answer questions, and truly bring the fort to life. Some of the interpreters wear period costumes and provide hands-on activities and demonstrations to engage children and adults. But they also continue to research and assemble more information on the fort, and this is critical. Although historians and archaeologists have been studying the fort for almost a century, they have only scratched the surface of the potential sources of information that are available for further research. For example, the pension records of the soldiers who served at the fort have not yet been studied. And who knows what may be hiding in the Public Records Office in England?

As research expands our understanding of Fort Montgomery, the OPRHP will update its interpretation to keep pace. Interpretive signs, illustrations, and even exhibits can be changed much more readily than reconstructed buildings. And just as important, these media will convey—in a way that reconstructions cannot—one of the most important facts about the site: that there is a great deal yet to learn about Fort Montgomery. Readers should come to experience the treasures of this great site themselves to understand Fort Montgomery and the men who fought there for America's independence.

This article originally appeared in *The Hudson River Valley Review*, Volume 20.1, Summer 2003.

NOTES

1. Brigadier George Clinton to Washington, July 11, 1777; Captain John Hodge to New York Council of Safety, July 13, 1777; William Bell Clark, William James Morgan, and Michael J. Crawford, eds. *Naval Documents of the American Revolution*, 10 vols. to date (Washington: U. S. Government Printing Office, 1964–), 9: 260, 281.
2. "Wm A. Patterson to Hon. &c," April 22, 1776; "A Plan of the Intended Works at Fort Montgomery By Wm A. Patterson 1st Lieut of the 15th Reg^{t}—April 22 1776," Sheffield Research files, from originals in the Massachusetts Historical Society, Boston, Mass.
3. William H. Carr and Richard J. Koke, *Twin Forts of the Popolopen: Forts Clinton and Montgomery, New York, 1775–1777*, Historical Bulletin no. 1. (Bear Mountain, N.Y.: Commissioners of the Palisades Interstate Park and the American Scenic and Historic Preservation Society, July 1937), 29. (It is unclear how many of these might have been at Fort Clinton.) "A Return of Ordinance Stores at Fort Montgomery this twentyeth Day of June 1777," *Public Papers of George Clinton, first Governor of New York, 1777–1795–1801–1804*, 10 vols., ed. Hugh Hastings (Albany: State printers, 1899–1914), 2: 45.
4. "Genl. Putnam, N°. 25," ibid.; George Clinton to Washington, Oct. 9, 1777, *Naval Documents*, 10: 94.
5. Continental Marine Committee to the New York Council of Safety, June 26, 1777, ibid., 9: 177.
6. Aug. 14, 1776, "Memorandum of Stores

Necessary for the Sloop Hudson & . . . Camden," Papers of the Secret Committee; George Clinton to Putnam, June 15, 1777; Captain John Hodge to the New York Council of Safety, July 13, 1777, ibid., 9: 118, 281; "Capt Hodge's Evidence, N 7," "Report of the Court of Inquiry on the Loss of Fort Montgomery" to Washington, April 5, 1778, McDougall Papers, United States Military Philosophical Society Records, 1789–1813, microfilmed by the New York Historical Society, Reel 2, USMA Library, West Point, N.Y., hereinafter cited as "Court of Inquiry."

7. Continental Marine Committee to the New York Council of Safety and to Captains Grennell and Hodge, June 26, 1777, *Naval Documents*, 9: 176–77.
8. Putnam to the New York Council of Safety, June 5, 1777; Phil. Livingston and Wm. Duer to Pierre Van Cortlandt, President of the New York Council of Safety, May 31, 1777; Hodge to Council of Safety, July 13, 1777; Cortlandt to the President of Congress, June 11, 1777, ibid., 9: 24, 42, 90, 281.
9. Orderly Book, King's American Regiment, 18 December 1776–12 November 1777, typescript, USMA Library, West Point, N.Y.; Hon. J.W. Fortescue, *A History of the 17th Lancers (Duke of Cambridge's Own)* (London: MacMillan and Co., 1895), 43–44; S. H. F. Johnston, *The History of the Cameronians (Scottish Rifles) 26th and 90th*, vol. 1, *1689–1910* (Aldershot, UK: Gale & Polden Limited, 1957), 148; W.S. Moorsom, ed., *Historical Record of the Fifty-Second Regiment (Oxfordshire Light Infantry from the Year 1755 to the Year 1858* (London: Richard Bentley, 1860), 16; H.H. Woollright, *History of the Fifty-Seventh (West Middlesex) Regiment of Foot, 1755–1881* (London: Richard Bentley and Son, 1893), 64–65; Colonel H. C. Wylly, C. B., comp. *History of the Manchester Regiment (Late the 63rd and 96th Foot)* (London: Forster Groom & Co., 1923), 65; W. Wheater, *Historical Record of the Seventh or Royal Regiment of Fusiliers* (Leeds: Private circulation, 1875), 72; journals, Oct. 5, *Mercury, Dependence*, and *Diligent*, Hotham to Admiral Howe, Oct. 9, and Clinton to General Howe, Oct. 9, *Naval Documents*, 10: 42–43, 96, 98.
10. Captain Machin's Evidence, N 5, "Court of Inquiry."
11. Commodore William Hotham to Admiral Howe, Oct. 9, 1777; Clinton to General Howe, Oct. 9, 1777; journal of *Dependence*, Oct. 6, 1777; George Clinton to New York Council of Safety, Oct. 8, 1777, ibid., 10: 42–43, 47, 70, 96, 98–99.
12. Hotham to Admiral Howe, Oct. 9, 1777; Clinton to General Howe, Oct. 9, 1777; journal of *Dependence*, Oct. 6, 1777; George Clinton to New York Council of Safety, Oct. 8, 1777, ibid., 10: 42–43, 47, 70, 96, 98–99; "Capt. Hodge's Evidence," "Court of Inquiry."
13. Arthur P. Abbott to Commissioners of the Palisades Interstate Park Commission, Feb. 16, 1930, and March 11, 1930. Palisades Interstate Park Commission files. Abbott's letters seem to be contradictory, at least without more information regarding the context of the letters. His first letter seems to support reconstructing the forts' buildings, while the second letter warns that "The desecration of these works by the obliteration of their most valuable and interesting features by 'restorations' is wrong and must not be done."
14. Thomas Palmer to New York Committee of Safety, April 27, 1776, in *American Archives*, by Peter Force, 4th series, vol. 5, 1095–96.
15. Thomas Palmer Map Number One of Fort Montgomery, in *Twin Forts of the Popolopen*, 23. The original of this map was in the possession of the New York State Library when it was destroyed by fire in 1911.
16. Lord Stirling's advice, incorporated in General Washington's directions to the Commissioners in the Highlands, in *American Archives*, 4th series, vol. 6, 792–93.

19

Revolutionary Road

Incident on Gallows Hill

THOMAS C. O'KEEFE

In the late summer of 1778, George Washington, commander in chief of the Continental Army, was very keen to protect the Hudson River Valley and the work-in-progress garrison that would eventually become the United States Military Academy at West Point. At the same time, Washington and his staff were making plans for the army's winter quarters.

Washington wanted to have his troops positioned within striking distance of Long Island Sound, from whence the British had previously attacked the Continental Army's supply depot in Danbury, Connecticut. Additionally, he was expecting the French fleet, which was coming into the Revolutionary War on the side of the Americans, to be in the waters off the Atlantic Coast, near either Boston or New York. The commander took all of these factors into account when deciding upon the location for the encampment of the Eastern Wing of the Continental Army.

In locating an area that would fit these imperatives, Washington relied on Major General Israel Putnam, who was Washington's senior officer in the Hudson Highlands and a native of Connecticut. Dr. James Thacher, an American surgeon who met Putnam in the Hudson Highlands in the summer of 1778, described his impressions of "Old Put":

> This is my first interview with this celebrated hero. In his person he is corpulent and clumsy but carries a bold, undaunted front. He exhibits little of the refinements of a well-educated gentleman, but much of the character of the veteran soldier.[1]

As a veteran soldier, Putnam knew how to delegate; in deciding upon winter quarters, Putnam looked for advice from another famous Revolutionary War military figure, Lieutenant-Colonel Aaron Burr, who had been an aide-de-camp to Putnam earlier in the war.

Burr was familiar with western Connecticut and the surrounding area from prior service in Norwalk and Fairfield, Connecticut, and in skirmishes on Long Island Sound. Burr also had an uncle in Redding, Connecticut, Stephen Burr. "Colonel Aaron Burr, one of General Putnam's aides and a frequent visitor to Redding, had suggested that Putnam look over the area for a future winter encampment during a Summer visit to General Heath's Brigade in Danbury. Putnam found the topography and location ideal."[2]

Major David Humphreys, another aide to General Putnam and also from Connecticut, set forth the rationale for Putnam's recommendation that the Eastern Wing encampments be centered around Redding, which is located north of Norwalk and south of Danbury:

> It was thought advisable by Washington to extend the winter quarters from Redding in Connecticut to Middlebrook in New Jersey nearly upon a line with West Point. The central body was stationed at Middlebrook where Washington, Greene, Knox

Fig. 19.1. Putnam's Escape at Horse Neck, engraving after Chappel, Johnson and Myles Publishers, New York, 1877. Library of Congress Prints and Photographs Division Washington, D.C.

> and Baron Steuben had their headquarters. General McDougall still commanded in the Highlands. General Putnam with the two Brigades of Connecticut, General Poor's New Hampshire Brigade, Col. Sheldon's cavalry and Col. Hazen's Infantry Corps were stationed at Redding Ridge near Danbury, Connecticut. . . . The campground is located about 17 miles north of Long Island Sound, twelve miles easterly from the New York State line and twenty-seven miles southeasterly from West Point.[3]

Surprisingly, despite its strategic location—and although there were to be thousands of troops stationed in Redding during the Revolutionary War—the town was spared from becoming the scene of any major battles.

But there was much action in the environs of Redding prior to these encampments. On April 26, 1777, the British had burned warehouses and barns in a brilliantly executed surprise raid on nearby Danbury, where munitions and military stores for the Continental Army were located. En route to the raid, the British Army—2,000 soldiers strong—passed through Redding in the course of a twenty-three-mile forced march from Compo Beach on the coast (near present-day Westport) to Danbury. When the British paused for a break in Redding, they rounded up a few Rebel hostages to hold for ransom and fired a shot or two at the gilded weathercock on the spire of the Episcopal Church.

After the British left town, Brigadier General Benedict Arnold (still a patriot at the time), turned up in hot pursuit of the British, briefly pausing near Redding Ridge during a miserable April rain storm to get his bearings before heading off to participate in the feckless rear-guard action by the Continental Army and Connecticut militia known as the Battle of Ridgefield. This action on April 27, 1777, was an attempt to block the retreat of the British from Danbury to the ships awaiting them in Long Island Sound.

But there was bloodshed on Redding soil during the war involving two young soldiers. One of them, a butcher from nearby Ridgefield who had joined the British Army, was hanged as a British spy. The other soldier, barely seventeen years old and in the Continental Army's 1st Connecticut Regiment, was shot as deserter. Both were executed on the same day atop the highest point of the road in Redding known today as Gallows Hill. Their deaths were meant to serve as examples to the other soldiers who served with them in the Redding encampments, just in case any of them were thinking of spying or deserting.

The question this article will address is whether this double execution on Gallows Hill was justified or was instead an expedient that

Fig. 19.2. A new and correct map of Connecticut: one of the United States of North America from actual survey, humbly dedicated by permission to his Excellency Samuel Huntington esquire Governor and Commander in Chief of said state. 1792. The University of Connecticut Libraries' Map and Geographic Information Center (MAGIC).

would not have been approved by Commander in Chief Washington had he been advised of all the facts and circumstances.

GEORGE WASHINGTON AND THE REDDING ENCAMPMENTS

Based on the history books, George Washington never slept in Redding, but a study of his Revolutionary War correspondence and General Orders issued by him reveals that he spent a lot of time worrying about what was going on with the troops stationed there.

Major General Putnam was Connecticut's most famous military man, who had achieved heroic stature in the nascent Continental Army for his bravery and exploits at the battles of Bunker Hill and Breed's Hill in June 1775. There Putnam had famously urged his troops to keep their powder dry until the British were well within range, uttering (according to legend) the famous phrase, "Don't fire 'til you see the whites of their eyes."

By the winter of 1778/1779, General Putnam served under Commander in Chief Washington as the head of the Eastern Wing of the Continental Army—approximately 3,000 men strong—responsible for protecting not only the Danbury supply depot north of Redding but the areas east of the Hudson River and from

Long Island Sound in the south to Connecticut, Westchester County, and West Point in the north. It was in that context that Putnam came to command troops in Redding.

The three Redding encampments were located near one another in the same general area of north Redding nearest to Danbury, just south of the Bethel border. The easternmost and main camp was in the Lonetown section of Redding, where Putnam Park now stands at the intersection of Connecticut Routes 58 and 107. Many artifacts remain in Putnam Park to permit visitors to imagine what these Revolutionary War encampments looked like, including the topography and size of these sites as well as the remains of firebacks, which were stone chimneys incorporated into the design of the soldiers' huts.

The huts were made of logs hewn from nearby woodlands. They measured fourteen by sixteen feet, and six feet high, with a door at the front facing toward the stream and a chimney at the rear. Each hut, spaced eight feet apart, accommodated twelve soldiers. Over 1,300 men occupied the huts. The evidence of how they were laid out can be seen in the exhibits in Putnam Park. There is also a reconstruction of what is thought to be officers' quarters, slightly more spacious than the troops' huts but rudimentary housing nonetheless. Officers' huts were spaced sixteen feet apart and located higher up the hill behind the huts of their subordinates.

The middle Redding encampment was located off Limekiln Road in woodlands on the side of a hill that sloped down to a stream, in the general area defined by present-day Whortleberry Road, Costa Lane, Gallows Hill Road, and Limekiln Road. This site remains undisturbed, preserved as open space by the Redding Land Trust.

The westernmost camp, which has been redeveloped, apparently was located in the general vicinity of present-day Deer Spring Road and Old Lantern Road, about a quarter of a mile north of the West Redding railroad station.

As of 1790, Redding had a population of only 1,503 people, so we can assume that the influx of troops probably tripled the local population during the winter of 1778/1779.

FALLEN FORTS IN THE HUDSON HIGHLANDS

It is significant to note that Putnam, notwithstanding his stellar reputation for bravery and resourcefulness in battle, was under a cloud and had become a bit of an embarrassment to Washington. In October 1777, on Putnam's watch, the British Army had captured Forts Montgomery and Clinton, located near each other on the Hudson River. Afterward, the Continental Congress, by a resolution dated November 28, 1777, had ordered a Court of Inquiry to investigate the affair.

Forts Montgomery and Clinton were twin forts, complete with redoubts and cannon emplacements that were built on rocky outcroppings on the west side of the Hudson River, located south of West Point and at the present-day Bear Mountain Bridge. These fortifications were part of the Continental Army's attempt to control the Hudson River and prevent the British Army in New York City from connecting with British forces under General John Burgoyne that were gradually making their way south from Canada toward Albany and the North River (as the Hudson was then known).

As the officer in charge of the Hudson Highlands, it was up to General Putnam to decide how to allocate the troops at his disposal given the lay of the land along both sides of the river. One consideration was that there were steep and narrow mountain passes on the river's west side in the vicinity of the two forts. Taken together with the forts' resources in terms of cannons and redoubts, that side of the river was arguably easier to defend than the opposite shore, which was less mountainous and populated with towns and villages, including Putnam's headquarters at Peekskill, Continental Village, and further north the Continental Army's main regional depot at Fishkill. The shortage of troops available to Putnam meant he had to hedge his bets.

He hedged in favor of protecting the east side of the river.

On September 29, 1777, the level of his troop strength shrank sharply when Putnam was ordered to transfer 2,500 soldiers to Washington's other commanders in the Upper Hudson and Pennsylvania. This left him with only 1,100 Continental troops and 2,000 of the less well-trained local militia to cover both sides of the river.

Meanwhile, British troops under Sir Henry Clinton headquartered in New York City were making their way by some fifty transport vessels upriver in Putnam's direction in an effort to relieve and reinforce Burgoyne's British forces, which were approaching Saratoga, north of Albany. Despite General Putnam's attempts to obtain local intelligence from sources on the river, no one in the Continental Army command structure could predict with certainty which side of river the northbound British forces would attack.

On the morning of October 6, 1777, the British seized upon this confusion and feigned an attack on Peekskill as a diversion to draw 500 of Putnam's troops to the east bank of the Hudson River. At the same time, under cover of fog the main elements of the British forces constituting in excess of 2,100 (and perhaps more) soldiers—Hessians, Loyalists, and British regulars—were ferried across to the river to Stony Point. From there they began a difficult march through the mountain passes to surprise the Americans and capture Forts Montgomery and Clinton.

Where was Israel Putnam while this legerdemain was going on? He and the troops under his immediate command were in the vicinity of the general's Peekskill headquarters, south and east of the twin forts. On the west side of the Hudson, two brigadier generals who happened to be brothers were in charge of the twin forts: George Clinton (who was also governor of New York State) commanded Fort Montgomery, while James Clinton was in charge at Fort Clinton. The two forts were connected by a pontoon bridge over Popolopen Creek that allowed communication and exchange of ammunition between them.

When it became apparent that the Americans were substantially outnumbered, the Clinton brothers sent desperate messages to Putnam for reinforcements. The first message was written by Governor Clinton at eight in the morning; it arrived at the Peekskill headquarters by late morning. Unfortunately, Putnam and his aides were already on a reconnoitering trip five miles south of Peekskill to Verplanck's Point, one of the spots where the British transports had landed a day earlier. By the time Putnam received the messages requesting reinforcements, it was late in the afternoon—too late to help the Clintons. Putnam had guessed the wrong side of the river to protect with the bulk of his forces.

In the evidence submitted at the Court of Inquiry conducted at the direction of the Continental Congress, several officers echoed the evidence of Lieutenant Colonel Marvin of the militia, who was at Fort Clinton, that none of the soldiers in the forts left their posts "until the enemy were within our walls and up on their backs, then everyone made his escape in the manner he could." Another participant in the battle testified that it would have taken as many as 2,000 soldiers to defend both forts properly.

The battle raged all day but the heroic Americans defending the forts were outnumbered three to one—the Clintons had perhaps 700 soldiers. With heavy artillery fire from the forts and eventually hand-to-hand combat, the losses on both sides were significant. The Americans suffered 350 killed, wounded, or captured. On the British side, forty were killed and 150 wounded. Although many Americans (including both Clintons) escaped the forts though the smoky haze and falling darkness, as many as 275 of their defenders were taken by the British as prisoners of war to New York City.

Putnam's aides at Peekskill had sent what reinforcements they could to the Clintons even before Putnam arrived back in Peekskill, but once it became apparent that the forts were lost, in an effort to deny the British even more trophies Putnam directed his troops to burn Fort Constitution, on the east side of the Hudson River, and head north to protect the Continental Army depot at Fishkill. Even so, British raiding parties pursuing the Americans by land and sea up the river found much to destroy, including the shipyards at Poughkeepsie, a number of small villages, and, as a final insult, the riverside manor house of the Livingston family.

Luckily for Putnam and the Continental Army, the embarrassment of the losses in the Hudson Highlands was leavened by the success of General Horatio Gates, commander of the Northern branch of the Continental Army. Following the second Battle of Saratoga on October 17, 1777, he had accepted the surrender of Burgoyne and his army of 5,871 British regulars and German mercenaries.

In a letter from George Washington to George Clinton dated October 25, 1777, Washington commiserated with Clinton, characterizing the situation after the burning of Kingston, on the west side of the Hudson River, in the aftermath of the collapse of Forts Montgomery and Clinton:

> I . . . feel much for the Havoc and devastation committed by the Enemy employed on the North River. Their maxim seems to be, to destroy where they cannot conquer and they hesitate not, to pursue a conduct that do dishonour to the Arms of Barbarians.[4]

The fall of these two Hudson River forts and the losses of men and material associated with the installations were of sufficient magnitude to convene a Court of Inquiry to examine what went wrong. But New York officials, who naturally were most affected by the forts' capture, were furious with Putnam for not managing to reinforce their defenders in time. The New Yorkers were so incensed that official letters were dispatched to Washington by prominent citizens like Chancellor Robert Livingston, the chief judicial officer of New York. In a letter to Washington dated January 14, 1778, Livingston states that Putnam, at the age of sixty, is too old and, further, New Yorkers do not want to be commanded by the Connecticut general:

> Your Excellency is not ignorant of the extent of Genl Putnams capacity, & diligence, & how well soever these may qualify him for the management of this work & most important command—the prejudices to which his imprudent Lenity to the disaffected, & too great intercourse with the enemy have given rise have greatly injured his influence—How far the loss of fort Montgomerry and the subsequent ravages of the enemy are to be imputed to him, I will not venture to say, as this will necessarily be determined by a court of inquiry whose determinations I would not anticipate—Unfortunately for him the current of popular opinions is this, & the neighbouring States, & as far as I can learn in the troops under his command, runs strongly against him. For my own part I respect his bravery, & former services, & sincerely lament that his patriotism, will not suffer him to take that repose to which his advanced age & past services, justly entitle him.[5]

Washington was uncharacteristically slow in responding to this letter, but when he did write back to Robert Livingston on March 12, 1778, he seemed to agree with Livingston. In explaining the problem of dealing with the aging Putnam, Washington wrote that "[Putnam] cannot see his own defects and make an honorable retreat from a station in which he exposes his own weakness."[6]

On March 16, 1778, Washington in effect took the action requested by Livingston and demoted Putnam, in substance if not in rank. In a letter to Putnam, Washington wrote that it was best for the general to stand down his command until the inquiry into the fall of

Forts Montgomery and Clinton was concluded. Washington told Putnam he took this action "owing to the prejudices of the people, which, whether well or ill grounded, must be indulged, and I should think myself wanting in justice to the public and candor towards you, were I to continue you in a command, after I have been almost in direct terms informed that the people of the State of New York will not render support and assistance while you remain Head of that Department."[7] (To make things worse for Putnam, his second wife died in October 1777.)

Because of the press of military business and out of deference to Putnam's personal loss, Washington had not pushed completion of the Court of Inquiry ordered by the Continental Congress, but by February 1778, Washington sent Major General Alexander McDougall with a request to tend to the matter. On March 21, 1778, Washington also formally appointed McDougall to take command of the Highlands until the Putnam matter had been concluded.

Based upon a review of Alexander McDougall's diary, McDougall met with the main protagonists—Governor Clinton and General Putnam—before the Court of Inquiry convened. The three men (as well as John Jay, then chief justice of the New York Supreme Court) all dined together at McDougall's quarters in Colonel Derek Brinckerhoff's house in Fishkill. The Court of Inquiry also was held in the Brinckerhoff house, which is located on New York Route 52, north of the intersection of present-day Interstate 84 and New York Route 9.

After these preliminaries with the principals, General McDougall met with the other members of the Court of Inquiry—Brigadier General Jedediah Huntington and Colonel Edward Wigglesworth—and opened the proceedings on March 30, 1778. According to McDougall's diary, by April 4, 1778, the Court of Inquiry had completed its work, having heard from Putnam himself as well as twenty witnesses from among the officers on both sides of the Hudson that fateful day.[8]

In response to the specific questions put to the Court of Inquiry by Washington, the members of the panel concluded as follows: the forts "were carried by Storm"; the British had about 3,000 soldiers and the Americans 700 in the forts during the day-long battle; although there were no regular returns of the day, seventy-five American soldiers were killed, forty were wounded, and 240 were taken prisoner by the British in the forts, totaling about 350 casualties, including 30 officers; Governor Clinton had made two requests by letter to General Putnam for reinforcements beginning at eight a.m. but not received by Putnam until five p.m.; no particular number of men had been requested by Clinton and "no succours were received."

It is clear from McDougall's papers that part of Putnam's defense was that he had been left with insufficient manpower following the loss of 2,500 troops sent away in late September 1777 pursuant to Washington's orders. And like the veteran soldier he was, Putnam had advised Congress even before the attack on the forts that "I would not be answerable for the safety of the forts" given the drawing away of these troops.

Putnam also noted in his evidence that the first of two messages sent by Governor Clinton asking for reinforcements was carried by a man who went over to the British the very next day. Since the messenger was not far away geographically from where Putnam was on his reconnaissance mission at Verplanck's Point, the suggestion is that treachery played its part in delaying Clinton's earliest request.[9]

The Court of Inquiry completed its substantive work promptly after hearing the witnesses and taking in the documentary proof. A point-by-point written response to the questions put to the Court of Inquiry by Washington was drafted as of April 5, 1778, by Brigadier General Jedediah Huntington and Colonel Edward Wiggelsworth, the two junior officers on the panel, and submitted to Major General McDougall for his review and approval. McDougall temporized a bit, apparently feeling that the junior officers had not fully responded to Washington's pointed queries and perhaps had gone a bit easy on General Putnam.

On May 21, 1778, General McDougall drafted his own report, a kind of mild dissenting opinion for Washington's benefit, although McDougall did not disagree with the conclusions of his fellow members of the Court of Inquiry. In the end, the court exonerated Putnam from all blame in the Hudson Highlands disaster, concluding that the forts were lost "not from any fault, misconduct, or negligence of the commanding officers, but solely through the want of adequate force under their command to maintain and defend them."[10]

Although the Court of Inquiry had completed its work and transmitted its report to Washington by the end of May 1778, by late July Congress had not acted one way or the other on the Putnam matter. Putnam was chafing at being in a kind of professional limbo while the Congressional inquiry hung over him and was apparently making a nuisance of himself, prodding Washington for an answer. In an extraordinary letter from Washington to the Continental Congress in Philadelphia on July 28, 1778, the Commander in Chief, with General Putnam hand-carrying the letter, basically passes the buck to them:

> This [letter] will be presented to Congress by Genl. Putnam. He arrived from Connecticut the day after I came into the Neighbourhood of this Camp [White Plains, NY]. As I have not received any Resolution of Congress, respecting the Court of Inquiry, which they directed and which was transmitted them, on the subject of the posts in the Highlands, taken last year, I am at a loss in what point of view to consider him. He wishes some decision in this instance and his journey to Philadelphia is for the purpose.[11]

Putting in a personal appearance seemed to work. On August 17, 1778, Congress accepted the findings of the report, and by September Putnam was given responsibilities by Washington in and around Connecticut and the Hudson River Valley. By November, Washington had appointed him to command the Brigades of Generals Enoch Poor, Samuel Parsons, and Jedediah Huntington in Redding.

MAKING CAMP

But it is clear from the letters and orders of Washington in 1778/1779 that the Commander in Chief planned to keep "Old Put" on a short leash after the debacle at Forts Montgomery and Clinton. Leaving nothing to chance, Washington worked hand-in-hand with Putnam in organizing the encampment at Redding based upon lessons learned during Washington's experience with the Continental Army a year earlier during the bitter winter of 1777/1778 in Valley Forge, Pennsylvania.

When it came to the construction of Redding encampments, Washington turned into a field architect, a one-man Army Corps of Engineers; this was not surprising since he had been a land surveyor and mapmaker in civilian life, so he knew the importance of the lay of the land.

In a letter to General Putnam dated November 25, 1778, just as the camps in Redding were being established, Washington notes that Putnam, in his prior letter, had not mentioned how his three brigades would be quartered. So Washington, unsolicited, proceeds to offer his advice as to how the camps should be situated so as to not unduly burden Redding's residents and promote military security:

> [W]ishing the Army to be as little burdensome as possible to the Inhabitants of the Country, and that the troops composing its several divisions may lie compactly together, in order to their greater security, and better discipline and government. It is my desire that they should hut themselves as they did last Winter at Valley Forge, wherever they can . . . with . . . proper attention to the manner of constructing the Huts. There

> were several last Winter at Valley Forge, which by the care of the officers were not only comfortable but commodious, and in which the men lived exceedingly well and preserved their health. These are considerations very important . . . the sooner the Troops can be fixed the better.[12]

No detail was too small for Washington who, as his letters and orders reveal, was a very precise man, who was concerned about the welfare of his troops. In one of his letters to Congress about blankets, written in early September 1778, he seems keenly aware of what it would be like to be in one of those rude little huts crammed together and shivering at night, writing: "Not a night will pass from this time [Sept. 7th], without the Soldiers feeling the want."[13]

In a follow-up General Order on hut construction dated December 14, 1778, Washington warns his officers against building the huts in a way that could lead to sickness among the soldiers: "Much of the sickness among the Troops seems to have been occasioned by the improper method adopted in forming many of the Huts last Winter, some being sunk in the ground and others covered with Earth . . . [the Huts are] to be roofed with boards, slabs or large shingles, that the men be not suffered to dig into the ground (except so far as to level the surface) or to cover the huts with earth or turf. The officers will likewise see that their men erect bunks or births to keep them off the ground and proper conveniences in their huts for the purpose of preserving their arms and accoutrements from being damaged."[14]

Still worried about construction of the huts and conditions in the encampments on Christmas Eve, 1778, Washington issued a further General Order, dated December 24, 1778, recommending engineering changes that the commanding officers should adopt to see to it "that ditches are made upon the upper side of every row of huts where on descending ground at about three feet distance from [the huts], and at every convenient place to make other ditches so as to carry off the water in front; this [it will be] observed, will secure the troops from any inundation of water and much contribute to the health and convenience of the whole camp."[15]

Ever sensitive to minimizing the impact of the Continental Army's encampments on the surrounding communities, the Christmas Eve General Order directed "[n]o firing or discharging of pieces, on any pretence whatever is to be suffered except at particular hours, which will be made known to the Army." It was to be a quiet Christmas in Redding in 1778.

Washington also was an early environmentalist, directing that "[t]he troops after having provided themselves with sufficient timber for hutting are to cut down no more green standing timber for firewood, until the logs, tops and old fallen timber be first used for that purpose."

In addition, Washington was almost like a quartermaster in chief, keeping tabs on those responsible for the care and feeding of his troops during the lean winter months when Congressional funding was insufficient and delayed, when boots and uniforms and blankets were scarce, and the army was sometimes reduced to eating horseflesh.

In a letter to General Putnam dated January 8, 1779, Washington was furious at reports that the Connecticut troops "had not fared so well as others, in the late distribution of clothing to the army." In the course of a discussion about the shortage of uniforms, Washington revealed that he was surprised to learn that procurement of uniforms locally through Connecticut sources had gone completely awry, all to the troops' detriment. Apparently, the uniforms of the Americans' French allies were of better quality and piling up in inventory at the Fishkill depot, while uniforms procured locally were not up to snuff and had been delayed, much to the chagrin and discomfort of the freezing, ill-clad Connecticut troops.

Washington knew that "the troops in general have had orders for a shirt and a pair of stockings per man for the hole, and a pair of shoes, for each that wanted it." The commander in chief was even alert to the shortcomings of the skimpy blankets being provided, obviously a crucial item for a soldier enduring a severe Northeast winter:

> The complaint, among other things, extends to Blankets . . . If I mistake not, I remember two [orders] successively given to General Parsons and for those of the largest and best quality, the latter parcels being of so small a kind, that it took two of one sort, and four of another to make one of full size, and besides this a deficiency of two or three thousand was found upon the whole quantity short of the Invoices. . . . If the Connecticut troops are in a worst predicament . . . they shall be put in the same situation as the other parts of the army. . . . It could not have been my intention to deprive the Connecticut troops of their proper share.[16]

In perusing the various letters of Washington and his General Orders during the Winter of 1778/1779, you cannot help but be struck by his mastery and detailed knowledge of how to run an army and his sincere concern for the welfare of the men who served under him in what he knew were very difficult conditions. On occasion he even stood up for the common soldier while chastising his sometimes ineffectual generals.

In sum, there can be no question that from the relative comfort of his own headquarters in Philadelphia during the winter of 1778/1779, Washington was determined to try to avoid the privations of Valley Forge a year earlier, ensuring that the Continental Army would be as comfortable as possible during the bad weather and healthy for the spring 1779 campaign.

MUTINY AT REDDING

Unfortunately, notwithstanding Washington's best intentions and plans, the harsh conditions in Redding that winter were as bad or worse than at Valley Forge the year before (some of the troops with General Putnam had been at both encampments). For all of Washington's planning, the troops suffered from shortages of everything, except bad weather.

Among the soldiers and officers in the Redding encampments were several diarists. In the main camp located at present-day Putnam Park, one diarist from the officer ranks, Lt. Col. Henry Dearborn, 3rd New Hampshire Regiment, kept track of the weather, noting several severe snowstorms in December. Summing it up, on December 27, 1778, Dearborn wrote "the weather seems more like Canada than Connecticut."[17]

On that same day, a mile and a half or so west of the Putnam Park encampment in the so-called middle camp, the brigade of General Parsons was running out of food. In a message to his troops on December 27, 1778, Parsons explains to his men that the flour and bread they need is stockpiled in nearby Danbury, but "the weather had been so extreme (mixture of rain and snow) that it is impossible for the teams to pass to that place. Every measure is being taken to supply flour, rum, salt and every necessary tomorrow."

The most famous of the Redding encampment diarists, Joseph Plumb Martin, a private in the 8th Connecticut Regiment in the middle camp who was to write about many battles in the Revolutionary War, endured all of these conditions, noting that "we now and then got a little bad bread and salt beef (I believe chiefly horse-beef for it was generally thought to be such at the time). The month of January was very stormy, a good deal of snow fell, and in such weather it was mere chance if we got anything at all to eat."

Additionally, the regimental paymasters of the Continental Army were historically slow in paying these troops. When they were paid it was in Continental script that was depreciating so fast that by the time the soldiers' past-due pay reached their families at home, its purchasing power was already diminished.

In light of these appalling conditions—and despite the horrendous weather—a movement within Brigadier General Huntington's brigade in the westernmost camp began to gather steam for a march on Hartford, the seat of the government some sixty miles away, to petition the legislature to improve the situation for the troops in the Redding encampments. When notified on December 30, 1778, of the unrest among the troops, Putnam rushed to the encampment from his headquarters elsewhere in Redding near Umpawaug Hill and gave a speech to the troops that calmed things down for the time being. The ringleader of the march on Hartford was imprisoned in a guardhouse. When he tried to escape, he was killed by one of the guards.

DEATH, PARDONS, AND THE LASH

Experienced soldier that he was, Washington had also previously communicated his views on camp discipline to his officers and was clearly not pleased when he heard of the nascent rebellion in Redding. Interestingly, and appropriately, Washington put a lot of the burden of enforcing military discipline on the line officers in charge of the camps and the field generals responsible for those line officers, emphasizing to his generals the importance literally of "being there amongst their troops."

In General Putnam's letter to Washington dated January 5, 1779, reporting on the rebellion Putnam had nipped in the bud with his stirring speech to the troops, he recommended the pardon of the ringleaders, plainly trying not to make things worse. The mutineers under arrest had sent a petition for pardon to Putnam, which the general was passing on to his commander in chief.

In his reply letter of January 18, 1779, Washington gave Putnam his general principles as to dealing with the ringleaders of a mutiny. In the end, however, Washington left the decision to General Putnam:

The mutiny of the Soldiers in Huntington's brigade was on its first appearance of a very alarming nature, but I am in hopes from the success with which your spirited exertions were attended in dispersing them, that there is no danger of further commotion.

The Conduct which a Commanding Officer is to observe, in cases of this kind in general, is to use every means for discovering the Authors of the mischief, to inflict instant punishment on them, and reclaim the rest by Clemency. The impression made on the minds of the multitude by the terror of the example, and their inability to take any resolution when deprived of their Ringleaders, are a sufficient Security against farther attempts. Humanity and Policy unite in prescribing such limits to Capital Punishments, when the Crime has been so general. With respect to the application in the present instance, and the doubt which arises from the foundation of Complaints which the men have, it is to be observed that their mode of pursuing Redress, is of so dangerous a tendency as to call for the exercise of wholesome Severity; and though the circumstances may require it, to be tempered with more lenity than in ordinary cases, such a subversion of discipline and Subordination cannot be passed unpunished. You will be best able to judge, from the degree of culpability of those in confinement, what measure ought to be taken respecting them, if there are any proper subject for execution among them, it is to be regretted that the matter has suffered any delay.

If the same causes should unluckily give birth to any future mutiny, the conduct abovementioned must be pursued; the severest and most summary example must be made of the Leaders, while a representation is made to the rest, in firm and at the same time conciliatory Language: That no measure compatible with our present

> circumstances is omitted for providing them, the Mutiny will not only be ineffectual in procuring a Remedy, but involve consequences infinitely worse than the evil complain'd of.[18]

Upon receipt of this letter, Putnam was plainly conflicted as to how to mete out a proportionate punishment for the mutiny in Huntington's brigade. Quite frankly, Washington's letter was not very helpful since it was couched in such ambiguous terms.

On the other hand, other letters of Washington showed a kinder and gentler commander in chief when he was faced with judging actual cases of military discipline. A letter to Congress dated August 31, 1778, just before the Redding encampments were laid out, reflects Washington's frustration that the range of disciplinary punishments used in the Continental Army was such—either 100 lashes at one extreme or capital punishment on the other—that he found himself frequently granting pardons for soldiers condemned to capital punishment in order to do justice to the circumstances as Washington saw them. Washington notified the Congress that he had asked his Board of Officers "to consider whether some mode might not be devised of equal or greater efficacy for preventing crimes and punishing Delinquents when they had happened less shocking to humanity and more advantageous to the States, than that of Capital execution."

To illustrate the quandary the Commander in Chief was dealing with in trying to temper justice with mercy, he gave the Congress a current statistic that faced him at headquarters: "there were eleven prisoners under sentence of death, and probably many more for trial." A General Order of Washington dated May 6, 1778, was typical of the way he dealt with pardons, including a recital of the rationale for showing mercy in the particular cases before him.

> The Commander in Chief being more desirous to reclaim than punish Offenders and willing to shew Mercy to those who have been misled by designing Traytors and that as many as can may participate the pleasures of the truly joyful day is pleased to pardon William McMarth of the Artillery and John Morrel of Colo. Henry Jackson's Regiment now under sentence of death and orders their immediate Release from Confinement, hoping that Gratitude to his Clemency will induce them in future to behave like good soldiers.[19]

With Washington's advice in the January 18th letter on his desk at Umpawaug Hill, Putnam temporized as to how to accommodate and reconcile Washington's General Orders—which were addressed to dealing with the ringleaders of the December mutiny and any future mutiny—with the facts on the ground, *i.e.,* keeping peace among the troops in the Redding camps.

SMITH AND JONES: SACRIFICIAL LAMBS?

And then the answer to his quandary presented itself to Putnam: not a mutiny but a possible spy situation where harsh punishment could be meted out as an example to the troops. Putnam's scouts in an outpost across the Connecticut border in Westchester County, New York, captured a man who was not supposed to be within their lines. They brought him to Putnam to be interviewed.

The prisoner was Edward Jones, originally from Wales, who had been a resident of nearby Ridgefield, Connecticut, before the Revolutionary War broke out. When war came, Jones, a Tory, joined with soldiers from his native country and became a butcher in the British Army. Like everyone else in charge of purveying goods for any army that winter, Jones was sent out to look for beef to feed the troops. He was captured by Putnam's scouts while on one of these procurement missions.

According to Brigadier General Parsons, Putnam interrogated Jones. After that, he was imprisoned in the guardhouse near Putnam's headquarters and court-martialed "for going to and serving the enemy as a guide and coming out as a spy." On February 4, 1779, Jones was found guilty of each and every charge. Putnam approved the sentence imposed on him by the court-martial: "execution . . . by hanging him by the neck till he is dead, dead, dead."[20]

Simultaneously within the Redding camps a case of desertion arose. John Smith, a sixteen- or seventeen-year-old with the 1st Connecticut Regiment was tried two days after Jones on February 6, 1779, at a General Court Martial "for desertion and attempting to go to the enemy." Smith, too, was found guilty and given the death penalty. However, he was to be "shot to death."[21]

Accordingly, Putnam had a spy and a deserter on his hands. Hanging one and shooting the other, he believed would, in the words of Washington's January 18 letter, make an "impression on the minds of the multitude by the terror of the example."

BLOOD STAINS IN THE SNOW

The manner in which the executions were carried out by Putnam was certainly calculated to make an impression on those who witnessed the sad and violent scene. The spy, Jones, was originally scheduled to be executed on Friday, February 12. It was postponed so that both executions could be held on the same day, Tuesday, February 16. One historian said that Putnam decided to "make a double job of it" and at the same time "make the spectacle as terrible and impressive as the circumstances demanded."[22]

On Sunday, February 14, the two prisoners were taken under guard to the Redding Meeting House, where a sermon was preached. The following day, the order was given to the brigade commanders that General Putnam "desires that the troops may appear clean and neat at the execution."[23]

Other lesser punishments also were meted out to various miscreant soldiers during this period, with one deserter sentenced to receive "one hundred lashes on his bare back" and reduced in rank, and another soldier, a horse thief, sentenced to sixty lashes. Both punishments were carried out in front of their respective regiments.

Having orchestrated a somewhat bloodthirsty atmosphere in the days before the executions, Putnam issued an order for calm intended to protect the prisoners in their final hours. He forbid the troops and local Redding residents from coming to the guardhouse on Umpawaug Hill to taunt and jeer the prisoners.

Charles Burr Todd, was a Redding resident and historian whose family had a house on Limekiln Road, not too far from the middle camp. The house was used by some of the officers during the encampment. Writing in the late 1880s and piecing together various and somewhat conflicting accounts, Todd reported the details of the executions, which were carried out on February 16, 1779, on what is now known as Gallows Hill, not far from the middle encampment. In some accounts, the spy was hanged first; in other accounts, the deserter was shot first. In any case, General Parsons described the circumstances as "revolting in the extreme."[24]

According to historian Todd, Putnam had assembled all the troops to bear witness to the executions. Edward Jones, the spy from Ridgefield by way of Wales, was hanged from a makeshift gallows erected about twenty feet off the ground. Before he was killed, Jones let it be known that "I am innocent of the crime laid to my charge."[25] He would not cooperate in his own undoing. The rope firmly around his neck, he refused to jump off the ladder/gallows, as Putnam had ordered him. Instead, some local youths were directed by Putnam to kick the ladder out from under Jones's feet.

The execution of deserter John Smith also was bungled. Smith was led to a spot about 200 yards from the gallows site; Putnam gave the order and three balls were shot through Smith's breast, causing him to fall to the ground. There, Smith's body twitched and convulsed until a soldier came forward to finish the job. He fired a round into Smith's forehead at such close range that the bullet set the boy's clothing on fire. Smith's body was placed in a coffin and every soldier under Putnam's command was forced to march past to review the teenager's smoldering remains. It was a grisly day's work for all concerned.[26]

DID THE PUNISHMENT FIT THE CRIME?

But the question raised in light of the deteriorating relationship between Generals Washington and Putnam in the winter of 1778/1779 is whether executing the Welsh butcher and the Connecticut teenager was the kind of punishment Washington had in mind when he gave Putnam his January 18th directive, which addressed dealing with ringleaders of mutinies, not the more garden variety cases of spies and deserters, which had plagued the Continental Army from its earliest days given the often horrible conditions endured by these young soldiers.

As usual, the punctilious Washington—apparently unaware of the capture of Smith and Jones—followed up with Putnam after a decent interval in a letter dated February 5, 1779, to see if the general had dealt with the December mutiny. Washington's persistence in keeping Putnam on his toes was, in part, plainly self-protective, since Washington did not want to deal with any more embarrassments from Putnam, to whom he had given a new lease on life with the Redding command.

In his February 5th letter to Putnam, written from his headquarters in Middlebrook, New Jersey, Washington noted the intervening letters he had received from Putnam on various subjects, apparently none of which reported on how Putnam had dealt with the mutineers. "I have your January [letters]. In one of my late letters I desired that you might take such steps with the mutineers in General Huntington's Brigade, as you, upon consultation with the principal Officers, should judge the most proper."[27]

With this letter from Washington in hand, Putnam could no longer dither. It would seem that as yet Putnam had not advised Washington about the spy from Westchester and the camp deserter, nor had he dealt conclusively with the mutineers. So the pressure was on Putnam to show his mettle to the Commander in Chief.

NOT PRESENT AND ACCOUNTED FOR

Significantly, at just this critical moment, Washington also was pressuring Putnam and the principal field generals serving under him—Generals Parsons and Huntington—for taking too much time off during the winter encampment, embarrassingly at the very time when discontent and a breakdown of discipline among the troops was manifesting itself across the board, whether by threats of mutiny or individual desertions.

Nothing infuriated the mild-mannered Washington more than the unpleasant discovery that his generals were not at their posts. Washington's standing orders were that at least two field generals must be in place at all times for each regiment except for extraordinary cases.

On February 10, 1779, Washington wrote another letter to Putnam, responding to correspondence from Putnam dated January 25th and 26th, one of which apparently contained a request by Putnam to take a leave of absence for personal reasons. Washington clearly did not tolerate fools gladly and expressed disappointment and genuine surprise that Putnam and, as it turned out, his field generals were taking leave simultaneously.

With a sternness that must have struck General Putnam to the core, Washington lectured and second-guessed the veteran general as to his supervision of the field generals under him and, in turn, the troops under them.

> The absence at this time of Gen. Parsons and Genl. Huntington, is a matter of some surprise. The intervals which the former in particular has already enjoyed and lately too, one would have though sufficient for the purpose of settling every thing of

> a private or domestic nature. We should not suffer ourselves to be led from the line of our service by a mere desire to see our friends, or to arrange affairs not really of the last importance.
>
> You need not be told of the disadvantages attending leaving a post of importance, even at a time, when we may suppose the season and other causes would check or prevent any operations of the enemy. But there are other considerations, which respect the discipline, the order, and, particular government of the command, and which require the constant attention of a superior officer.
>
> However, as you think it advisable to throw out a sheet anchor I could wish to accommodate matter to your request. You will therefore on Genl. Parsons and General Huntingtons return, (which you think will be some time in March) if you find the service will then admit of your going home, use that opportunity. But you will make your stay as short as possible, as it is altogether uncertain when you may be wanted.[28]

In early March, Washington returned to the subject of excessive leave time, commenting offhand in a letter to Putnam dated March 6, 1779, "I hope Generals Parsons and Huntington are with their Brigades."[29]

But Washington's final comment to Putnam on military discipline in his February 10th letter should have taken root in Putnam's soul as reflecting the core values of Washington's military jurisprudence, which blended justice with mercy, while leaving the ultimate punishment to officers on the ground. Commenting on an unrelated affair of military discipline that had presented itself, in his February 10th letter Washington put it much more simply to Putnam than he had in his letter of January 18th. "It appears to me a mixed case, and such a one as may be better decided by . . . those on the spot."[30]

A REQUEST FOR CLEMENCY

With all this as background, on February 16, 1779, Putnam made the decision to adhere to the results of the courts-martial earlier in February and execute Smith and Jones, apparently without ever seeking Washington's further views on the individual cases as to whether they should be handled with the pardon mechanism Washington so often employed as "less shocking to humanity and more advantageous to the States, than that of Capital execution." By imposing capital punishment on Smith and Jones, General Putnam had taken the hardest possible line, treating the men as if they were ringleaders of a mutiny—which they were not—and punishing them accordingly.

Reverend Nathaniel Bartlett, who was the longtime pastor of the Congregational Church in Redding and ministered to the Redding camps, tried to intercede with General Putnam on behalf of Smith, a local boy, to obtain a stay of execution for the teenager until General Washington could be consulted. Putnam ruled out clemency, apparently without ever presenting it to Washington.[31]

It is clear from a letter to Brigadier General Parsons from Washington dated April 30, 1779, that requests for leniency in death penalty cases did go to Washington directly on occasion from the Redding camps. And when faced squarely with capital punishment for one of his soldiers, Washington tended toward leniency. In the case of a Sergeant Gray, discussed in the April 30th letter to General Parsons, Washington advised Parsons that "it appears by testimony to the Court that there may have been a temporary insanity which led to the commission of the crime, and for the other considerations alleged, I have thought proper to remit the sentence of death."[32]

And as Washington had written to Congress in August 1778, his custom was to frequently grant pardons since he regarded capital punishment a waste of a good soldier who might otherwise be reclaimed if given a reprieve.

Did Putnam do the right thing in hanging the spy and shooting the deserter, and in not submitting the case to Washington for his consideration? Or was Putnam unduly influenced in imposing these extreme sanctions—which Washington had prescribed for ringleaders of mutinies—by the thinly veiled criticism of his performance by Washington that had been coming through loud and clear from the time of the fall of Forts Montgomery and Clinton in October 1777, through the organization of the Redding encampments, and continuing in the somewhat patronizing January and February 1779 letters from Washington, questioning Putnam's mettle and his leadership skills in managing his troops?

What would Washington have done if Reverend Bartlett's request for a stay of execution had been granted and a request for clemency formally presented by Putnam to him? Obviously, we do not know because, it seems, General Putnam was simply too proud to ask, not willing to further burden the superior who, Putnam probably sensed by then, had already put up with quite enough from him.

What we do know is that just a few days after the executions in Redding, Putnam continued to embellish the heroic legend of "Old Put" when, on February 26, 1779, he barely avoided capture by an enemy raiding party in present-day Greenwich, Connecticut, at a place called Horseneck Heights, by saddling up his horse and descending down the edge of a rocky cliff to the valley below. A sculpture memorializing Putnam's daring escape is located outside Putnam Park. Had General Putnam not eluded capture, he might have found himself on the sharp end of military justice.

As it was, command of the three camps at Redding in the terrible winter of 1778/1779 was General Putnam's last hurrah. Washington and Putnam continued to communicate, but Washington's tone continued to be one of vague disappointment, chastising Putnam on occasion for failure to get his troops in readiness for the spring 1779 offensive and expressing alarm at the diminished number of rank-and-file soldiers from Connecticut available to secure the Hudson River. Putnam had a paralytic stroke in December 1779, which forced his retirement from active duty. He died on May 29, 1790, at 72 years old.

There are statues and monuments all over Connecticut dedicated to General Putnam, from Hartford to his hometown of Pomfret. Counties all over America are named after him. Putnam Park in Redding is a permanent memorial to the folk hero general.

There are no historic markers for the bloodstains in the snow on Gallows Hill.

The author wishes to thank Redding's Historian, Charley Couch, for the enthusiasm and invaluable assistance he provided during the research for this article.

This article was originally published in *The Hudson River Valley Review*, Vol. 28.1, Autumn 2011.

NOTES

1. William Farrand Livingston, *Israel Putnam, Pioneer, Ranger and Major-General, 1718–1790* (G.P. Putnam's Sons, 1901), 380, hereafter cites as *Livingston*.
2. See generally the "Park History" portion of Putnam Memorial State Park, putnampark.org website, which is devoted to Putnam Memorial State Park, the oldest state park in Connecticut.
3. Frank Landon Humphreys, *Life and Times of David Humphreys: Soldier - Statesman – Poet* (G.P. Putnam's Sons 1917), Vol. 1, 120–21.
4. George Washington to George Clinton, October 25, 1777, George Washington Papers, Series 3, The Continental Army Papers. All references in this article to letters and General Orders from and to George Washington and his fellow officers can be found within this archive, Manuscript

Division, Library of Congress, Washington, D.C. http://memory.loc.gov./ammen/gwhtml/gwhome.html.

5. Robert Livingston to George Washington, January 14, 1778.
6. George Washington to Robert Livingston, March 12, 1778.
7. George Washington to Israel Putnam, March 16, 1778.
8. The following quotations and remarks are taken from the evidence offered in the Court of Inquiry; see "Report of the Court of Inquiry on the Loss of Fort Montgomery" to Washington, April 5, 1778, McDougall Papers, United States Military Philosophical Society Records, 1789–1813, microfilmed by the New-York Historical Society, Reel 2, USMA Library, West Point, N.Y., hereinafter cited as "Court of Inquiry".
9. Major General Putnam's Evidence, No. 25, the written evidence given by General Putnam before the Court of Inquiry.
10. Journal of the Continental Congress, August 17, 178, 803–04; see also *Livingston*, 375.
11. George Washington to the Continental Congress, July 28, 1778.
12. George Washington to Israel Putnam, November 25, 1778.
13. George Washington to the Continental Congress, September 7, 1778.
14. General Order, December 14, 1778.
15. General Order, December 24, 1778.
16. George Washington to Israel Putnam, January 8, 1779.
17. These quotations from the diaries of soldiers in the Redding encampment, and many more such entries, can be found on the Putnam Memorial State Park, putnampark.org/website in the "Winter Encampment" portion of the website.
18. George Washington to Israel Putnam, January 18, 1779.
19. General Order, May 6, 1778.
20. Charles S. Hall, *Life and Letters of Samuel Holden Parsons; Major General in the Continental Army and Chief Judge of the Northwestern Territory, 1737–1789* (Otseningo Publishing Co., 1905), 213, hereinafter cited as *Parsons*.
21. Ibid., 214.
22. Charles Burr Todd, *The History of Redding, Conn.* (The John A. Gray Press and Steam Type Setting Office 1880), 60, hereinafter cited as *Todd*.
23. *Parsons*, 214.
24. Ibid., 214.
25. *Todd*, 60–61.
26. *Todd*, 58–64; see also William Edgar Grumman, *The Revolutionary Soldiers of Redding* (Hartford Press, 1904), 82–84, for an alternative account of the courts-martial and executions of Smith and Jones.
27. George Washington to Israel Putnam, February 5, 1779.
28. George Washington to Israel Putnam, February 10, 1779.
29. George Washington to Israel Putnam, March 6, 1779.
30. George Washington to Israel Putnam, February 10, 1779.
31. *Todd*, 61–62.
32. George Washington to Samuel Holden Parsons, April 30, 1779.

20

Soldier of '76

The Revolutionary War Service of a Connecticut Private in the Campaign for New York

WILLIAM SULLIVAN

CONNECTICUT FURNISHED over a third of the men who fought the British Army for control of New York in 1776. Militiamen and short-term enlistees known as "levies" made up the majority of these troops. During this campaign, General George Washington came to the conclusion that these temporary soldiers would never win the Revolution. "To place any dependence upon Militia, is, assuredly, resting upon a broken staff," he asserted.[1] Washington penned this disparaging assessment just nine days after the first sounds of British cannon at the Battle of Kips Bay had led to the panic and flight of the Connecticut levies. Among those who ran that day was Private Moses Tuttle. His experience as a soldier during the campaign of 1776 demonstrates that while the performance of temporary troops proved dismal at times, their willingness to enter the field of battle against great odds and in spite of hunger, poverty, and disease helped sustain the Revolution through its early stages. In addition, his regiment's valiant effort at the Battle of White Plains helped to blunt a British thrust at the Hudson River Valley.

Government documents preserve the story of Tuttle's service to our country. In 1832, at the age of seventy-eight, he appeared at the Court of Probate in Cheshire, Connecticut, and gave a full account of his military experience in order to obtain a federal pension. At this time, the government granted such pensions to Revolutionary War veterans who offered proof by sworn affidavit of at least six months of service.[2] The approval of the pension application of Moses Tuttle confirms the overall validity of his claim.[3]

A second source corroborates and gives further detail to the statement given by Tuttle. Joseph Plumb Martin served in the Tuttle's regiment during the 1776 campaign. In 1830, Martin published one of the few memoirs of the American Revolution written from the viewpoint of an ordinary soldier. This book, *Private Yankee Doodle: A Narrative of Some of the Adventures, Dangers and Sufferings of a Revolutionary Soldier, Interspersed with Anecdotes of Incidents that Occurred Within His Own Observation*, generated little interest beyond Martin's neighbors in Maine at the time. However, historians now consider it the most complete and accurate account of a soldier's life in the American Revolution.[4] Martin's narrative, along with the deposition of Tuttle, provides a fascinating account of the experience of a soldier of 1776.

Moses Tuttle was born on November 15, 1753, one of ten children raised by Moses and Sybil (Thomas) Tuttle in Wallingford, Connecticut.[5] His military career most certainly began before the outbreak of hostilities with the British in 1775. The law compelled all able-bodied males to own a firearm and drill with their neighbors in militia units. During the War for Independence, these units served as a police force to quell domestic unrest, enforce loyalty to the Patriot cause, and, when needed, respond to local incursions of the British army.[6]

At times the rebellious colonies called forth volunteer militia units to reinforce the regular "continental" regiments of General Washington's army or to perform a mission outside of the state when the need arose. Connecticut issued such a request during the winter of 1775 and 1776. At this time, the siege of Boston occupied much of Washington's army. Many suspected that the next British assault would be aimed at capturing the harbor facilities of New York City. Therefore, Washington ordered his second in command, Major General Charles Lee, to obtain volunteers from the Connecticut militia and prepare defensive works in New York City. The Connecticut Council of Safety enlisted approximately 1,500 men for a three-month term to help in "The York affair for Genl. Lee."[7]

Moses Tuttle enlisted for this mission in the early part of December 1775—eight months after the first shots had been fired at Lexington and seven months before the colonies declared their independence from Great Britain. Tuttle explains that his "company of volunteers formed in Cheshire," Connecticut, with Captain Stephen Rowe Bradley commanding. As few as twenty-five to as many as 104 men generally constituted a company, the basic building block of an eighteenth-century army.[8] Tuttle states in his affidavit: "I do not know if I belonged to any particular regiment" (a unit of eight to ten companies). He did have a clear recollection of the pay, however: forty shillings a month and no bounty (a bonus for signing up).[9]

Tuttle's pension application does not include any explanation as to why he took up arms against the British. The lack of bounty money largely discounts financial considerations as a prime motivation. Young men volunteering for service at this time generally did so out of idealism, the longing for adventure, and pressure from their fellow townspeople. Of all these factors, devotion to the revolutionary cause may have been the most important to Tuttle. According to Don Higginbotham's study, "The patriotic response early in the war tended to be enthusiastic, especially that of the New England militia."[10]

The twenty-two-year-old Tuttle fits the description of a typical recruit for the time and place of his enlistment. As a young, single man without property, New England society considered him expendable in times of war. His enrollment into a state company of militia instead of the Continental Line also matches an expected pattern. Since Continental soldiers signed on for long terms and could expect to march far from home, they tended to come from the lower classes of society. States generally manned units with those persons who had the most to lose from a long leave of absence: propertied farmers, artisans, or men like Tuttle who were about to attain such middle-class status.[11]

Tuttle most likely reported for duty with his own clothing as a uniform and needed to furnish a musket. The best models available were British Army "Brown Bess" flintlocks that had been issued during the Seven Years War (1754–1763) to colonial militia. Some men carried flintlocks inherited from conflicts fought as many as sixty years prior to the Revolution. Still others relied upon locally manufactured "Committee of Safety" muskets patterned after the "Brown Bess" or crudely designed hunting flintlocks known as "fowling pieces." In addition to his musket, Moses needed to provide his own knapsack, blanket, canteen, flint, pouch or cartridge box, priming brush and pick, and a tomahawk. When he joined a Connecticut regiment, Joseph Martin reports that his grandparents provided him with "arms, and accouterments, clothing, cake, and cheese aplenty . . . and a pocket bible." Unfortunately, like most American soldiers of the day, both Tuttle and Martin probably lacked the most important weapon of the eighteenth century—a bayonet.[12]

Once enrolled, the authorities had trouble deciding what to do with Bradley's company of volunteers. General Lee and his force of Connecticut militia departed for New York in late January. However, as Tuttle points out they were soon "Ordered to return to Milford." They "Again marched to New York" and "Crossed the Kingsbridge" but were "Again ordered back but the order was countermanded and marched to New York."[13]

This frustrating series of marches and countermarches up and down the Boston Post Road is explained by a dispute between General Lee and New York's governing Committee of Safety. Lee wanted to secure the city from British attack as quickly as possible. However, the New York Committee of Safety worried about the consequences of such an action. A large number of Loyalist citizens lived in New York who would most likely perceive Lee's force as an invading army. This would probably lead to many families fleeing the city in the dead of winter and might provoke a violent reaction from those loyalists who remained or a bombardment of the harbor by the small squadron of British ships stationed nearby. Therefore, the Committee of Safety demanded that the command of the incoming soldiers be turned over to them to dispel the perception that New York was about to be invaded by Connecticut. Eventually, the Continental Congress intervened on Lee's behalf in the dispute, and the Connecticut militia began entering the city on February 4, 1776.[14]

New York City in 1776 clung to the southernmost tip of Manhattan Island and crowded some 25,000 inhabitants into a one-mile-square radius. By the time Captain Bradley's company arrived, many families had already boarded up their homes and fled. A local reported that the newly arriving soldiers would "break open and quarter themselves in any houses they" found "shut up."[15]

While in New York, Tuttle states, "we engaged in cutting post lines" and "Barricaded some of the streets." He also remembers that "there were some other troops in the city at the time, though not many," including a company from Hartford, Connecticut.[16] The work described by Tuttle indicates that his unit most likely took part in carrying out General Lee's order to barricade every street that led to the Hudson River.[17]

The need to complete the task of readying New York for battle intensified during the spring. The British army departed from Boston on Saint Patrick's Day, 1776. Sensing their next move, Washington began transferring his army to New York. On March 28, the first troops of Washington's regular army appeared, and Major General Israel Putnam dismissed the Connecticut militia. Tuttle remembers being "verbally discharged" on "the first of April."[18]

He remained at home for only a brief respite before volunteering to serve again. With the attack on New York City appearing imminent, Connecticut responded to a desperate request to provide reinforcements to Washington's army by authorizing the formation of seven battalions of "New Levies" to serve until December 25, 1776.[19] "Levies" were state troops who would sign up for a short, specified period of time. Organized into state companies and regiments, this "state line" acted as a reserve force to the more permanent regular army regiments that formed the "Continental Line." Moses Tuttle became a levy on June 24, 1776, when he enlisted as a private in Captain Nathaniel Bunnel's Seventh Company of Volunteers of the Fifth Connecticut Battalion.[20]

A group of highly regarded officers commanded this regiment. Colonel William Douglas, a New Haven merchant and farmer, used his own funds to help raise the force. The thirty-four-year-old veteran of the French and Indian Wars placed his family fortune in jeopardy and would eventually give his life to the cause of liberty.[21] The other two field officers clearly earned the respect of the men. The often critical Private Joseph Plumb Martin describes Lieutenant Colonel James Arnold as a "fine officer and a brave soldier."[22] When the British captured Major Phineas Porter in the subsequent campaign, "his loss was much regretted by the men of the regiment."[23] These commanders earned such praise despite their reputation for toughness. At the close of the Battle of Harlem Heights, an enlisted man who had not eaten for two days grumbled about his hunger within earshot of the Lieutenant Colonel. Arnold reached "into his coat pocket, took out a piece of an ear of Indian corn burnt as black as a coal. 'Here,' said he to the man complaining, 'eat this and learn to be a soldier.' "[24]

To show their rank, the officers affixed epaulettes to the shoulders of their jackets and colored, rosette-shaped badges known as cockades to their hats. Field officers like Douglas wore red, the captains white, and officers below this rank green. However, upon entering their first battle, Arnold and Porter would remove their cockades. When asked why, Arnold "replied that he was willing to risk his life in the cause of his country, but unwilling to stand a particular mark for the enemy to fire at."[25] The historic record yields no precise description of what uniforms, if any, the enlisted men wore as they marched into battle.

In total, 614 officers and enlisted men joined Douglas's regiment. Although the state filled out the officer corps completely, the recruitment drive failed to meet the goal of manning each company with eighty-three "rank and file" soldiers. The actual number of corporals and privates varied between fifty-eight and seventy-one per company. Connecticut came up 138 enlistments short of the full 752-man regiment that it had hoped to field.[26]

Rarely did any of the colonies succeed in fully manning their regiments. Drawing men away from their farms for any extended period of time to face the hardships of military service proved a challenge as the war dragged on. Connecticut anticipated having difficulty in recruiting for the 1776 campaign. In addition to the going rate of forty shillings per month, each man enrolling as a private in Douglas's regiment received a bounty of three pounds as an inducement to enlist. Furthermore, the authorities compensated volunteers with money for providing their own muskets, blankets, knapsacks, bayonets, and "cartouch-boxes." The state even promised to pay one penny per mile marched to and from the campaign in lieu of rations, and "one days pay for every twenty miles between home and the general rendezvous, going and returning."[27]

Under these terms, Tuttle earned at least thirteen pounds ($43.36). His five months of service would come to ten pounds, plus he earned the three-pound bounty for signing on, and gained a small sum for fifty-two miles of marching. Without a surviving payroll record for Captain Bunnel's Company, it cannot be determined whether or not he received money for bringing his own equipment into camp. However, the other scattered accounting records from the regiment show that most men did furnish themselves with weapons and other items that entitled them to compensation.[28]

Even with the bounty money, Tuttle's earnings were minimal. If he had served a full six months, his wages and signing bonus would have totaled fifteen pounds—the approximate figure an unskilled laborer could expect to earn over the same period of time. A skilled artisan in Connecticut would command at least twice this income for six months' work.[29] Clearly, Tuttle did not enlist for riches. In exchange for risking his life, the authorities promised him only the wages of a common laborer.

Regrettably, as was all too common in the Revolution, Connecticut fell well behind in actually paying what they promised to the soldiers. A payroll record from one of Douglas's companies shows that the state still owed every pence of the wages earned by the privates at the end of their six-month term. Another accounting book demonstrates that Connecticut did not distribute back pay until the following year.[30]

The issue of back pay created lingering bitterness among the soldiers. Decades later, Joseph Martin still remembered, "We were . . . promised six dollars and two thirds a month, to be paid us monthly." But he did not receive the money until "August, 1777 when paying ceased." To add to the seriousness of the injury inflicted, Connecticut paid him in the form of "Continental currency." This paper money quickly lost value. The holder of a Continental dollar received only twenty cents of actual goods from merchants in 1777, down from fifty cents per dollar in 1776. This extraordinary rate of inflation made the shameful act of not paying the soldiers on time particularly cruel. In his memoir, Martin presents a stinging commentary on the injustice of the matter. He explains that by the time he got his hands on the wages owed, six dollars and sixty-seven cents "was scarcely enough to procure a man a dinner." He points out that "Had I been paid as I was promised . . . I needed not to have suffered as I did . . . there was enough" food "in the country and money would have procured it if I had had it." This state of affairs led Martin to regret that he ever joined the army for:

> It is provoking to think of it. The country was rigorous in exacting my compliance to *my* engagements to a punctilio, but equally careless in performing her contracts with me, and why so? One reason was because she had all the power in her own hands and I had none. Such things ought not to be.[31]

While Moses Tuttle surely also grumbled about his pay falling in arrears, he at least could share his unhappiness with familiar company. Since recruitment happened at the local level, neighbors and usually family welcomed the men who joined the patriot army. Of the seventy-four men who joined Captain Bunnel's Company, seventy came from Tuttle's hometown of Wallingford and the other four hailed from New Haven, Connecticut. Ties of kinship also bound these soldiers. Six members of the Hotchkiss family joined the company as did four Hitchcocks, three Merrimans, and two Meriams. While Moses is the only "Tuttle" to appear on Bunnel's roll, it is of interest to note that he would soon marry into the Hitchcock clan. In addition, the rolls of the other companies in the regiment list the name Tuttle six times.[32]

Moses Tuttle began his second tour of duty on a lonely mission. He states, "I went down to New York previous to the rest of the company as a guard to the baggage—the only soldier on this duty. I was quartered in New York near the North River, just above what was called Tea Water Point.[33] Besides the baggage, the Connecticut Assembly also allowed "four hogsheads of rum, two hogsheads of molasses and two barrels of sugar" to make the trip in spite of its embargo on "West Indies goods."[34] Eventually, the entire regiment joined up with their supplies and quartered "near the East River" to await the anticipated British attack.

Beginning in late June, the British navy and army began to arrive in great numbers on Staten Island. From their positions on Manhattan Island, the Americans watched as the invasion force swelled to nearly 32,000 men—the largest British expeditionary body of the century. To help create this army, King George III "rented" around 8,000 soldiers from four German princes. The most numerous of these blue-coated troops came from Hesse-Cassel, and thus the Americans came to call all of these mercenaries "Hessians."[35]

Washington lacked the strength to meet this threat. His army would eventually grow to nearly 30,000 men. However, outbreaks of dysentery and other debilitating illnesses throughout that summer left nearly a quarter of these troops unfit for combat. To defend New York he never counted more than 21,000 "effectives" in his army, many of whom were untested militia. The complete absence of a navy to oppose the thirty warships deployed by the British also dimmed any hope of defending Manhattan Island and its approaches. Military wisdom dictated that Washington abandon New York City given the situation. Politically, however, he could not yield such a prize without a fight.[36]

For two months while the British forces assembled and prepared, Tuttle and his unit trained in New York City. Martin recounts being "called out every morning at reveille beating, which was at daybreak, to go to our regimental parade in Broad Street." Broad Street was east of and parallel to Broadway and ran from the Exchange on Dock Street to Wall Street. On the parade grounds the regiment practiced "the manual exercise, which was the most that was known in our levies, if they even knew that."[37]

Martin's reference to the "manual exercise" indicates that the men practiced drilling, loading, and firing their weapons in formation, although the shortage of powder prevented them from actually discharging the musket. Today we generally view drilling as a way for the military to instill discipline and make a good show. However, in 1776, soldiers used the maneuvers learned while drilling in battle. Due to the tremendous inaccuracy of the smoothbore musket, eighteenth-century tactics called for officers to mass the men in lines ranked two or three deep. Soldiers needed to maintain this formation as they marched forward and closed to within 100 yards or less of their enemy. Since few would bet a shilling that they could hit a man-sized target at fifty yards, the combatants fired a simultaneous volley with the hopes that the wall of lead bullets they produced would strike and thin the ranks of the enemy. The unit would then reload, following a series of practiced commands so as not to get in each other's way, and fire again. A well-trained regiment could reload and fire three times a minute, enough to perhaps hold off the much-feared bayonet charge of the British. Unfortunately, despite the constant drill practice endured during the summer of 1776, Tuttle and the other levies remained woefully unprepared for battle when compared with their peers in the King's service.[38]

After the morning drill, the soldiers would get their provisions for the day. The menu never varied. Day after day the men consumed salted meats and hard bread.[39] While it did not compare to what they ate at home, Martin felt the food "was not bad; if there was any deficiency it could in some measure be supplied by procuring some kind of sauce."[40]

After preparing and eating their meals, the men of Washington's army spent most of their time during the summer of 1776 on guard duty or building forts and entrenchments. Tuttle probably endured long periods of labor and many tedious hours on sentry before turning in for the night. He most likely retired to sleep in a house abandoned by a Loyalist family in the vicinity of Stone Street in lower Manhattan. Shortages compelled most men to sleep two to a blanket.[41]

Efforts to instill discipline over the men during their idle hours failed. Lectures from ministers and officers did little to curtail the spread of venereal diseases from the thriving New York prostitution trade. The stealing of property by enlisted men became rampant despite the threat of punishment. Farmers, angered at the theft of their produce, stopped traveling to the city to sell their crops and livestock. This denied the army the vegetables and fresh foods needed to provide a proper diet to the men. With only bread and meat to eat, many soldiers suffered from malnutrition.[42]

To Washington, the most serious breakdown in discipline came on July 9, 1776. The day ended with a solemn reading of the new Declaration of Independence to each assembled brigade. Once dismissed, the men joined the locals in a riotous celebration that resulted in the destruction of property. The incident left the commander in chief both shocked and angered.[43]

Washington's injured sense of good order aside, the worst threat posed by the lack of discipline came in the area of sanitation. Many soldiers ignored the pleas of their officers to dispose of their waste properly. A horrified General Nathanael Greene found that the most ignorant made it a practice to relieve themselves into the ditches before their entrenchments. The men suffered for such insolence. The tainted water and soil created an overpowering stench and led to the frightful proliferation of disease that laid waste to a large portion of the army.[44]

Washington could ill afford such losses with the threat of British attack increasing. Throughout the summer, the men frequently found their tasks interrupted by calls to prepare for battle.

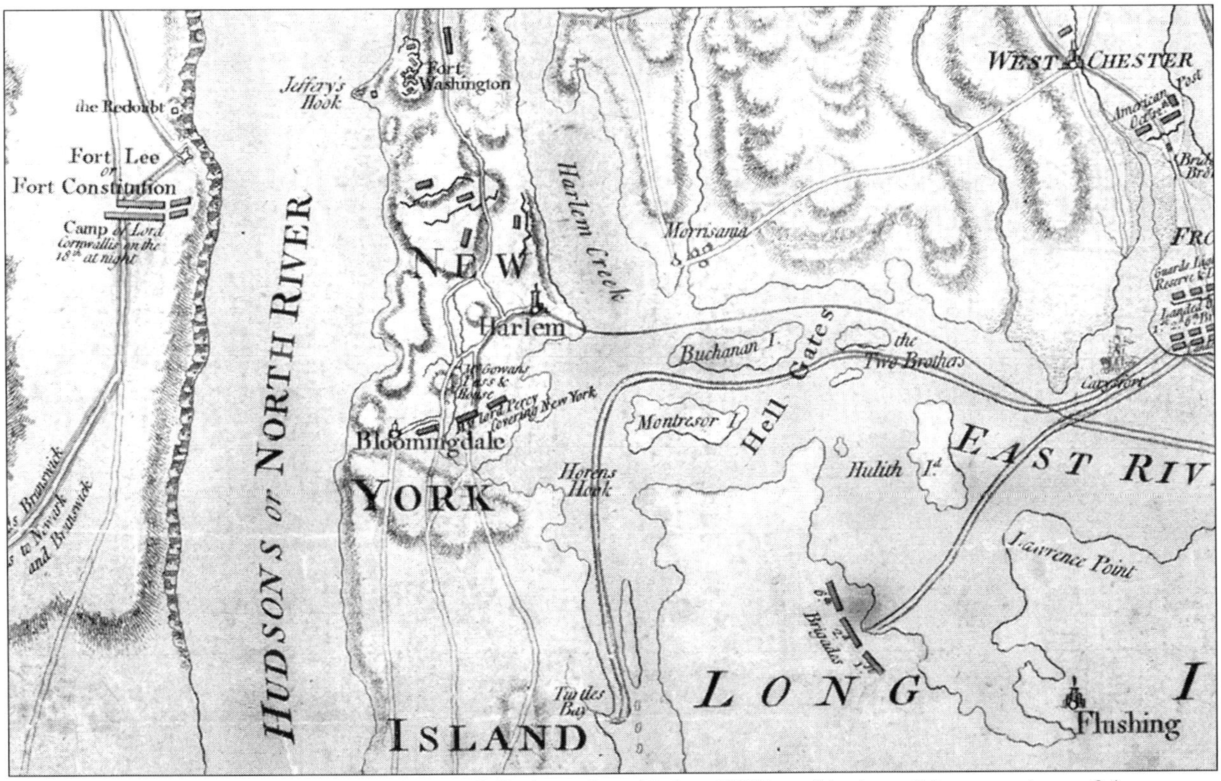

Fig. 20.1. Detail showing New York City and Harlem, from Faden, William, "A plan of the operations of the King's army: under the command of General Sr. William Howe, K.B. in New York and East New Jersey, against the American forces commanded by General Washington, from the 12th of October, to the 28th," Feb. 25, 1777. The Lionel Pincus and Princess Firyal Map Division, The New York Public Library, Astor, Lenox and Tilden Foundations.

Without adequate intelligence of Howe's intentions, Washington oftentimes responded to rumors of British movements and sounded the general alarm for all men to get to their posts. Inevitably, they would wait for an assault that never came. The one exception to this pattern came on July 12 when two British warships, the HMS *Rose* and HMS *Phoenix*, sailed up the Hudson River and then back down again, exchanging cannon fire with the rebel gunners that lined both shorelines. The ships emerged intact from the engagement, and the city suffered only light damage.[45]

The real hammer did not fall on New York until late in the summer. On August 21, the ever-cautious General William Howe moved a large portion of his British army to Long Island to begin his long-awaited conquest of New York. The onset of real action generated tremendous excitement in the American camps. Tuttle's commanding officer, Colonel Douglas, wrote to his wife that "our troops are in . . . high sperits and it is a general voice, Let them come on us as soon as they can or dare!"[46]

Howe dared to challenge the American army. He moved his troops into position on Long Island with the intention of dislodging the Americans from their fortifications on Brooklyn Heights. Should this high ground fall to the British, they could easily bombard the city from the east. Fearing this outcome, Washington reinforced his lines on Brooklyn Heights by ordering several regiments, including Douglas's men, to cross the East River and join the Americans defending Long Island. Tuttle, "being in charge of the sick," remained behind in the city and avoided the "American disaster" that followed.[47] In the battle of Long Island, Howe

Fig. 20.2. The retreat of Continental forces from Long Island. Drawing by H. A. Ogden, printed 1905 by John D. Morris & Company.

Fig. 20.3. The British Fleet in the Lower Bay. Harper's Magazine, August 1876.

outmaneuvered and routed the poorly deployed Rebel army on August 27. General Putnam held Douglas's regiment in reserve until the closing stages of this engagement.[48]

Tuttle missed the battle that cost the American army 1,100 men. He explains that

> I was ordered to go on to the Island the same morning that Washington's army was floated back to New York on a makeshift fleet of vessels to save themselves from total destruction. I and others would have gone over sooner, had it not been for the dreadful rain which lasted three or four days.[49]

With Brooklyn Heights firmly in Howe's hands and the Royal Navy free to roam the East River, New York lay vulnerable to attack. The British paused to discuss peace terms with a delegation from the Continental Congress. While nothing came of these talks, debates within the Connecticut militia produced disappointing results. During open meetings, many discouraged soldiers voted to go home. Approximately 6,000 of the 8,000 Connecticut militiamen in New York wound up returning to their farms for the fall harvest.[50]

Tuttle, however, remained. He and his regiment lingered in the city until September 3, when they marched up to the stores at Turtle Bay (north of the city and near Kips Bay). "Here, the flour and cannon balls were carted off as fast as possible—we did not get much of the cannon balls off—but did considerable of the flour. The rest of the flour we dashed and threw into the river. Into this service we pressed all the wagons we could raise."[51]

At this point, General Washington found himself in the midst of a difficult situation. The closest defensible ground lay to the north of New York City in the densely wooded area of upper Manhattan Island. Prudent military strategy suggested an immediate withdrawal of his 9,000 soldiers to Harlem Heights. However, Washington needed time to transport supplies out of the city and wait for the Continental Congress to confirm his opinion that New York should not be set ablaze. Thus, 5,000 men remained in New York City while the rest, including Tuttle, formed a thin line along the eastern shores of Manhattan Island. One decisive landing by the British along this coast and a dash across the island would trap much of Washington's army in the city.[52]

General Howe eventually seized upon the opportunity presented and selected Kips Bay, a cove located between present-day Thirty-Second and Thirty-Eighth Streets, as the perfect landing area for his troops. Tuttle lay directly in this line of attack, "in the entrenchment thrown up by the army south of the stores" at Kips Bay. Martin asserts that the entrenchments "were nothing more than a ditch dug along on the bank of the river with dirt thrown out towards the water."[53] From this position on Sunday morning, September 15, 1776, Tuttle observed:

> [T]he enemy's boats from the Island put off for our shore . . . As soon as the boats came within the British shipping (five warships, including the HMS Rose) and our entrenchments, the shipping opened a tremendous fire upon us, likewise with the boats. We were commanded to retreat and did not stop until we got to Harlem Heights. This retreat was made in great confusion, people huddling out of the city, the flying army, wagons with the sick, etc . . .[54]

And so, Tuttle saw his first action in the embarrassing battle of Kips Bay. British and Hessian troops landed unopposed following the bombardment that sent the Americans to flight. Witnessing Connecticut soldiers run that morning, an exasperated General Washington shouted to "take to the wall" and form a defensive position. With no response, he ordered them to "take the cornfield." With men still fleeing and the British about to capture the commander, Washington exclaimed, "are these the men with which I am to defend America? Good God! Have I got such troops as these?"[55]

"Such troops as these" would have a second chance to prove themselves the next day. The American army slipped out of the trap that the British had set, abandoned New York City, and reformed itself on Harlem Heights, where the men dug in. In the early morning hours of September 16, a scouting party of 120 riflemen under the direction of Lieutenant Colonel Thomas Knowlton moved a mile south of Harlem Heights and probed the British lines. At dawn, a skirmish between Knowlton's Rangers and Howe's advanced sentries broke out. Knowlton ordered his men to stand. They fired eight rounds into the ranks of the advancing British. Finding themselves outnumbered three to one and nearly outflanked, Knowlton withdrew in good order. When the Americans fell back, the British unwisely followed and came dangerously close to Washington's main lines. From the top of Claremont Hill, the bugler of the British troops sounded the "fox chase"—a tune intended to insult the once-again retreating Americans as trapped quarry.

This time the quarry decided to become the hunter. Washington sensed an opportunity. The British force lay just south of the American army on the other side of a valley known as the Hollow Way. His staff believed that the enemy consisted of no more than 350 men, and they stood one mile in advance of any support that Howe could send. Given this situation, Washington hatched a scheme to encircle and trap the British. He ordered a small body of troops into the Hollow Way to bait the enemy into the valley. At around 11 a.m. the British moved forward to engage these troops. Meanwhile, Knowlton's

Rangers, reinforced by three companies of Virginia riflemen under a Major Leitch, attempted to make their way behind the British troops without being detected. The encirclement failed. Knowlton turned right too soon and struck the Redcoats at their right flank instead of their rear. Both Knowlton and Leitch fell fatally wounded in this assault. Nonetheless, the surprise attack shocked the British, who fell back a distance before rallying in a buckwheat field.

For the next hour and a half, the two forces exchanged fire in a deadly contest for farmer Vandewater's field. The British hurried reinforcements to the battle. Washington also began committing his reserves. Eventually, he turned to Douglas's men. Tuttle recalls that his

> Regiment engaged and we drove them (the British) back and up a long hill. While we were pursuing them up the hill they took off the drag ropes from one of their cannon and let it roll back upon us. We opened to the right and left, and let it roll without doing any damage, and we took the cannon.[56]

The British retreated to their main lines. Tuttle and his fellow levies—the same men who had run the day before—now stood victorious and gave a cheer. Fearing that they could be cut off and destroyed, Washington called his troops back to Harlem Heights. Tactically, therefore, the Battle of Harlem Heights was nothing more than an extended skirmish. The two sides did not permanently exchange ground. However, the first defeat Washington inflicted on the British gave his men an enormous boost of morale.

Victory did not come without cost. Washington's army suffered between sixty and 130 casualties. Of these, Martin believed that the regiment lost "eight or ten killed and a number wounded."[57] Documentary evidence supports Martin's rough calculation. The only surviving muster roll of the regiment lists four dead and two missing on September 16, including Private William Merriams of Captain Bunnel's company. Three more died over the next ten days, presumably from wounds suffered in battle. In addition, the regiment reported three missing and a Major Porter as captured at Kips Bay the previous day.[58] Estimates of British losses at the Battle of Harlem Heights vary, but the best source—a letter from one of their officers—reveals that fourteen British soldiers died and 157 fell wounded.[59]

For nearly a month after the battle, Tuttle and the rest of the American army remained on Harlem Heights while General Howe plotted his next move. During this time, conditions worsened considerably. While Tuttle says nothing of the deprivation in his affidavit, Martin describes a miserable existence in his memoir:

> We remained here till sometime in the month of October without anything very material transpiring, excepting starvation and *that* by this time became quite a secondary matter; hard duty and nakedness were considered the prime evil, for the reader will recollect that we lost all our clothing in the Kip's Bay affair. . . . It now began to be cool weather, especially the nights. To lie as I did almost every night (for our duty required it) on the cold and often wet ground without a blanket and with nothing but a thin summer clothing was tedious.[60]

Inadequate food, clothing, and shelter took a tremendous toll on the men of Tuttle's unit. Colonel Douglas designated an average of 219 men as "sick" when filling out his weekly strength reports. This left only sixty percent of the unit available for duty. The number of "rank and file" sent out of camp to recover in makeshift hospitals rose from just nineteen on September 21 to 160 on October 20. The army also discharged a growing number of Douglas's regiment, as many fell gravely ill or needed to recover from battle wounds. A total of ninety-two soldiers obtained permission for early dismissal from the service.[61]

Moses Tuttle leaves us a disturbing line from his account of the time he spent on Harlem Heights: "A man was brought up to be shot." Martin recalled the same event, but with much more detail. According to his account, Sergeant Ebenezer Leffingwell from Connecticut had been ordered to the rear during the battle of Harlem Heights to secure more ammunition. When Colonel Joseph Reed found Leffingwell running away from the action he took him for a deserter and demanded he return to the lines. When the sergeant insisted on completing his assigned mission, Reed drew his sword. Leffingwell responded by cocking his musket. This incident resulted in Leffingwell being charged and convicted of mutiny. Martin reports that the announcement that the man was to be executed caused much discontent among the common soldiers who felt that a grave injustice had been done. A tense drama unfolded as the "Connecticut troops were drawn out and formed in a square and the prisoner brought forth. After being blindfolded and pinioned, he knelt upon the ground" and watched the executioner's squad come forward. At the last moment, a Chaplain read a reprieve which saved the man's life, but only after "repeatedly using this sentence, 'crimes for which men ought to die,' which did much to further the resentment of the troops already raised to a high pitch."[62] This near execution occurred on September 22—the same day the British hanged Nathan Hale as a spy.

Besides this event, much of the month at Harlem Heights passed without any further comment from Tuttle beyond "Here, we stayed for some time." The stalemate between Washington and Howe finally broke on October 12, when the British loaded a portion of their army on ships and leapfrogged past the American positions, landing at Throgs Neck and then Pell's Point. Once again, the British threatened to trap the American army on Manhattan Island. Once again, the deliberative Howe moved too slowly to tighten the noose. Despite a critical shortage of horses and wagons, Washington escaped the snare by moving the main part of his army from Harlem Heights to White Plains, a strategic village that controlled the roads coming from New England and going up the Hudson River Valley. Tuttle recollected making "a few halts" on his way to White Plains, where the record indicates he arrived on October 21.[63]

The regiment that Colonel Douglas offered to assist in the defense of White Plains was hardly ready for the battle that would soon ensue. On October 25, only 200 of the rank and file reported for duty "present and fit"; 160 of the enlisted and a quarter of the officers lay sick. The need to look after the ill, post sentries, and attend to other duties out of camp occupied another eighty-seven of the enlisted. In total, Douglas could call upon only around 270 men to fight in the impending battle of White Plains. Disease, death, and discharge had cut the strength of his unit by more than fifty percent since the regiment's formation in July.[64]

Washington prepared his defenses at White Plains for a week while the British army gathered its strength for an attack. The depleted, tired, and hungry Continental army threw up makeshift entrenchments made of cornstalks and dirt. To substitute for bayonets they attached iron pikes to long poles. As the 14,000 British and Hessian troops assembled before them, Washington informed his officers: "Gentlemen . . . do the best you can."[65]

On October 28, 1776, the British made their move. Howe made Chatterton's Hill, which lay on Washington's extreme right, the objective of an offensive designed to seize high ground and place artillery on the American Army's flank. To counter this threat, Washington called upon Joseph Spencer, an inept sixty-two-year-old Connecticut Major General nicknamed "Granny" by his troops. Spencer commanded 2,500 soldiers, including Tuttle and his regiment. Washington ordered this detachment to move forward of the American lines and delay the Hessian troops advancing on Chatterton's Hill. Spencer's men crossed the Bronx River and took up a defensive position behind a low stone wall.[66]

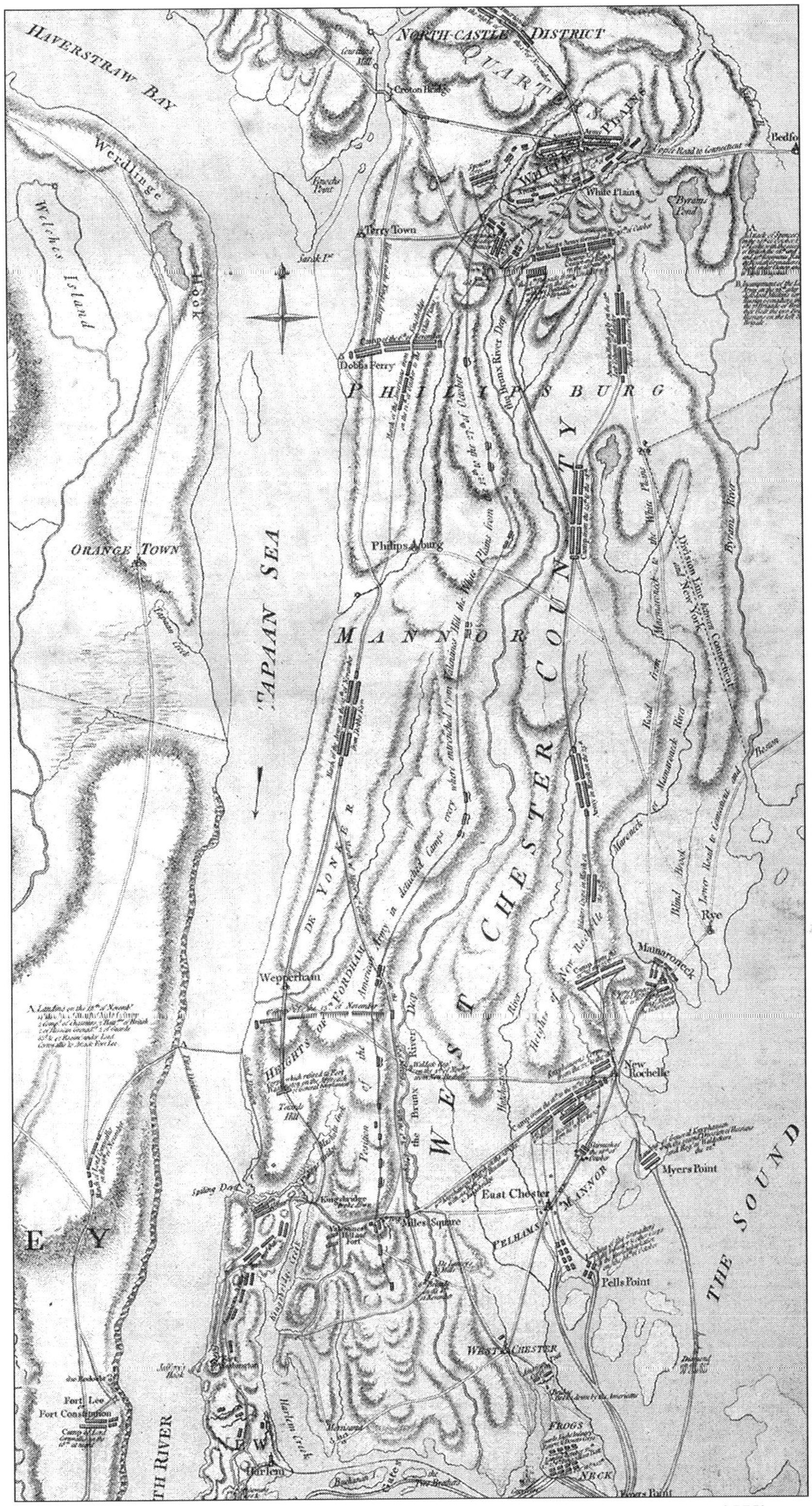

Fig 20.1. Detail showing the distance and terrain between Harlem and White Plains, from Faden, William, "A plan of the operations of the King's army: under the command of General Sr. William Howe, K.B. in New York and East New Jersey, against the American forces commanded by General Washington, from the 12th of October, to the 28th," Feb. 25, 1777. The Lionel Pincus and Princess Firyal Map Division, The New York Public Library, Astor, Lenox and Tilden Foundations.

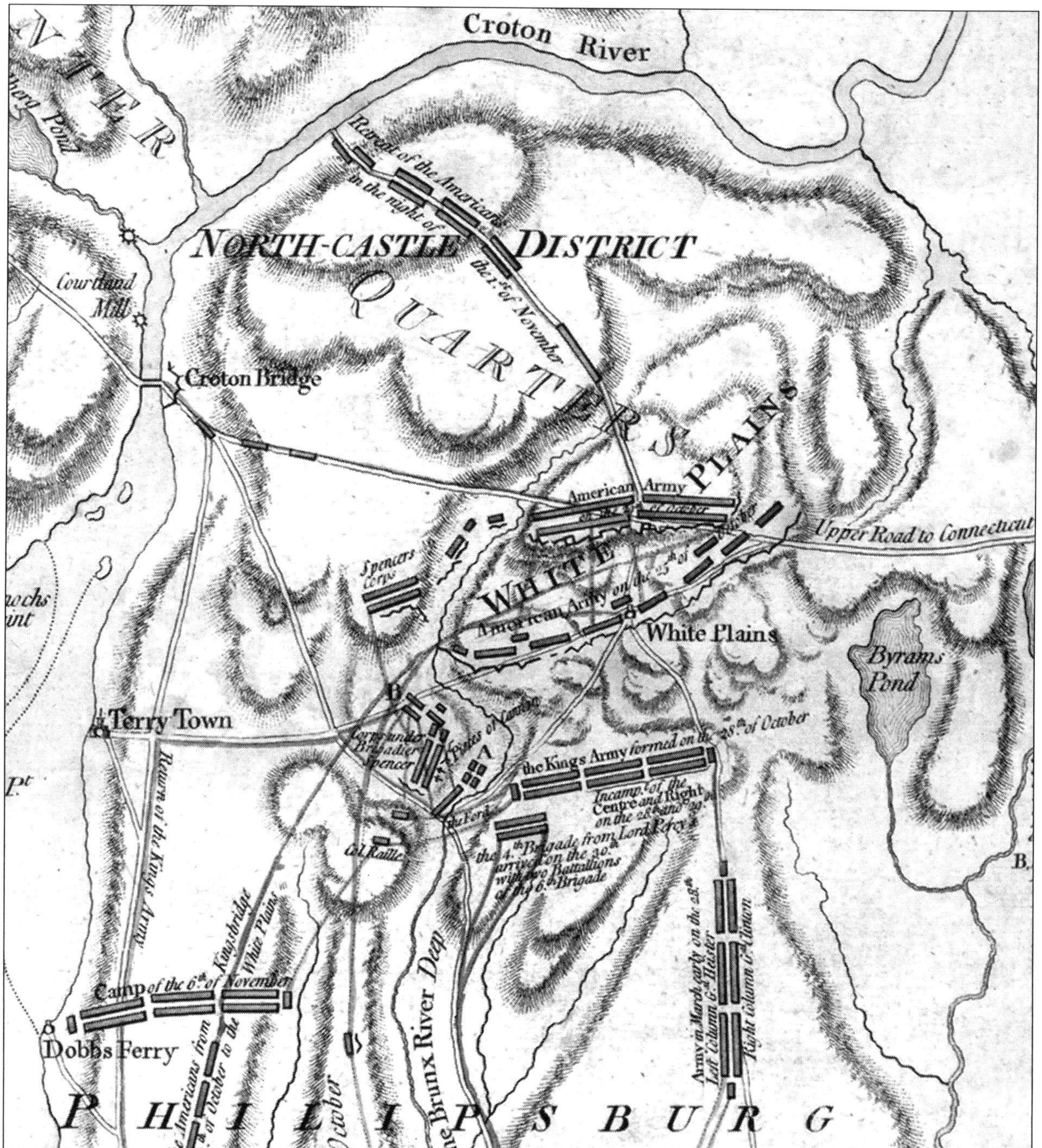

Fig 20.5. Detail of White Plains from Faden, William, "A plan of the operations of the King's army: under the command of General Sr. William Howe, K.B. in New York and East New Jersey, against the American forces commanded by General Washington, from the 12th of October, to the 28th," Feb. 25, 1777. The Lionel Pincus and Princess Firyal Map Division, The New York Public Library, Astor, Lenox and Tilden Foundations.

Tuttle remembers the enemy "came upon us from eastward." The initial volley from the Connecticut troops "broke and scattered them at once."[67] One participant vividly recalled that Douglas's regiment fired a volley at the Hessian grenadiers from a distance of "20 rods" (about 110 yards). The shots "scattered them like leaves in a whirlwind; and they ran so far off that some of the regiment ran out to the ground" and collected weapons, ammunition, and rum from the fallen Germans. The Americans had enough time to drink a round of captured rum before the enemy "came on again."[68]

Martin states that his regiment remained behind the protective stone wall for some time exchanging fire with a party of Hessian troops who used the slope of an apple orchard to shield themselves. Located just fifty yards away, the enemy advanced just far enough above the rise to get a round off and then fell back below the ridge to reload. The Americans did their best to fire "as soon as they showed themselves above level ground, or when" the Hessians "fired, to aim at the flashes of their guns." The regiment engaged in this manner "for some time" and lost relatively few men.[69]

Unfortunately, while the Connecticut men held these troops at bay, the Americans noted that other enemy soldiers "would run from our front and get round our wings to flank us."[70] Martin laments that:

> When finding ourselves flanked and in danger of being surrounded, we were compelled to make a hasty retreat from the stone wall. . . . when forced to retreat we lost in killed and wounded, a considerable number. . . . We fell back a little distance and made a stand, detached parties engaged in almost every direction.[71]

Spencer's men continued to fight a furious action. Major Benjamin Tallmadge reports: "As stone walls were frequent, our troops occasionally formed behind them and poured a destructive fire into the Hessian ranks. It, however, became necessary to retreat wholly before such an overwhelming force."[72]

Tuttle remembers that when "repulsed . . . a part of our men" were "driven through to the river, and among the rest the chaplain of our regiment, Dr. Trumbel, lost his wig in the river and never afterward wore one."[73] The memoir of Benjamin Tallmadge corroborates the story of the Chaplain's fall into the Bronx River. Major Tallmadge states:

> When I reached the bank of the river, and was about to enter it, our Chaplain, the Rev. Dr. Trumbull, sprang up behind me on my horse, and came with such force (as) to carry me with my accoutrements, together with himself, headlong into the river.[74]

The two men barely avoided capture by the advancing Hessians. Following the retreat, Tuttle saw no further action that day. He "got back to camp a little after noon."[75]

Now in his third and final battle, Tuttle had enough confidence in his knowledge of military affairs to offer his own analysis of the tactics employed that morning. He surmised:

> [T]he Americans would have been more successful here if the reserve came on to the assistance of that part of the Army engaged. But, they hung back until there was such confusion that the men could not be reformed.[76]

Tuttle raises a valid point in his critique. However, it must be stressed that the Connecticut troops displayed tremendous courage and fulfilled their mission. Spencer's men held the wall as long as they could and then continued to inflict casualties as they withdrew.[77] This delayed the British onslaught long enough for Washington to prepare a defense of Chatterton's Hill.

In the end, Chatterton's Hill fell to the British. However, to dislodge the reinforced patriots from this position, the King's troops needed to carry on a prolonged artillery bombardment and launch a massive assault by infantry and eventually cavalry units. In total, Spencer's delaying action and the struggle on Chatterton's Hill cost the British well over 200 troops and the Americans nearly 175.[78] Five or more of Douglas's regiment fell in the battle.[79] Martin remembered the death of one of these soldiers. Just before the battle, Martin relates that:

> [O]ne man who belonged to our company said 'Now I am going out to the field to be killed,' and said more than once afterwards that he should be killed, and he was. He was shot dead on the field. I never saw a man so prepossessed with the idea of any mishap as he.[80]

Despite such bloodshed at the Battle of White Plains and having gained strategic ground, Howe failed to press his advantage. Another opportunity to finish off the Rebels passed as Howe bombarded the endangered American lines but held his troops back from another offensive.[81] Martin states that the artillery on Chatterton's Hill lay "not more than half or three fourths of a mile" from Douglas's regiment. "As might be expected," the cannons "entertained" the men "with their music all the evening." However, the anticipated attack by the British infantry never came. Martin feels that:

> The British were very civil, and indeed they were after they had received a check from Brother Jonathon for any of their rude actions. They seldom repeated them, at least not till the affair that caused the reprimand had ceased in some measure to be remembered.[82]

This insight best explains why Howe moved so cautiously throughout the New York campaign. Perhaps Howe had still not forgotten a day he had spent in Massachusetts the previous year. As a field commander at the Battle of Bunker Hill, he had watched in horror as entrenched American troops gunned down 1,126 British soldiers in just ninety minutes.[83] Since that time, he attempted to avoid direct assaults upon the enemy when it occupied any type of earthen work.

Washington's army thus stood somewhat unmolested after retiring to a new defensive position north of White Plains where it could block any enemy movement up the Hudson River Valley. Martin found the ground there to be "springy" and after three days of severe wind and rain "the water . . . was nearly over shoes, which caused many of us to take violent colds by being exposed upon the wet ground after a profuse perspiration."[84]

Following the damp conditions near White Plains, Tuttle counted himself among those to fall ill. His final march took place on October 31, when Washington withdrew to North Castle, New York. Here, Tuttle

> was taken sick and was in the hospital. My father came after me and got written permission to take me home. I cannot say whether I had verbal or written discharge as my father managed all of the business. It was about the last of November.[85]

His father's intervention may have saved the life of Moses Tuttle. The "hospital" to which he refers was a breeding ground of disease. Men afflicted with dysentery, tuberculosis, pleurisy, and smallpox crowded head to toe in such institutions. The cries of men recovering from bullet extractions and amputations added to the misery. The best cure for one's illness in such a situation consisted of getting as far away from the hospital as possible.[86]

Tuttle returned to Connecticut and recovered. In his pension application, he remembered: "The other men" of his company "got home a month later, said they were discharged Christmas day." Not all of the regiment returned. At least twenty-two had died, five remained missing, and Major Porter languished in captivity. Captain Bunnel's Company marked the names of four dead on its muster roll.[87]

In the months that followed the homecoming of Douglas's regiment, Connecticut conducted another recruiting drive. The state wished to fulfill the request of the Congress for eight Connecticut battalions to become a part of Washington's Continental Line. It abandoned the practice of short-term enlistments. Instead, men had to sign on for either three years or the duration of the war.[88] Having barely survived his previous five months of service and perhaps still recovering from illness, Tuttle understandably passed on the offer.

We cannot make definite conclusions as to what Moses Tuttle felt about the part he played in the American Revolution. His pension application is silent on that matter. Whatever thoughts he shared with his wife Thankful, whom he married in 1778, or their seven children have been lost.[89] However, the record of his service suggests that he must have felt considerable pride. He had volunteered twice, faced death on the battlefield three times, and almost lost his life to sickness. Yes, his unit had run at the first sound of cannon at the Battle of Kips Bay. However, they redeemed themselves at Harlem Heights and White Plains where they fought the British regulars and their German mercenaries with valor and competence. Furthermore, despite the cold, hunger, poverty, and maladies the regiment endured, their muster roll chronicles only one official desertion. While maligned by many, the militia and levies had performed a valuable role in the New York campaign. The revolution lived only so long as Washington's army remained in the field, and that army endured only because thousands of temporary soldiers like Tuttle agreed to fill out its ranks. As he told his story in court to obtain his deserved pension, Moses Tuttle must have looked back upon this record and felt a high degree of satisfaction for having served as a soldier of 1776 in New York.

This article originally appeared in *The Hudson River Valley Review*, Volume 28.1, autumn, 2011.

NOTES

1. George Washington to John Hancock, President of Congress, September 24, 1776, *The Writings of George Washington*, ed. John C. Fitzpatrick, vol. 6, (Washington, D.C.: U.S. Government Printing Office, 1931–1944), 110.
2. Initially, enlisted men had received pensions only if they were disabled in the war. In 1818, Congress extended eligibility to those veterans of the Continental forces who demonstrated a financial need. Congress dropped the financial need requirement in 1828; in 1832 it allowed nondisabled veterans of state line and militia units (such as Tuttle) to apply for a pension for the first time. The 1832 law—"An act in addition to an act to provide for certain persons, engaged in the land and naval service of the United States in the revolutionary war, approved March 18, 1818"—allowed veterans with at least two years of service to receive the full monthly wage they had earned during the war for the rest of their lives. Those with between six months and two years of service received a portion of their former wage. For a discussion of pension records and other Revolutionary War narratives see Alfred F. Young, "George Robert Twelves Hewes (1742–1840): A Boston Shoemaker and the Memory of the American Revolution," in *The New England Working Class and the New Labor History*, eds, Herbert G. Gutman and Donald H. Bell, (Chicago: University of Illinois Press, 1987).
3. Revolutionary War Pension File of Moses Tuttle, National Archives, Washington, D.C.; Moses Tuttle is listed on the "Roll of a Regiment of New Levies from Connecticut Commanded by William Douglas," 1776, Record Group 93, War Department Collection of Revolutionary War Records, M246–27. He also appears on a "Travel Roll" of the 7th Company in the same collection of records.
4. George F. Scheer, Editor's Introduction to Joseph Plumb Martin's *Private Yankee Doodle: Being a Narrative of some of the Adventures, Dangers and Sufferings of a Revolutionary Soldier*, (New York: Little Brown and Co., 1963), 5–6.

5. Date of birth from Pension file of Moses Tuttle; other family records from George Tuttle, *The Descendants of William Tuttle*, (Rutland VT: Tuttle and Co., 1883). Moses was from the village of Cheshire, which was a part of Wallingford at the time.
6. Connecticut Colony, *The Public Records of Connecticut from April, 1636 to October, 1776,* (Hartford: Brown and Parsons, 1850–1890), vol. 12, 248–49; vol. 14, 3–4; Don Higginbotham, "The Strengths and Weaknesses of the Militia," reprinted in *Major Problems in the Era of the American Revolution*, Richard Brown, Editor, (D.C. Heath, Co., 1992), 239–50; James B. Whisker, *The Colonial Militia: The New England Militia 1606–1785*, (Edwin Mellen Press, 1997).
7. Connecticut Colony, *The Public Records of Connecticut*, Vol. 15, 225; Barnet Schecter, *The Battle For New York*, (Walker Publishing, 2002), 67–69, 78, 80.
8. Bradley eventually became a U.S. Senator from Vermont. See "Descendants of Danyell Broadley de West Morton," www.bradleyfoundation.org. Connecticut raised unusually large companies of 100 enlisted men and four officers (a captain, two lieutenants, and one ensign) at the war's outset. They soon reduced this to sixty-five enlisted men per company and four officers. Keith C. Wilbur, *The Revolutionary Soldier,* (Globe Pequot Press, 1969), 64; Brendan Morrissey, *Boston: 1775*, (U.K., 1993), 27, 32, 44; Harold Peterson, *The Book of the Continental Soldier* (Stackpole Co., 1968), 253–54.
9. Tuttle Pension File. Forty shillings = two pounds which came to $6.67 according to Martin, 237.
10. Higginbotham, "Strengths and Weaknesses of the Militia," 241.
11. Jackson Turner Main, *Connecticut Society in the Era of the American Revolution*, (The American Revolution Bicentennial Commission of Connecticut, 1977), 18; Higginbotham, "Strengths and Weakness of the Militia," 241.
12. Martin, *A Narrative,* 33. Some Connecticut soldiers had an official brown or red uniform coat in the opening stages of the war. However, many militiamen wore their civilian clothes. By the summer of 1776, a simple homespun or linen "hunting shirt" became a common "uniform" that a soldier might dye a particular color to match those of his regiment. Wilbur, *The Revolutionary Soldier,* 8, 10; Schecter, *Battle for New York,* 143–45; Harold L. Peterson, *The Continental Soldier* (Stackpole Co., 1968), 23–35, 74.
13. Tuttle, Pension Application.
14. Correspondences between General Lee and the New York Committee of Safety, Papers of Charles Lee, New York Historical Society, 1871.
15. George F. Scheer and Hugh R. Rankin, *Rebels and Redcoats*, (World Publishing, 1957), 195.
16. Tuttle, Pension Application.
17. Scheter, *Battle for New York,* 80.
18. Tuttle, Pension Application.
19. Connecticut Colony, *The Public Records of Connecticut,* vol. 15, 417.
20. Moses remembered joining in May. The Muster roll of Captain Bunnel's Company pinpoints his date of enlistment as June 24 (Roll 246–27). We can forgive Moses for perhaps being mistaken on this small detail since over fifty years had elapsed. The terms "battalion" and "regiment" were used interchangeably during the Revolution. Technically, a battalion at that time referred to a regiment that had eight instead of the standard ten companies, either because two companies had been detached as the British often did, or because the unit was raised with only eight companies as was the case with Douglas's regiment. Peterson, *The Book of the Continental Soldier,* 253–54.
21. Schecter, *Battle for New York,* 98–99.
22. Martin, *A Narrative,* 40.
23. Ibid., 51.
24. Ibid., 53.
25. Ibid., 53, 24.
26. Connecticut Colony, *Public Records of Connecticut,* vol. 15, 417; Muster Rolls from

Colonel Douglas's Regiment of Levies, M246–27.

27. Connecticut Colony, *Public Records of Connecticut,* Vol. 15, 418; Pay Roll Record of Captain Prentices Company. Pay Roll record of Captain Peck's company, Travel Log of Captain Bunnel's Company, M246–27. A cartouche box held the soldier's ammunition.
28. Martin tells us that the two pound monthly salary came to $6.67, so one pound equals $3.34.
29. Robert A. Gross, *The Minutemen and Their World,* (New York: Hill and Wang, 1976), 60. Gross reports that a common laborer earned 2 shillings per day. Assuming a six-day work week, he would earn 312 shillings in six months, slightly more than fifteen pounds. Main, *Connecticut Society in the Era of the American Revolution,* 35–36. Main establishes that skilled wage earners brought in four or five shillings per day.
30. Payroll Records of Captain Peck's and Captain Prentice's Companies, M246–27.
31. Martin, *A Narrative,* 237–38. Inflation rate discussed in Parker, Wyman W., *Connecticut's Colonial and Continental Money,* (The American Revolution Bicentennial Commission of Connecticut, 1976), 41.
32. Muster Roll of Captain Bunnel's Company, M246–27.
33. Tuttle, Pension Application.
34. *Public Records of Connecticut,* Vol. 15, 436.
35. Schecter, *Battle for New York,* 92–93.
36. Thomas Flexner, *Washington: The Indispensable Man* (New York: Little Brown and Company, 1969), pgs. 77–79; Schecter, *Battle for New York,* 121.
37. Martin, *Narrative,* 34. Martin belonged to Captain Samuel Peck's 3rd Company of the 5th Connecticut Battalion.
38. Robert Middlekauff, *The Glorious Cause* (New York: Oxford Press, 1982), 298–301.
39. Fischer, David Hackett, *Washington's Crossing* (New York: Oxford University Press, 2004), 86.
40. Martin, *Narrative,* 34.
41. Schecter, *Battle for New York,* 90. Martin, *Narrative,* 36, identifies Stone Street as his quarters. We can assume the regiment was stationed together in the same vicinity.
42. Fischer, *Washington's Crossing,* 86.
43. Middlekauff, *Glorious Cause,* 328, Fischer, *Washington's Crossing,* 29.
44. Fischer, *Washington's Crossing,* 87.
45. Ibid. 83–89; 88–89.
46. Douglas quoted in Fleming, Thomas, *Liberty,* (New York: Viking, 1997) 187.
47. Tuttle, Pension Application.
48. Martin, *Narrative,* 39–42; Flexner, *Indispensable Man,* 80–82, Fleming, *Liberty,* 186–94.
49. Tuttle, Pension Application. The record supports Tuttle's claim of a driving rain. See McDowell, Bart, *The Revolutionary War,* (National Geographic, 1976), 93.
50. Higginbotham, Don, *The War of American Independence,* (Northeastern University Press, 1983), 159.
51. Tuttle, Pension Application.
52. Flexner, *Indispensable Man,* 80.
53. Martin, 45. This cove has been filled in.
54. Tuttle, Pension Application. The order to withdraw was nothing more than a rumor.
55. Higginbotham, *War of Independence,* 160; Flexner *Indispensable Man,* 83–84; Middlekauf, *Glorious Cause,* 348.
56. Tuttle Pension Application.
57. Johnston, Henry P., *The Battle of Harlem Heights,* (New York: 1897), 56–91; Martin, *Narrative,* 53; Flexner, *Indispensable Man,* 84; Middlekauff, *Glorious Cause,*. 349.
58. Muster Rolls of Colonel William Douglas's Regiment. Undated, but apparently from December 1776. M246–27. In the Revolution, being marked as "wounded" on a return of strength record indicated that a man was very severely injured. Thus, Martin's claim that a number were wounded probably indicates that they were only slightly wounded by eighteenth-century standards.
59. Johnston, *Harlem Heights,* 193.
60. Martin, *Narrative,* 56.
61. "Strength Returns from Colonel Douglas's

Regiment of Foot," September 13–October 20, M246–27.

62. Martin, *Narrative,* 54–55; Colonel Reed, Washington's adjutant, told a very different story in court. He twice found Leffingwell running and hiding from action and struck him in the hand and face with his sword. He afterwards found him cowering in a ditch and claimed that Leffingwell confessed to his desertion. See Schecter, *Battle for New York*, 216.
63. Martin, *Narrative,* 60, Higginbotham, *War for Independence,* 161. Middlekauf, *Glorious Cause,* 351.
64. "Weekly Return of Strength," October 26, 1776, M246–27.
65. Schecter, *Battle for New York*, 235–37.
66. Middlekauf, pgs. 351–52; Potts, Louis, *American National Biography*, Edited by Garraty and Carnes, (Oxford, 1999) 451–52; Snow, Richard, "Stand-off at White Plains," *American Heritage*, (April, 1973), 41.
67. Tuttle, Pension Application.
68. "An unknown American participant in the battle" quoted in "They Were There," *American Heritage Magazine*, (April, 1973), 44.
69. Martin, *Narrative,* 61.
70. "An unknown American participant in the battle," *American Heritage*, 44.
71. Martin, *Narrative,* 60–61.
72. Tallmadge, Benjamin, quoted in Scheer and Rankin, *Rebels and Redcoats*, 195.
73. Tuttle, Pension Application.
74. Tallmadge, Benjamin, *Memoir of Colonel Benjamin Tallmadge* (New York Times and Arno Press, 1968, originally published 1858), 14.
75. Tuttle, Pension Application.
76. Ibid.
77. Snow, "Stand-off at White Plains," 41.
78. Ibid.
79. Pinpointing casualty figures in the American Revolution can be a daunting task, with incomplete and conflicting evidence. In this instance, the weekly "Return of Strength" for November 1 places the number of wounded over the previous seven days at one and the dead at four. However, the Muster Roll of Douglas's Regiment notes October 28 as the date that four of the men listed were wounded and the death of one man. The roll has no one dying between October 29 and November 1.
80. Martin, *Narrative,* 61.
81. Schecter, *Battle for New York*, 240.
82. Martin, *Narrative,* 61.
83. Casualty figure from Morrissey, *Boston,* 66.
84. Martin, *Narrative,* 62.
85. Tuttle, Pension Application. The Regiment's Muster Roll identifies the date of his discharge as November 24, 1776. Over the course of six months, eighteen of Captain Bunnel's company were similarly discharged. Fifteen of them left between October and December.
86. Wilbur, *The Revolutionary Soldier*, 74–75.
87. Muster Roll, M256–27. These figures must be considered absolute minimums as the Muster Roll seems to understate the actual losses. The only existing "Returns of Strength" records from the regiment number seventeen as having died between September 13 and November 1. The Muster Roll finds only fifteen dead between such dates.
88. Martin, *Narrative,* 67.
89. Tuttle Pension Application; Prospect, Connecticut, Vital Records.

21

Valcour Island

Setting the Conditions for Victory at Saratoga

GREGORY M. TOMLIN

THE HUDSON RIVER VALLEY'S rich Revolutionary War history evokes images of fortress West Point, the sensational trial and hanging of British Major John André in Tappan, and General George Washington's emotional address to his officers at New Windsor. Just thirty miles north of the valley, another important event occurred: the American victory at Saratoga in 1777. When asked to provide a specific event or date in the American Revolution where the specter of victory shifted from the British to the colonists, many scholars cite the Battle of Saratoga. Colonial military historian Richard Ketchum credits British General John Burgoyne's surrender on October 17, 1777, as essential for convincing the French government to ally with the Americans. In Ketchum's view, without Saratoga "there is no telling what might have happened," since the absence of the alliance may have led the Americans to sue for peace due to the sustained economic strain of two years of conflict and the deterioration of their fighting forces.[1] For the Hudson River Valley, this decisive battle also denied the British control of the river that they had hoped to secure in order to split rabblerousing New England from the crops and manpower of the Middle and Southern colonies.

While the importance of Saratoga is not disputed, some historians contend that Burgoyne's surrender is directly traceable to the Battle of Valcour Island, which delayed an earlier British attack in the fall of 1776, thereby providing the Americans with an additional year to prepare their defenses for the British northern invasion of New York.[2] This unique naval battle fought on Lake Champlain, seventy miles north of Saratoga Springs, should be considered the opening phase of the Saratoga campaign, making it a relatively obscure engagement that deserves greater attention by students of the American struggle for independence.

Studies of naval operations during the Revolution commonly focus on European sea battles in the West Indies, Captain John Paul Jones' exploits in British waters, Admiral François Joseph Paul de Grasse's success in the 1781 Battle of the Chesapeake, or the transatlantic logistics responsible for sustaining the Continental Army. Rarely do the riverine or lake operations of "green-water" navies significantly influence the outcome of a campaign, let alone a war; however, the Battle of Valcour Island proves to be an exceptional case due to the centrality of the Richelieu and Hudson Rivers to both British and American strategies during the Revolution. Among the most notable scholars to draw attention to this engagement is naval historian Alfred Thayer Mahan who more than a century ago opined, "The little American navy on Champlain was wiped out; but never had any force, big or small, lived to better purpose or died more gloriously."[3]

To appreciate the magnitude of the battle it is first necessary to understand the military value of the lake. Situated in upstate New York,

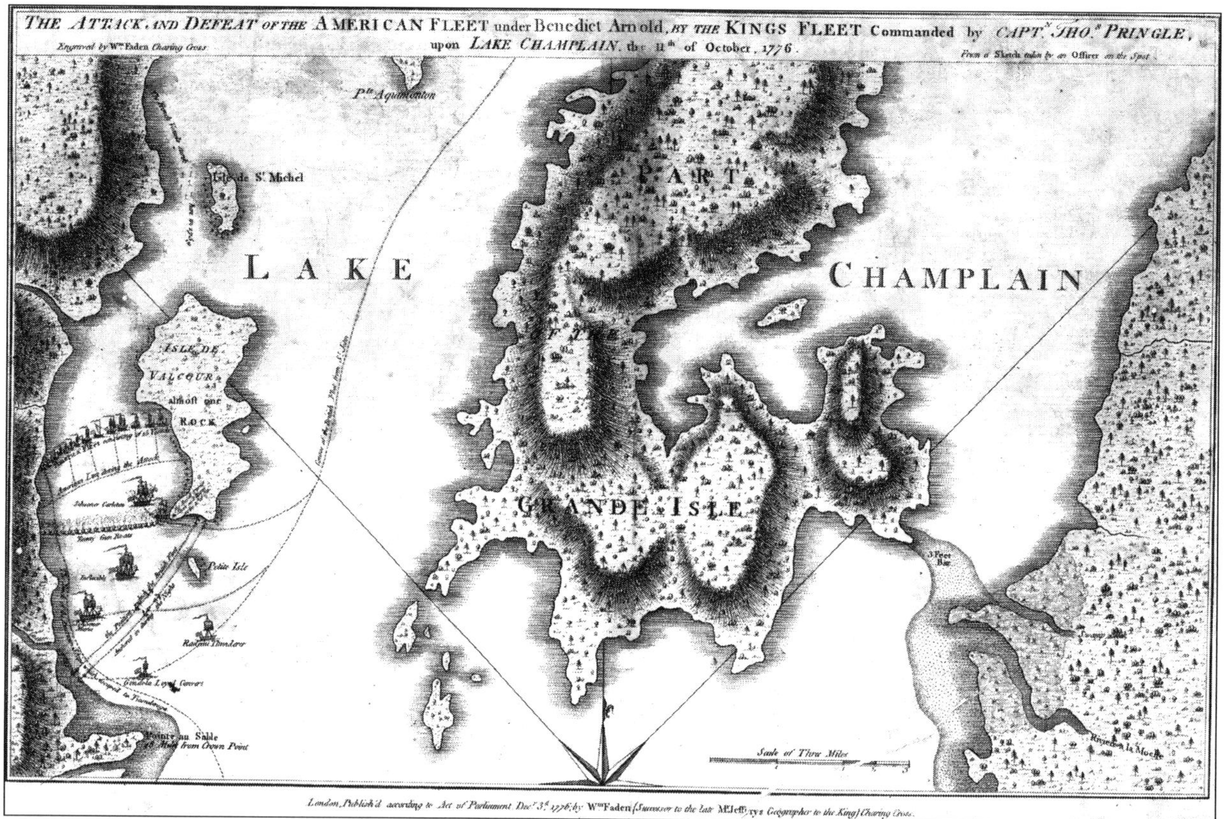

Fig. 21.1. The Attack and defeat of the American fleet under Benedict Arnold by the King's fleet Commanded by Sir Guy Carleton upon Lake Champlain in "11th" of "Octr." 1776. From a sketch taken by an officer on the spot. Engraved by Wm. Faden, Charing Cross. Scale ca. 1:70,000. Library of Congress Geography and Map Division Washington, D.C.

Lake Champlain is accessible from Quebec by sailing up the St. Lawrence River to the Richelieu River, which opens into the northern tip of the lake. Due to rapids and falls along the Richelieu, however, large vessels could not sail the entire route.[4] The southern basin of the 110-mile-long lake is situated sixty miles from the Hudson River, which traverses through most of New York prior to draining into the Atlantic Ocean at New York Bay.[5] In the early years of the Revolution, these inland waterways served as key terrain for the British, who sought to isolate the rebellious New England colonies through a two-part strategy: occupy the major ports in Boston, Newport, and New York in order to block coastal resupply, and simultaneously secure the Hudson and Richelieu rivers to prevent access to the Middle and Southern colonies. Military historian Russell Weigley observes that the British fascination with the rivers stemmed from the absence of geographic objectives that, if seized, would contribute to the destruction of the Continental Army and colonial militias.[6] For example, even if the British captured the colonial capital of Philadelphia, the Continental Congress would relocate or possibly scatter prior to admitting defeat.

In the late summer and early fall of 1776, the British army executed a two-pronged assault in New York designed to secure the Hudson River. While British General William Howe fought Washington's Continental Army at Long Island, Harlem Heights, and White Plains, General Guy Carleton simultaneously led a British column from Quebec toward Fort Ticonderoga, an impressive Vauban-style citadel constructed by the French (Fort Carillon) at the southern end of Lake Champlain during the Seven Years' War (1754–1763), which the French subsequently lost at the end of the conflict. If all went according to plan, Carleton's troops would defeat the American garrison at Ticonderoga and continue marching to Albany where he expected to meet Howe and his forces, who would have marched north along the Hudson from New York City. Combined, their regiments would complete the envelopment of New England.[7]

American generals recognized the threat that British control of the Hudson would pose, and they sought to limit the advance of the enemy's approach from either Quebec or Manhattan by fortifying Ticonderoga as well as West Point, a natural defensive position fifty miles north of New York City on the Hudson.[8] Washington ordered contingents of his army to augment the militias in manning the ramparts of Ticonderoga and West Point. The Continental commander in chief assumed tremendous risk by further reducing the size of his field army to strengthen these forts; of the original 20,000 men under his command at the beginning of Howe's invasion of New York, fewer than 3,000 remained by the time the army escaped across the Delaware River into Pennsylvania in December 1776.[9] Earlier that summer, however, Congress appointed Major General Horatio Gates, Washington's former adjutant, to head the Canadian command, and he departed Albany on July 5 to assess his troops firsthand. He arrived first at Crown Point, a fort ten miles north of Ticonderoga on Lake Champlain. Much to his disappointment, he discovered a devastated American garrison. Describing the scene to John Hancock in a letter, Gates suggested that his new forces "had more the Appearance of a General Hospital, than an Army form'd to Oppose the Invasion of a Successful & enterprizing [*sic*] Enemy."[10] A committee dispatched to the citadel by the Continental Congress painted a similar image in their report to their colleagues in Philadelphia: here was an army "in a distressed condition," wanting of the most basic necessities and likely to turn their guns on locals to seize enough flour to prevent starvation.[11]

Despite their appearance, the ragged men at Crown Point had demonstrated a tenacious fighting spirit during the ill-fated expedition to Quebec in the winter of 1775 to 1776. Commanded by Brigadier General Richard Montgomery, 1,200 American soldiers converged on the city from Maine and Montreal to lay a five-month siege in the hopes of capturing it and enticing the French Canadian populace to join the American cause. Despite shortages of able fighting men and supplies, the British garrison under Carleton held out until the St. Lawrence River thawed, allowing for the arrival of both British and Hessian reinforcements in May 1776. On New Year's Eve, 1775, Montgomery perished after being shot in the head by a musket ball while leading the siege.[12] In addition to the loss of the commanding general, nearly two-thirds of the American force died before Colonel Benedict Arnold led the surviving 400 soldiers by foot through the wilderness in a retrograde operation to Ticonderoga.[13] After learning of the feat, one British writer lauded praise on his adversary: "Their perseverance was astonishing in their circumstances. . . . Arnold, who had hitherto displayed uncommon talents in his march into Canada, (which may be compared to the greatest things done in that kind) discovered on this occasion the utmost vigor of a determined mind, and a genius full of resources."[14] When Gates arrived later that summer, he found the survivors nursing combat wounds or, worse still, succumbing to the ravages of small-pox, typhoid, and malaria.

Gates' opponent, Carleton, commanded a force of nearly 10,000 men whom he forward deployed to St. Jean, a town on the Richelieu fifty miles north of Lake Champlain. Despite being freshly knighted for his stalwart leadership as governor-general during the besiegement of Montreal, Carleton proved to be a cautious field commander, and his pause at St. Jean would be the first of several examples used by his critics to suggest that he was a better general of the defense than the offense.[15] With roads nonexistent, his army needed to travel by water to the south end of Lake Champlain before crossing briefly over land to access the Hudson. However, Carleton worried that the fortifications at Crown Point and Ticonderoga would impede his movement, and he doubted that his British and Hessian troops could successfully assault either site by land. His concern especially peaked when his spies grossly overestimated the number of Americans garrisoned within the forts, placing the total at 20,000 Continentals.[16] Had his intelligence been more accurate, perhaps Carleton would have gained the confidence necessary to risk the hardships of an overland attack in lieu of waiting to sail the length of the lake.

Two successive major delays impeded Carleton's expedition into New York during the summer and early fall of 1776, the first being the absence of sufficient water transports on the lake. Although workers began laboring dexterously under the supervision of Royal Navy Lieutenant John Shank in July at the hastily refitted dock of St. Jean, construction of the required 200 landing craft to accommodate the regiments and several warships to carry artillery and protect the infantry required three months. Known as bateaux, the flat-bottom vessels used as transports were little more than extended rowboats, being thirty-six to forty feet in length and six to seven feet in width.[17] In addition to the small amphibious assault craft, Carleton ordered several prefabricated small war ships from England that Shank put together at St. Jean. To his credit, the general had ordered the ships in 1775, when he first envisioned the need for a fleet on Lake Champlain to ensure British dominance in the region.[18]

Carleton originally asked Vice Admiral Samuel Graves, who resided in Boston at the time, for the components to build two sloops of war and 400 bateaux as well as for enough knowledgeable men to construct and operate the vessels. However, when the admiral could not accommodate the governor of Quebec, he forwarded the request to the Admiralty. Although policymakers in London reduced the quantity Carleton appealed for, they did provide materiel with the relief fleet that arrived at Montreal's port in May 1776 and followed with additional provisions in June.[19] Since Canada is rich in timber, the navy did not need to weigh down its ships with such bulky and heavy material but, instead, only those components made exclusively in England. Several warships were also dismantled and carried over a newly made road to St. Jean, where they were put back together in a "remarkable feat of engineering." Captain Charles Douglas, commander of the St. Lawrence fleet, argued that these ships would be essential to securing a decisive victory by overwhelming the inferior American ships.[20]

The firepower of the British lake fleet proved considerable. Shank built twenty gunboats capable of holding a twenty-gun mix of 24- and 9-pounders, and two gondolas with seven 9-pounders each. Two American schooners, captured by the British in June 1776, arrived overland to be reassembled, fitted with a dozen 6-pounder guns apiece, and christened the *Carleton* and the *Maria*, the latter in honor of the governor's wife.[21] Workers also carried components of the 180-ton frigate *Inflexible* to St. Jean, a ship so heavy that, upon completion, it could not carry the additional twenty-seven tons of its eighteen 12-pounder guns until it sailed down the Richelieu and into the lake. Perhaps work crews could have more expediently built two or three smaller vessels in the time required to transport this single massive ship, but Carleton insisted on this addition to the fleet and refused to deploy his vessels onto the lake until his builders completed the *Inflexible* because he remained concerned about the wildly exaggerated strength of the opposing fleet.[22] Shank's men constructed one final vessel, the radeau *Thunderer*, completely from scratch at St. Jean, and this nearly flat-bottom platform carried the fleet's heaviest armaments: six 24-pounders, six 12-pounders, and two howitzers.[23]

Although impressive in their ingenuity, the time required to construct the fleet kept the British at St. Jean until late September, all the while giving the Americans an opportunity to improve their own defenses on Champlain. The second British delay, one entirely out of their hands to control, began just as Carleton's fleet attempted to sail down the Richelieu. For twenty consecutive days, winds from the south denied them access to the lake, and sailors could not defy their leeward challenge by zigzagging downstream due to the narrowness of the river.[24] On October 9, 1776, the fleet finally reached the northern rim of Champlain, and a reconnaissance vessel spotted an American fleet awaiting the invaders twenty-five miles further south on the west side of Valcour Island. From July through September, while Carleton prepared his forces and then waited for the winds to mercifully change, Gates established a dual mission for his own troops: fortify the most suitable land-based positions on the south end of Lake Champlain, and build a fleet to oppose the imminent British invasion force.[25] The American commander handed responsibility for defending the lake over to his deputy, recently promoted Brigadier General Benedict Arnold.

While popular history concentrates on Arnold's infamous treason, the officer's contributions to the American war effort have increasingly gained recognition in contemporary historiographies. After he fled West Point on September 24, 1780, upon learning that the Continental Army had discovered his arrangement with the British to change sides, the United States government deliberately scourged Arnold's name from the annals and monuments of Revolutionary War history.[26] However, James Martin, a historian who wrote *Benedict Arnold, Revolutionary Hero: An American Warrior Reconsidered*, credits his personal interest in the general to an elementary teacher's villainous portrayal of the man: "Not since Judas, I recall one of them saying, had a human being left so wicked a mark on the pages of history."[27] Martin, as well as authors Thomas Desjardin and James Nelson, argue in their recent monographs that Arnold's meritorious service quite possibly made him the best general of either side (and certainly the best general to serve on both sides!) during the Revolution, and they question the methodology of other historians who examine his performance strictly through the prism of treason.[28] For his distinguished service in the Quebec campaign, Desjardin calls Arnold "America's Hannibal."[29] Indeed, few generals of any era led troops through as many forced marches, or sustained as many wounds without retiring from the field, or, as will be detailed momentarily, commanded desperate engagements from the frontline of a battlefield and the helm of a sailing ship.

Gates asked Arnold at the end of July 1776 if he would be willing to serve as commodore of the fledgling American fleet on Lake Champlain. Arnold had already told Washington a month earlier that the only way to secure the lake would be the construction of a fleet of at least twenty to thirty "Gundaleos Row Gallies & floating Batteries," so he readily accepted Gates' offer.[30] Arnold also recommended that the Continentals expand their defenses by constructing a fortification on Isle-aux-Noix, a small island in the Richelieu about ten miles north of the river's mouth on Lake Champlain; however, Gates denied the request to stretch his meager forces even further.[31] Martin observes that, with such a high probability for failure, Arnold embraced a mission at which most Continental officers would have balked.[32]

Recognizing the importance of ships, either to defend the lake or withdraw troops further south, Gates hoped that Arnold would improve the quality of the craftsmanship and the efficiency of the production of vessels coming from the meager American dockyard at Skenesborough, located twenty miles south of Ticonderoga on the South River. Construction began in the spring, prior to either Gates' or Arnold's arrival, when Major General Philip Schuyler feared that he would need to evacuate the remnants of the American forces from the failed Quebec expedition. However, this initial progress under the supervision of Dutchman Jacobus Wynkoop proved unimpressive.[33] Gates' inspection of the first two gondolas to sail north to Ticonderoga clearly prompted his decision to replace Wynkoop with Arnold. After examining the first two vessels on July 15, he lamented that the sixty carpenters at Skenesborough "must be very ill-attended to, or very ignorant of their business, not to do more work."[34] Arnold enthusiastically assumed his new duties, and he increased the number of craftsmen at the American dock from sixty to 200. In a glowing letter to Washington, Gates expressed his optimism with the performance of his new commodore: "he has perfect knowledge in Maritime Affairs, and is besides a most deserving, and Gallant Officer."[35] Responding to Gates on August 14, Washington opined that he trusted "neither Courage nor Activity will be wanting in those to whom the business is committed—If assigned to Genl Arnold, None one [*sic*] will doubt of his Exertions."[36] Arnold derived much of his earlier reputation from rallying men to defy insurmountable odds, and the situation for the Americans on Champlain seemed no less daunting. Arnold's scouts reported the British activities at St. Jean, and he knew that he faced an enemy growing in size and lethality.

Production output increased dramatically under Arnold's supervision between early August and October 11, leading to the completion of eight gondolas, three row-galleys with triangular sail, three schooners, the cutter *Lee*, and the sloop *Enterprise*.[37] The gondolas comprised the backbone of the fleet, each forty to fifty feet in length with a forty-five sailor crew to man the 12-pounder howitzer mounted on the bow, two to four 9-pounder cannons on the sides, and eight swivel guns mounted on deck.[38] Arnold created a scheme of operations that distributed the labor of ship construction throughout the area: craftsmen at Skenesborough built hulls; army engineers at Ticonderoga made gun carriages; soldiers at Crown Point shaved oars, and scouts located new sources of timber in the nearby woodlands. Completed hulls floated along the South River to their next stop on Arnold's assembly line, Ticonderoga, for rigging and arming. Gates' chief engineer and artillerist, Colonel Jeduthan Baldwin, supervised operations at Ticonderoga and described in his diary how consuming this task became: "I have my hands and mind constantly employed night and Day except when I am a Sleep [*sic*] and then sometimes I dream."[39]

Although Arnold corrected for the shortage of shipbuilders, acquiring sufficient shipbuilding material remained vexing throughout the summer. Procurement of military materiel, in fact, proved the bane of most Continental officers throughout the Revolution. A year earlier, as Arnold helped Montgomery prepare for the Quebec campaign from Ticonderoga, Arnold complained about his inability to fund his logistical requirements: "I am reduced to great extremity, not being able to pay off the people who are in great want of necessities, and much in debt."[40] In 1776, he used his prewar business connections in Connecticut to acquire sailcloth and cordage.[41] His envoys sent to Philadelphia in search of larger artillery pieces, however, proved less successful, leaving him with only six 24-pounder guns to divide between the three galleys and one 12-pounder gun for the bow of each gondola.[42] Acquiring sufficient rigging material proved to be the greatest material shortage, and even though nearly all shipbuilding ended in late August, the galleys were not fully rigged until October 11. Illness, most likely malaria, also contributed to the decline in productivity in late August, and hull construction completely ended on October 2 with the departure of the galley *Gates* from Skenesborough.[43]

Arnold could motivate the shipbuilders at Skenesborough, but he also had to train inexperienced men for sea duty. He faced three challenges: his soldiers-turned-sailors were inexperienced, the British outgunned his fleet, and the gondolas did not possess maneuverability. Not only were his crews unfamiliar with sailing, but most were from the dregs of the regiments stationed at Ticonderoga and Crown Point. When tasked by Gates to provide volunteers for the ships, officers volunteered their undesirable soldiers, the troublemakers whom commanders readily released to improve the cohesion and discipline of their own units within the tight confines of a fort.[44] Once the builders completed the vessels, Arnold could train them on sailing and maneuvering on the South River and Lake Champlain, but a severe lack of gunpowder prevented him from training them in the skill most essential to nautical warfare: naval gunfire.[45] Indeed, it is hard enough to train disciplined gunners how to shoot howitzers on land, but the practice of shooting artillery from a vessel moving on a body of water is exponentially more difficult to master. With gunpowder stores low, Arnold feared the troops at Ticonderoga would not have enough to defend themselves against the advancing 10,000 British and Hessian soldiers, and he privately believed that if a resupply did not arrive before the appearance of the enemy fleet, Gates would be forced to withdraw.[46]

The American generals more or less kept their concerns over the gunpowder shortages to themselves and continued to plan for the defense of Lake Champlain. On August 7, Gates issued his orders to Arnold: "The Preventing the Enemy's Invasion of our Country is the ultimate End of the important Command which you are now intrusted [*sic*]."[47] Two months later the commodore deployed his fleet to the half-mile wide channel between the west bank of Valcour Island and the New York shoreline. In a letter to Gates on October 10, Arnold shared his thoughts on the tactical situation. The position of the Continental's navy on the lake appeared to Arnold "an object of the utmost importance." The high cliffs and thick woodlands of the two-mile-long and mile-wide Valcour Island concealed his fleet from a southbound armada, and Arnold believed that the narrowness of the channel would prevent the British from massing their fleet against his. He also expressed his preference for the value of the galleys over the gondolas: "I am of Opinion that Row Gallies are of the best construction & cheapest for this Lake."[48]

Despite deploying scouts in August and September to survey British construction operations at St. Jean, Arnold received inaccurate intelligence that purported the British as being well behind the Americans in the race of ship construction for the anticipated engagement.[49] Indeed, American intelligence remained poor until the day of the naval battle. Neither Gates nor Arnold thought a British attack very likely due to the onset of winter, and Arnold decided that he would return the fleet to Ticonderoga if the British did not emerge by mid-October.[50] One of Gates' spies, Sergeant Stiles, returned on September 30 from a reconnaissance mission to describe the appearance of earthworks and cannon batteries on the Isle-aux-Noix north of the Richelieu's mouth on Lake Champlain. Gates interpreted these as indicators that the British were assuming a defensive posture and would not attack until the following year's campaign season. On the eve of the green-water battle, Arnold still did not realize that Carleton had deployed his fleet, much less that it was closing in on his position, because the Americans had recently lost the two canoes designated for scouting parties.[51] Fortuitously, Arnold dispatched the schooner *Revenge* north of Valcour Island early on the morning of October 11, where it quickly spotted the British fleet sailing on the eastern side of the island.

When the *Revenge* returned to the American position at eight o'clock the same morning to describe the composition of the approaching enemy, David Waterbury, a general sent by Gates to assist Arnold, encouraged the commodore to retreat south on the main lake. Arnold disagreed, preferring to follow his original plan to remain between Valcour Island and the New York shoreline, despite learning that the British fleet greatly outnumbered his own. He believed that his fleet occupied the most tactically advantageous position. By forming a concentrated front to the enemy, with flanks resting on either shore he could avoid becoming surrounded by enemy ships.[52] Positioning the gondolas and galleys in a tight defensive crescent in the channel at nine-thirty in the morning, Arnold ordered Colonel Edward Wigglesworth, his third in command, to sail south in the *Royal Savage* to draw the British ships northward toward the American gunships as they passed the eastern shore of Valcour Island.[53]

Captain Thomas Pringle of the Royal Navy commanded the British fleet from his flagship *Maria*, which also carried Carleton. Behind the schooners, the gondolas, the radeau, and the frigate trailed forty bateaux holding 1,000 soldiers, and a mosquito fleet of canoes carrying 650 Indian allies, led by Major Thomas Carleton, the commanding general's younger brother.[54] The remaining 7,000 troops stood by with their bateaux at Point au Fer, at the northern end of the lake, awaiting orders to sail to Crown Point once Pringle destroyed the Continental fleet.[55] As the British fleet closed, Arnold signaled for Wigglesworth's sailing ships to rejoin his defensive line. However, due to mishaps by the crew aboard the *Royal Savage*, the schooner missed lining up several times, became isolated south of the American fleet, ran aground, and faced the direct fire of several British vessels, including the *Invincible*. Seeking protection from the west shore of the island, most of the crew abandoned the schooner prior to the arrival of a boarding party from the British gondola *Loyal Convert*.[56]

Near one o'clock, the *Carleton* led seventeen gunboats towards the American line; all the while Arnold's vessels concentrated their fire on the British schooner. Effective fire nearly destroyed the *Carleton* before two British boats towed it out of range of the American defensive line. Pringle did not bring the *Maria* into the fight, a decision likely influenced by an American cannonball impacting against its quarterdeck and severely injuring Carleton's brother, Thomas.[57] The fearsome *Thunderer* also proved less formidable because its flat-bottom design prevented it from sailing into the wind to reach the Americans. Aboard the radeau, Lieutenant John Enys commented, "We fired some few Shot at the time we first Saw their fleet but believe it might have been just well let alone."[58] The devastating fire against the Americans originated mostly from the gunboats, which closed within 700 yards of the enemy to form their own line of battle. On the flanks, Indians and British soldiers disembarked to provide musket fire from the shoreline of New York and Valcour Island, although the Americans found this "more annoying than destructive."[59] The British continued firing broadsides into the American line until about five o'clock, when Pringle ordered the ships to withdraw out of range in order to establish a blockade south of the American position, which would prevent Arnold's mangled fleet from escaping to Ticonderoga.[60]

Assessing his damage reports at dusk, Arnold clearly recognized that his fleet sustained terrible damage: the *Philadelphia* sank around six o'clock; the *Congress* lost its mainmast and began taking on water; the *Washington's* senior leadership were all dead or wounded, and all of the officers, except for the captain, died on the *New York*.[61] Arnold lost sixty men, or ten percent of his crews, in the day's engagement, and they had expended seventy-five percent of their ammunition.[62] The errors derived from poor seamanship and the lack of gunnery training prior to the battle directly contributed to the loss of American vessels and the inaccuracy of their fires against the British fleet. Arnold later bemoaned to Gates that the battle "suffered much for want of Seamen and Gunners."[63] In fact, the crews never managed to bring forty-eight of their guns into action on October 11 because they could not maneuver their watercraft into range of the enemy fleet.[64] The British also suffered approximately sixty dead and wounded, but their superior numbers made this loss of personnel less detrimental to their ability to continue prosecuting the battle. Both of the fleet's largest vessels, the *Thunderer* and *Inflexible*, suffered structural problems that concerned their captains, who informed Pringle that they would be unable to participate in hostilities until repaired. As his own vessels formed a semicircle to the south of Arnold's fleet, Carleton ordered the severely damaged *Royal Savage* to be destroyed, and the British used the American schooner's own gunpowder to burn it to the waterline.[65]

At seven o'clock that night, Arnold assembled his captains aboard the *Congress* to provide further orders. The Continental fleet would escape in the night, he told them resolutely; surrender was not an option.[66] Amazingly, the vessels formed a line in the darkness using one hooded lantern at the stern of each ship to pass between the British line and the New York shoreline of Lake Champlain.[67] At daybreak the British identified the rear element of the withdrawing fleet well beyond artillery range, and a "greatly mortified" Carleton ordered a quick pursuit.[68] However, unforgiving winds prevented even the fastest British ships from intercepting them. Pringle later explained that the Americans managed to escape due to the "extreme obscurity of the night," but three of his captains wrote in 1779 that their commodore's negligence in positioning his fleet too far away from the New York shoreline provided Arnold with ample room to escape.[69] One disappointed British artillery officer concurred, writing in his wartime journal that if Carleton had not consolidated his gunboats the night prior, Arnold would not have found a water gap wide enough to sneak past.[70]

Early on the morning of October 12, as his crews patched up leaks and rebuilt masts from their temporary sanctuary near Schuyler Island, nearly ten miles south of Valcour Island, Arnold wrote to Gates: "The whole fleet will make the utmost dispatch to Crown Point, where I beg you will send ammunition and your further orders for us. On the whole, I think we have had a fortunate escape."[71] Indeed, Arnold enjoyed a very narrow escape. Had the British immediately pursued, they would have discovered easy prey since the American fleet continued to disintegrate. Surveying the damage on the *Providence*, its captain ordered it scuttled. The *New Jersey* ran aground, and a Canadian raiding party captured it the following day. For reasons still unclear to historians, the crew of the *Lee* abandoned their cutter, which the British soon captured.[72]

By the following day, Arnold's luck began to turn for the worse. The winds shifted to come from the south, and the British resumed their pursuit. When his spotters reported that they identified eleven sails on the horizon, Arnold ordered the hospital sloop *Enterprise* to place three crew members on each oar so that it could make its way to Ticonderoga safely ahead of the enemy fleet. Arnold then signaled his remaining vessels to prepare to engage the British at nine o'clock in the morning. The two fleets closed at ten o'clock, but the second battle did not commence until noon. When three British vessels surrounded the *Washington*, Waterbury surrendered without firing a shot. With Pringle's fleet turning in pursuit of Arnold's flagship, the American commodore led the *Congress* and the remaining four gondolas into Ferris Bay, on the southeastern shore of the lake, ten miles from Crown Point. Run aground, he ordered the cannons to be dumped overboard and the vessels burned, so as to avoid capture by the enemy. The British closed in but did not seek to prevent the destruction of the vessels or the escape of their crews.[73] Marine Sergeant James Wilkinson of the *Congress* later recounted the dramatic affair:

> [Arnold] set [the ships] on fire but ordered the colours not be struck, and as they grounded, the marines were directed to jump overboard, with their arms and accoutrements, to ascent a bank about twenty-five feet elevation, and form a line for the defense of their vessels and flags against the enemy, Arnold being the last man who debarked. The enemy did not venture into the cove, but kept up a distant cannonade until our vessels were burnt to the water's edge.[74]

The remaining 200 Continentals followed Arnold on the ten-mile trek to Crown Point, a march that narrowly escaped an Indian ambush.[75] Upon arriving they discovered that the *Trumbull, Enterprise, Revenge,* and *New York* had also reached the fort. Arnold convinced Colonel Thomas Hartley, the garrison commander, that they could not hold the fort. The vessels' crews helped the troops burn the buildings prior to withdrawing from Crown Point to the much more formidable citadel at Ticonderoga.[76] Carleton's soldiers seized the vacated Crown Point on October 14, and the British fleet sailed within three miles of Ticonderoga.[77] Shortly after their arrival at the stone fortress, several British rowboats, flying the flag of truce, approached the fort to return Waterbury and the surviving crews of the *Washington* and *Philadelphia*, completely stunning the Americans.[78] Gates and Arnold still anticipated an attack against Ticonderoga, and Schuyler, back in Albany, hastened to order an additional 1,000 militiamen from nearby states to reinforce the garrison and bring its strength to nearly 10,000 defenders.[79]

As the Americans struggled to reinforce artillery batteries on both sides of the South River and construct a log boom across the southern mouth of Lake Champlain, Carleton thoroughly surprised Gates and Arnold by turning his fleet around and returning to Canada on October 20. His ground forces also sailed from Crown Point between November 13 and 15.[80] Carleton still believed that 20,000 Americans stood behind the walls of Ticonderoga. His conviction in the necessity of reinforcements prior to laying siege to the fortress appears to have weighed more heavily in his decision to withdraw than did his concern for the advent of winter.[81] However, the specter of freezing temperatures also proved daunting. Old Man Winter has led to the isolation and destruction of many an expeditionary force whose commander callously dismissed the threat. As one British officer under Carleton explained, "After the 15th November on account of the frost, which begins to set in with great violence about that time . . . Canada is as much shut out from all communications with the rest of the world as possible, particularly then, as the country from Ticonderoga was in possession of the enemy."[82] Recalling their isolation in Montreal during the Americans' siege the previous winter, many British leaders did not wish to become as vulnerable as their enemy had by taking a similar risk for themselves.

Nevertheless, British records suggest that Carleton's lethargy "had prevented the frontier of New England from being burst open."[83] Major General William Phillips, Carleton's chief of artillery, had conducted numerous reconnaissance missions of the American position at the south end of the lake while the navy constructed the fleet. He doubted that 20,000 troops opposed them from within Ticonderoga. At a minimum, Phillips vented after returning to England, the British should have retained a foothold at Crown Point to expedite preparations for resuming offensive operations in the spring of 1777.[84] Upon receiving reports from Canada, King George III and Prime Minister Lord North both felt that a more aggressive officer than Carleton would not have waited so long to attack the Americans on Lake Champlain in the fall of 1776, and such an officer would have certainly continued to pursue the defeated Americans after sinking Arnold's fleet off of Valcour Island and in Ferris Bay. Lord Germain, Secretary of State for America in North's cabinet, never particularly cared for Carleton, and he seized the opportunity of the retreat from Crown Point to shuffle the army's chain of command in North America. Prior to the next campaign season, Germain selected Burgoyne as commander of the next expedition from Canada into New York in the spring of 1777.[85]

By accepting Gates' offer to serve as commodore, Arnold assumed responsibility to delay the British long enough to enable Gates to establish a suitable defense at Ticonderoga in order to prevent Carleton from seizing Albany and uniting with Howe's forces. Despite the tactical loss and the destruction of his fleet, Arnold's delaying action succeeded because of his officers' "Spirited Conduct During the Action."[86] Military historian Joseph Mitchell contends that, "It may be true that the year saved at Lake Champlain . . . saved the Revolution."[87] The British did not advance towards Albany for another year, and it is unlikely that Gates could have defeated Burgoyne at Saratoga, or even Carleton had he remained in command, without the ten-month reprieve. Without the high-profile British defeat at Saratoga, most scholars agree that France would not have seen the prospects of an American victory as sufficient enough for Louis XVI's government to declare war on the British.[88] Alfred Thayer Mahan considers the Battle of Valcour Island to be one of the two decisive naval battles of the American Revolution (the other being the 1781 Battle of the Virginia Capes) because it directly led to the French alliance. Mahan defends the necessity of France and Spain's entry into the war on the American side: the European allies provided a counterbalance to British sea power, making it possible for the American forces to receive military supplies and resume, although minimally, its transatlantic trade.[89]

It is improbable that Arnold's fleet could have won the Battle of Valcour Island. Given the significant disparities in men and cannon, as well as the critical shortage of gunpowder for training during the summer months, the American fleet could not have accomplished more than a successful delaying tactic against the British, which it did accomplish on October 11, 12, and 13, 1776. Today the gondola *Philadelphia*, one of the American flotilla's gunboats from the battle, is the oldest intact warship displayed in North America. It is located at the Smithsonian's National Museum of American History in Washington, D.C.[90] The small boat stands in silent memory of a battle hardly remembered in the annals of American Revolutionary War history, perhaps because of its association with the infamous Benedict Arnold. Nevertheless, the engagement proved critical for setting the conditions for victory at Saratoga, and it also offers fascinating insight into the dynamism and courage of the men of the Revolution as well as the significant contributions of the American green-water navy to the protection of the Hudson River Valley and to the country's struggle for independence.

This article originally appeared in *The Hudson River Valley Review*, Volume 29.1, autumn 2012.

NOTES

1. Richard M. Ketchum, *Saratoga, Turning Point of America's Revolutionary War* (New York: Henry Holt, 1997), xi.
2. For one example, see James M. Volo, *Blue Water Patriots: The American Revolution Afloat* (Lanham, Md.: Rowman & Littlefield, 2006), 208–12.
3. Alfred Thayer Mahan, "Major Operations of the Royal Navy, 1762–1783," in William Laird Clowes, *The Royal Navy: A History from the Earliest Times to the Present*, Vol. III (London: Sampson Low, Marston and Company, 1898), 368.
4. James L. Nelson, *Benedict Arnold's Navy: The Ragtag Fleet that Lost the Battle of Lake Champlain but Won the American Revolution* (Camden, Maine: McGraw Hill, 2006), 169.
5. In 1823 completion of the Champlain Canal connected the lake with the Hudson River. Constructed simultaneously with the Erie Canal, it served as a link in the system between Lake Erie and the Atlantic.
6. Russell F. Weigley, *The American Way of War: A History of United States Military Strategy and Policy* (Bloomington: Indiana University Press, 1973), 22.
7. Piers Mackesy, *The War for America, 1775–1783* (1964; Lincoln: University of Nebraska Press, 1993), 94–95.
8. Benson J. Lossing, *The Life and Times of Philip Schuyler*, Vol. II (New York: Sheldon & Co., 1873), 135, Special Collections, U.S.

Military Academy Library, Jefferson Hall, West Point, NY; hereafter cited as USMA Special Collections.

9. Allan R. Millett and Peter Maslowski, *For the Common Defense: A Military History of the United States of America* (1984; New York: Free Press, 1994), 68–69.

10. Letter, Horatio Gates to John Hancock, July 16, 1776, an enclosure to Gates' letter to George Washington, July 16, 1776, *The Papers of George Washington: Revolutionary War Series*, Vol. 5 (Charlottesville: University Press of Virginia, 1993), 339.

11. Continental Congress Committee report, quoted in Frederic Jesup Stimson, *My Story: Being the Memoirs of Benedict Arnold: Late Major-General in the Continental Army and Brigadier-General in that of His Britannic Majesty,* (New York: Charles Scribner's Sons, 1917), 207.

12. In 1818, the nephew of Montgomery arrived in Quebec, requesting to exhume his uncle so he could be laid to rest in the United States. With the permission of the British military commander, friends of the deceased located the grave, recovered the body, and processed through several U.S. towns before reburying the general in St. Paul's Chapel on Broadway in New York City; see *The Sword of Brigadier-General Richard Montgomery, A Memoir*, J. M. LeMoine, ed. (Quebec: Middleton & Dawson, 1870), 29, USMA Special Collections.

13. For an excellent account of the Battle of Quebec, see Thomas A. Desjardin, *Through a Howling Wilderness: Benedict Arnold's March to Quebec, 1775* (New York: St. Martin's Press, 2006). For the day-to-day experience of one Continental officer who survived the campaign, see *The Invasion of Canada in 1775: Including the Journal of Captain Simeon Thayer, Describing the Perils and Sufferings of the Army under Colonel Benedict Arnold, in Its March through the Wilderness to Quebec*, Edwin Martin Stone, ed. (Providence: Knowles, Anthony & Co., 1867), USMA Special Collections. Dr. Isaac Senter, Arnold's troop physician also maintained a log of the expedition; see *The Journal of Isaac Senter, on a Secret Expedition against Quebec, under the Command of Col. Benedict Arnold, in September 1775* (1846; Philadelphia: Historical Society of Pennsylvania, 1969).

14. Annual Register, 1776, p. 16, quoted in Edwin Martin Stone, "Introduction," *The Invasion of Canada in 1775,* xvii, USMA Special Collections.

15. Carleton would not learn of his knighthood until his wife joined him in Montreal from England in early November 1776. See John R. Bratten, *The Gondola* Philadelphia *and the Battle of Lake Champlain* (College Station: Texas A&M University Press, 2002), 72.

16. Ketchum, *Saratoga*, 41.

17. Bratten, *The Gondola* Philadelphia, 37

18. Nelson, *Benedict Arnold's Navy*, 163.

19. Mackesy argues that part of the reason Carleton received less materiel than he requested stemmed from Lord George Germain's personal dislike of the general. As Secretary of State, Germain found Carleton to be a less competent commander than Howe, and, upon receiving Carleton's reports during the siege of Montreal, he argued that the governor-general painted a much bleaker picture of the situation facing the British garrison and of the American capabilities than reality would suggest. See Mackesy, *The War for America*, 56–57.

20. Bratten, *The Gondola* Philadelphia, 37–39.

21. The two schooners were originally British vessels that the Americans captured in November 1775; see Ibid., 59.

22. Nelson, *Benedict Arnold's Navy*, 288–89.

23. Bratten, *The Gondola* Philadelphia, 59.

24. Ketchum, *Saratoga*, 41.

25. Nelson, *Benedict Arnold's Navy*, 227.

26. One example of how the United States

sought to remove Arnold's service record from the history of the American Revolution can be seen in the Old Cadet Chapel at West Point. Bronze plaques line the right wall of the nave, each naming one of the thirty-six generals who served in the Continental Army. The inscription on last plaque beneath the choir loft reads, "Major General, born 1740," without providing Arnold's name or the date of his death.

27. James Kirby Martin, *Benedict Arnold, Revolutionary Hero: An American Warrior Reconsidered* (New York: New York University Press, 1997), xi.
28. See the introductions of the studies in, Desjardin, *Through a Howling Wilderness*; Martin, *Benedict Arnold, Revolutionary Hero*, and Nelson, *Benedict Arnold's Navy*.
29. Desjardin, *Through a Howling Wilderness*, 187.
30. Letter, Arnold to George Washington, June 25, 1776, *The Papers of George Washington: Revolutionary War Series*, Vol. 5, 96.
31. Stimson, *My Story*, 208.
32. Martin, *Benedict Arnold, Revolutionary Hero*, 249.
33. Bratten, *The Gondola* Philadelphia, 18, 23.
34. Horatio Gates, quoted in Ibid., 4.
35. Letter, Gates to Washington, July 29, 1776, in *The Papers of George Washington: Revolutionary War Series*, Vol. 5, 500.
36. Letter, Washington to Gates, August 14, 1776, in *The Papers of George Washington: Revolutionary War Series*, Vol. 6 (Charlottesville: University Press of Virginia, 1994), 21.
37. Bratten provides period sketches of most of the specific American and British vessels that participated in the Battle of Valcour Island. While some were drawn by shipbuilders on site, others were done by the British Admiralty after Carleton's men captured several of the ships; see Bratten, *The Gondola* Philadelphia, Chapters 2 and 3.
38. Nelson, *Benedict Arnold's Navy*, 228.
39. Jeduthan Baldwin, *The Revolutionary Journal of Col. Jeduthan Baldwin, 1775–1778*, Thomas Williams Baldwin, ed. (Bangor, Maine: De Burians, 1906), 63.
40. Arnold, entry for June 24, 1775, *Benedict Arnold's Regimental Memorandum Book: Written while at Ticonderoga and Crown Point, 1775* (Philadelphia: Collins, 1884), USMA Special Collections.
41. Letter, Richard Varick to Washington, August 3, 1776, in *The Papers of George Washington: Revolutionary War Series*, Vol. 5, 555.
42. One design flaw possibly caused by building hulls and gun carriages in separate locations was that the stem of each gondola needed to be sawed down at Ticonderoga to provide clearance for the 12-pound guns; see Bratten, *The Gondola* Philadelphia, 160.
43. Ibid., 32–34.
44. Martin, *Benedict Arnold, Revolutionary Hero*, 248.
45. On October 1, 1776, Arnold wrote Gates a "Memorandum of Articles which have been repeatedly wrote for, and which we are in the extremest want of," which included 1,740 artillery rounds of grape and shot. See memorandum, Arnold to Gates, in *Horatio Gates Papers, 1726–1828*, microfilm, 3:1082.
46. Martin, *Benedict Arnold, Revolutionary Hero*, 253.
47. Gates, orders to Arnold, August 7, 1776, in *Horatio Gates Papers,* microfilm, 3:315.
48. Letter, Arnold to Gates, October 10, 1776, in *Horatio Gates Papers,* microfilm, 3:1158.
49. Stimson, *My Story*, 216.
50. The British clearly surprised the Continentals, evidenced by Gates' letter to Philip Schuyler written on the morning of October 11, 1776: "Nothing remarkable has lately happened in this quarter." See *Horatio Gates Papers*, microfilm, 3:1164.
51. Letter, Arnold to Gates, October 10, 1776, in *Horatio Gates Papers,* microfilm, 3:1158.
52. Stimson, *My Story*, 219.

53. Nelson, *Benedict Arnold's Navy*, 294–95.
54. James M. Hadden, *Hadden's Journal and Orderly Books: A Journal Kept in Canada and Upon Burgoyne's Campaign in 1776 and 1777*, Horatio Rogers, ed. (Boston: Gregg Press, 1972), 18–19.
55. Bratten, *The Gondola* Philadelphia, 58.
56. Letter, Arnold to Gates, October 12, 1776, in *Horatio Gates Papers,* microfilm, 3:1184.
57. Nelson, *Benedict Arnold's Navy*, 304–05.
58. John Enys, quoted in Bratten, *The Gondola Philadelphia*, 63.
59. Bratten, *The Gondola Philadelphia*, 64.
60. Nelson, *Benedict Arnold's Navy*, 306.
61. Letter, Arnold to Gates, October 12, 1776, in *Horatio Gates Papers,* microfilm, 3:1184, and Lossing, *The Life and Times of Philip Schuyler*, 139.
62. Martin, *Benedict Arnold, Revolutionary Hero*, 279.
63. Benedict Arnold, quoted in Bratten, *The Gondola Philadelphia*, 65.
64. Nelson, *Benedict Arnold's Navy*, 298.
65. Bratten, *The Gondola* Philadelphia, 65–66.
66. Letter, Arnold to Gates, October 12, 1776, in *Horatio Gates Papers,* microfilm, 3:1184.
67. Martin, *Benedict Arnold, Revolutionary Hero*, 280.
68. Lossing, *The Life and Times of Philip Schuyler*, 141.
69. Thomas Pringle, quoted in Bratten, *The Gondola* Philadelphia, 66.
70. Hadden, *Hadden's Journal and Orderly Book*, 24.
71. Benedict Arnold, quoted in Bratten, *The Gondola* Philadelphia, 67.
72. Nelson, *Benedict Arnold's Navy*, 318–20.
73. Martin, *Benedict Arnold, Revolutionary Hero*, 283–84.
74. James Wilkinson, quoted in Bratten, *The Gondola* Philadelphia, 69.
75. Confiding in Schuyler about Arnold after hearing of his escape to Crown Point, Gates wrote, "Few Men ever met with so many hair Breadth Scapes [*sic*] in so short a space of time." See letter, Gates to Schuyler, October 15, 1776, in *Horatio Gates Papers,* microfilm, 3:1223.
76. Baldwin, *The Revolutionary Journal of Col. Jeduthan Baldwin*, 80–81.
77. Nelson, *Benedict Arnold's Navy*, 319–20.
78. After their release, the prisoners spoke so highly of the medical care and treatment that they received from Carleton that Gates feared they would influence the other men under his command to think more favorably of the British. Therefore, Gates promptly ordered all of the former prisoners of war to be sent home; see Bratten, *The Gondola* Philadelphia, 71.
79. Letter, Schuyler to Washington, October 16, 1776, in *The Papers of George Washington: Revolutionary War Series*, Vol. 6, 579–80. Specific militia numbers are provided in Lossing, *The Life and Times of Philip Schuyler*, 144.
80. Hadden, *Hadden's Journal and Orderly Book*, 34.
81. Bratten, *The Gondola* Philadelphia, 71–72.
82. Anonymous British officer, quoted in Ketchum, *Saratoga*, 42. To add to the concerns of the British, the first snowfall of the season occurred on Lake Champlain in late September; see Bratten, *The Gondola* Philadelphia, 54.
83. Mackesy, *The War for America*, 107.
84. Ketchum, *Saratoga*, 42.
85. Mackesy, *The War for America*, 106.
86. Postscript to letter, Arnold to Gates, October 12, 1776, in *Horatio Gates Papers,* microfilm, 3:1184.
87. Joseph Mitchell, *Military Leaders in the American Revolution* (McLean, Va.: EPM Publications, 1989), 32–33.
88. Volo is one of the few historians who argue that the French Council of State had already determined that it would support the Americans as a way to restore the balance of power in Europe disturbed by the Seven Years' War, and that the French government would have intervened without the victory at Saratoga; see Volo, *Blue Water Patriots*,

232. Nevertheless, it seems more likely that the French would not have declared war on the British if they thought that the American rebellion would imminently collapse, and Gates' victory at Saratoga indicated to French elites that the Continental Army remained a viable threat to British forces.

89. Alfred Thayer Mahan, *The Influences of Sea Power upon History, 1660–1783* (1890; New York: Barnes & Noble, 2004), 289.

90. Bratten recounts the salvaging of the *Philadelphia* from Lake Champlain on August 9, 1935; see Bratten, *The Gondola* Philadelphia, Chapter 6.

Contributors

CLARE BRANDT is the author of *An American Aristocracy: The Livingstons* and *The Man in the Mirror: The Life of Benedict Arnold.* A graduate of Radcliffe, she is a past president of the Friends of Clermont and resident of Rhinebeck, New York.

DENIS P. BRENNAN is a lecturer at Union College. He earned his Masters and Doctorate at the State University of New York at Albany. His doctoral thesis, "The Printer's Stand: William Lloyd Garrison and the Liberator," won the University's Distinguished Dissertation Award in 2003 and is currently under contract for publication in 2013.

EDWARD J. CASHIN received his BA from Marist College in 1952 and his Masters and Doctoral degrees from Fordham University. In 1963 Cashin was appointed assistant professor of history and Academic Vice President. After 1968, Cashin left to work as a professor of history at August College and eventually chair of the history department until his retirement in 1996. After retirement Cashin founded the Center for thc Study of Georgia History at Augusta State University and carried out research in Georgia history until his death in 2007.

GREGORY SMITH holds a Bachelor of Arts degree from the State University of New York at Albany, and Masters of Arts degree in U.S. History from the University of Alabama. He is the Historic Preservation Program Analyst for the New York State Office of Parks, Recreation and Historic Preservation.

JAMES M. JOHNSON, the author of *Militiamen, Rangers, and Redcoats: The Military in Georgia, 1754–1776* (Mercer University Press), is the Executive Director of the Hudson River Valley Institute and the Dr. Frank T. Bumpus Chair in Hudson River Valley History at Marist College.

JONATHAN CLARK was a graduate of the University of California at Berkeley who went on to become a Professor of History at Vassar College, specializing in Revolutionary War and colonial history until his death in 1983.

KENNETH SHEFSIEK is the Executive Director of the Geneva Historical Society. He previously served as the Museum Curator at the Huguenot Historical Society in New Paltz, New York.

LINCOLN DIAMANT was the president of Spots Alive, Inc., a New York-based television cost-management firm, and a contributor to the *Journal of Military Affairs* and the *Croton Review*. Diamant published numerous books and articles, many of which focused on the American Revolution. This interest continued until his death in 2009.

NEIL LARSON is an architectural historian specializing in Hudson Valley vernacular buildings. Formerly a field worker for the National Register for Historic Places and the director of Hudson Valley study Center at SUNY New Paltz, Mr. Larson now works as a freelance consultant for historic preservation and museum services.

R. BETH KLOPOTT earned a Ph.D. in local and regional history from the University at Albany (SUNY). She is a historical consultant and grant reviewer for the National Endowment of the Humanities.

THOMAS S. WERMUTH is the Vice President for Academic Affairs and Dean of Faculty at Marist College. Dr. Wermuth is also the author of *Rip Van Winkle's Neighbors: The Transformation of Rural America in the Hudson Valley, 1720–1850.*

WILLIAM P. MCDERMOTT, a local historian, is president of the Town of Clinton Historical Society. He is the author of *18th Century Documents of the Nine Partners Patent* and the editor of *Clinton, Dutchess County, New York: A History of a Town.*

MICHAEL DIAZ has worked at numerous historic sites and museums in the Hudson River Valley. He received his B.A. in History from Marist College and his M.A. in Public History from SUNY Albany. He recently taught at Indiana State University.

MAJOR GREGORY M. TOMLIN is currently an instructor in United States Military Academy's Department of History. He has co-authored *The Gods of Diyala: Transfer of Command in Iraq* as part of the Williams-Ford Texas A&M University Military History Series, with Caleb S. Cage.

FRANK DOHERTY is a retired Dutchess County businessman. He and his wife purchased the Buck farm, onetime home to Pearl Buck, in 1972 and his interest in the history of the home and the area began his literary career. He recently published his tenth volume on the 18th-century settlers of the Beekman Patent, from which many of the Loyalists on the prison ships came.

THOMAS C. O'KEEFE is a business lawyer who practices in the U.S. Virgin Islands and New York. His military experience consists of being drafted out of Cornell Law School to serve in the artillery in Vietnam with the 199th Light Infantry Brigade, the 1st Cavalry Division and the 25th Divison. Mr. O'Keefe's home in Connecticut is adjacent to one of the Redding encampments, which sparked his interest on this subject.

WILLIAM SULLIVAN teaches at Northwestern Regional High School in Winsted, Connecticut, and Tunxis Community College in Farmington, Connecticut. His articles on labor history have appeared in *Connecticut History.*

MAJOR COLIN WILLIAMS is a serving officer in the U. S. Army and a former assistant professor of history at the United States Military Academy. He graduated from West Point in 1998 as a field artillery officer and is now all-but-dissertation at the University of Alabama. Major William expects to receive his doctorate within the year.

Index